The Folk Arts in Renewal

The Folk Arts in Renewal

Fisherfolk Resources

PATRICIA BEALL
MARTHA KEYS BARKER

ILLUSTRATIONS BY RUTH WIETING

HODDER AND STOUGHTON
LONDON SYDNEY AUCKLAND TORONTO

Biblical quotes, unless stated otherwise, are from the Revised Standard Version.

All enquiries about materials copyrighted by Celebration Services (International) Ltd should be directed to Celebration Services (International) Ltd, 57 Dorchester Road, Lytchett Minster, Poole, Dorset BH16 6JE. Further reproduction is not permitted without written permission from the copyright holder.

Fisherfolk music is found in the songbooks, *Sound of Living Waters, Fresh Sounds* and *Cry Hosanna*, all published by Hodder and Stoughton, and *Hey Kids, Do You Love Jesus?*, Celebration Records. The songbook titles are abbreviated throughout: SOLW, FS, CH and HK. Page numbers are not given for *Cry Hosanna* as they were not available at the time of publication.

Cover Photographs:
The Post Green Fisherfolk Team – Säde Kallionen
Festival of the Arts in Worship, York Minster – St. Michael-le-Belfrey, York
The Cumbrae Fisherfolk production of 'Jonah' – Christine Allan
A Community of Celebration Family Carnival – David Gustafson

Cover Design: Ruth Wieting

British Library Cataloguing in Publication Data
Beall, Patricia
The folk arts in renewal.
1. Public worship 2. Folk arts
I. Title II. Barker, Martha Keys
264 BV15

ISBN 0 340 25154 9

 Phototypeset in V.I.P. Baskerville by Western Printing Services Ltd, Bristol. Printed in Great Britain for Hodder and Stoughton Ltd., Mill Road, Dunton Green, Sevenoaks, Kent by Lowe & Brydone Printers Ltd., Thetford, Norfolk.

Dedication

To our parents

James and Valerie Beall
'Jim and Val'

William and Margaret Keys
'Mr. Bone and Miss Peggity'

Images of family life
bright kaleidoscope of love and joy
colour our memories

Love

encouragement offered
counsel given
acceptance extended
selves sacrificed

Joy

lingering meals, with laughter and storytelling
rambling houses, with open doors, winding stairs
familiar festivities, song, games, homemade plays
depth of worship, at home and at church

Images of family
life, coloured love and joy
fill our hearts' memories

Acknowledgements

After several months of writing we were confronted by Clare Morris, a four-year-old member of our community, 'Are you *still* working on that book?' she asked, disbelievingly, 'I don't think making a book is *that* hard.' The next day she proudly presented us with a gift – a book she made *by herself*. 'Making a book is very simple,' she confided, '*I* just used staples for this one.'

Making *this* book, we discovered, was not so simple as Clare's helpful example. It required not only staples, but also time, energy, care, love, and perseverance from many sources. Here we acknowledge some of those sources.

We are especially grateful to Jeanne Hinton, our editor-friend, who offered the perfect balance of critique and encouragement. Her faithful involvement with us despite her own demanding publishing schedule was a strength to us personally and a decisive factor in the completion of the manuscript.

We give thanks for the kindness of Brother Roland and the Community of the Transfiguration for the use of their wee cottage, 'The Snoopy Hut', when we needed a quiet place to work. Its 'prayed in' atmosphere and restful simplicity gave peace to our spirits and wings to our writing.

At a crucial time, the Post Green community in Dorset welcomed us into their life for three months of intensive work. We particularly thank Christopher and Jennifer Lees who made their lovely country home available to us. We also express warmest appreciation to Susan Abbott and the Panorama household, with whom we shared meals, daily prayers, and well-timed birthday celebrations. This gave us the support of a rich family life and the much-needed spice of festivity in the midst of our work.

We gratefully acknowledge the Post Green Resources department who performed the massive job of proof-reading the materials section. This task was an unexpected addition to their normal workload, and meant sacrificial use of their time, skills, and energy.

As we state in several places, this book represents the fruit of the Fisherfolk ministry. We express our appreciation to each of the Fisherfolk for their gifts, commitment, hard work and willingness to experiment. From these have come many of the materials, ideas, and illustrations. We particularly thank those who contributed workshop ideas, exercises and techniques to the workshops section: Conway Barker, Maggie Durran, Max Dyer, Sandy Hardyman, Grace Krag, Margi Pulkingham and Ruth Wieting.

We are especially grateful to Ruth Wieting for her delightful people who dance and move through these pages. Her careful attention to the details of movement and gesture, and her helpful suggestions for clarifying verbal descriptions have been an invaluable resource. Her unflagging willingness and sunny cheerfulness have been a source of personal encouragement.

The preparation of the final manuscript was expedited greatly by the willing proof-readers who offered their spare time to assist us: Pat Allen, Jodi and Howard Clark, Val Nobbs, and Rick Roberts. We especially thank Margaret Bryan our Millport neighbour who, while working at her own full-time job, spent evenings typing the bulk of the manuscript. We also thank Louis Newton who typed the materials section. His careful work, incisive comments and helpful, humorous notes affixed to copies kept us from falling into theological pitfalls through the careless placement of a comma. His wry humour, even under time pressure, has been a constant refreshment.

We thank Arabella Kornahrens for reading and commenting on the manuscript, the Post Green Graphics Department for assistance with artwork and cover photographs, Barbara Gilbert for her administrative aid, and Margaret Love and Rusty Denman for their help and encouragement in the initial stages.

In addition to those who gave specific and nameable help, we express our appreciation to each member of the Community of Celebration in Millport for their constant love, daily prayers, and encouraging words. We particularly thank each one in our households who shouldered extra responsibilities and cared for us in ways too numerous to mention.

Finally, it would seem a serious omission not to express our awareness and appreciation of the Holy Spirit's presence with us. To whom else can we credit the many 'coincidences' along the way: the dinner conversation that clarified a point, the chance comment that illustrated an idea, the arrival of a letter with a pertinent article at just the right time? We have also known the Spirit's comfort in the natural beauty in which we have been privileged to write: the green hills and ever-constant, ever-changing sea of Cumbrae, the rolling, fertile farmlands of Dorset in spring. In these surroundings we have seen the Spirit's creativity which we trust will refresh and encourage you through these pages.

Isle of Cumbrae
May 1979

MARTHA KEYS BARKER
PATRICIA BEALL

Contents

PART IV APPENDICES

Part I The Folk Arts

CHAPTER 1

Treasure in our Field

Fisherfolk History

'THE WAY IN' COFFEE-BAR

2 July 1969. Houston, Texas. The garage and garden of the large frame house on North Main Street was swarming with people. Like a three-ring circus, a variety of activities were happening simultaneously: groups were painting the interior of the garage, cutting and laying carpet, hanging and adjusting lights, arranging tables and chairs. Inside, a singing group was rehearsing, undaunted by loud traffic noises coming through the open windows, the whir of large fans, and the attacks of persistent mosquitoes. In the kitchen, several people were busily preparing a hamburger supper for twenty-five. In just two days, 'The Way In' coffee-bar was to open its doors for the first time.

In the midst of this preparatory flurry were the authors, Martha and Patricia. Though we had known each other since childhood, our individual decisions to spend the summer of 1969 in Houston had been the result of our individual pilgrimages. At our respective universities we had heard about the Church of the Redeemer – an inner-city, Episcopal church in Houston – where renewal had begun in the early sixties. For each of us the news of this renewal held a particular hope, which a brief spring visit to the church had encouraged.

Patricia knew the Lord had called her to be 'a minister'. Even in the Methodist church which ordains women, she felt limited by the traditional roles this implied: Christian education director, missionary, ordained minister. None seemed an adequate outlet for her gifts of creativity and communication, nor for her desire to unite theatre and the gospel. She opted for a career plan which included ordination, hoping that by the time she had finished her education some new pattern of Christian ministry would emerge. During our visit at Redeemer, she saw the effectiveness of community as the basis for ministry. Each member played a vital part in the church's life. As each one offered unique and diverse gifts, resources of time, money, and abilities were released for ministry. Patricia saw that when many people shared together, ministry was lifted from its narrow province of roles and became a way of life for a whole group.

Martha's primary motivation was her desire to be part of an alive and caring church. The daughter of an Episcopal priest, she grew up experiencing both the strengths and weaknesses of the church. Having seen renewal of worship and ministry in groups outside the Church, she was concerned to find new life within its structures as well. Her hope for change within the Church was sparked when she heard about the renewal of the Church of the Redeemer. While visiting Houston, she saw that her hope was a possibility. Here, in an Episcopal church, were people living together in love and peace; the power of Christ's love among them was tangible. And their love did not stop with themselves; it reached out to include those who came to them looking for help, healing, a place to belong.

As a result of our first visit the question was posed for each of us: might this be the place to offer ourselves to serve the Lord fully? Determined to discover the answer, we planned to spend the summer in Houston. We trusted that living in the church's extended family households and participating in 'The Way In' would help us to make our decisions.

The ministry group of 'The Way In' was a heterogeneous one. Led by Graham Pulkingham, the rector of the Church of the Redeemer, and Bill Farra, a young law student, the group included teenagers of families involved in the church, young adults – university age and older – who were living in the church's households, and several students from other universities, who had also come to Houston for the summer. Eleven of the group had gone to New York City for intensive training in street ministry. They returned with a vision for sharing their faith with the young people of Houston. And, as Houston was fast becoming a crossroads in the 'Hippie Trail' to California, their vision also included those passing through on their restless way to unknown destinations further west. They also realised that in order to penetrate the 'word-weariness' of many young people, a new language was needed – a language of sounds and rhythm, of imagination and visual perception, of movement and drama.

A new language

It was from this original gathering of twenty-five persons and the need for a new language that our use of the folk arts evolved. Therefore, we begin the consideration of the folk arts in worship, teaching, and festivity with a brief sketch of 'The Way In' coffee-bar, its effect on the parish worship life, and the beginnings of the

Fisherfolk ministry. This, we hope, will answer some of the questions we're often asked: 'What is the purpose for using the arts?'; 'How can we start?'; 'Do we need formal training?'.

Quite simply, involvement in the folk arts grew from fellowship with each other, and from a desire to share that fellowship with those who came to 'The Way In'. To prepare ourselves for each evening's ministry, we gathered together daily for a variety of purposes. We discussed the previous evening, planned and rehearsed the entertainment, studied the Bible and prayed, and dealt honestly with any problems in our relationships to each other. To interact at this depth daily with a group of twenty-five persons was no easy task. We were from a variety of backgrounds and experiences. Frequently we had to work through differences of approach and expectation as well as personality conflicts. For many of us, therefore, these daily gatherings were the most intense interpersonal encounters we had known. In them we were confronted with both acceptance and rejection, faith and failure, joy and pain. In the midst of working and sharing together, we were aware of the Lord's love amongst us in a new way.

To share what we were learning and experiencing, many of us began to write songs, poetry and dramas. As we shared these expressions in the coffee-bar, we found they spoke to our clientele deeply. Often individuals responded by asking questions that called us to open our lives further to them: 'I felt exactly the way you talked about – tell me more.'; 'How do you know God loves you?'; 'I don't believe anyone loves me – but what you said about how you people love each other – I can see that's true. How do you do it?' The folk arts became a natural channel to open communication between us and the folk who wandered into 'The Way In' that long, hot summer.

An atmosphere of trust

As a ministry team, an atmosphere of trust and acceptance grew amongst us, and with it came a freedom to be spontaneous and open with each other. This had a marked effect on our explorations in the folk arts. Several of us had worked with drama, some had written poetry or composed songs; others were novices. The acceptance we experienced together enabled all of us to venture into things we'd never done before: taking part in drama, writing a poem and reading it to others, experimenting with dance. These vulnerable first offerings were received, and often suggestions were offered for changes or improvements. Honest praise and sensitive critique encouraged us to continue to develop our abilities and to exercise our new-found freedom. Several times, in the midst of her solo entertainment spot, one guitarist would spontaneously sing a new song which had occurred to her at that very moment. Often, while contributing our thoughts about a central theme for the evening, we would find that two or three people had similar ideas to share in song and poetry. It was an exciting time as we unearthed gifts that had been lying dormant and watched new potential emerge before our eyes.

Changing orientation

In this context our orientation toward competition underwent a transformation. The purpose of the group was not excellence of performance for its own sake, but communicating the gospel with honesty and vitality. This focus reduced the element of competition in our approach to the folk arts. Though we spent many hours in rehearsal, we were not striving to be recognised as the most accomplished guitarist, or the most talented actress. We were simply concerned that in everything we did, the media enhanced the message. Liberated from the excessive pressure of artistic competition, any of us who had previously found such competition daunting were able to participate fully and creatively with a minimised fear of failure.

THE CHURCH FAMILY

Young people who had been challenged by the coffee-bar ministry began to attend the Sunday morning service at the Church of the Redeemer. Though we were using an experimental liturgy and a folk music setting for holy communion, the form of the service was similar to most Episcopal churches. The main difference was a warm and enthusiastic atmosphere, and guests often commented that they felt especially welcomed and loved. However, as the coffee-bar clientele joined us, we realised that some of the old words and old hymn tunes were too remote from their experience to be meaningful. We felt they would be more at home in a service which included some of the folk expressions familiar to them from the coffee-bar.

Even had there been no visitors from 'The Way In', those of us in the coffee-bar ministry wanted to share the fruits of our creativity with the church family in the context of worship. At Graham's invitation, we gradually incorporated folk art expressions into our Sunday morning worship. Taking care not to rush or push, we introduced only one element at a time: a poem to call us to worship, an original song to augment a scripture reading, a folk dance to sum up a time of thanksgiving. Because the folk arts were an important part of the coffee-bar ministry, they were received by the whole church family; before long they were a familiar element in Sunday morning worship.

Throughout the parish, as in the coffee-bar ministry, people were coming to know and love each other more deeply. The increased depth of relationships brought a new dimension into worship. Rather than being a completely pre-planned production, our services developed into a dialogue, sensitive to the special needs of our congregation at that particular time. This dialogue was expressed in various ways: spontaneous prayers during the set intercessions gave voice to personal and corporate concerns; sermons, rather than being exclusively monologues, at times became dialogues with two persons discussing their understanding of a scriptural passage; questions from the pulpit were no longer strictly rhetorical, but at times were designed to solicit genuine response from the congregation. Both exploration in the folk arts and growth in relationships were shaping and moulding worship into new forms.

The folk arts in teaching

Those involved in teaching in the parish also began to utilise the folk arts in various teaching circumstances: with children and youth, in family services, in outreach. Using the folk arts in this way was a result of natural evolution rather than sudden transformation. No group sat down and concluded: 'We remember a teaching better if it includes a graphic illustration,' or 'We are more likely to be touched deeply by something we experience than by something we only hear about.' But we noticed that several weeks after we'd performed a play in the coffee-bar, we were still quoting from it, laughing about the amusing behaviour of some of the characters, and finding parallels between their exaggerated responses and our own everyday ones. 'I was like Asparagus today!' one of the group shared (referring to a recent play in which a personified asparagus insisted on her own way), 'then I realised what I was doing, laughed at myself, and stopped pushing for *my* idea.' Our identification with the characters, and our laughter helped us to recognise and to change behaviour patterns. The folk arts were proving to be a valuable teaching tool.

We also observed that the children were remembering the sketches – not only for their humour, but also for their teaching content. The children's questions and observations about characters and situations provided a springboard for continuing discussion. Dramatic illustrations in which children and young people participated were incorporated into family services. Actually *doing* something in the services gave them a new sense of importance and involvement. Church wasn't 'for adults only': it was an arena in which they had a significant part to play.

As the potential of the folk arts was developed, we planned our services with creative possibilities in mind, weaving dramatic or graphic illustrations into teachings whenever possible. Our planning was no longer limited to discussing the points we wished to convey. We considered how to appeal to the senses, the imagination and the emotions, as well as to the intellect. Thus, the folk arts became not just an occasional diversion, but an integral part of both our worship and teaching.

Family festivities

In addition to their key role in worship and teaching, the folk arts also gave us a new arena to simply enjoy each other. As a congregation we drew together in many ways, and a 'family feeling' grew among us. Increasingly we wanted to be together whenever possible – particularly to celebrate special occasions: Christmas, New Year, birthdays, weddings, farewells, or 'just because' times. Stories, drama, dance, music were now an important ingredient in our family festivities. We were amazed to see those who were usually reticent come out of themselves to join in a humorous drama. Others who felt too clumsy to dance were encouraged to venture into a simple folk dance with others who were 'just beginners' too. The animated telling of a story would draw all of us into a common experience of delight.

Without intending to do so, we were developing an alternative to the passive consumerism of television and film. Rather than organising entertainment *for* the children, we involved them in *doing* it with us: they created characters for the play, they decided the best way to tell a story, they suggested or wrote songs for all of us to sing. The joy of planning and presenting entertainment for the whole church family gave us a sense of accomplishment. It was a powerful incentive to continue to draw ideas from each other, rather than to accept whatever flickered across our television screen. We saw a major transformation in the children and in ourselves from the isolated attitude of television watching which regards others as an intrusion. We began to appreciate each other as vital and sought-after participants in our corporate creativity. Thus, an intimate family atmosphere and experimentation in the arts nurtured each other; the family atmosphere encouraged the most timid to venture forth into new areas, and enjoying the fruits of creativity drew us closer as a church family.

THE TRAVELLING MINISTRY

Experiencing this welcoming family atmosphere and fulfilment in ministry, both of us, Patricia and Martha, made the decision that Houston was indeed the place to offer ourselves to serve the Lord. Transferring to universities in Houston, we moved permanently into extended family households and continued our involvement in the coffee-bar and parish, as we completed our education.

The vitality of the Church of the Redeemer's community lifestyle and ministry was becoming a newsworthy topic. Graham was receiving many invitations to share the church's experience and the principles of renewal with other churches and fellowships throughout the

United States and abroad. To meet this need, the assistant rector of the parish began to shoulder more responsibility together with other capable lay leaders. And Graham began to travel, initially with Bill Farra, to provide Bill with in-depth training in lay ministry. After a year, Graham expressed his need for a larger, more diverse group to travel. Such a group could provide a fuller demonstration of renewal as they led in worship and continued development in the folk arts. In 1972, Martha became part of a travelling team of seven persons who had been trained through the coffee-bar ministry in various areas of artistic expression and worship leadership. Patricia travelled on a similar team of three persons.

That same year, after speaking at several conferences in England, Graham received a joint invitation from the Bishop of Coventry, the Rt. Rev. Cuthbert Bardsley, and a vicar in his diocese, to bring his household to live for an extended period in the Potters Green parish, to apply the principles of renewal there. Accepting the invitation, Graham and his household of sixteen persons moved to Potters Green, a suburb of Coventry, in the autumn of 1972. In February 1973 they were joined by the travelling team of seven. Soon christened 'The Fisherfolk', the team was quickly booked for months in advance. To meet the growing need, seven others from the Houston church, including Patricia, were added to the team in June 1973. By this time accommodation in Coventry was inadequate to house such a large group. Yeldall Manor, a disused convent in Wargrave, near Reading in Berkshire, was made available to the community through the kindness of the Abbot of Nashdom Abbey. The time seemed right for the indigenous leaders of the Potters Green parish to function independently. Three of the original group, including a young curate, remained in Coventry while the majority of the community took up residence at Yeldall Manor in the winter of 1973. The Bishop of Oxford welcomed the community into his diocese and in this new setting several English families joined them for a period of one or two years of training in community lifestyle and leadership.

The Fisherfolk

The addition of several English members to the Fisherfolk in the next year enabled three teams to form. Travelling extensively, we developed resources in the folk arts to encompass diverse situations: parish weekends, school assemblies, coffee-bars, festivals of the arts, youth groups, workshops, family camps, conferences, cathedral festivals of praise. At times our use of the arts met with some initial suspicion as a 'gimmick'; but on many occasions they proved to be a catalyst to draw together groups and congregations. In many situations, rather than performing, the Fisherfolk team functioned as a stimulus for a local church or fellowship. We organised workshops to provide an arena for experimentation. Our primary task was drawing out ideas from the group and, if necessary, shaping them into a cohesive expression. In some situations we co-ordinated several workshops to present a unified performance for a special gathering. For many groups this was a new and fulfilling experience. Participating in the folk arts unlocked a new spontaneity in worship and a fresh appreciation of their potential as a group.

RENEWAL IN THE CHURCH

As the Fisherfolk travelled, both in England and abroad, we experienced a phenomenon so widespread that we can only attribute it to the work of the Holy Spirit. In a diversity of places and amongst a variety of people we observed a common longing: for deeper fellowship, for freedom in worship, for in-depth Bible teaching, for a style of leadership that utilises all the gifts of the body of Christ. In many churches and fellowships we found people gathering together at times other than formal Sunday morning worship. Sharing meals, praying, studying the Bible, relaxing together, they were experiencing friendship and acceptance, encouragement and support. From their Bible study they were discovering the principles of a life of faith and applying them to their lives and relationships. Opening their lives to each other, they were receiving direction, counsel and correction.

As their fellowship deepened, worship was taking on new significance. Freedom and spontaneity in singing and praying aloud, joyful outpourings of praise and thanksgiving, and well-balanced exercise of gifts of the Spirit, were some of the signs of renewed worship. Accompanying this renewal was an eagerness to draw their children and young people into a fresh experience and understanding of the Lord and of his purposes in their lives. Many groups were exploring the folk arts as a means to express new depths of praise and to involve children and youth.

Concerning leadership, many questions were being raised. Ordained and lay persons were looking for ways to combine their gifts and abilities to provide a richer, fuller ministry. Rather than the traditional hierarchical approach, a mutual sharing of responsibilities and authority was being sought. Instead of expecting only the ordained persons to meet a congregation's needs, emphasis was being placed on utilising the gifts of each member.

Following the Spirit

We visited several churches and fellowships whose atmosphere felt similar to our Houston church. These were groups who knew each other well, who were sharing in each other's daily lives, who were struggling with common problems and supporting and encouraging each other in their faith. We were strengthened as we saw our experience of the church as a family was not limited to a single parish in Houston, Texas, but was occurring simultaneously in many other places. The Holy Spirit was moving certainly and beautifully to restore an experience of friendship and family within the church. We were aware that, rather than initiating a movement or programme of church renewal, we were simply co-operating with the Spirit's direction.

This realisation removed from us the burden of trying to be innovative. We didn't need to strain to come up with a brilliant idea for a particular group. In a relaxed environment where people felt free to experiment, creativity flowed freely. Our main task was to set a warm atmosphere and then allow the group to work. If things bogged down, we would provide direction or suggest a different approach, but we didn't have to control the group to assure results. We were always aware of the Creator Spirit moving among God's people, speaking to and through them.

In the context of this activity of the Holy Spirit, the folk arts served a variety of purposes. They opened new avenues to expression of worship and praise. They provided new methods of teaching and instruction. They drew people together in an atmosphere of enjoyment, experiment and festivity. Throughout the course of the book, we will consider each of these aspects in depth.

TREASURES IN YOUR FIELD

The materials in this book are the treasures we have unearthed both in our community worship and through the travelling ministry of the Fisherfolk in England, Scotland, Ireland, Wales, Sweden, West Germany, Australia, New Zealand and the United States. They are the result of our interaction with many people in many places. At times it is impossible to give individual credits as a play, dance or poem evolved from a group process.

These materials are also the result of a change of emphasis in the Fisherfolk ministry. Through 1975, we were involved in extensive, full-time travel. Consequently, we received many requests for our resources: music, plays, mimes, poetry, dances and graphic expressions. Because of the intensity of our travelling schedules, the production of materials for others' use was not possible. We realised a change was necessary. In 1975, we set up a business, Celebration Services (International) Ltd., designed to make our resources available to others. In the same year we were offered the use of the property of the Cathedral of the Isles and the adjoining college in Millport, the Isle of Cumbrae, off the west coast of Scotland. The isolated situation seemed ideal for the needs of the new business: the making of recordings, the publishing of songbooks, the writing of creative resources; and the property also provided a permanent base for our international travel. At the invitation of the Bishop of Argyll and the Isles, Graham Pulkingham was made the provost of the Cathedral and in the summer of 1975 about one-half of the community made the move to Scotland. At the same time others of the community moved to the Post Green Community where production of resources, primarily teaching materials, was already established. From that base a team of Fisherfolk continued to travel in England.

In presenting these materials we are well aware that it is not by the mere use of them that worship, teaching and festivity are renewed; they are simply media through which renewal may be expressed and encouraged. As you use the resources we hope you will be challenged, as we have been, to look deeper within yourself and those around you to find gifts and abilities awaiting discovery. We trust these materials will help you draw forth the treasures hidden in your field.

The children of Abraham learn to journey as they wander with faithful Abraham. Abraham tells them where he has been. That is their common past. But now they travel on together. That is their future. Together, the generations offer each other a mutual nurture. . . . The Church lives not only because adult passes on experiences to child, but because both adult and child share new experiences, which are interpreted in the light of the tradition. The tradition itself is renewed in the process.

Not to nurture a child in the tradition of his family is to deny him that part of his self-hood which should be given to him. It is to deny him the past, which is his own past, out of which his creation of his own unique self-hood should take place. . . . One of the most important principles of a truly Christian nurture (is) to give the past but not to close the future.

BRITISH COUNCIL OF CHURCHES
FROM *The Child in the Church*

When we think we know
the direction our lives should go
to bring your kingdom to man,
often we end with things arranged
to prevent change;
Wind of Spirit, wind of change
You move at will to rearrange
our goals, our priorities, our vision.

'Wind of Spirit, Wind of Change'

CHAPTER 2

Wind of Spirit

The Folk Arts Past and Present

Challenging, changing, rearranging, urging, nudging, wooing, the Spirit is continually initiating new perspectives and stimulating growth. As we began tracing our development of the arts in preparation for writing this book, we recognised the Spirit's hand, nudging and urging us through a variety of circumstances – some obvious and some not-so-obvious. Of course, we knew a primary impetus had been our experiences in 'The Way In' coffee-bar and Fisherfolk travel, but as we talked we realised other major influences and felt they should be explored as well.

Chief among these has been a renaissance of interest and participation in the arts which has made them more accessible and familiar to a wider range of persons. As part of this general resurgence of interest, there has been particular emphasis on what we term 'the folk arts'. By 'folk arts' we do not necessarily mean basket-weaving and quilt-making, though these may be included. We refer to arts performed 'by the people and for the people' – i.e. the arts of the non-professional. Evidences of this participation by the 'folk' are all around us: the gathering of *ad hoc* groups to do national dancing or folk singing, the proliferation of drama and mime troupes, the steady stream of books on folklore and folk craft. Through our involvement in a variety of countries and cultures, we have seen a common thread running through this interest in the folk arts – a desire either to maintain or to regain a knowledge of one's folk culture, to learn the folk music, dance, stories, customs and wisdom of one's forbears. The term 'folk art' therefore embraces both these aspects: art done by 'folk' or the non-professional, and art related to one's folk culture or background.

Closely related to the folk arts renewal is the movement to return to one's 'roots' – to discover some link with one's heritage. This movement has also had its effect on our use of the arts. It has particularly focused our attention on the essential role of the arts in pre-literate or semi-literate cultures as the media through which history, knowledge, and a sense of identity are preserved and handed down from generation to generation. More specifically, it has sharpened our awareness of the importance of the arts in maintaining our Judeo-Christian heritage.

In this chapter then, we look more closely at these formative influences including the renewal in the arts, particularly the folk arts, the search for roots, the use of the folk arts in our Jewish and Christian heritage. We also consider the challenge of the folk arts in the present renewal in the church.

RENEWAL IN THE ARTS

Indications of a re-awakening of interest in the arts in the last thirty years appear from many sources. The annual report of the Scottish Arts Council for 1977–78 provides some measurement of the extent of this revival. According to the report, in the year 1977–78 the Scottish Arts Council received the following:

1) A basic grant of £4.95m for revenue purposes (an increase of 14.6% over last year's £4.32m).
2) An additional £20,000 for special purposes.
3) An additional £58,000 for Housing the Arts.

Commenting on this continual increase in the budget allotted for the arts, Lord Balfour of Burleigh, the Chairman of the Scottish Arts Council, observed that since 1944–45 Parliament has increased the amount of the grant to the Council from £175,000 to £4.95m, a rate of increase enjoyed by few other bodies. He noted that these statistics indicate not only a continual increase in interest over the last thirty years, but also a constant growth in support for the arts and in demand for both quantity and quality of performance.[1]

Similarly, in the United States, interest in the arts has mushroomed. Returning for a visit in 1976 after a four-year absence, we were immediately struck by the proliferation of opportunities for involvement in the arts which had occurred just during that time. In the course of a month's stay in a moderate-sized city, we were inundated with opportunities as both participants and spectators: a travelling mime troupe offered Saturday workshops, a modern dance group performed and lectured on technique, several excellent plays and poetry readings were presented. As we travelled in other cities we discovered that interest in mime particularly had grown to such an extent that in almost every city we found an abundance of new mime groups and training schools.

On an international scale there is also evidence of a major

resurgence of involvement in the arts. The International Edinburgh Festival, which attracts artists and audiences from all over the world, continues to grow in popularity each year. In addition to the official programme, the Fringe, which promotes works by experimental groups, has constantly grown in both size and quality since its humble beginnings. Attending the Festival in 1976 opened our eyes to the international scope of renewal in the arts. The city was jammed with people of many nationalities, and an English-speaking person seemed the exception rather than the rule.

In these surroundings we also saw the arts relieved of their image as rarified, esoteric and unattainable. Every theatre, auditorium, courtyard and public park was filled with performances and exhibitions attended by jostling crowds of young back-packers, families, and tourists – creating the atmosphere of a large folk festival in which everyone felt at home.

The causes of the new popularity are several. Televising of orchestras, ballet, mime, and drama have opened the arts to a larger audience. Increased standards of living and availability of leisure time certainly contribute. But, at the heart of the revival, we feel, is a search for something more basic.

THE SEARCH FOR ROOTS

The re-kindling of interest in the arts is intertwined with an emerging desire within twentieth-century persons to make contact with our 'roots'. Alienated from a sense of our own history, isolated from family or life-long friends, we are robbed of continuity with our past. Having little knowledge or appreciation of the traditions that have nurtured us, we tend to see ourselves as merely another product of our age with its emphasis on transience, mobility, efficiency. Consciously or unconsciously we feel a need for roots to withstand the battering, disintegrating forces of our impersonal, technological society. As the folk arts have traditionally been a vehicle for maintaining contact with one's heritage, it is not surprising that the search for roots and the renewal in the folk arts are companions.

Oral tradition

Our hunger to know our origins is powerfully evidenced by the response to Alex Haley's novel, *Roots*. His saga of the African, Kunta Kinte, has struck a chord in the hearts of the rootless – both black and white. As the first black American to trace his ancestry to his African origins, Haley's story touches within us a longing to know the chain of history and personality in which we are a link. Haley's own search was motivated by the stories of his grandmother which had been passed from generation to generation. Central to his grandmother's stories was the figure of Kunta Kinte and his fierce determination to remember the land and people from which he was abducted by white slavers. He entrusted his knowledge of his origins, his language and people to his daughter, Kizzie, who perpetuated the family tradition. Kizzie's knowledge enabled her family to maintain dignity within a system that attempted to force them into sub-human existence. Their example illustrates the tremendous unifying power of knowing one's roots, as one tries to preserve an identity against overwhelming odds.

In his pilgrimage to investigate the land of his grandmother's stories, Haley succeeded in pinpointing and visiting Juffure, the village from which Kunta Kinte disappeared. The 'griot' of Juffure, the historian and storyteller of the tribe, still told the story of Kunta Kinte who was seized by slavers while chopping wood to make a drum – the same story Haley had heard from his grandmother. This story provided the 'missing link' between Haley and his African ancestor, and authenticated the oral tradition which he had received. Haley's experience illustrates the importance of the folk arts in sustaining a people's identity. In Juffure and other tribal societies, storytelling is not merely an entertainment; it maintains the vital connection between past and present. Other folk art expressions – dance, drama, song, poetry, drawing and painting – are also media through which the tribe remember their history, strengthen their traditions, and express their relationship to nature and God.

Folk culture

Travelling in the Fisherfolk ministry, we have experienced this search for roots through the folk arts in widely varying places and people. In the central Dalarna area of Sweden, strong emphasis is placed on preserving the traditional costume, customs, dance and music. On Lake Siljan, in the heart of Dalarna, men and women dressed in the traditional costume row to church across the lake in a brightly painted boat – an ancient custom in that area. Craftsmen in small cottage workshops still hand-paint wooden clogs and carved animals in colourful designs typical of the area. On Midsummer's Day we joyfully participated in the festival surrounding the maypole. People from all over the area gathered to observe and join in the dancing. Each dance told a story familiar to all who were present, uniting them in a common tradition. For our Swedish friends it was obvious that this yearly folk festival kept alive a sense of continuity with the past and strengthened a common bond in the present.

The Midsummer festival is one that has continued for generations; other customs have only recently been revived. About ten years ago, Swedish young people began to realise that sweeping changes – social, political, economic – while positive in many ways, had unfortunately also swept away their sense of tradition as a people, including many of their folk festivals and customs. A dramatic sense of rootlessness, a lack of certainty about one's identity, ensued. Those who were alarmed about this impoverishment began a campaign to revive folk arts and customs. They appealed to the old people, the keepers of the traditions, to tell them the folk tales, to teach them to play the old instruments, and to sing the traditional folk songs. The fruit of their persistence is now seen in large folk festivals throughout the country where old and young share in the music, dances and folk tales of their ancestral past. Here is an occasion where the old find a place of respect and importance, while the young experience a sense of identity and continuity with their past. In this arena the folk arts are the key to unlock the treasures of a rich inheritance, to assure its survival from generation to generation.

In Sweden the renaissance of interest in the folk arts has been motivated by a concern to balance the effects of rapid modernisation; in Nigeria, a completely different cultural milieu, a similar resurgence has been stimulated by concern to preserve tribal traditions in the face of a comparable trend towards technological development. Our friend, Peggy Harper, for many years a university professor in dance and drama at the University of Ife, Nigeria, shared with us her work of studying and preserving tribal dances. In the course of their projects, she and her students travelled to many remote villages, filming and recording tribal dances and music. They interviewed tribe members concerning the historical significance of the dances and their function in the tribe's present life. Returning to the university, the classes then created dance-dramas based on the tribal dances and rituals they had filmed. For the students, the productions supplied a vital link with the traditions that had nurtured them; for members of the tribe who viewed the completed performance, seeing their dances enacted on stage affirmed the continuing importance of their life, even within the context of a modernised educational system.

Such affirmation encourages tribal societies to preserve the quality of their life which could easily be lost in the struggle to emerge as a developing industrial nation. Thus, the folk arts act as mediator between the tribal societies and the educational system, enabling them to view traditions and progress as mutually supportive, rather than opposing forces.

JUDEO-CHRISTIAN HERITAGE

In addition to these contemporary examples, we also have the witness of our Judeo-Christian heritage as eloquent evidence of the folk arts' role in preserving history and identity. The Jews, like other tribal people of their day, developed a strong oral tradition. The Old

Testament continually reiterates the importance of explaining to one's children the significance of historical events in Israel's life. Psalm 78 which recounts the deliverance from Egypt and the desert wanderings begins:

> I will open my mouth in a parable; I will utter dark sayings from of old, things that we have heard and known, that our fathers have told us. We will not hide them from their children, but tell to the coming generation the glorious deeds of the Lord, and his might, and the wonders which he has wrought! He established a testimony in Jacob and appointed a law in Israel, which he commanded our fathers to teach their children; that the next generation might know them, the children yet unborn, and arise and tell them to their children, so that they should set their hope in God, and not forget the works of God, but keep his commandments. Psalm 78:1–7

Such reminders were vital to the continuing life of the Jews. Their history was not only the account of a people, but also the record of the mighty acts of their God. These two strands were intertwined and inseparable. By recalling God's disclosure of himself through their history, and by transmitting their knowledge to the next generation, the Jews both sustained themselves as a people and preserved the revelation of God's purposes in human history.

Folk arts in oral tradition

In the Old Testament we see the primary importance of oral tradition in Jewish life in the yearly celebration of the Passover. The deliverance of the Jews from Egypt was the crux of their national life; their remembrance of the exodus was a crucial event in maintaining their national identity. Throughout their history, in the Passover observance they acknowledged their dependence upon God and affirmed their distinctiveness as God's chosen people. Prohibitions against foreigners or strangers keeping the feast assured that the occasion was reserved for the Jews alone, and affirmed the observance's unique role in preserving their identity.

The Passover illustrates the folk arts' key role in oral tradition as its ritual employs dramatic and storytelling techniques. The occasion commences with the youngest child asking, 'Why is this night different from all other nights?' Then, through traditional questions, the children draw from their father the story of the first Passover and the history of their people. Use of dramatic dialogue and storytelling is essential to the educational aspect of the celebration. From an early age a Jewish child plays a vital role in an important event. The surroundings of family, the familiar ritual and the dramatic technique communicate not only historical facts, but the importance of those facts. The father's obvious excitement as he tells the tales of their forefathers – Abraham, Isaac, Jacob, Moses – gives the children a sense of pride in their origins. His dramatic recital of the original Passover engenders awe towards the God they worship. Thus, the folk arts play a crucial part in the dramatic effect of the Passover. And eloquent testimony to the observance's cohesive power is borne by the Jews' preservation as a people through their incredible history of dispersion and persecution.

Folk arts in worship

The folk arts have also played a significant role in Jewish worship, where drama, poetry, music and dance have given voice to the full gamut of human experience. Nowhere is this more evident than in the poetry and music of the psalms. As the words of the psalms were sung in worship, a breadth of experience was expressed – from David's heartfelt confession, 'For I know my transgressions and my sin is ever before me,' to the exultation of Psalm 150's 'Let everything that breathes praise the Lord!' The psalms both recalled the memories of the exiled Jews: 'By the waters of Babylon, there we sat down and wept, when we remembered Zion' (Psalm 137:1), and provided a vision of the restoration of the nation: 'O Israel, hope in the Lord! For with the Lord there is steadfast love, and with him is plenteous redemption. And he will redeem Israel from all his iniquities' (Psalm 130:78). As a record of God's presence in every dimension of human existence, the psalms served as a continual reminder that God was not confined to a small segment of life marked 'religion'; he was fully involved in the whole of life.

Dance is also recorded as a means of expressing joy and victory in Jewish worship. Deliverance from slavery in Egypt was celebrated in song and triumphant dance: 'Sing to the Lord, for he has triumphed gloriously; the horse and his rider he has thrown into the sea!' (Exodus 15:21). David's exultation as he brought the ark of the Lord into Jerusalem moved him to dance with complete abandonment which couldn't be quenched, even by the disapproval of his wife! And Psalm 150 also calls the worshippers to 'Praise the Lord with timbrel and dance' (Psalm 150:4). The use of the arts in both worship and teaching is explored more fully in Chapters 5 and 6.

Folk arts in teaching

Throughout the Old Testament, the Lord's word to his people is proclaimed through dramatic technique, and graphic illustration. Jeremiah was instructed to go down to the potter's house to hear God's word. There he witnessed the potter's craft, a vivid portrayal of God's intent for Israel: 'O house of Israel, can I not do with you as this potter has done? says the Lord. Behold like the clay in the potter's hand, so are you in my hand, O house of Israel.' Similarly

Ezekiel was commanded to present a dramatic portrayal of Israel's impending exile: 'Son of man, prepare for yourself an exile's baggage, and go into exile by day in their sight; you shall go like an exile from your place to another place in their sight. Perhaps they will understand, though they are a rebellious house' (Ezekiel 12:3). And Hosea's dramatic enactment of the Lord's judgement extended to his marriage to a harlot, 'For the land commits great harlotry by forsaking the Lord' (Hosea 1:2). Such dramatic action and proclamation certainly must have attracted attention and stimulated controversy. Though the evidence shows that Israel did not change as a result, they were not without a clear, pointed and inescapable illustration of God's intent.

Moving from the Old Testament to the New, we see dramatic storytelling technique employed by Jesus in his teaching. A master storyteller, he spoke to the common person by weaving his teachings from the familiar elements of daily life – a lost coin, sheep gone astray, men working in fields. His simple examples, spoken with authority, fixed his teachings in the minds of his hearers, who remembered them and passed them on.

Jesus was especially adept at utilising everyday events to teach about his Father's life and love. His sense of dramatic timing enabled him to seize the potential of even awkward situations. For instance, while dining with Simon, the Pharisee, a woman known to be a sinner washed his feet (Luke 7:38–50). Jesus took the opportunity of his host's criticism to tell a story of two debtors who were forgiven their debts. Involving Simon in judging which debtor will love the master more, he skilfully made his point. In one well-timed story he both assured the woman of her forgiveness and suggested to Simon his own need.

Storytelling also enabled Jesus to make strong statements about the religious establishment in an indirect manner. For example, in Luke 20 he told the story of a landowner who let out his vineyard to tenants to warn the people about the religious leaders who challenge his authority. However, he did not openly accuse the leaders. The application of his word to their lives was left to them: the conclusion that 'he had told the parable against them' was their own.

The effectiveness of these folk art teaching methods is considerable when we realise that Jesus's teachings were not written down in the Gospels until at least thirty years after his death and resurrection. His use of dramatic illustration and vivid storytelling kept his teaching alive in the minds of his disciples until they were written down. Thus, they form a vital link between Jesus's teaching and the Gospel record transmitted to us.

The arts in church history

The relationship between the church and the arts has been an unsettled one. At times, the church has courted the arts as a respected lady capable of enhancing its life; at other times, the church has scorned the arts as a woman of ill-repute. Though space does not permit a detailed study of religious art history, we will briefly consider some examples of the relationship between the church and the arts, limiting our discussion to developments in English history.

In the Middle Ages several forms of religious drama flourished. Liturgical drama was performed in Latin in many churches; Miracle plays depicted the lives of the saints; Morality plays dramatised man's struggles with temptation, doubt, fear; Mystery plays enacted the main events of biblical narrative. From the point-of-view of the lay person, the Mystery plays were the most significant. Their production was a non-professional and communal affair in which each craft guild was assigned a particular play in the cycle. On the appointed day, each play was mounted on a large wheeled stage and driven through streets and market-places. One can imagine the spectacle: the colourful costuming and stage decoration, the music which accompanied the various scenes, the streets swarming with enthusiastic onlookers as the carriages plied their way through the crowds.

In his introduction to the Chester Mystery Plays, Maurice Hussey describes the variety of artistic richness which brought such excitement into ordinary life: 'They were made up of comedy, spectacle, pathos, activity, colour and music. In the medieval play cycle there was . . . (an) . . . inter-relation of the arts: verse, solo and choral music with the tonal colours of different musical instruments were to be heard while the visual spectacle was unfolding.'[2] In addition to their artistic variety and the communal spirit which their production aroused, the plays served the vital function of making biblical narrative available to the lay person. Even with touches of local colour and possibly fanciful additions, the content of the plays imparted a knowledge of biblical material that would otherwise have been inaccessible to the illiterate. In the words of Hussey: 'The plays could provide bridges across which the imperfectly educated could and did reach the central truths of their faith. . . . The play cycle indeed offered in its texts a synthesis of the hopes and faith of medieval man and in its performance each year a perfect summary of his culture.'[3]

Clearly one of the primary attractions of the plays was the mobilisation of the populace which their production engendered. When the plays were halted by order of Elizabeth I because of their decidedly Catholic traditions, they were replaced by plays performed by professional actors. This removed the ordinary folk from the status of performers and reduced them to mere spectators. The play's ability to involve and instruct the lay person was dealt a severe blow.

During the Elizabethan period, the religious themes of the Mystery and Miracle plays were superseded by the more psychological and historical emphases of Shakespeare, Marlow, and Jonson. Through their genius, court plays and the public stage made monumental advances, but the biblical content of the medieval plays was not translated into these arenas. Music was the primary art form through which spiritual thought found expression during this period. Indeed the musical brilliance of William Byrd, Orlando Gibbons and Thomas Tallis has continued to inspire the church through the ages.

Towards the end of the Elizabethan age, taste in drama grew generally more corrupt. The dramatists following Shakespeare and his contemporaries catered to their audiences' preferences. The ensuing decadence of the theatre gave a firm foothold to the Puritans' opposition to drama, though as one historian of the period points out: '. . . no "decadence" was primarily responsible for the success of the Puritans' final attack on the stage. . . . their objection was to the drama as essentially immoral in itself (not merely to immoral plays), and necessarily conducive to the most fatal of all sins, idleness.'[4] The Puritans' objection to music was more conditional. They forbade its use in church, but apparently enjoyed and appreciated it in the domestic sphere. Dance also, was not completely taboo, but the Puritans did condemn the lasciviousness which it sometimes occasioned. In this prevailing attitude towards the arts, religious feelings found expression in only one permissible art form. Through the poetry of Milton, Puritan spirituality was given artistic expression. Thus, in their preaching-centred worship the Puritans had no room for artistic enhancement. The use of drama, dance, or music in religious instruction or worship was not a possibility in the Puritan mind. Their negative feelings about the arts, and particularly towards the arts in worship, left their imprint.

A resurgence of Puritan seriousness and spirituality in the Victorian era also adversely influenced the development of the arts both in the Church and in society in general. In his *Illustrated English Social History,* G. M. Trevelyan succinctly appraises the Puritan strain in Victorian England and its effect on the arts: 'An individualist commercialism and equally individualistic type of religion combined to produce a breed of self-reliant and reliable men, good citizens in many respects – but "Philistines" in the phrase popularised by their most famous critic in a later generation. Neither machine industry nor evangelical religion had any use for art or beauty, which were despised as effeminate by the makers of the great factory towns of the north.'[5]

Thus, it is only fairly recently that a general revival of interest in the arts is motivating a re-evaluation of the arts in the church. And more specifically, within the last fifteen years, in the current renewal in the church, the potential of the arts for communicating biblical truth and enlivening worship is again being explored.

WHAT IS THE FOLK ART RENEWAL SAYING TO THE CHURCHES?

The present renewal in the church brings with it many changes, including a new perspective on the arts. Rather than dismissing the arts as something evil in themselves, the church is recognising them as a tool with potential for either good or evil. Though the arts have often been used to communicate confusion, alienation, and conflict, they can be harnessed to communicate God's love for his creation and his involvement in human lives. To recapture the arts for this purpose is a challenge for the church today.

Responding to this challenge, groups are springing up in many churches to work in dance, drama, music, mime, poetry and the graphic arts. Issuing from these groups are folk art expressions reflecting the groups' experience of both alienation and reconciliation, both confusion and resolution, both conflict and healing. Combined in the most effective expressions are a solid biblical perspective and contemporary language and style. Because of their contemporary flavour, the folk arts are re-establishing the church's communication with those for whom traditional language and style of presentation are remote. Therefore, rather than providing esoteric interest for the connoisseur, the folk arts are again bringing Christian teaching and worship into the language and experience of 'the folk'.

In addition to enabling the church to communicate more effectively to others, the folk arts also have something to say to the church itself. The folk arts renewal indicates the existence of deep needs in modern women and men – the need to discover our own resources for creative and artistic expression, and the hunger to get in touch with the sources of tradition and heritage that have shaped and nurtured us. These needs signal new directions in which the church must move.

First, the folk arts renewal affirms a basic truth: creativity is an essential aspect of our humanity. The folk arts assert that a portion of the human personality must be expressed in creative and expressive action. Thus, dance, song, poetry, drawing, decoration, craft are not just cultural niceties; they are basic human expressions. This truth presents a challenge to the church: will the church stir up this latent creativity and employ it in the service of the Creator, or will we be content to release it to the service of other masters, while we continue to complain about the boredom of worship services, and the ineffectiveness of Christian education?

Secondly, as the folk arts are opening treasures of heritage and identity to our friends in Sweden and Nigeria, why shouldn't they unlock similar riches for the family of God? Today, when the church seems to be going through an identity crisis, don't we need the anchor of a deeper knowledge of our heritage as God's people? Don't we need to be reminded of the family qualities and characteristics of our ancestors: faithful Abraham and Sarah, righteous Noah, bold Deborah, steadfast Mary? Now as never before, don't we need the encouragement of the stories of God's constant guidance and protection of his family, as we seek to be his family in our day? And can we afford not to tell the tales of our family history using the full gamut of creativity and expression available to us – songs of hope and faith, stories of courage and victory, dances of joy and praise?

Believing that these challenges must be met by the church, we have selected the material in this book to assist God's family to explore the depths of our family legacy. Through such exploration we trust we will find the encouragement and faith to sustain us and remind us that we, who were 'once no people, are now God's people' (1 Peter 2:10).

NOTES

1. Scottish Arts Council Report '78, pp. 2–5.

2. Maurice Hussey, *The Chester Mystery Plays* (Heinemann, London, 1957), p. xi.

3. M. Hussey, *Ibid*., pp. viii, xii.

4. Godfrey Davies, *The Early Stuarts 1603–1660* (Oxford University Press, London, 1959), p. 398.

5. George M. Trevelyan, *Illustrated English Social History* (Penguin Books, Harmondsworth, 1964), p. 60.

A folk approach implies openness to indigenously created songs and hymns, a continual search for materials that will express the myths and symbols and facts of Christian and biblical existence, and a flexible form in which these can be transmitted to the congregation. What characterises the folk approach is the primary value placed upon simplicity and accessibility . . .

STEPHEN C. ROSE
FROM 'Folk Approach to Church Music'
The Christian Ministry[1]

. . . because Christians have been made new in Christ, they are now in a position to appreciate God's true intention for man and the world, and create beauty in art as a result. So we will pray as we work. We will pray to the Lord for help – to open our eyes to the real possibilities, to open our eyes to see how we can achieve the best for our fellow human beings, to help us in creating according to the best that is in us.

H. R. ROOKMAAKER
FROM *Modern Art and the Death of a Culture*

CHAPTER 3

Keys

Unlocking the Folk Arts

Then Traveller, whose feet were tiring, whose head ached with his journey, saw before him a large house. The windows were amber lights of warmth and welcome, beacons in the darkening sky. Smoke curled from the chimney, the evening breeze carried the scent of thick stew and freshly baked wheat bread. At last, companionship and refreshment! He approached the front door, noticing appreciatively the sign in the garden: GO RIGHT IN. Turning the doorknob expectantly, he was surprised when the door failed to open. He tried again, and again, thinking the door stuck; and then suddenly realised that it must be locked. 'Hah!' he said. 'Go right in!' Peering through the large window, he saw still another door, its lock clearly visible. Even if he got through the first door, he would still have to unlock the second. 'Go right in,' he repeated crossly. 'But how?!' Weariness and disappointment frustrated him, and he pounded on the door and pulled the knob fiercely, futilely, exclaiming aloud:

The door is locked, I can't get in!
The door is locked, I say,
I find no way
To open it!
I'm weary,
I've come a long way.
But the door is locked,
I can't get in!
Where are the keys!

How discouraging, to travel so far and be thwarted! This story may parallel feelings about implementation of the folk arts, particularly if the ventures are new ones. Perhaps you have caught sight of the house, welcomed the invitation and approached, but now wait outside. In this chapter we focus on guidelines which will unlock the folk arts. These key principles are simplicity, spontaneity, use and development of resources, planning and placement, and skilful use of humour.

SIMPLICITY

Folk art is often unsophisticated, uncomplicated. A child's drawing may capture the essence of a teaching point, a simple song crystallise the direction of an entire group. Leave the great productions, the intricate harmonies, the polished dance routines to the professionals – at least initially! Occasionally the lengthy, elaborate drama will be appropriate; ordinarily it's the three-minute narrated mime or forty-second reading that's needed. As you become more experienced, projects can develop in depth and detail; but early on, approach them as basically as possible. Look for the simplest way of conveying a point or presenting a concept. This will have a stabilising effect, helping to keep projects and projections at a realistic level.

How is this principle of simplicity applied? Imagine that you are in a planning group. Depending on the project, ask the appropriate questions: What do we want to communicate? What folk art form(s) (drama, mime, dance, story, etc.) would be most effective, or most attainable for us at the moment? Which songs would build the theme? Which scripture contains the essence of the intended teaching point? Your discussion will probably result in many good suggestions, as well as some that are obviously unusable. Give yourselves enough time to sift through the ideas, remembering it won't be possible to develop all of the good ones. Decide on one idea and refine it to its simplest shape. Consider factors like number of people required, preparation time necessary or available (the amounts often differ!), location of presentation, streamlining of style or techniques. Be able to summarise, in one statement, the purpose or concept of your project. Allow time, when preparing or rehearsing, to think as you work. If progress seems to bog down or pressures build up, pause to ask yourself questions: What do we want to convey? Are we still working toward that, or have we got sidetracked? Where are we now? Was our original idea too complicated? Is our teaching point becoming confused? Don't hesitate to halt so you can reassess the direction and shape of your work.

Simplicity then, is a keynote. It's easily forgotten, so sound it often!

SPONTANEITY

Spontaneous development is a unifying, satisfying group experience. The idea that suddenly emerges, the suggestion tentatively offered and appreciatively received, the new instrument to experiment with, the poem impulsively shared and then worked with – from such raw stuff can come rich expressions charged with vitality. Occasionally a group will go in an entirely new direction: a shift from the working pattern previously structured, a different dramatic ending than the one envisioned in the planning session, an idea that deepens or broadens the concept being developed. Why is it that some groups share such lively experiences? Flexibility, in leaders, time and atmosphere, is frequently the hidden factor.

Leaders

Both the attitudes and practices of those who lead have all to do with spontaneity in a group. Leaders and teachers either narrow or widen the range of possibility. They confirm or refute people's negative or hesitant opinions of themselves, they preclude or include spontaneous group interaction. Chapter 17 develops this point in depth.

Time

Lack of time can discourage spontaneity. Leave 'space' when structuring rehearsals, workshops, planning meetings. Be sure of your overall intent, but allow enough room within the structure for people to feel comfortable and even adventuresome. Particularly if your people are inexperienced or apprehensive – or if you are! – there will be a tendency to arrange activities and goals too rigidly. Participants will feel boxed in rather than directed. They may also feel that as individuals they aren't really necessary, that they're just automatons reproducing someone's programming.

Avoid these impediments by planning the details of your project as fully as possible while still leaving the way open for group contribution. Participants know their ideas are welcome when leaders solicit suggestions and modify arrangements. At the same time, maintain orderly progress. Group meetings shouldn't be a whirl of unfettered suggestion-making, constant discussion, undisciplined idea implementation! Some possibilities can be experimented with straight away, others will have to wait until another day or another group.

Atmosphere

Spontaneity is rather like a shy doe, likely to disappear if threatened or overwhelmed. A light, open atmosphere, relaxed and easy, is conducive to people being able to think and work creatively. Similarly, a stilted, formal atmosphere, or one that emphasises competitiveness, will stifle or restrict natural abilities. Martha recalls how this latter approach discouraged her: 'In my childhood I experienced the results of a competitive approach in my study of the piano. I remember vividly the clammy palms and thumping heart of public piano recitals and competitions. Other children thrived on the contests and attention, but I was very self-conscious. These occasions were a source of great anxiety.'

People are especially vulnerable when attempting something new or working hard to perfect something. If they feel condescended to or laughed at, their natural inhibitions will only increase. Sometimes people 'freeze', unable to even think clearly. But in a warm environment, where acceptance, caring and appreciation are obviously held in greater esteem than competition or success, people are succoured, nurtured, released.

To encourage spontaneity, work towards the goal of flexibility. Good leaders should be willing both to plan prodigiously and to change freely. Remember, these are the folk arts, and it's good to let the folks have a chance! Equally, responsible participants will learn to offer their ideas freely, without demanding that they all be applied. As your group works out this principle of flexibility, you'll find your relationships, enjoyment and projects flourishing. Spontaneously you will find the group developing an extra part in the drama, or discovering the instrumentation that solidifies the style of a song, or working out the teaching device that seemed so elusive.

USE AND DEVELOPMENT OF RESOURCES

'But we don't have anything to work with!' 'What we need are some dramas, or new songs, or____________(fill in the blank).' Churches and schools frequently declare resource material one of their greatest needs, and rightly so. Clearly developed material of good quality supplies direction, establishes a working structure and conserves precious preparation time. It also works as a stimulant, engendering new ideas and discussions.

The material in Part II can be used not only in performance but also as a springboard. After learning the basic folk dance steps, rearrange them, making dances for your favourite songs. Study the structure or non-structure of the poetry, and have your own writing workshops. Examine the lyrics of the suggested songs, particularly those based on scripture, and then write your own lyrics, using scriptures of special personal meaning.

People often have, within their own situations, the potential to create material they know they need. But they may fail to recognise their own potential. In churches, schools and communities all over the world, we have found that groups have a wealth of latent ability, enthusiasm, desire and talent, and hidden in the most unexpected fields! The man who has faithfully kept the books for twenty-seven years may have a box of his own poetry under his bed; the woman who's always organised the suppers so well and so cheerfully, humming and whistling as she works, may have within her heart melodies which would be delightful songs.

The secret of creating your own material is positive expectation. Expect material to emerge from your people, material unique to your culture, your environment, your common concerns. If a few leaders or key people begin expecting fresh and lively expressions in worship and teaching to come from their local group, and look for hints of such potential, they will almost certainly find it! Perhaps not a cellist, as anticipated, but the secondary school flute player, to provide a musical background for a dramatic scripture reading. There may be no trained dancers in obvious sight, just a handful of people with a desire to experiment. Meeting, praying and talking together will result in surprises: the experienced mentor suddenly materialising from apparently nowhere, a book to give needed guidelines, a grandmother 'who was a leading ballroom dancer in her day, and knows just a few steps that might be helpful. . . .'

Providing an arena to develop people's abilities and latent gifts is just as important as believing that they have them. Workshops (developed at length in Chapter 17) are just such an arena.

In summary, do use material and resources already developed, and also pursue the idea of creating your own. Be open to new ideas, new expressions, new experiences, new participants and leaders. Cultivate a faithful expectation of the Lord. He has promised to supply everything we need, which means we should either pray for specifics or ask him to show us his provision. Correspondingly, regard yourselves and others expectantly. We ourselves are often the Lord's means for meeting needs or answering prayer. It won't be too long before you find yourselves becoming a resource centre for others. . . .

PLANNING AND PLACEMENT

Skilful use of the folk arts, particularly in worship, depends upon planning and placement. A mime may convey the intellectual point, but if inappropriately placed it will disrupt the flow of the entire service. One of your groups may have just developed a wonderful new reading, but if its content leads in another direction than that of the morning's scriptures, people will be confused rather than edified. Similarly, songs unrelated to dramas or graphics unrelated to times of prayer will have a disintegrating rather than heightening effect. The dance group may be lovely once the dance has begun, but a great deal will have been lost if the dancers had to clatter their way forward, or if time gaps were created because they weren't sure of the available space. One of the pleasures of some services may be their familiarity: certain prayers said at certain times, people knowing when to move, to sing, to remain quiet. Just as rigid adherence to tradition can be deadening, so interrupting an expectable rhythm abruptly or insensitively works an unnecessary hardship. The end product of instances like these is a fragmented service seeming more like a three-ring circus or variety show than a corporate, unified expression and experience of worship.

Sensitive planning is one way to avoid such unfortunate occurrences. A service planning group, meeting regularly or irregularly, helps eliminate the possibility of fraction or friction. Such groups have varying forms. In many churches the ordained minister and music director are primarily responsible for worship. They may plan a project and then commission its execution, liaising with a group or appointed leader; or they may invite others to join their planning meeting. Other churches and communities are now structuring groups that combine service planning with aspects of pastoral care. New expressions of worship are incorporated as such a group senses the need for a drama rather than a spoken sermon, a new song rather than a familiar one. In other instances, groups working within the church may offer to those responsible for the worship some new idea or project; and sometimes, *ad hoc* groups are established, such as one that begins in late October to prepare a series of Christmas presentations.

A crucial factor for co-ordinating new expressions in worship is good communication. Since it's easy to confuse or misunderstand what people say or mean, those who are in planning meetings must work hard at building effective communicating channels. They must also be diligent to be sure that the channels are kept open.

Whatever structure your local situation has or requires – and structures often change – the important principles are: perceptive awareness of the entire congregation; sensitivity to the rhythm and shape of the worship; careful planning; clear communication; at least one rehearsal in the actual location.

SKILFUL USE OF HUMOUR

In a worship service, a story-instead-of-the-sermon began with 'Once upon a time . . .' Afterwards, three-year-old Susann turned to her mother wide-eyed, saying, 'Mummy, Martha said "Once upon a time" in *church*!' Even at her tender age, Susann had already realised that there are certain ways of speaking in certain situations, and that church is a place where 'fairy tale' words usually aren't heard.

Are we as aware as Susann of the narrow limits we have imposed upon ourselves? Frequently our spontaneity of expression or activity is confined by the rigidity of our institutional structures. In churches or schools we are meant to walk quietly, sit or stand at marked intervals, respond as expected, directed or socialised. At sports events however, we see people as they really are: enthusiastic, spontaneous, concentratedly involved, bound together in a common cause, relatively oblivious – sometimes to a negative extreme! – to the judgements of others. View the same people in a church or school, and they are likely to be stiff and reserved, a bit uncomfortable, and distracted with awareness or fear that others may be watching them critically. In church, answering the minister's rhetorical questions would prove an embarrassment to all present, as would asking our own questions to clarify a misunderstood sermon point. Perhaps we wouldn't really mind the appearance of a spontaneous dance during the offering, or an impulsive diversion from the expected rituals – if there was anybody spontaneous or impulsive enough to do something! Or a hearty laugh, rather than the sedate chuckle, as an anecdote tickled our fancy. . . .

It's the hearty laugh, or lack of it, that shows us how far removed from our humanity we can become in institutional environs. Often the laughter heard in social or public situations, particularly schools, is the rather brittle, mocking sort that occurs because of a mishap or at the expense of someone's embarrassment. But the warm, shared laughter that comes from a common experience of delight is another kind entirely, and can be a powerful linking force. Humour also helps dig out our stiffened, sometimes buried, humanity. In the context of worship it adds an element of relaxation and naturalness sometimes lacking, and in pastoral situations it can aid in Christian nurture. In education its effectiveness is almost unparalleled, particularly when used in dramas and mime, for people enjoying themselves learn more quickly and better.

Using humour is certainly not an original idea. Providing a vehicle for an indirect approach, it has been used throughout the ages. Libraries are filled with books and stories that communicate forcefully and pointedly because of their humorous tones. In both theatre and circus, the clown has always been a major symbolic figure with import far beyond his actions and words. Traditionally, ministers and after-dinner speakers have used humorous anecdotes to spark interest or stress a point.

Humour has an inherent, perhaps instinctive, appeal. We like to think ourselves fully in control of our lives and of the lives of those close to us. In actual fact, life is filled with complications and incongruities. When the unexpected suddenly rears its unharnessed head, we are left breathless and exposed. We realise anew what we have sometimes suspected: we cannot control. It is easier to cope with this realisation, easier to perceive it in perspective, when we encounter it through humour.

Humour aligned with dramatic action forges a practically irresistible combination. Dramatic action alone is compelling: few souls are stout enough to resist the appeal of a story unfolding before them. People become involved with the characters, identifying with or rejecting their situations, actions, reactions. Dramatic action which incorporates humour is even less resistible! It will usually make a point with greater impact than the verbal approach, which often means 'drilling' concepts into people.

Techniques of humour

Exaggeration, gentle satire, even slapstick are effective humorous devices. Personification of inanimate objects is another. Imagine, for instance, a drama featuring a large red tomato with human characteristics of thought, energy and activity. This tomato devotes its life to stealing vitamins from the sun, water from the smaller plants, and warmth from the soil. Watching the tomato's actions, seeing its selfishness and insecurity and the resultant havoc, can give us interior glimpses into our own actions and attitudes. But because they have been presented to us in such an inoffensive object as a garden vegetable, we don't feel personally insulted. We are able to experience self-awareness exclusive of the fear or humiliation that fingers are pointed at us. Discovering our weaknesses in this indirect manner is less threatening or painful than being confronted with them in other ways. 'How Can the Body be Complete?' p. 237, is an example of this personification technique.

Personification and correction

Correction is an important aspect of pastoral care, yet also one of the most sensitive. Most of us have had painful experiences that have left us somehow wounded or vulnerable: at certain times our responses to other people or situations may be laced with anger, fear or defensiveness. These self-protective responses may be especially activated if we feel threatened or criticised by correction. Sometimes, particularly in one-to-one counselling relationships, the person being advised may reject what the counsellor says and end up directing intense personal bitterness towards the counsellor. In other circumstances the correction may be misunderstood, or dismissed as unnecessary or boring.

Humorous drama (including mime, gesture and movement) however, creates a relatively uncharged atmosphere conducive to some types of correction. Humour as a dramatic device helps defuse possible antagonistic responses, and the personification technique helps remove the tendency to respond defensively.

A healthy experience of correction will include at least three steps: awareness (self-recognition), the genuine desire and decision to change (repentance), and personal acknowledgement and ownership (confession) of characteristics or behaviour pointed out. Integrating these steps, and present in all of them to greater or lesser degree, is catharsis, or release of emotional tension. The drama with a red tomato is a simple idea, but it can set this extremely complex human process into motion. Humour is helpful because it establishes a reliable foundation: it makes a focal point. The laughter caused by the red tomato is not only our intellectual response, it is also a channel for our emotional responses. Guilt, shame and anxiety may all have been stirred by this seemingly innocuous red tomato, and they can be released through our laughter. We laugh at the tomato, but we also laugh at ourselves and the human condition. Our laughter contains not only amusement but also the painful recognition of our own attitudes and actions. The very fact that we are able to laugh, that the tomato provides a focus and direction, eases our pain. This easing is itself a release of tension, which opens even wider the way for change in our thought and behaviour. Sometimes the need for reassurance of our acceptability (forgiveness) is also stirred: the emotional tension is not fully released. At this point counselling may be uniquely effective.

Humour well-handled makes some types of correction simple and almost painless. But humour is a tool to wield with care and skill. Like any other incisive instrument, it can cut cleanly and surely or slice and sever painfully. If used cruelly or manipulatively, its effect can be devastating.

> A sudden blur to the left of his head, followed by a broken metallic clank, caused Traveller to look down in quick surprise. Lying at his feet, clearly visible in the soft light shining through the house's windows, was a ring of keys. 'Just what I need!' he exclaimed, stooping to pick it up. He selected an octagonal brass key and eagerly fitted it into the heavy brass lock of the front door. It turned smoothly, and he stepped through the door that opened before him. Holding the keyring high, he found the silver key that fitted the second door's lock.

NOTE

1. Copyright 1979 Christian Century Foundation. Reprinted by permission from the March 1979 issue of *The Christian Ministry*. See also p. 48.

The Bible is an untapped reservoir of living water waiting for the poetic imagination of the churches to immerse itself and surge forth . . . I believe that the folk process provides an exceedingly effective mode of getting at biblical reality. If a text can be turned into a song – a good song – then it can come alive for the people.

STEPHEN C. ROSE
FROM 'Folk Approach to Church Music'
The Christian Ministry

. . . a God who has been experienced in joy, who has touched our lives by his presence, the living God who speaks to his people and communicates with them, who acts and manifests his presence in his marvellous deeds on their behalf.

PAUL HINNEBUSCH, O.P.
FROM *Praise: a way of life*

The creative arts have a vital part to play in proclaiming the Word which once became flesh. Drama, dance, mime, painting, photography, architecture, tapestry: all of these can tell the glory of God and proclaim his handiwork.

DAVID WATSON
FROM *I believe in Evangelism*

Chapter 4

Source and Resource

The Scriptures in Our Lives

'But how do we start?
We believe we do have the potential . . .
to enliven our worship and teaching
to gather in small groups to share and work
to produce our own material
. . . but we don't have any ideas!
Where do you get yours?!'

This question is easily answered by noting titles of Fisherfolk dramas, songs and poetry: 'Jonah', 'Only Be Strong, and of Good Courage', 'Mr. Noah', 'Put On Love', 'The Good Shepherd', 'Peter', 'Ho, Everyone That Thirsteth', 'The Woman at the Well' . . . the catalogue could go on and on. Time after time, our ideas and inspirations have come from the Bible.

Panorama, history, drama, theology, the recording of God's word – we find the Bible is all of these. But how do scriptural stories, obviously set in cultural and sociological contexts entirely different from our own, relate to contemporary life? In what ways are the scriptures foundational, informative and directional? How do they specifically provide vision and insight?

In this chapter we list five basic concepts, all of which are developed and amplified in the scriptures. We have found that most of the material we create is related to one or more of these themes, which include God's identity, God's speaking, accepting our humanity, God's people and God's kingdom. In each section we share points which have been of particular significance to us, as well as examples of their applications in our lives and ministry. Additionally, we relate to each concept one or more of the questions posed above.

GOD'S IDENTITY: THE PERSONAL GOD

The scriptures are foundational . . .

> 'Now as Saul journeyed he approached Damascus, and suddenly light from heaven flashed about him. And he fell to the ground and heard a voice saying to him, "Saul, Saul, why do you persecute me?" And he said, "Who are you, Lord?" And he said, "I am Jesus . . ."' Acts 9:3,4

'Who are you, Lord?'

At some point in our lives, each of us who were Fisherfolk had asked that question. Not all of us had started with it, some had been stirred by prior questions: 'What is life about?' 'What should I do with my life?' 'How does one cope with such seeming absurdity?' 'Who am I?' This last enquiry was often of special significance. Many of us were propelled into a search for God when answers to this question rang hollow. In seeking our own identity, we were led into the question, 'What – or who – is beyond me?' We found that lacking knowledge of God, we lacked real knowledge of ourselves. At some point then, each of us had been intrigued, confused, quickened or overwhelmed by the deep and broad questions of life, meaning, purpose.

'Who are you, Lord?'

God answered us each personally, just as he answered Saul. And though the answers came in varying fashion, for each of us it was the same: 'I am Jesus.' He was the Way, and as we followed him we were led into other relationships: knowledge of God as loving Father, experience of God as Holy Spirit, kinship with welcoming brothers and sisters in God's family. Jesus led us, but we had much to learn about relating to God and others trustingly, lovingly, comfortably. The Bible soon came to our aid! It is essentially a book about relationships, telling the open-ended story of God's relationship to people, of people's growing awareness of his love. God is continually offering himself to people, and in the Bible we encounter those who love him, those who reject him, those who obey him, those who betray him.

This God is not a disinterested watchmaker, sitting in celestial objectivity. He is rather the God of David, the poet-King of Israel. Reading David's psalms is like reading his private journal, so full are they of the intimacies of his relationship with God. God was loving, chastising, forgiving; David was faithful, rash, trusting, strong-willed. If ever a relationship endured stress and discomfort, as well as enjoying fidelity and delight, it was David's and God's.

This God is not an angry tyrant, watching eagerly for human

error; he is rather the God of Hosea, a prophet of Israel. Through Hosea God spoke words of infinite tenderness, wooing love, pained grief. Nor is this God a fair-haired youth slipping through hazy cine camera lenses. He is rather the God of Zaccheus, the despised tax collector disdained by the Jews but sought out by Jesus. This God, who became human, is constantly involved with his world, longing for his creatures to be involved with him. To that end he creates, perseveres, rescues and destroys. He speaks, directs, intervenes, arranges. This God is personal and passionate; it is he who answers 'I am Jesus!' when we, struck down or blind, cry out 'Who are you, Lord?'

The scriptures became a living guide, confirming our experiences and leading us into new ones. As we met others who asked the same questions that had absorbed us, we were eager to share the answers that we had found satisfying. The scriptures, our own experiences and the arts formed our communication. In Psalm 139, for instance, David records a profound awareness of God's love for him. While reading this psalm, Jodi, one of the Fisherfolk, realised anew God's love for her. She wrote a song, paraphrasing David's words for the verses, using words of reassurance that God had spoken to her as the chorus. The result was a series of questions and statements that she could sing to others:

Do you know that I love you?
Do you know that I care?
Do you know my love won't give up,
Anytime, anywhere,
I'll always care for you.

When you're walking, when you're sitting down
When you're talking, or standing around
I'm beside you, I'm behind you,
From beginning to end, I am there.

In your mother's womb as you grew,
I watched lovingly over you.
I have made you well, wondrously,
All my thoughts toward you grow hour by hour.[1]

God's love is personal. We experience it personally, we offer it to others personally. We ourselves were reminded of this through our forty-minute production of 'JONAH'.[2] Using drama, music, dance, mime and storytelling, it is a contemporary rendering of the Old Testament parable about Israel.[3] God asks Jonah to go to Nineveh, to warn the people about his unhappiness and displeasure with their wicked lives. Jonah refuses and flees. After a hefty tussle 'twixt God and man, involving an horrific three days in a large sea creature's belly, Jonah accepts the mission. The news of God's concern for them and his imminent destruction of their city, unless they change their lives, transforms the pagan Ninevites. The entire populace, including the king, humbles itself before the God of Israel. But Jonah is furious and storms off to sulk in the nearby desert hills. From his point of view, God is the exclusive possession of the Israelites and should not have forgiven their enemies.

One presentation of 'JONAH' is particularly memorable for us. It was during a large cathedral service attended by several hundred people. Mike was the Fisherfolk taking the off-stage, never-seen character of God. Throughout the drama Mike had spoken and reasoned, entreated and pleaded with Jonah, played by Gary. The citizens of Nineveh were shattered and lonely, portrayed by isolated, mechanical dancers. But Jonah had been unmoved by the Ninevites' pathetic lives. Mike, as God, had witnessed Jonah's stony-hearted rejection of human need, the self-righteousness that prevented compassion. Jonah had likewise stiffened his heart to the Ninevites' profound, lyrically danced repentance and tender reconciliations; again Mike had perceived the depth of Jonah's resentment towards God's charity and forgiveness. Now Jonah sat outside Nineveh's city walls, solitary and angry, alienated from God and humans, embroiled in wrath because of the death of the small tree that had given him brief respite from the burning sun. Beginning the final scene, in which God entreats Jonah time and again to forsake his anger, Mike's realisation of the magnitude of God's mercy was overpowering. His voice broke and he wept as he said the final words:

> O Jonah! Can't you see what has really happened? You're angry because a tree died, a tree *you* didn't plant, *you* didn't weed, *you* didn't water! A tree you had nothing to do with, except you sat under it for one day! Can't you see how I feel . . . about a city filled with thousands of men and women that *I* created, that *I* love, that *I* care for? A city of homes and animals and schools and lives, a city where people are confused and angry and scared and lost? O Jonah! You are angry for the death of one little tree – yet you're also angry because I didn't *cause* the death of thousands of people and creatures! Ah, Jonah, you weep when a tree is destroyed, but I weep when my people are destroyed!

Later Gary told us what it had been like for him. 'When I heard Mike's voice, begging me, pleading with me to change, I almost couldn't keep my character. I had such a strong sense of God's love, God's travail, as he seeks us out, that it took all of my will to remain

Jonah, the iron-hearted man who refuses God.' Talking with people in the congregation, we learned they had been swept with peculiar intensity into the powerful dynamics between God and Jonah. Their experiences paralleled Mike's and Gary's. All this made us realise that Mike's willingness to be touched by the Spirit had allowed him to be a channel through which the Spirit spoke to others. People had heard God through Mike's voice, characterisation, compassion.

At our lodgings that night, Gary shared a further awareness. 'Mike,' he said, looking directly at him, 'because it was your voice speaking God's words, it made me aware of you personally. I thought of how long we've known each other, of how much we've been through together.' Gary stopped, grinning a bit sheepishly, and we all chuckled. We too had been part of their relationship. Both Mike and Gary are gifted musicians, which had been an immediate and fast bond between them, but their differences in personality and opinion had caused more than one altercation. 'We've disagreed with each other, and misunderstood each other, and been afraid of each other. Yet we've also respected and accepted each other, and trusted each other. Through it all, what we've learned is how to really love one another. So, when I was playing Jonah, and had to just sit there, staying angry, hurling words of rejection and rage towards you, refusing to respond to your love – it was almost impossible! The more I thought about it later, the surer I was that Jonah, in his relationship with God, had gone through things of equal, if not greater, depth. And,' Gary paused again, looking around at us, shaking his head in puzzled sorrow, 'I just don't know how Jonah could have held out against God's love.'

Incongruous though it is, there are times when, like Jonah, we hold ourselves aloof from God. 'I Stand and Knock', p. 141, contrasts our sometimes stand-offish, regimented attitudes towards God with the full involvement he longs to have with us; and 'gooseberry pie', p. 170, depicts the inevitable futility we experience if we give our worship to something or someone other than God. Conversely, in two poems which combine traditional biblical imagery with contemporary language, 'Friday', p. 175 and 'the self-giving God', p. 178, we find descriptions of the enormous personal cost paid by God to ensure that we would have the opportunity of receiving his love.

The scriptures disclose God's identity and personality. They reveal his attitudes and desires, his hopes and plans, his intentions towards people. The arts help us translate these into messages spoken and heard personally.

GOD'S SPEAKING

The scriptures are directional . . .

The scriptures provide vision and insight . . .

Imagine a wealthy and powerful ruler. His enormous palace is set in grounds stretching mile after mile, his court is crowded with ministers of state, foreign ambassadors, professors, artists, servants. Banks are filled with his gold, silver and securities, leaded vaults protect rare and valuable jewels, his estate contains vast oil reserves. Yet all is shrouded by a strange languor. The servants are motionless, occupying the same places hour after hour. The representatives and diplomats are speechless, inactive day after day. Educators are wordless, their knowledge stilled; artists are unproductive, their work not even begun. All are waiting, waiting . . . for some word from the ruler. But there is none. There is no command, no direction, there are no enquiries, no indications of will or desire. The ruler's riches and resources are apparent, but how to employ them is a mystery. The ruler's status and authority are unquestioned, but how to serve him is unknown. The great prince is silent, mute.

Contrast that ruler with God, who is eager to communicate! Countless statements in the Bible detail God beseeching his people into dialogue. Many passages begin with God saying one of these: 'Hear me, my people', 'Listen to me', 'Incline your ear and hear what I say', 'Hearken to me'. The scriptures show God speaking across history's spectrum in a variety of ways: through creation, through individuals, through his son Jesus, through circumstances, through the human imagination. The scriptures are both a channel through which God speaks and a confirmation of his many channels. In the following section we relate parts of our own dialogue with God to our use of the arts, showing how the scriptures have clarified our hearing him.

Creation

Several Fisherfolk have felt particular affinity with the natural world. Its mysteries, beauties, anomalies have captivated their sense of awe and imagination. Yet this is not unusual, because for generations people have discovered God through nature. In Romans the apostle Paul refers to the created world as one of the more obvious ways God communicates with humankind: 'For what can be known about God is plain . . . because God has shown it. . . . Ever since the creation of the world, his invisible nature, namely his eternal power and deity, has been clearly perceived in the things that have been made.'[4]

Genesis records how things were made: God spoke, and the heavens, the oceans, land appeared; God spoke, and living creatures, plants, animals, beasts, came into being. Responding to these mysteries of creation, some of us have written poetry or songs which express our wonder and delight. The scriptures tell of the presence and power of the Holy Spirit in creation; is it any wonder that the Spirit continues to speak through creation, inspiring us?

One spring morning in Texas, Martha found gentle words of praise and an unknown melody going through her mind. Singing it aloud, she recognised that the imagery came from years lived in a small, Western Pennsylvania town. The melody's lyricism was a fitting accompaniment to memories of dawn-dappled hills as the sun rose over the mountains:

Soft as the sun shines through my window,
soft as gath'ring shadows in my hair,
soft as the morning glory, morning glory broke.
I woke and found you softly waiting there.

Although she never sang it aloud, the melody would occasionally waft through Martha's mind. Spring came again, and now Martha and other Fisherfolk were living in England. One evening Jodi asked Martha to listen to a new melody. She had been working on it for several days but didn't have any ideas for words. Jodi sang her new tune but wondered at the odd, increasingly stunned look crossing Martha's face. Breaking off, she asked if anything was wrong, whereupon Martha exclaimed, 'One morning when I was alone in our house in America, I heard the same melody! And I have words for it!' Together, Martha and Jodi completed 'Morning Glory':[5]

Clear as the sun on rippled waters,
clear as the bird-calls on the air,
clear as the waters laughing, waters laughing broke.
You spoke, I heard you clearly standing there.

Bright as the sun behind the mountain,
bright as the fiery death of day,
bright deep night's flaming glory, flaming glory spoke.
I broke and knew you bright beside me would always stay.

Sometimes an idea developed by one person has a domino effect on others. One of Maggie's poems contained both light-hearted and poignant natural images: 'mottled stickleback', 'crystal streams', 'silly camel', 'echoes of the starlight', 'shadows of the moon', 'howling night wind'. It went beyond nature however, to encompass God's intent for his people: 'But you I made my children to walk and hold my hand.' When Jodi read the poem she told Maggie that she had been reading J. B. Phillips's translation of Romans 8, which also combined the ideas of the natural world and the children of God. Jodi set Maggie's poem to music and made a chorus from Phillips's words: 'And all creation's straining on tiptoe, just to see the sons of God come into their own.'[6] The cheery, sing-along song was shared with the rest of the community during an informal communion service. As Margi listened, she thought it ideal for a children's dance. One evening she and Maggie collected together all the community's children and together they worked out the interpretative circle dance that now accompanies 'On Tiptoe', p. 262. The dance is a practical blend of simplicity and challenge. As long as a leader knows it, children can follow spontaneously; yet it isn't repetitively boring because the picturesque words ensure variety. Soon other children, in the parishes and towns we visited, were dancing along. But the story doesn't stop there. A couple of years later a group of Fisherfolk lived at a diocesan conference centre in Rättvik, Sweden for a summer. Although we were learning Swedish, our ministry involvements couldn't wait until we had mastered it. So mime came into its own! We developed several mimes portraying scripture stories or concepts, concluding each with a summarial or provocative one-line quotation. 'On Tiptoe', based on the Romans scripture Jodi used for the song's chorus, is one such mime.

Leaders, laws and prophets

> 'Samuel! Samuel!' the voice called. Awaking, the boy cried 'Here I am!' and then ran to the room of Eli, the old priest who was both father and teacher to him. 'Here I am,' Samuel repeated, 'for you called me!' 'No I didn't,' Eli replied. 'Go back to bed!' Obediently the boy returned to his room. But 'Samuel!' he heard again. The incident occurred twice more before Eli realised that the boy was not imagining things. Someone was indeed calling the boy . . . and it was God. 'Say "Speak, Lord, for your servant listens!"' Eli instructed him. The next time the voice called, Samuel responded as Eli had said.[7] Then God began with Samuel the dialogue that lasted the whole of Samuel's life.

This story about Samuel is representative of many Bible stories. God often spoke to and through individuals, conveying his plans and hopes. Early on he spoke to Abraham, Isaac and Jacob, guiding their lives and families. He spoke to Moses, making him the leader of the enslaved Hebrews. But God spoke in other ways as well. After freeing the Hebrews from slavery, God had to free them from the habits of idolatry learned in Egypt. To accomplish this he spoke again, this time in the form of law. Surrounded by smoke, spoken in flame, carved into stone, God's word gave the Hebrews a desperately needed values system. When they faithfully fulfilled the social, moral and religious requirements of the code, the Israelites' obedience welded them into a unique nation. But the Israelites became increasingly careless about keeping the law; frequently they were flagrantly disobedient. God continued to speak to them, this time through prophets. It was at great personal cost, however, that Old Testament figures such as Jeremiah, Ezekiel and Isaiah heard and spoke God's word, for they were trapped between a philandering, promiscuous people and a God jealous for fidelity. The Israelites were reluctant to hear God's word and rebellious against obeying it. They found it far easier to slander and slay the prophets who relayed that word than to acknowledge the God who spoke it. The group participation story on p. 194, 'The Faithful God of Daniel', makes clear the high price exacted from those who had pledged themselves to be faithful to God.

'The Potter',[8] a dance drama with music and poetic narrative, is based on words God spoke to Jeremiah about Israel.[9] This is another presentation evolved through friendship and collaboration. Its basis is a poem written by a very discouraged Patricia, who used Biblical imagery to express her despair. Jodi heard the poem and wrote an answer. This response told of a caring, concerned Potter who works with anything, even 'grey, grey lumps of clay', even 'a hard heart made of clay'. Thereafter, Patricia and Jodi often used the poems in dialogue talks about acceptance and love. More than six years later, a Fisherfolk team was reflecting on the scriptural idea of the potter and the clay. Jonathan had just written a song based on Jeremiah 18, and the team decided they wanted to develop the concept more fully. They found copies of the poetry, then Margi worked out a dance mime to both song and poems. The end product is more than a valuable teaching tool: it is also a chronicle of God speaking to us both through his word and through each other.

The Word made flesh

In Jesus, God's words lived on earth. No longer echoing through insubstantial vastness, nor chiselled by the Spirit onto stone, nor whisper-shouted to select few, God's word was tangible, knowable, accessible to all. It was spoken to humans in a way they could understand, through Jesus, another human. In the words of one of Tim and Jonathan's songs:[10]

> This same Jesus, we saw and we felt,
> His eyes met our eyes, His hands held our hands.

The gospels not only tell the story of Jesus, they also tell the stories of those who knew him. Reading these stories and reflecting upon them, we have frequently written about the people who encountered Jesus. A poem on p. 177, 'The Woman at the Well', is a cameo portrait of a rejected, self-rejecting woman, and her response to Jesus's tender and unprecedented acceptance. 'Revelation', p. 151, parallels the story of blind Bartimaeus, who waited by the side of the road for Jesus. When Jesus came, Bartimaeus implored his mercy and healing, and Jesus's words released him from his agony of fear, isolation, blindness.

Personal reflection on Jesus's love has called forth equally deep responses from us. 'Come, Lord Jesus'[11] and 'Never in my life'[11] are songs on the theme of Jesus's friendship. The reading 'Lord of Gentle Hands' p.162, and 'By Their Fruits', the congregational drama on p. 243, develop gospel accounts of Jesus's suffering and death.

Other New Testament books show that God continued to speak to and through individuals, but now there was a greater sense of interdependency. As the Holy Spirit joined people to God, the possibility and responsibility of hearing him speak was broadened. It was opened to all, rather than belonging primarily to a leader or prophet. The early Christians experienced themselves as members of a single body. Balanced and co-ordinated functioning was possible only when each shared with others whatever the Lord had said. Dreams, visions, unusual directions from the Holy Spirit abounded, and it was only as all spoke and all shared that God's word and intent were known. And sometimes, even when people had shared together, God's word didn't become clear to them immediately.

We ourselves have experienced this. Take, for example, a dream Arabella had in the autumn of 1970. At that time Betty Jane Pulkingham was involved in the coffee-bar ministry, where we were developing new ways to communicate the gospel. 'O Betty Jane!' Arabella said one evening. 'I dreamed about you last night! And when I woke up and realised what I'd dreamed, it was so outlandish I just laughed out loud! And,' she said, her eyes twinkling and her forehead furrowed in a mock frown, 'so obviously *out of the question*! But I've remembered the dream all day, and I think the Lord may want to say something to us.'

By now everyone's attention was fully captured. Other dreams of Arabella's had seemed ridiculous or humorous, but more than one had confirmed the Lord's direction. 'Well, Betty Jane,' she continued, 'I dreamed you had a baby!' And then she had to stop, interrupted by our shouts of laughter and muffled exclamations. Having already had six children, the youngest of whom was but two years old, Betty, sensibly enough, considered her days of child-bearing well over. So did Arabella, who was the childrens' nanny! Now we understand why the dream had been declared 'out of the question'. 'It was a boy,' Arabella carried on, 'and you named him, of all things . . .' she paused dramatically, '. . . Clyde!' This elicited further chuckles because all of Betty's children had either family or biblical names, and Clyde was neither. Then we sobered, considering what the Lord might be saying. In actual fact, none of us could make any sense of the dream and so, after fruitless pondering, we forgot it.

Forgot it, that is, until a community meeting in April 1974. Some Fisherfolk were now travelling for as long as three months at a time, and we increasingly needed an out-of-the-way home for recuperation after such lengthy tours. Wargrave, so close to London, was not such a place. As Graham Pulkingham described a prospective home in Scotland, he tried to define its location for us without aid of a map. 'It's an island off the west coast,' he said. 'Between the mainland and the island runs the Firth of Clyde.' A sudden stillness swept over us. 'The Firth of . . . *whom*?' enquired Arabella. 'Clyde,' repeated Graham. 'The Firth of Clyde.' 'My dream,' Arabella said into the silence. 'My dream, back in Houston in . . . in . . . when was it? The first year of the coffee-bar.' Only then, years later, did we understand God's mysterious word spoken in Arabella's dream. From the stage of the 'Way In' had come a renewal ministry which had 'sung and danced' its way across oceans. Seeds of the future had lain secret and dormant as Betty Jane and the rest of us prayed, talked, wept and worked together, communicating God's good news in ways that were meaningful to us. Those seeds had bloomed during our years in England, now they were to bear fruit in our research and development location on the Firth of Clyde in Scotland. 'You had a baby, Betty Jane. It was a boy, and you named him, of all things, *Clyde*!'

Yes, God still speaks in and through human flesh. The scriptures verify that the human imagination, with its capacity for dreams, vision and contemplation of the future, is one channel through which God speaks to people. Whenever one of us hears God through our imaginative abilities, we share with the others what that word seems to be. Sometimes, God's word or intention becomes clear to all of us, and we act accordingly. Other times, as was true with Arabella's dream, we are sure only of our lack of understanding. In those instances we reaffirm that times and plans are in the Lord's hands and that we must take no other action than prayer and patient waiting.

'Tableaux of Faith', p. 291, is a mini-survey of biblical people who heard and believed God's word. The Bible itself is the chronology of God's speaking, the history of his word to his people and the world. We find its precedents and guidance invaluable as we communicate with God and others.

> Listen, can't you hear the Lord speak to you?
> Listen, can't you hear him call your name?
> Listen, can't you hear the Lord speak to you?
> He wants to tell you what to do.
> He wants to show you who you are.
> He wants to fill you with his life.
> Listen, can't you hear the Lord speak to you?[12]

ACCEPTING OUR HUMANITY

Scripture stories, set in cultural and sociological contexts entirely different from our own, relate to contemporary life . . .

The scriptures provide vision and insight . . .

We . . . who are so often selfish and fearful,
who are so often unreliable in our responses to others,
inadequate in our abilities . . .
We are the people of God, the inheritors of his life and power?
No, surely not!
But God says it is so.

In us . . . who are sometimes bold in false bravado, reckless in assumed arrogance,
who sometimes disappoint those we love as well as ourselves . . .
The Spirit of God dwells in our flesh, the love of God is revealed to the world through our humanity?
No, surely not!
But God says it is so.

From us . . . who cannot always counter the challenge that we are fools, because we sometimes suspect it ourselves . . .
From our lives comes the kingdom of God?
No, surely not!
But God says . . .

Sometimes our negative thoughts seem more believable than God's word! But we are not the first to have such doubts. In the Bible we meet men and women with similar apprehensions and uncertainties. They also struggled with self-rejection and anxieties, they also felt themselves inadequate. But time and again God worked through their humanity, not despite it. The scriptures help us learn to love and accept ourselves, to appreciate our own humanity.

Consider Gideon.[13] Because of their unfaithfulness, God allowed the Israelites to be oppressed by their enemies. Seasonally, their crops and produce, their livestock, their land were wasted by powerful, marauding Midianites. One day, desperately attempting to salvage his wheat crop, Gideon took the grain into his wine press, hoping to thresh it undiscovered. The angel of the Lord appeared with the greeting, 'The Lord is with you, mighty man of valour!' Ignoring the latter for the moment, Gideon's unhesitating response was 'Right! And if he's with us, why are things so awful?'

When circumstances are not as we had hoped, when situations are thoroughly muddled, do we echo this response? 'If you were really involved, Lord, this couldn't have happened . . .' or 'I just can't believe that things would be this way if God really cared . . .' Yet continuing with Gideon, we see that God was involved and did care. The angel next told Gideon the Lord wanted him to lead an army against his enemies. And now Gideon's true response to the appellation 'mighty man of valour' surfaced. Again he answered in uncomprehending disbelief. 'Me? But my clan is the weakest of our whole tribe, and I'm the weakest member of our whole family!'

In other words, Gideon was a born loser, the least of the least. He was apparently the weakest of more than one million men; yet God had chosen him as his leader. It was obviously not because Gideon's family had a noble reputation or because Gideon himself was famed for his unflinching courage and military skill. God wanted someone who would trust and obey him, and he valued these characteristics more highly than background, skill, education or personal achievement. 'Go forth in this might of yours' meant 'You know you're weak, and absolutely dependent upon me. You yourself can achieve nothing.' This is a far cry from our cultural values which highlight personal accomplishment, self-sufficient strength, individual heroism!

Encouraged by God's reassurances, Gideon destroyed an altar built to a false god. When the Midianites and several other tribes allied and made preparations for retaliation, Gideon sounded the alarm for men to join him. But soon he was uncertain that even God could be victorious against such awful enemies. Gideon concocted a test: 'Lord, I'll put this sheepskin on the ground tonight. In the morning, if it's wet and the ground's dry, then I'll believe you're really going to do what you've said.' God fulfilled Gideon's request: the next day the ground was unnaturally dry and the sheepskin soaked. But Gideon was still afraid. He tested God again, this time asking that the sheepskin be found dry on dew-wet ground. Thus it was not until the third day, after God had twice proved himself, that Gideon made the battle plans.

Do we see ourselves mirrored in Gideon? 'I'm not really sure you'll do what you've said, Lord. Give me a sign.' 'Let's make a deal, Lord. If you come through with your part, maybe we can come through with ours.' Yes, as we struggle with faith and obedience, the knowledge that others chosen by God had similar struggles is reassuring to us. Gideon's unbelief shouldn't be a model for us, but his honest relationship with the Lord could. Witnessing Gideon's struggles with self-image and self-acceptance helps clarify our own.

Let's look again at Jonah. We may be tempted to judge him too quickly, offended by his flagrant refusal to obey God. But if we project ourselves into a setting with similar political realities, we may be more sympathetic with Jonah's initial reactions. Pretend yourself the citizen of a small, provincial country. Your nation has a widespread, often deprecated reputation for worshipping a strange, alien god, one totally unlike any other god worshipped by any other people. Right next door to you is an immense nation, unfathomably wealthy, overwhelmingly powerful. For as long as you can remember, that country has menaced and intimidated yours, sending harassment parties through the border areas, stealing or raping your women, threatening and provoking your small armies. And the most frightening part of that foreign nation is its capital. The imperial centre, an architectural showcase of magnificence and renown, it is massive and opulent, the nation's cultural focus. It's also filled with the sort of idolatry and debauchery that receive the death penalty in your own nation.

One Wednesday morning while you're working in the garden, hoping to get the potatoes hoed before lunch, God speaks to you. He tells you to go to that foreign land, to the capital in fact, to proclaim his word. Why, a border crossing alone could result in your death: your enemies would slay you just for sport! But to go to the very heart of that country, to confront all that wealth, arrogance and power? To bear the reprehensible defilement that would certainly accompany any contact with such pagan filth? And to say that *God* was watching them? God *who*? Those people wouldn't have a clue what you were on about!

Perhaps, in Jonah's situation, we too would say, 'Me, go there? Not on your life!' and then get as far away as possible as fast as we could. God's people from the past sometimes help us realise our loyalties are divided between obeying God and preserving our lives, between fulfilling his command and protecting ourselves. Or we may grapple with anger, finding ourselves unreasonably infuriated by God's love for others. We needn't follow Jonah's example of fear and resentment, but we can find hope in the realisation that God was merciful and patient with him. Examining the relationship between trust and obedience in Jonah's life will help us define it in our own.

In the New Testament we encounter Mary, Jesus's mother, living between revelation and darkness, knowledge and ignorance. 'Why Doesn't He Come?', the dramatic dialogue on p. 140, frames questions the first disciples might have asked after Jesus's death. Another meditation on this theme of balancing the known and the unknown is 'leaping', a poem on p. 156.

We discover Peter, alone and dazed, stopping at a campfire to warm himself. We hear him accused of friendship with an arrested political criminal and suspected religious saboteur; we watch as, fearful and confused, he attempts to return to his former life of fishing and net mending. 'As Peter', p. 155, tells a parallel story of a person's struggle to trust in a loving, caring God when the circumstances of life seemed to indicate otherwise.

We also find Paul, in the Book of Acts, sanctioning murder without trial. We see him securing the legal and religious rights to arrest any Jews not conforming to tradition and heritage. Paul may help us recognise similar motivations in ourselves: he may show us the depth of security we find in depending on traditions and systems. 'The Unforgiving Servant', p. 233, is another New Testament story based on impersonal legalism. The main character in this parable did not appreciate the value of mercy, so found it impossible to be merciful to another.

There are countless others: Matthew, Mary Magdalene, Thomas, Stephen, 'ordinary' people who loved and served the living God. Many of them were self-rejecting or had suffered rejection from others, many of them had painful pasts to overcome. Some were uncertain of their abilities, others over-confident. But as they continued in relationship to God, they learned to love and accept themselves and were gifted with the grace to love and accept others. We ourselves may swing, sometimes widely, sometimes narrowly, between acceptance and rejection of ourselves and others. Yet God is stable and unchanging. His firm intent is that we love him, ourselves and others, and he will help us realise it. Gideon, Jonah, Mary, Peter, all the others – God asked them for trust, not understanding; obedience, not ability; weakness, not strength. He asks the same of us today. Knowing these people from the past helps our response in the present.

GOD'S PEOPLE: THE FAMILY OF GOD

The scriptures are foundational, informative, directive . . .

The short winter afternoon was disappearing into five o'clock darkness. Our planning meeting was almost over – at least, the clock said it was. In actuality, we weren't sure. The mission we were participating in was lengthy and rapidly growing in complexity. Hundreds of school children, evangelised by love and music, had been turning up for the workshops and evening meetings; we wanted others on the mission team to share actual leadership with us, which meant extra planning and additional review meetings; there were teachings, dramas and music to plan and prepare for the open services. The clock did say five, the scheduled stopping time, but in fact we needed at least two more hours. It was cold, we were weary, our bodies, minds, emotions were stretched to straining – and there were still five days to come. Suddenly one of the Fisherfolk uncurled from his cramped position on the floor, rose and started for the door. There was something peculiar about his silence and we sensed he wasn't just going for coffee. 'Ah . . . where are you going?' Jodi asked.

Our friend halted, his back to us. Then he said softly, 'I'm leaving.' 'I beg your pardon?' gasped Jodi. 'I'm leaving,' he repeated, full voice now. 'I've had it. I can't take any more. There's too much to do, and not enough time, and I can't cope with it.' There was a momentary pause as we took in his words, and then Jodi faltered, 'But . . . but you can't just *leave.* We need you! What would we do without you?' 'I don't know,' he acknowledged, 'and I don't even know if I care.' Another silence. Then Jodi, who seemed the only one capable of responding, spoke again. 'But, where's your commitment?' she asked. 'I don't have it any more,' our brother answered. 'It's gone.' Silence . . . then all at once Jodi was on her feet, planning notes and Bible scattering on the floor, eyes flashing as she faced him. 'You're right,' she said, suddenly strong and sure. 'You *don't* have it any more. *I* do! You gave it to me, and I took it. And I'm not giving it back!' Now our dear friend was speechless. He stiffened, remained motionless for a few seconds. Then he relaxed, his hand dropping from the doorknob, his eyes filling with tears as he came back to our circle. 'That's true,' he agreed softly. 'So please help me.'

In a few words, Jodi summarised the wonder of God's grace among us. The Holy Spirit had made us more than friends, more than people who managed to work together consistently. In Christ's love, we had become brothers and sisters. Our lives, our relationships, our jobs had been unified at a deeper level than any of us could verbalise or theologise very accurately. But it was real, and we knew it. We had given ourselves to God and through him to each other; despite our differences, fears, anxieties, God had made us a family.

Reading and studying the scriptures, we found historical precedence for our experience. Both Old and New Testaments emphasise God's intent to form a people who will love him freely, worship him faithfully, obey him humbly. Tracing the formation of this people, we see that ultimately they become members of God's own family.

Initially we find Adam and Eve, created to know and love God, to live intimately with him. Then Abraham, to whom God revealed his intention of creating a people who could share his very life. Noah and his family were the centre of God's new beginning, God's hope for a creation and people faithful to him. The Hebrews were in bondage to the wealthy and powerful Egyptians, but God miraculously delivered them, then shaped them into a nation. Finally, through his son Jesus, God fulfilled his plan for humankind. God's people would no longer be limited to one race, one nation. The life and death of Christ meant all people, not just the Israelites, were freed from slavery to death.

This effected more than liberation, it created kinship. Just as people born into natural families are united by blood kinship so people born into God's family are united by Spirit kinship. Jesus opens God's family circle to humanity: the Holy Spirit makes people members of God's family. They become sons and daughters of God, brothers and sisters to each other. This, in fact, is what we experienced, just as the early church. Those first Christians were confident they had been engendered by one Father, ransomed by one Brother, made alive by one Spirit. For ages such powerful bonds as blood kinship, marriage, culture, race, nationality had united people – and separated them. But the Holy Spirit joins people in a bond of love capable of surpassing all natural bonds. Despite immense natural, cultural, national differences, members of the first church were united by the Spirit's distinctive power. They identified themselves as a family and addressed each other as 'brother' and 'sister'. Their human circles, just as ours, had been opened by the Spirit.

Knowledge of ourselves as God's people is one of our most profound awarenesses. An exuberant song and dance, 'Once no people',[14] p. 260, is based on Peter's words to early Christians: 'For you are a chosen race, a holy nation, a royal priesthood. Once no people, now God's people, proclaiming His marvellous light.' Our awareness is not static but ever changing, ever deepening, as the Spirit challenges us to new dimensions of love and commitment. The story beginning this section makes it clear that there are times when it is a genuine *endeavour* to 'maintain the unity of the Spirit' Paul describes in Ephesians. Appendix 4 is a listing of some aspects of life in God's family, together with material contained in Part II that develops them. Topics include the riches of God's promises and provision, diversity and unity among God's people, human resistance and repentance, relationships within God's family. Other aspects are God's relationship to his people, individual relationships to God, the relationship of God's people to the needy, the rejected, the dispossessed. It's possible to talk about the intended quality of these relationships but it is much more difficult to enflesh the talks with realistic examples. In a dramatic situation however, definite visual images are constructed. Thus the musical 'Ah! There's the Celebration'[15] is our attempt to convey visually, experientially and musically our ever-increasing awareness of the mission and role of God's people. Developed for the Edinburgh Festival Fringe, the full-length performance centres around several people whose sense of family pervades all aspects of their lives. Some have jobs, others care for the home. The Family is encouraged by Jesus, who is always present, and nurtured by each other's love; nonetheless, circumstances subject members to stress, misfortune and tragedy. Their lives become intertwined with the broken, the poor, the worldly-wise; they find their love and faithfulness constantly stretched by new confrontations.

The Family finds no easy answers. Gingerly they respond to painful questions, slowly they realise that, should those questions be asked again, perhaps a whole new set of answers would have to be given. Sometimes the Family finds no answers at all: they are left with searing questions. The Family suffers, it changes. Gradually its life is marked by qualities of maturity and hope not formerly present. One senses the Family is shifting orientations. Members no longer seem to expect immunity from adversity, nor are they so shocked when it comes. An excerpt from the title song expresses the musical's theme:

For the joy and for the sorrow,
Yesterday, today, tomorrow,
We celebrate.

For the sun and for the rain,
Through the joy and through the pain,
We celebrate.

Ah! There's the celebration:
Celebrate the whole of it!

As emphasised earlier in this book, knowledge of family background and heritage strengthens God's people's sense of identity. The scriptures impart this knowledge, helping us to 'celebrate the whole of it'.

GOD'S KINGDOM: VALUES AND LIFESTYLE

The scriptures provide vision and insight . . .

. . . cultural contexts different from our own relate to contemporary life.

God's word may clash with our cultural values, our own traditions, our background. What then? God's word may contain a directive, requiring action innately foreign to our experience or expectation, perhaps offensively foreign to the experience or expectations of family and others. What then?

As indicated throughout this chapter, the values of God's kingdom can be at sharp variance with those that perpetuate human institutions or stabilise societies. Sometimes the divergence is so great that God's people must make costly choices between the two standards. In such instances, or in preparation for them, knowledge of scriptural principles, models and precedents is essential and upbuilding.

Old Testament writings are often concerned with social injustice, religious faithlessness, cultural seduction. To obey God, one often had to leave or change everything. Consider Abraham. Surely God's sudden word to him, 'Go, leave your country, your family, your home; and I will lead you'[16] was the last command Abraham would have expected! It challenged every value, traditional, cultural and personal, that structured and gave meaning to his life. Yet he responded obediently, leaving his property, his father's household, his inheritance, his relatives and friends. 'Abraham and Sarah', p. 221, is a drama that raises in contemporary language issues these two may have grappled with before journeying in a direction and land unknown. Noah is another superb example. His society was corrupt and violent but he himself 'was righteous and walked with God'.[17] He was also willing to risk complete rejection and ridicule from those around him rather than disobey God. 'Mr. Noah'[18] is a mini-musical which makes clear the conflict that ensued when Noah began building the ark, a strange vessel never before seen, and collecting animals. Other Old Testament examples are found in the prophets, who were frequently at painful and dramatic variance with prevailing social norms.

The New Testament finds entire gospel segments, such as Matthew 5, 6 and 7 or Luke 6, confronting the ideals, standards and practices of Jesus's time. They confront ours no less. The parables of Jesus, which frequently cite cultural prejudice, religious hypocrisy and economic craftiness and deprivation, are as contemporary in meaning and application as when first spoken. The Prodigal Son mimes, Chapter 13, and 'The Unforgiving Servant', p. 233, mark the differences between Jesus's teaching and more predictable attitudes. Other New Testament books record activities and testimonies of the early church. They chronicle the first Christians' radical change, their literal revolution, in both attitude and action. Peter's vision described in Acts 10 is just one example of the cultural differences that God bridged between people. Religious values, social standards, relationships between men and women, economic patterns – all were transformed. 'The Hat Race', p. 214 and 'How Can the Body be Complete?', p. 237, are dramatic presentations which explore reversal of assumed attitudes.

In conclusion, we stress that when using the scriptures as the basis for any folk art expression, be sure you have read and studied them carefully. Be faithful to what you find, drawing out what is there; and be diligent not to read ideas, situations, concepts into them. Share and work with others as you develop material from the scriptures, for each person can offer experience and insight that is just a little different from anyone else's. Chapter 16 contains practical guides for writing scripture-based material.

NOTES

1. Recorded on 'Celebrate the Whole of It', Celebration Records.

2. Script enquiries: Celebration Publishing.

3. The Book of Jonah.

4. Romans 1:19–20.

5. Recorded on 'God Make Us Your Family', Celebration Records.

6. Romans 8:19.

7. I Samuel 3.

8. Available in Fisherfolk Kit 3, 'The Stone Quarry', Celebration Publishing.

9. Jeremiah 18:1–10.

10. 'Jerusalem Bound', recorded on 'On Tiptoe', Celebration Records.

11. Recorded on 'On Tiptoe', Celebration Records.

12. 'Listen, Can't You Hear the Lord Speak to You?', recorded on 'On Tiptoe', Celebration Records.

13. Judges 6.

14. Recorded on 'On Tiptoe', Celebration Records.

15. 'Ah! There's the Celebration', Celebration Records.

16. Genesis 12:1.

17. Genesis 6.

18. Available in Fisherfolk Kit 1, 'All Aboard the Ark', Celebration Publishing.

We usually think of praise only in terms of sound: words and song and joyful music. Perhaps we ought to think of it also in terms of light and colour and form. . . . To celebrate something is to cause it to shine forth. In celebrating, we make use of light and colour, sound and form, motion and touch, flavour and fragrance. . . . To praise God is to celebrate him, using every method we can in making him shine forth.

PAUL HINNEBUSCH, O.P.
FROM *Praise: a way of life*

Authentic form and expression of our liturgy grow out of our response to what God is doing in our midst. . . . People always worship out of their life-experiences. . . . Liturgy alone cannot renew a church or change a person. It can focus, deepen and nurture the faith already there. . . . If the liturgy is authentic, it will reflect those intersections where the gospel meets life. It will note crises, acknowledge events, interpret common concerns, and nurture Christian growth.

WILLIAM B. ODEN
FROM *Liturgy As Life-Journey*

CHAPTER 5

Living Praise

Folk Arts in Worship

'Not this dreary hymn again . . . it must be the organist's favourite. We seem to sing it every other week . . . always reminds me of Gran's church . . . it's been months since I've written her . . . maybe this afternoon after dinner . . .'

'Wonder how much longer he's going to talk . . . we've got to get out to the golf course before three if we expect to get a full round in . . . he's made that point before . . .'

'I hope the oven switches on in time for the roast to be well-done when we get home . . . I wonder which would be better, carrots and sprouts or cauliflower . . . Michael doesn't like sprouts and Sarah doesn't like cauliflower . . .'

Such distracting thoughts are probably not unfamiliar to many Sunday morning worshippers. Our attention is not compelled by the contents of a typical service, so our minds wander to other matters. Contrast this with the excitement before a football match, the intensity of a film, or the warmth of a family celebration. At such events all one's energies are focused on the present moment. One's mind, body and emotions are fully engaged. Time passes unnoticed. Can worship be as compelling as these events?

In our experience, the answer to this question depends upon our expectations. What should we expect of worship?

To answer this question we look at both Old and New Testament expectations and experiences. Our purpose is not to find a blueprint for contemporary worship, but to glean principles which may be applied in our own historical and cultural setting. In relationship to these principles we explore the ability of the folk arts to fulfil our expectations and renew our experience of worship.

Worship: functional or expressive?

Considering the question of expectation, Martha remembers with some amusement an incident from her childhood:

'I was staying overnight on a Saturday with a school friend who attended the Roman Catholic church. I was intrigued with the number of different masses – one every hour through the morning. At our church we only had two services and I always went to the same one – the family service. I asked my friend how she decided which mass to attend. "Well, if we have a lie-in and go at 10:00 a.m. or 11:00 a.m., we'll have to be there for an hour," she informed me, making an unpleasant face. "But, if we get up early and go to the 8:00 a.m. or the 9:00 a.m., we'll get the other priest. He gets through it in twenty minutes!" The incentive of getting through with church won, and we chose to get up a bit earlier in order to endure as little "worship" as possible!'

The decision was a pragmatic one. Why waste the day in church if one could perform one's duty to God in twenty minutes and have most of the day for one's own plans? But this approach to worship is an all-too-typical one. It reveals an underlying expectation of worship as essentially a functional event. By functional, we refer to those activities which serve a utilitarian purpose; ploughing a field, washing clothes, buying groceries, building a house – these are functional. Those who classify worship as a functional event see it as a series of actions to be performed in a prescribed way in which the doing of the acts, or the saying of the words, in themselves, accomplish a certain function. Thus, one feels that simply enduring the saying of the words for the allotted time fulfils one's weekly obligation. If this is the case, then by all means, let's have done with the ordeal in twenty minutes and get on with something more interesting.

Worship as it appears in all societies, however, is classified as an expressive occasion rather than as a functional one. Expressive events are those with no particular functional purpose, such as family gatherings, birthday or holiday celebrations, games and recreation. In the context of an expressive event the functional needs and demands of daily life are minimised, the pressures and duties of work and family are disregarded. One is able to relax sharp role and status distinctions, and to simply enjoy oneself. In such a relaxed, enjoyable atmosphere one's expressive capacities are drawn forth. In folk cultures which we previously discussed, expressive events incorporate singing, dancing, reciting poetry, telling stories. Such events meet an important human need: to occasionally step outside the requirements of survival, business, family life, and to experience oneself in a different dimension of enjoyment, festivity, and spontaneous expression.

As an expressive event, worship has much in common with other such events. In the words of Karl Barth: 'Confession is a serious act; but in its freedom from purpose it has more of the nature of a game or song than of work or warfare . . . as confessors we are not concerned with any end but only with the honour of God.'[1] So, when God's people gather to worship, they are not fulfilling an onerous duty. God's family assembles to acknowledge his love and to give thanks for his mighty acts in their lives; their expectation should be simply to enjoy God and each other. The atmosphere of worship should bear some resemblance to a family gathering where appreciation for each other is expressed in a warm, welcoming environment, gentle laughter, the telling of stories or the playing of favourite games. In such welcoming surroundings, the folk arts may easily become part of the worship event. As in other expressive events, creative abilities are drawn forth; song, dance, drama, and poetry may naturally express the praise and thanksgiving of God's family.

This expectation of worship may seem far removed from our contemporary experience, but worship as an expressive event was obviously enjoyed by the Jews. Throughout the Old Testament we are given glimpses of worship which is anything but functional and dull. Particularly in the psalms we are presented with a vibrant picture of whole-hearted worship:

> Shout for joy to the Lord, all the earth. Serve the Lord with gladness; come before him with joyful songs. Enter his gates with thanksgiving and his courts with praise; give thanks to him and praise his name.
>
> Psalm 100:1–2,4 NIV

> Let us go to his dwelling-place; let us worship at his footstool – arise, O Lord, and come to your resting place, you and the ark of your might. May your priests be clothed with righteousness; may your saints sing for joy.
>
> Psalm 132:7–9 NIV

> Praise him with the sounding of the trumpet, praise him with the harp and lyre,
> praise him with tambourine and dancing, praise him with the strings and flute,
> praise him with the clash of cymbals, praise him with resounding cymbals.
>
> Let everything that has breath praise the Lord. Praise the Lord.
>
> Psalm 150:3–6 NIV

Worship was not a grim affair; it was a time of joy – a celebration. This sense of celebration is reinforced in the accounts of the offering of sacrifices. These were not sacrifices in the contemporary sense of depriving oneself, in fact, at times they were occasions for festivity, as described in the Deuteronomy accounts:

> But you are to seek the place the Lord your God will choose from among all your tribes to put his Name there for his dwelling. To that place you must go; there bring your burnt offerings and sacrifices, your tithes and special gifts, what you have vowed to give and your freewill offerings, and the firstborn of your herds and flocks. There, in the presence of the Lord your God, you and your families shall eat and shall rejoice in everything you have put your hand to, because the Lord your God has blessed you. Deuteronomy 12:5–7 NIV

Evidence may also be found for the presence of great animation and even *noise*, in the context of worship. In the Chronicles story of the army of Jehoshaphat we are given an example of extremely lively worship. When confronted by a vastly superior enemy, Jehoshaphat sent a *choir* (of all things!) at the head of his army to 'sing to the Lord and to praise him for the splendour of his holiness' (II Chronicles 20:21 NIV). Their praise was so energetic that their enemies, frightened and confused by the noise, proceeded to kill each other. One can hardly imagine such a response to contemporary lukewarm hymn singing!

Comparable animation and enthusiasm is also seen in New Testament worship. Though we find little that describes actual worship procedures in the New Testament, we may gain some insights by reading between the lines. In Paul's letters to the Corinthians we see that the main problems in worship seem to be the ordering and discipline of enthusiasm. There was obviously freedom for each person to participate in the worship, rather than exclusive control by a few. Such freedom existed in fact, that several were speaking at once, causing general confusion:

> What then shall we say, brothers? When you come together, everyone has a hymn, or a work of instruction, a revelation, a tongue or an interpretation. All of these must be done for the strengthening of the church. If anyone speaks in a tongue, two – or at the most three – should speak, one at a time, and someone must interpret. If there is no interpreter, the speaker should keep quiet in the church and speak to himself and God . . . For God is not a God of disorder but of peace.
> I Corinthians 14:26–28,33 NIV

Since the Corinthian church was a Gentile church, it was probably not typical of the worship of the Jewish Christian congregations which were influenced by the synagogue; for by that time, the earlier spontaneity of Jewish worship had been superseded by more formal temple ritual. Still, in this description of Corinthian worship we glimpse, in its least disciplined form, the enthusiasm which infused the worship of all the early churches to some extent. The presence of such enthusiasm indicates an expectation and experience of worship as an expressive event. This picture is reinforced by other passages where Paul states his expectation of the worship of the early churches:

> Do not get drunk on wine, which leads to debauchery. Instead, be filled with the Spirit. Speak to one another with psalms, hymns and spiritual songs. Sing and make music in your heart to the Lord, always giving thanks to God the Father for everything, in the name of our Lord Jesus Christ.
>
> Ephesians 5:18–20 NIV

It is not clear whether he is referring to a specific worship event or to worship as a part of daily life. One can imagine either – a worship event with people singing freely and spontaneously, or an everyday scene with people working together, encouraging each other as they work with favourite hymns and psalms. In either case, worship is certainly expected to be enjoyable, relaxed, and spontaneous rather than dutiful and dull.

How can we restore this expressive nature to our worship? A careful consideration of the qualities of other expressive events provides us with some direction.

The folk arts: a stimulus to expressive worship

An expressive event communicates on many levels through a variety of stimuli. At a football match, excitement and competition are engendered not only by the playing of the game, but by the total environment: waving flags, supporters wearing team colours, frenzied cheering and shouting, enthusiastic singing. Similarly, in a family Christmas celebration communication is multi-faceted. The Christmas tree and colourful decorations transform the sitting room from its usual functions to the setting for extra-ordinary events. The familiar scent of evergreen branches mingled with the aroma of cooking turkey; Aunt Margaret playing Christmas carols on the piano; mother wearing her red velvet dress with a sprig of holly in her hair; brightly wrapped parcels appearing underneath the tree. The message is communicated to every sense: something special is happening!

Compare these events with the usual worship setting. Rows of pews restrict one's view of the other participants. Cold and uncomfortable buildings necessitate wearing bulky coats which increase one's sense of isolation. Insufficient or poorly situated lighting casts shadows and creates a general sense of gloom. Plodding or erratic music with archaic words feels strangely out-of-step with the rest of our lives. These factors certainly create an environment, but it is one which conflicts with the good news it is trying to communicate.

The elements of sight, sound and movement that communicate to all our senses may be brought into worship through the arts. As we walk into the church colourful banners may arrest our attention and lend an air of festivity (see p. 464). Our sense of expectation is further aroused by the reading of a poem which proclaims the Lord's presence amongst us. Contemporary music sensitively combined with traditional hymns interjects a note of freshness and immediacy. A simple, interpretative dance stirs our desire to offer ourselves fully in worship.

Introducing these elements enables participants in the worship event to receive the message of new life in Christ non-verbally as well as verbally. Non-verbal communication is crucial to another aspect of the expressive event – its ability to involve the entire person. As mentioned earlier, in the expressive event one's attention, energy, emotions and mind are fully engaged in the present moment. At the football match, for instance, one's attention is riveted on the ball, one's energy and emotions are occupied responding to the fortunes of one's team and cheering them on, one's mind is engaged in following the plays, anticipating the game strategy, evaluating the chances of victory. One is not likely to be worrying about last night's argument or anticipating tomorrow's office demands.

However, in worship we are not so integrated. Our diverse faculties are not drawn together in the activity of the event; our minds wander, our backs ache, our emotions are unemployed. This lack of integration is due to several influences. Accustomed to worship which is primarily cerebral, we are suspicious of anything which suggests emotionalism, so we design our services to be devoid of anything that would appeal to the emotions. The influence of a negative Puritanical attitude towards the body pervades worship, making us feel that physical expression is out-of-place. Finally, the force of habit is a formidable foe. Worship which employs all our faculties is an unfamiliar experience. We would have to change our expectations and adapt to new experiences. We prefer to choose the path of least resistance: 'Let's keep things the way they've always been.'

From many sides, however, the church is beginning to get the message: worship must appeal to the whole person if the church is to keep pace with the powerful effects of other media in the lives of modern persons. We must begin to synthesise the faculties of mind, body, and emotions in our worship.

The folk arts can play a key role in the synthesis. A part in a simple drama, for instance, requires the use of several faculties: the mind is stimulated as one considers the personality of the character one is portraying; the body's motor abilities are required for stage presence, entrances and exits, and the fine points of characterisation. The emotions are employed to convey the character and one's response to other characters. The use of dance in worship likewise calls for an integration of capacities. In selecting music one's mind must make judgements regarding the intent of the dance within the service. Working out appropriate movement utilises one's physical co-ordination, sense of rhythm and technical expertise. Actual performance summons one's emotional energy and communication skills. Presenting a dance or drama in the context of worship also involves the minds, imaginations and emotions of those who observe, as they perceive and respond to the dramatic action, characterisation and movement.

Using one's body in worship – through dance, drama, mime – may be particularly liberating to those whose primary concentration has been on intellectual development. A vivid illustration of this point occurred at a university where the Fisherfolk led a ten-day festival of the arts in worship. At the first of the series of dance workshops, one student shared with us his desire to overcome his inhibitions regarding physical expression. We assured him that the workshop was designed for that purpose, and that we would be especially sensitive to his needs. Throughout the week, in the small, supportive workshop group, he became increasingly free to move, to experiment, and to feel comfortable with his body. As we planned the final worship service, we considered the need for someone to play the part of a man whom Jesus healed. After discussing the participants in the various workshop groups, we all felt our friend from the dance workshop was the one for the part. Though we realised his shyness would make it difficult for him initially, we felt it would provide just the right challenge for his new freedom.

Our confidence in him was amply rewarded. Throughout rehearsals his facility in movement and dramatic expression continued to unfold. After a moving performance in the final service, he came to us, his face shining: 'Playing the part tonight, I really felt what the blind man experienced when he was healed by the Lord. And I know I've been healed as well, because I was free to *move* in front of all those people!'

As our friend entered into the character of the blind man, he experienced Christ's healing extended to both the blind man and to himself. His awareness of God's love motivated a deep response which he expressed in worship and thanksgiving. In microcosm, this incident illustrates another basic principle of worship which we wish to consider: worship is the appropriate and natural response to the revelation of God's mercy towards his creation.

Worship: our response to God's mercy

In the Old Testament passages of Deuteronomy Moses unites the ideas of worship and mercy as he articulates the Lord's expectations of his people. As he calls Israel to obedience to the Lord's statutes and to single-hearted worship, Moses links this expectation to their experience of the Lord's mercy.

> And now, O Israel, what does the Lord your God ask of you but to fear the Lord your God, to walk in all his ways, to love him, to serve the Lord your God with all your heart and with all your soul, and to observe the Lord's commands and decrees that I am giving you today for your own good? To the Lord your God belong the heavens, even the highest heavens, the earth and everything in it. Yet the Lord set his affection on your forefathers and loved them, and he chose you, their descendants, above all the nations, as it is today.
>
> Deuteronomy 10:12–15 NIV

Similarly, when Israel strays from its fidelity to the Lord the appeal is made through the prophets to remember the mercy by which they were led and preserved as a people:

> When Israel was a child, I loved him, and out of Egypt I called my son. But the more I called Israel, the further they went from me. They sacrificed to the Baals and they burned incense to images. It was I who taught Ephraim to walk, taking them by the arms; but they did not realise it was I who healed them. I led them with cords of human kindness, with ties of love; I lifted the yoke from their neck and bent down to feed them.
>
> Hosea 11:1–4 NIV

On the basis of this mercy, Hosea pleads with them to forsake the worship of the Baals, and return to the Lord.

In the New Testament, Paul also unites worship and the revelation of mercy. Throughout chapters nine to eleven of his letter to the Romans, he writes of God's infinite mercy toward the Gentiles – his inclusion of them with his chosen people in his plan of redemption. At the culmination of this theme he enjoins the church in Rome:

> 'Therefore I urge you, brothers, in view of God's mercy, to offer your bodies as living sacrifices, holy and pleasing to God – which is your spiritual worship.' Romans 12:1 NIV

In Paul's estimation, following the revelation of such great mercy, worship is the only appropriate response. Rather than a dreaded chore, therefore, worship is a spontaneous and whole-hearted offering of oneself. The ability to make this response, however, depends upon our keeping alive the awareness of God's mercy. In this connection the arts may also be of importance.

The folk arts stir awareness of God's mercy

In our discussion of Jewish oral tradition, we saw that storytelling and ritualised dramatic portrayals stirred the Jews' remembrance of the Lord's mercies and motivated them to worship. In our experience, the folk arts can function in a similar way today. The 'Tableaux of Faith' p. 291, for instance, illustrates the folk arts' ability to vividly recall the history of God's mercy to his people. Created for a large cathedral service with several workshop groups participating, the tableaux portray God's mercy in a variety of circumstances. In our original presentation each workshop group focused on a particular story: a music group prepared a song, 'Abraham, father of the faithful', a drama group enacted Joshua's victory at Jericho, a dance group depicted the Day of Pentecost, while a choral reading group prepared dramatic readings to link and to interpret the various sections. When the entire presentation was woven together, we beheld a panoramic view of God's mighty acts. Both those who participated and those who observed were overwhelmed by the breadth and depth of God's love. The awareness of our inheritance as descendants of those faithful people called forth rich praise to fill the cathedral.

In our community's worship life we have used the folk arts in a comparable way. Once, when facing important decisions about our future, we felt the need to reflect upon God's guidance in our community history. Rather than simply discussing the topic, we employed a combination of media to refresh our memories. Slides reminded us of the variety of places God had led us and sustained us. Poetry and personal reminiscences recalled the Lord's direction through circumstances, seemingly-chance conversations, dreams and visions. Short dramas enacted difficult situations where the Lord had provided the necessary persons, resources or ideas. Strengthened by these visual and dramatic reminders, we freely offered our thanks for God's faithfulness in our past and looked forward to the future with renewed trust in his guidance and mercy.

Perceptions of God's mercy may also be sharpened through dramatic enactment of individual encounters with Jesus. For example, in a Fisherfolk training course, members of the course led others through a dramatic account of Jesus healing the lepers. In preparation for the exercise the painful physical symptoms and the social stigma of the disease were related in appalling detail. Following this participants were assigned their parts: some were lepers, some were healthy persons, one man was Jesus. The lepers were then clothed in rags and given bells to warn others of their dreaded presence. The healthy persons were instructed to jeer at the lepers, but to take pains to avoid contact with them. As the tension between the lepers and their persecutors intensified to an almost unbearable point, 'Jesus' entered. The lepers swarmed around him, clamouring to be healed. Jesus, breaking all social conventions, spoke to each one, touched them, and cleansed them of their disease. For those playing the parts of lepers, the exercise was a profound experience; the touch of Jesus had transformed their lives. Spontaneously they responded in thanksgiving to Jesus and praise to God. Later, in an evaluation session several shared that they had experienced being touched and loved in a special way through the drama. Identifying with the rejection experienced by the lepers, they had become aware of God's love in areas of their lives which they had felt were unacceptable. The man who played Jesus was also deeply moved. 'I experienced so much compassion for all of you,' he shared, 'I felt your pain so strongly and wanted to touch each person, to release you from your agony. It changes how I understand the Lord. I know his love on the inside now.'

Knowledge of God's tender love for us 'on the inside' is a vital ingredient in the renewal of worship. Obviously, the folk arts can be a motivating force in apprehending this knowledge. For renewal to continue to grow and flourish, it must also be rooted in a supportive common life, which we consider in the next section.

Worship: the fruit of a common life

For both the Jews and the primitive church, worship was not an isolated event, unrelated to the rest of life. It was not a once-a-week affair in which one encountered persons who were virtually unknown. Rather, it was the celebration of persons who shared a common identity and a common life. The relationship between worship and the common life was a crucial one; the life they shared nourished their worship, and worship in turn strengthened the bonds between them.

The Jews, for example, experienced a close relationship between their identity as a people and worship. They were acutely aware that their existence as a people was the result of the Lord's mighty acts: he had delivered them from Egypt, he had guided and fed them in the wilderness, he had established his covenant with them and had given his Law to order their lives. Through their history they gained a unique self-understanding: they were God's chosen people. Worship was the primary way they recalled his acts on their behalf and remembered the requirements of his Law. Therefore, worship was a crucial factor in maintaining their identity as a people.

This becomes especially clear when we read the punishment for those who enticed others to worship other gods (Deuteronomy

13:6–11). The practice of stoning may seem excessive to us, but it indicates the critical function of worship as a cohesive force in Jewish society. Whenever the Jews emulated the practices of their idol-worshipping neighbours, they began to lose their unity as the people of God. When they worshipped the Lord faithfully, their worship nourished and sustained their common life and identity.

Their common life also influenced their worship. The life of the Jews as a nation was meant to reflect the nature and purpose of the Lord. Thus, in the same Mosaic discourse we mentioned in our discussion of God's mercy (Deuteronomy 10:17–19), the relationship between nature and the Jews' ethics was clearly established:

> For the Lord your God is God of gods and Lord of lords, the great God, mighty and awesome, who shows no partiality and accepts no bribes. He defends the cause of the fatherless and the widow, and loves the alien, giving him food and clothing. And you are to love those who are aliens, for you yourselves were aliens in Egypt. Deuteronomy 10:17–19 NIV

As the Lord had showed himself merciful to the Jews when they sojourned in Egypt, so the Jews were to show mercy to the sojourner among them. When the Jews' common life was consistent with their understanding of God, their worship was honest and acceptable to him. At times, however, the temptation crept in to separate behaviour and worship; the Jews acted contrary to the dictates of the Lord, but still performed the rituals of worship. Responding to this separation, the prophets gave voice to the Lord's unqualified disapproval, as in this passage from Isaiah:

> Your New Moon festivals and your appointed feasts my soul hates. They have become a burden to me; I am weary of bearing them. When you spread out your hands in prayer, I will hide my eyes from you; even if you offer many prayers, I will not listen. Your hands are full of blood; wash and make yourselves clean. Take your evil deeds out of my sight! Stop doing wrong, learn to do right! Seek justice, encourage the oppressed. Defend the cause of the fatherless, plead the case of the widow.
> Isaiah 1:14–17 NIV

Here the prophet expresses God's anger at the contradiction between Jews' pious practices and their oppression of the poor and helpless. The God of the Jews had revealed himself as one who cared for the weak and disadvantaged. To worship him as God and yet live in a manner which did not reflect his character represented an intolerable divorce between the Jews' common life and their worship. As a result of this division, both life and worship suffered. Life was removed from the tempering and corrective influence of worship; and worship became a mere formality. Both life and worship fell short of the Lord's intent for his people.

In the early church common life and worship were also interdependent. Reading the New Testament from the point-of-view of our contemporary experience of 'church' as an organisation which we attend, it is easy to miss the significance of this inter-relationship. In order to understand the New Testament, we must have some appreciation of the situations to which its epistles are addressed. These churches were not merely collections of families and individuals worshipping God once a week in the same building; they were a group of people with a distinctive identity. In the course of a day their lives were intertwined in a variety of ways, as is clear in the description of the first church in Jerusalem:

> Those who accepted his message were baptised, and about three thousand were added to their number that day. They devoted themselves to the apostles' teaching and to the fellowship, to the breaking of bread and to prayer. Everyone was filled with awe, and many wonders and miraculous signs were done by the apostles. All the believers were together and had everything in common. Selling their possessions and goods, they gave to anyone as he had need. Every day they continued to meet together in the temple courts. They broke bread in their homes and ate together with glad and sincere hearts, praising God and enjoying the favour of all the people. And the Lord added to their number daily those who were being saved.
>
> Acts 2:41–47 NIV

Obviously, in the first church, there was a close correlation between fellowship and teaching, between eating meals together and attending the temple. Worship was clearly a source of nourishment to the daily-increasing church, and fellowship was an impetus to worship and praise. Whether other New Testament churches followed the example of the Jerusalem church is, of course, debatable. But whether or not other churches had *all* things in common, they certainly shared a common life in a broad sense. By common life we understand a system of deep relationships between persons which is not limited to religious activities, but encompasses the whole of life. This generally implies daily involvement, possibly including worship and fellowship. Throughout the New Testament there is ample evidence for this quality of common life in the early churches.

The importance of peace and unity in a common life, makes the maintaining of loving relationships a high priority. In fact, in several places there is strong evidence that the harmony of relationships between people directly affect an individual's or church's ability to glorify God in worship. In his sermon on the Mount, Jesus was adamant about this relationship: 'Therefore, if your are offering your gifts at the altar and there remember that your brother has something against you, leave the gift there in front of the altar. First go and be reconciled to your brother; then come and offer your gift' (Matthew 5:23–24 NIV). Likewise, in his epistle to the Romans, Paul underlines this connection: 'May the God who gives endurance and encouragement give you a spirit of unity among yourselves as you follow Christ Jesus, so that with one heart and mouth you may glorify the God and Father of our Lord Jesus Christ. Accept one another, then, just as Christ accepted you, in order to bring praise to God' (Romans 15:5–7 NIV).

Awareness of this connection between a peaceful and united common life and worship leads one to consider whether disregarding this relationship may not contribute to the lack of vibrancy and depth in much contemporary worship. Most congregations do not share a common life. They may share certain activities or ideas, but they do not have a common identity. They have not committed themselves to anything beyond casual involvement which can be easily changed if required by employment or family demands. Therefore, the importance of harmony in relationships is often ignored; churches are like any other organisation with its cliques, factions, and misunderstandings.

Further, in our propensity for dividing the spiritual and the material, we have separated worship from human relationships almost entirely. We expect to have a 'spiritual experience' only when we are able to dissociate ourselves from all outside distractions. This separation has introduced a brand of piety which, even in the context of public worship, attempts to devote one's entire attention to God by ignoring as far as possible those sitting nearby. While such single-hearted devotion may be the appropriate attitude for private meditations, it robs corporate worship of its distinctive purpose – to remind the church of its identity as the body of Christ.

As we stated earlier, in many places this orientation is changing. Churches are re-discovering the relationship between a common life and worship. The importance of healthy relationships among the members of the body of Christ is being emphasised. People are re-organising their lives to give priority to involvement in the church family. In such a context, what role can the folk arts play? How can they strengthen a common life?

The folk arts: a catalyst in relationships

As previously mentioned, in our Houston experience and our travelling ministry we found that the folk arts and our common life mutually nourished each other. As we shared together in the Houston church family, we were liberated to express ourselves in the folk arts. And working together in the folk arts gave us more opportunities to draw together, to discover each other's abilities and to enjoy each other. In travelling we experienced a similar phenomenon. In churches where renewal was beginning, people were eager to find new ways to express themselves in worship. Church members who knew each other well often discovered new things about each other through participating in workshops together. Following workshop sessions, surprised and delighted comments were often heard: 'What a beautiful banner design – I had no idea you drew so well!'; 'Did you study drama? Your portrayal of that character was superb!'; 'I didn't think we had any talent in our group – but the drama we came up with really says a lot about us as a church. We could do more with drama here.' Through brief workshop encounters, the potential of individuals and whole groups was unlocked.

Such a one-time experience probably will not effect lasting change in relationships, but it can certainly open the way for further development. Often after Fisherfolk weekends we receive letters from groups thanking us and asking for more ideas as they have decided to continue exploring in the folk arts.

When a group decides to work regularly in the folk arts, they open the way for many opportunities to develop relationships. From these relationships a new quality of freedom and openness may be introduced into the worship of the whole congregation. What are some of the ways this may happen?

As developed in Chapter 3, a group working in the folk arts will be a ground for developing sensitivity to the needs of others. As people work together, sharing their feelings, ideas, responses, a forum is created for opening one's personal experiences to others. Such sharing draws a group together into a deeper understanding of others as persons, and into an appreciation of the strengths and weaknesses of each member.

Also, in any group disagreements or difficulties in communication will arise from time to time. If people are free to express their feelings and to pursue resolution in relationship to each other (not in complaint sessions to someone else later!), the group can be strengthened by these conflicts. As difficulties are resolved and communication established, strong bonds of trust will develop. Occasionally groups may encounter difficulties which they cannot resolve themselves. In such circumstances they may ask for the assistance of other members of the church family. In this way, relationships between the group and others in the church will also be strengthened.

Clearly, the fruits of group work are more extensive than improvement of expertise and technique; they also include growth in openness, sensitivity and trust which strengthen the fabric of a church's common life. Building relationships will also enrich the worship life of the congregation. As a group expresses the fruits of their explorations in dance, drama, mime, music or graphics, the church will experience not only their expertise, but also the depth and strength of their relationships. This inter-relationship of fellowship and worship is clearly illustrated by the worship of St. Michael-le-Belfrey, an Anglican parish in York. The church's dance group which beautifully enhances their worship, has developed a strong basis of fellowship among its members. From this foundation, their dancing in worship communicates not only the dancer's individual freedom and expertise, but also their supportive relationships. As Anne Watson, one of the members of the group, shares:

> We have been moulded together through pressure of working out dances for services. We've experienced a crisis together, and now a new feel has come into the group, a much deeper commitment and openness; and so a oneness. The original togetherness because of task has changed into a togetherness because of fellowship.[2]

The dancers' sensitivity to each other and to the congregation is apparent as they dance. Rather than being a performance, the dance draws others in; even as a 'non-dancing' member of the congregation, one feels included in their graceful expression of worship. The original co-ordinator of the group, Kay Taylor, comments on this relationship between dancers and congregation: 'We are much encouraged by more and more people telling us how they have been helped and spoken to in different ways through the dances. We are aware of a real response to our reaching out, and an understanding and identifying has happened which has released in people deep feelings that otherwise have been hidden away.'[3]

As 'hidden away' feelings are touched by worship, one ceases to be a spectator; one becomes a participant. Identifying with the actions and feelings of others, we begin to feel 'at home' with each other. For this 'at home' feeling to grow and flourish, one must also experience some connection between worship and the activities of one's daily life.

Worship and daily life

Again we look to the example of the Jews and the early church. For the Jew, worship was not just an occasional event, it was an integral part of everyday life. The Lord was involved in every activity, no matter how trivial it might seem. To encourage this awareness, the Law prescribed blessings associated with many daily activities: eating, farming, travelling, family life. Nothing was considered 'secular', or beyond the care and protection of the Lord.

The close connection between daily affairs and worship was also symbolised in the special events of worship. At the primary religious feasts of the year, offerings were made to the Lord from the produce of one's flocks and fields. The passover included a sacrifice from one's flock or herd; the feast of weeks incorporated a grain sacrifice; and the feast of tabernacles called for an offering from the threshing floor and wine press (Deuteronomy 16). Through the association of religious practice and one's daily labours, an intimate relationship between the necessities of daily life and worship was maintained.

A comparable unity between daily activities and worship is seen in the early church. In Paul's teaching worship is not confined to religious observances; it is an attitude that permeates all of life. Thus, in his letter to the Colossians he exhorts them: 'Let the word of Christ dwell in you richly as you teach and admonish one another with all wisdom, and as you sing psalms, hymns and spiritual songs with gratitude in your hearts to God. And whatever you do, whether in word or deed, do it all in the name of the Lord Jesus, giving thanks to God the Father through him' (Colossians 3:16–17 NIV). In this passage, as in the one from Ephesians 5 (quoted in the section concerning worship as an expressive event, on p. 75), it is not clear whether Paul is referring to a particular worship event, or to the conduct of daily life. But the injunction to 'do it *all* in the name of the Lord Jesus, giving thanks to God the Father through him' clearly indicates his expectation that all activities be infused by an attitude of worship.

In specific acts of worship we can also see a relationship between daily activities and the worship event. The Jewish practice of offering the fruits of one's labours in worship is echoed in the celebration of the Lord's supper. The elements of bread and wine are the fruits of their labours as well as the common ingredients in any meal. Elaborate ceremonial trappings had not yet removed the Lord's supper from its similarities to other familiar Jewish religious meals, so the procedure was in most ways, a familiar one.

Contrast this integration between the everyday and the sacred with our contemporary experience of almost complete separation between the two. Our daily life generally reflects little of the attitude of thanksgiving which Paul encourages, and our worship bears little relationship to our daily activities. Most religious observances employ language and traditions that have no relevance to the rest of our lives. In an industrialised, technological society, the elements of bread and wine no longer serve as an offering of our life and labours. How can we bridge the gap between our worship and the activities of our life?

In some churches and communities an awareness of the symbolism of the bread and wine of the Lord's supper is being recaptured by using bread and wine made by members of the congregation or community. At our community home in Millport one of our primary means of support is running the island bakery. In our community eucharist therefore, we find it meaningful to use the bread we have baked ourselves. The small crusty loaf does represent the labours of our hands and the totality of our lives which we offer to the Lord. However, in most situations this symbolism is not particularly relevant. As labour is mechanised and computerised, it is difficult to offer anything which symbolises the labours of our hands. Where can we find appropriate offerings of our daily life?

The folk arts: symbols of our lives

The folk arts are certainly one area to be explored in this connection. Groups working together to create a dance, drama, mime or song to be used in worship experience a sense of fulfilment as they offer the fruits of their work together. We have found that graphic expressions often fulfil the need for a visual symbol of our self-offering. On parish weekends groups have worked together to make banners. Pooling their ideas, imaginations and abilities, the group designs and creates a banner which may depict the theme of the weekend, or include a verse of scripture that is especially significant to the group. At the climax of the weekend, the Sunday morning worship, a special festive procession parades into the church carrying the banner. The colourful work of art is not only attractive to the eye, it is also a visual symbol of the group's life and labour.

The importance of such visual symbols is particularly seen with children. At one children's service during a worship conference we asked each child to bring with them something they had done that day: a toy they'd played with, a book they'd read at school, a ball from their after-school game. At the offertory, each child came forward to present their special offering. Through this involvement the children brought the activity of their day into the service, and experienced being an integral part of the worship. And not only the children felt involved. Adults commented afterwards that the children's offerings reminded them to offer the activities of their day to the Lord as well.

The gap between our daily life and worship may also be diminished by the use of drama that draws its inspiration from the everyday experiences of the congregation. In our community's daily worship we often find our best teaching illustrations come from our daily involvements: working in our offices, baking and selling bread, tending the garden or milking the goats. When a group gathers to prepare a teaching, recalling these simple incidents often helps to crystallise a teaching point. One person's frustration in struggling with an unco-operative office machine may have been relieved by the thoughtful attention of a fellow worker. A short dramatisation of the situation is sufficient to remind us all of the importance of being sensitive to each other's needs even in the midst of busy-ness or pressure. Another's inability to cajole the goats into a new portion of the field may suggest a dramatic illustration. A sketch depicting the goats' obstinacy may remind us of our own reluctance to change, even when the change is to our advantage. Incorporating our everyday experiences into worship clearly reminds us of the Lord's presence in our daily concerns. The laughter that often accompanies such a sketch is the result of identification with the feelings or predicament portrayed. It is the 'I know just how he feels!' response. Drama which provokes this response in the context of worship helps to break down the barrier between our 'real' lives and our worship. We know that the Lord is concerned with our daily disappointments and triumphs; worship gives us a context in which to express them.

In conclusion, we re-iterate that the folk arts are not intended to be a magic wand, capable of transforming worship in a single stroke. However, they effectively complement the worship of churches and fellowships that are searching for ways to deepen their awareness of God's mercy, to increase their involvement as a church family, and to further integrate their worship and their daily life. In this context, the folk arts facilitate worship as an occasion in which the church family joins together to offer all their human faculties – bodies, minds, emotions – and the whole of their lives to God and to each other in an atmosphere of thanksgiving and celebration.

NOTES

1. Karl Barth, 'Freedom Before God', *Church Dogmatics* III. 4.53 quoted in Joseph C. McLelland, *The Crown and the Crocodile* (John Knox Press, Richmond, Virginia, 1970), p. 149.

2. Anne Watson, quoted in 'A Place to Grow', *Towards Renewal*, Issue 3 (Summer 1975), p. 17.

3. Kay Taylor, quoted in 'A Place to Grow', *Ibid*., p. 17.

All scripture quotes in this chapter are from *The New International Version of the Bible* (Hodder and Stoughton, London, 1979).

What sort of people does the world need? We have no right to indoctrinate people, but we have every right and we have the duty to provide the kind of experience needful for helping people to find themselves and that human interdependence without which the world cannot survive. At present we are educating people as if they were greyhounds, running competitively in parallel tracks. We need to educate them as if they were living in a group. And not to be afraid of love.

ROY STEVENS
FROM *Education and the Death of Love*

It is a truism to say that the media in general, and TV in particular . . . are incomparably the greatest single influence in our society today, exerted at all social, economic, and cultural levels.

MALCOLM MUGGERIDGE
FROM *Christ and the Media*

The task of the teacher is to prepare the pupil for the time of separation, which must come, so that the pupil may find within himself such resources as enable him to follow the direction in which the teacher has started him without any further aid. It is not only that the time of separation must come; it is a good thing that it should come, for otherwise that inward strength, which it is the purpose of education to develop, will never be exercised.

WILLIAM TEMPLE
quoted by MICHAEL HARPER
IN *Let My People Grow*

CHAPTER 6

Signs of the Times

Folk Arts in Education

When aren't we bored? (Choose as many as apply)

1. When something catches our fancy
2. When something makes us think
3. When something relates to our experience
4. When something disturbs our prejudices
5. When we're enjoying ourselves

Of all the above, perhaps the most universal truth is point 5. Yet for many people, education and enjoyment have not been linked. 'It's boring' is the most common reason people give for not liking school, for wanting to skip the sermon at church, for not attending a lecture. Yet 'It's boring' is a convenient generalisation encompassing many factors. *What's* boring?, one must ask. Often the teacher or topic receives the blame, whereas the fault is really to be found in the presentation style. Approach and method make all the difference to whether or not one is bored.

In Chapter 5 we saw how the folk arts help 'unbore' worship by heightening and humanising it. They encourage participation, involvement and physical activity. Since these same elements are significant in learning situations, using the folk arts can yield maximum educational success with a minimum of effort. Additionally, certain aspects make them particularly valuable as teaching techniques. They don't require a high degree of expertise or long hours of preparation, which means they can be used spontaneously or with a modicum of rehearsal. This ready availability renders them ideal for a variety of circumstances, for people of any age. Such diverse teaching situations as religious education classes, study groups, youth clubs or coffee-bars, instruction during general worship, Sunday school or scout groups, school assemblies, can all benefit from the folk arts' colourful appeal and lively presentations. Quick application is another advantage: after presenting a drama or teaching a song, one can immediately pick up on the intended point.

Still other reasons make the folk arts useful in education. The following relates them to factors which influence or impede positive learning experiences.

EDUCATION AND ENJOYMENT

Let's consider a few general reasons why people may not enjoy learning. Many folks had negative experiences as children, and so their natural eagerness for learning has been discouraged or lost. Sometimes, particularly in relationship to the arts, people have inhibiting memories of the well-intentioned teacher who said, 'Just smilc but don't sing, you can't carry a tune,' or the adult who suggested, 'Why don't you sit this one out? I think you must have two left feet (ha, ha).' Still others have experienced so much pressure to be successful in the educational system that learning became a competitive task, quite unrelated to pleasure.

But why should learning be enjoyable?

Firstly, people learn more quickly and with less effort when they're enjoying themselves. They don't get distracted, wishing they were somewhere else or hoping the time will pass quickly. People learn best when they are wholeheartedly involved, when their concentration can be focused and their energies channelled. Enjoyment nurtures this single-mindedness.

Secondly, the nature of an enjoyable experience is that it stimulates desire for repetitions. When learning is pleasurable and engrossing, not tedious and endured, a genuine desire for further learning is kindled.

Thirdly, enjoyment and pleasure are of special significance in a world as impersonal and confusing as ours. Educator Roy Stevens, calling for an element of celebration in the overall educational system, emphasises the importance of enjoyment in education: 'If we are able to help people, the basic task is to help them enjoy themselves (not the worst thing in the world, though many people in education seem to think so). In a world of suffering and corruption, it is all the more important to celebrate the life and hope and love we have, the clearness, the honesty, the candid acts of loving.'[1]

The folk arts are a natural aid to combining enjoyment and education. They are helpful in restoring and encouraging natural enthusiasms, and particularly effective with people who have had discouraging past experiences. They help shift emphasis from competition and success to group involvement and enjoyment. 'Anything worth doing is worth doing badly' might be a suitable motto for using the folk arts. The initial concern should be that people are encouraged to experiment, to take chances, to attempt. Through such exploration and trial and error they will find the freedom to try again, to work harder, to perfect. Polished presentations can come later, enabled by well-planned rehearsals and sensitive leadership. But that is not the starting point. The overriding attitude should be to allow people to seek and find, unhampered by the requirement of success. Ironically, the very fact that the folk arts are not success-oriented often releases people to be extremely successful when using them!

There is one unique pleasure the folk arts offer the learning experience. It is the joy we find in watching people we know and love as they sing, read, act, dance. This is indeed a simple pleasure but a rich and deep one, touching and stirring the very heart of our humanity. It helps us to be aware of and celebrate 'the life and hope and love we have'.

CHRISTIAN RESPONSIBILITY AND RESPONSE

To advocate enjoyment is not to imply frivolity. Christian education is of crucial importance. Christian commitment includes not only worship and witness but education. God's people are to communicate clearly and scripturally the calling, the mission, the traditions of those who follow Christ. They must teach the young and newly converted, they must challenge and nurture those already mature in Christ.

Yet Christian education, perhaps even more than secular, has suffered from sterile methods and dull, predictable forms. Its language has frequently been archaic, specialised or uncomfortably trendy, its presentation styles stale and uncompelling.

Those concerned with Christian education can readily identify with the necessity of re-evaluating and enlivening teaching methods. In this era of communication they ask themselves, 'How well do we communicate?' Those outside the church ask another question, 'What do you communicate?'

The past two decades have exposed the church, no less than every other social and political institution, to conflict and radical confrontation. Statistics have been compiled and volumes written on the role of the church in contemporary society, the decline in church attendance, church growth, and applications to theological colleges, the powerful impact of the mass media, the implication for the church of shifting social values. Indeed, the Assembly Report of the World Association for Christian Broadcasting, which in 1968 met in Oslo, summarises the twin influences of the media and social change:

> The very role of the church as a communicator has been undergoing change. Until recently the church was in a more domin-

> ant position and did much to shape the social structure of its environment. Its influence on moral and social standards was both direct and indirect. It prompted social and political causes. In some ways it set limits and otherwise influenced many of the performing arts.
>
> Now for some years, becoming increasingly noticeable with the widespread use of the commercial film, and even more pronounced since the introduction of television, the role of the church has undergone change. It no longer is at the centre of the stage. Other forms of persuasion have become extremely powerful. The voices of the commentator, the entertainer, the dramatist and musician, seen and heard over television, have become more forceful influences on the population as a whole. These secular voices, largely beyond the control of the church and frequently expressing themselves along lines that challenge and sometimes set aside the church's traditional attitudes, are not only more widely seen and heard but, because they use multi-media impact, their influence has become more penetrating and persuasive.[2]

The years since this report's publication have continued to verify its basic observations. As Christians then, we face a dual challenge: to fulfil our own standards and responsibilities for Christian education and nurture, and to respond to the queries and influences of our culture.

IMPACT OF THE MASS MEDIA

A brief examination of the impact of the mass media will help us gain perspective about communication and education. The traditional 'language' of education is based on scribal and verbal skills: reading, writing, lecture, recitation. Both secular and Christian educators have spoken and taught this language. For thousands of years it has been the common method; perhaps, until this century, its effectiveness has not been widely questioned.

Our age however, is unprecedentedly influenced by the mass media. We are so familiar with them that often we are unaware of how radically they have altered human society. Our plethora of electric and electronic communicating devices has broken down walls which formerly protected, excused or isolated. As Marshall McLuhan summarises in *Understanding Media*:

> The telephone: speech without walls.
> The phonograph: music without walls.
> The photograph: museum without walls.
> The electric light: space without walls
> The movie, radio, and TV: classroom without walls.[3]

Divisions and limitations once preserved by time, distance and ignorance have been eradicated.

Telephones, record players, tape recorders, televisions, home cine films give us the ability to equip ourselves for both entertainment and education. We can rent films, learn foreign languages, keep fit, get a university degree, all in our individual homes. We now have the power to create and control our own environment. In the comfort and seclusion of our private world we can lounge about, talk, perhaps fix a snack, without disrupting any of our entertaining/educating machines. If we're dissatisfied with what's on the telly, we just change the channel. If we don't like the record or tape we're playing, we replace it. If we're uncomfortable, we move around, turn the heat on or off, find another cushion, stretch out full-length.

Contrast such mobility and independence with most formal learning situations in churches or schools. Then we usually sit in one position in one seat, we often have only one rather immobile person to look at, we generally listen to only one soon-monotonous voice. Frequently the surroundings are sterile or institutional, decorated impersonally, if at all. Compared to our homes, this 'learning environment' is an incongruity, a strange arena in which we submit ourselves to physical and psychological endurance tests.

Audio-visual perception

Television is the medium which presents the greatest challenge to education's traditional methods. It has changed our standard of sense perception: we are now accustomed to sight (images, movement, colour) accompanied by sound (dialogue, music, special effects). Our senses have become conditioned to a sophisticated interplay. We now expect a variety of ever-shifting images, we want the immediacy of action.

This predisposition to audio-visual perception makes literal-verbal perception seem cumbersome and tedious. We may find it hard to read without missing out passages or skipping ahead to 'find out what happens'. Verbal communication is clumsy and wearying, it seems to require great effort to express ourselves and tremendous tenacity to listen to others. It's as if our mind has gone numb: it's hard to follow what someone says, particularly a teacher-or-preacher someone for more than about ten minutes.

Long-term television watching is the norm. In Muggeridge's *Christ and the Media* we learn '. . . studies reveal that in Britain the average adult watches television for sixteen to eighteen hours a week, which represents about eight years of the human life span or one-seventh of the time we are awake.'[4] Anthony Smith in *The Shadow in the Cave* quotes from *Broadcasting Magazine*: 'The average American child watches television for six hours per day, and the adult for two and a half.'[5]

Children who have grown up with television often suffer extreme learning difficulties when confronted by the usual textbook/blackboard/writing method. They are used to having images presented to them, so it's hard for them to imagine word pictures. They are experienced in perceiving graphic concepts but awkward at working with word concepts. They are much more familiar with the impulsive or irrational than with the logical. Many of these children do not learn to read properly, which means they do poorly in their school work. Yet these same ones are able to repeat unerringly, detail by detail, the entire action of a television programme viewed the night or even week before. Again McLuhan has a word for us: 'It is a matter of the greatest urgency that our educational institutions realise that we now have civil war among these environments created by media other than the printed word. The classroom is now in a vital struggle for survival with the immensely persuasive "outside" world created by new informational media. Education must shift from instruction, from imposing of stencils, to discovery – to probing and exploration and to the recognition of the language of forms.'[6] And, in *Understanding Media*: 'If we ask what is the relation of TV to the learning process, the answer is surely that the TV image, by its stress on participation, dialogue, and depth, has brought . . . new demand for crash-programming in education. Whether or not there will ever be TV in every classroom is a small matter. The revolution has already taken place at home. TV has changed our sense-lives and our mental processes. It has created a taste for all experiences in depth. . . .'[7]

Television: a double illusion

The statistics verifying how much we watch television must provoke the question 'Why?!' What does television offer that we voluntarily give so much time to it?

McLuhan asserts that the answer is found in the nature of the medium. 'Television demands participation and involvement in depth of the whole being. It will not work as a background. It engages you.'[8] And later: 'In television, images are projected at you. You are the screen. The images wrap around you. You are the vanishing point. This creates a sort of inwardness . . .'[9]

McLuhan stresses participation; we must question what sort it is as well as the effects. 'Inwardness', McLuhan's own word, is a clue to both. Television certainly requires full sensory participation: eyes, ears, emotions are all active. We feel as if we're participating in real life. In fact, this is a double illusion.

Firstly, television relays not people but arrangements of symbols, sounds and images. When we see a person on television, we're actually seeing not the person but a picture, a synthetic reproduction, of the person. Secondly, the people thus telecast are either unreal (characters, animated figures) or unrelated to us personally (entertainers, commentators).

But it's hard to remember that these people are unreal or that we don't know them. Television, film and radio create pseudo relationships. The profusion of talk shows, interviews and personal reports familiarises us with people we've never met, people we probably never will meet. But we feel as if we know them. The following incident, related by Philippe Halsman in his book *The Frenchman*, is not unique:

> On leaving (the restaurant) I found myself face to face with a horse-faced gentleman. With the feeling of seeing a dear friend again, I seized his hand and shook it violently. 'Bon soir, Fernandel! (Hi, Fernandel),' I cried. 'Comment ça va (What's cooking?)?', and I pressed him against my chest. 'I am here only for one night,' Fernandel answered . . . 'Tomorrow I return to Canada. But before I leave for France, I'll stop again for a day in New York.'
>
> I stopped slapping his back, blushed, stuttered a polite 'Good night,' and disappeared with extraordinary speed . . . I had suddenly realised that I had never met him before. Seeing Fernandel innumerable times on a movie screen had tricked me into the illusion that he was one of my oldest friends.[10]

Another effect of the pseudo relationship syndrome is that long hours of television watching may enervate us out of actual relationships. Watching two or three programmes consecutively will consume most of the emotional energy we would otherwise invest in relating to others. Such an evening, or several of them, can leave us feeling that 'real people' are unreasonable and overly demanding. The numbness to verbal communication, that weariness with talking and listening mentioned earlier, comes into effect here. We can feel unable to cope with close relationships and irritated about impersonal ones.

Television gives us 'the illusion of participation together with immunity from interaction. . . . One may weep or laugh or hate or fear and escape the necessity of acknowledging the physical existence and the reciprocal demands of those others who arouse emotion. Reality, on the other hand, is beset with people and things that resist, react, counter-thrust, encroach, demand.'[11] Television then, offers us the illusion of involvement with reality and others without the demands that such involvements actually require.

Imagination and fantasy

In-depth television viewing tends to dull adult imagination even as it creates fantasy. The habit of sitting and watching as people and situations move before us has caused much of our own imaginative ability to atrophy. Obviously other factors than just television contribute to this. Many people have jobs which are repetitive and prescribed, precluding spontaneous or creative thought. Dull employment further propels the dulled imagination cycle: we hope television programming will supply the meaning or stimulation lacking in our work. Oppositely, some jobs are extremely demanding intellectually or emotionally; at the day's end we use television as an anodyne, seeking relief by observing events and characters that require nothing from us.

On the level of the rational and intellectual, we know that television people and situations aren't real. Yet the power of the double illusion is so great that these people and situations become real on the level of the affective and emotional. We find ourselves arranging schedules around our favourite programmes, eager not to miss the next development. At odd moments we find we are thinking of certain characters, wondering what they will say next, how they will respond to their current predicament. These idle thoughts, stemming entirely from leisure-time fantasy, may be the extent to which most adult imaginations are ever stirred. Similarly, the content of most television programming rarely compels us to direct action. Our energy supply depleted, consumed by what we watched, we just switch off the set and retire.

Children conversely, are stimulated to action by television. It affects their imaginations the way adrenalin affects the body. Children think less categorically, more subjectively than adults, with finer lines between the possible and the impossible. They watch an abundance of adventure/police/detective/space exploration programming which exposes them to unreal situations wherein time is eclipsed, people are endowed with superhuman abilities, the improbable is somehow always achieved. All this gears them to adventure, excitement, action!

The results are less than laudable. Young children are still developing in reasoning ability and are inexperienced in real life encounters. Their inability to fully discern between fact and fiction means they inadvertently allow what they watch on television to establish their real life norms. These young ones judge life and others by the standards of their media models. Often it's only when they enter school that the process of sorting out begins. A kindergarten teacher, describing the difficulties of their necessary disillusionment, stresses that the children are genuinely shocked when repetitions of TV feats don't occur. They become seriously disoriented by the realities and seeming limitations of human life.

Additionally, the content of much mass media programming militates against Christian principles. The value of human life and relationships is generally held in low esteem, and materialism and success, at others' expense, is idolised. Effective problem solving, for instance, is practically non-existent: at the point of conflict people either shoot each other or walk out, slamming the door. Neither 'solution' is an example for growth and maturity, both obviously exclude basic human caring and responsibility for others. Such casual violence is repugnant, such self-centred withdrawal immature. They are incompatible with a gospel that directs us to love and serve others, giving ourselves for them. Yet these models are repeated time and again.

The World Association for Christian Communication grappled with this issue:

> Take as one example the impact of television on children. In a country like America, the present generation of youth have been raised in a hearing and viewing environment. They are surrounded from morning till night by music or what passes for music and by films and television. Now within their hearing and viewing are many unreal and entirely fanciful interpretations of life. Cartoons making use of trick photography create an imaginary world where the hero makes use of magical powers and his success is due to a fanciful manipulation of laws over which he, as a real person in real life, has no control. Such viewing hardly prepares youth for the demands of a complex modern society. The most that can be said of an almost endless series of them that is offered for his entertainment is that they strongly appeal to one's imagination.
>
> Yet these are what shape life. They take the place of Christian Education for multitudes of children. They make almost any rational or disciplined approach to the demands of life seem tame and uninteresting.[12]

Recognising the power and appeal of the communicating media, the effectiveness of imagery, action, movement as educating techniques, the attractions of in-depth involvement and participation, let us turn those principles and devices to our own use. The folk arts, which appeal to both adults and children, will help immensely. They capture imagination, depend upon participation, are non-existent without real, 'live' people, and they draw the vivid mental pictures not easily forgotten. Let's tell our Bible stories dramatically, teach our concepts with mime and dance, enact our parables visually, impress our values graphically. Let us, as McLuhan recommends, recognise and use 'the language of forms'.

To do any less is to ignore the signs of the times. As Jesus pointed out, answering the Pharisees and Sadducees who came to test him, 'When it is evening you say, "It will be fair weather; for the sky is red." And in the morning, "It will be stormy today, for the sky is red and threatening." You know how to interpret the appearance of the sky, but you cannot interpret the signs of the times.'[13]

We are able to forecast the weather not only of local areas, but of foreign countries, entire continents, outer space! Now, more than ever, we must interpret the signs of the times. Our society gives us overwhelming signs, radical proofs, of the need for vital, stabilising Christian education. If it had the answers, it wouldn't query and challenge the church! In Jesus's time, the religious establishment resisted his words. Let us, as God's people in these times, receive and obey them.

SPECIALISATION AND INTEGRATION

In an earlier chapter we saw how one's roots and traditions contribute to one's sense of identity. Here we briefly examine the relationship between social trends and education.

Using the folk arts in education is certainly not new. There is an ancient precedent for such use; it is actually the oldest mode of education known in human society. Long before they could write or talk, people told stories through movement, sound and dance. Humankind matured and added poetry, in the form of songs comprised of rhythm, rhyme and vivid imagery, to its communication resources. These two basic patterns, used together, were the means of remembering entire histories and imparting cultural traditions, i.e., the means of educating.

Techniques of survival, the significance of the natural world, the meanings of life, death, growth, change, leadership and responsibility: all were interpreted and clarified through song and dance. By watching and then learning these expressions, the young experienced continuity with their past and identification with their future. The knowledge imparted by their elders exposed them to challenges they would face and equipped them for mature decision-making. Intensified participation, as the children grew older, was an affirmation of their place in society as well as their own acceptance of the responsibility of carrying on the traditions. Finally, as they themselves became the elders, in turn teaching the young, they gave their own children the unbroken, unifying heritage which had nurtured and educated them.

Young people today do not experience this kind of unbroken heritage and integrated education. Our culture is complex, not simple, and characterised by specialisation. This is recognisable even in our educating systems. Individual competition and personal achievement are encouraged much more than supportive unity and mutual endeavour. The success syndrome, the subtly pervasive 'achievement at first attempt' philosophy, the dreaded fear of failure or, even more binding, its actualisation, are social attitudes infecting even our youngest.

As early as the primary level some children, realising they are more skilled in certain areas than in others, find security in their 'good' subjects and are threatened by insecurity about their 'bad' ones. They concentrate on the former and shy away from the latter, fearful of failure or rejection if they can't excel. Similarly, the needs of technology and pressures of career planning often require students to make an early decision between the arts and sciences. Once the two roads have diverged, they may never meet again. Those who choose the arts may discover a later fascination with sciences, but their previous choices prevent further exploration. Or, those who selected the sciences may arrive at middle age confident in their expertise but unable to enjoy a symphony or appreciate poetry.

This specialisation syndrome has even compartmentalised the human personality. It's a peculiarity of Western culture to divide and polarise. Following this inclination, our society has generally emphasised the intellectual, the analytical, the practical to the detriment of the emotional, the intuitive and the imaginative. Wholeness of personality however, requires the integration of these faculties. If the purely analytical and rational is insensitive to the emotional and affective, the result is likely to be rigidity, harshness, ruthlessness. If the creative and expressive is not informed by the rational, that result is likely to be sentimentality, petulance, manipulation. Many sources, psychological, sociological, theological, urge us to balance and synthesise the two. Social as well as individual health depends on it.

Visiting schools and universities, we have met scores of people whose ability to think was their only well-developed personality aspect. These people were ill at ease with their bodies, their posture withdrawn and awkward, their movements tense and self-conscious. Although students and instructors had had the advantages of the most outstanding educational opportunities our society offers, they had never learned to be comfortable with their own bodies. Most had played or been trained in sport yet the benefits had never been integrated into their lives overall.

Just as telling as physical awkwardness is awkwardness in relationships. Many of these same people were ill at ease with others. They managed conventional social relationships without too much discomfort but, when trying to express personal concern, they were often inept and embarrassed or overly aggressive. They had never learned the basic steps which would lead them to physical ease, nor the basic patterns of meaningful interaction.

We use people from educating institutions as example, but they are not exceptional. Look around, at those we pass in the streets, those we work next to, those we meet in restaurants and churches and parks. We see the same discomfort, the same disjointedness. There is the orchestra conductor who freely sways, dips, whirls as he leads, but is stiff, mechanical, unrelaxed when walking to the podium or bowing to the audience. There is the potential athlete, body honed and well-trained, verbal ability painfully undeveloped. There is, possibly, the reflection we see as we look in the mirror.

What we view, in all these situations and with all these different people, is the result of our culture and often our educating. The fruit of society and systems is frequently dis-integrated, uncomfortable people who have not learned to appreciate the fullness of their humanity, who have never learned a balanced use of mind, feelings, body. Roy Stevens says, 'Instead of being like a unifying experience, education is like a continuous programme of those quizzes and contests to find the best "brain", which have confirmed the public idea of education as being something to do with being like an encyclopedia, instead of a full human being.'[14]

The folk arts as educating techniques reflected the integration of earlier societies. They can help us shatter the compartmentalisation of our society. The folk arts combine the intellectual, the emotional, the physical; they develop several aspects of the human personality simultaneously. The facility and ease which result from such balanced development affects one's life overall. Individuals who learn to express themselves spontaneously in storytelling and drama, for instance, will have more facility in expressing their own thoughts and feelings. People who have learned to move rhythmically and gracefully will be more aware of their bodies and more comfortable with them. People who discover they don't have to be specially gifted in music to learn to sing easily and naturally will find music becoming an expressive part of daily life.

As these diverse facets of human potential are drawn out and become 'usual', awareness and appreciation of our humanity widens and deepens. The arts no longer are rarefied and removed, they become part of life. Education is also taken out of a box, the one labelled 'thinking only'. Soon it becomes normal to teach and learn using many different forms.

This normalcy helps liberate people as they choose a career. If one is relaxed and familiar with a variety of expressions and experiences, one is cognisant of potential in many areas. Such people won't be so prone to clinging to the area in which they seem most capable or at least proficient. Even when they have made a choice, they will still be able to keep developing in areas other than their speciality.

Drama, dance, mime, music, art – all are valid and valuable teaching tools. As Christians increase their use of them, they will aid in changing the idea of education from an 'encyclopedia' to a process and experience that nurtures the 'full human being'.

EDUCO: TO DRAW OUT OF

The Latin root of our word 'to educate' is *ducere*, which means 'to lead out, to draw out, to develop'. This captures the intent and dedication of many teachers. They see themselves as catalysts, eager to unearth and spark the potential of others.

Still, it's all too easy for those who teach and those who are taught to become locked into their respective roles. As developed in Chapter 7, the folk arts help break down role barriers. They encourage relaxed relationships, enabling people to see and know each other first as people and only secondly as specialists, authority figures, students, learners. Also, because the folk arts depend on the contributions and involvement of everyone who is participating, they give learners and teachers alike a shared experience. The former find their ideas not only acceptable but necessary, the latter find extra opportunities to express approval and commendation. Teachers also discover new reasons for respecting and appreciating those they teach, as formerly unknown aspects of personality and ability emerge.

The folk arts also draw potential out of teachers. They provide a stimulus, sometimes lacking once one reaches adulthood, to keep growing and developing. It's not just young people or students who need such an impetus! The person who has concentrated on drama may never have done much with music, the one who has trained in maths may like working with young people but never have thought himself likely to lead in spontaneous prayer. As these people use folk art forms as teaching tools, they will find their own abilities broadening. They will not only be leading those they teach into new endeavours, they themselves will also be exploring along the way. The folk arts then, can act as a personal catalyst for teachers, giving them the opportunity to venture into areas in which they may be completely inexperienced.

Many teachers and leaders however, have experienced in both life and education the very specialisation out of which they are keen to lead others. They themselves may be locked into narrow roles, expectations, limitations. Perhaps they are still wary of areas which were threatening in their own student days, perhaps they have become so comfortable in their ability to conduct a class or lead a discussion that it's easy to forget that other abilities are still undeveloped. The teacher with such graceful carriage may actually feel quite inept with dance or movement, the scripture teacher who draws out such hidden truths may quail at the thought of appearing in a drama, speaking words other than his own well-researched ones.

Such teachers can find the folk arts uniquely helpful. By using them they will recognise their own attitudes or stereotypes, and will also have specific yet low-key possibilities for change. As these people write their first dramatic dialogue, or consult others more musical than they for assistance in using rhythm and percussion, or take part in their first dance, perhaps alongside those they teach, they will experience a new flexibility and freedom. These teachers and leaders will have a greater personal satisfaction, as old barriers break down, and they will experience greater depth and interdependency in personal relationships, as they learn from others and with others. If they have struggled with the common psychological pressure to have all the answers, to be the infallible expert, to be entirely self-sufficient as a teacher or leader, they will find the strain of this pressure diminishing. With the folk arts, it's not just the 'learners' who learn!

The folk arts then, provide an alternate 'language' to education's traditional one. They enliven learning experiences, making them more enjoyable, and they draw on the effectiveness of certain principles of mass media communication. At the same time, they stress participation and personal interaction on the level of the real, not the fantastic. Folk art forms also stress the integrated use of the human personality, countering the specialisation trend so characteristic of our culture. Lastly, the folk arts are helpful in drawing out and developing potential in both teachers and students. They are distinctively useful in assisting Christians to answer the questions 'How well do we communicate?' and 'What do we communicate?'

NOTES

1. Roy Stevens, *Education and the Death of Love* (Epworth Press, London 1978), p. 102.

2. James E. McEldowney, Ed. *FRAM: A Report of the Oslo Assembly, June 1968* (The World Association for Christian Communication, London, 1968), p. 9.

3. Marshall McLuhan, *Understanding Media* (Routledge and Kegan Paul Limited, London, 1964; Sphere Books 1967; Abacus 1973), p. 302.

4. Malcolm Muggeridge, *Christ and the Media* (Hodder and Stoughton, London, 1977), p. 1.

5. Anthony Smith, *The Shadow in the Cave*, A Study of the Relationship between the Broadcaster, his Audience and the State (Quartet Books, London, 1976), p. 222.

6. Marshall McLuhan and Quentin Fiore, *The Medium is the Message* (Penguin Books, Harmondsworth, 1967), p. 100.

7. Marshall McLuhan, *Understanding Media*, p. 354.

8. Marshall McLuhan and Quentin Fiore, *The Medium is the Message*, p. 125.

9. *Ibid.*, p. 125.

10. Philippe Halsman, *The Frenchman* (Simon and Schuster, New York, 1948, 1949), Introduction.

11. *FRAM*, p. 56.

12. *FRAM*, p. 10.

13. Matthew 16:1–3.

14. Roy Stevens, *Education and the Death of Love*, p. 153.

If those living in the northern hemisphere, worn out by activities, were to lose the source of the spirit of festival – when that festival is still so alive in the hearts of the peoples of the southern continents. . . . If festivity faded away from the body of Christ, the Church, where on earth could there still be found a single reality of communion for the whole of mankind?

BROTHER ROGER
FROM *Festival*

CHAPTER 7

Family Gathering

Folk Arts in Festivity

In earlier, less sophisticated days, entertainment was a corporate activity, enjoyed by the whole family or community. Dogs barked, children raced in and out, babies laughed or cried as people shared food and conversation, sang and danced, told stories and played games. Such simple pleasures, shared between those of all ages, have largely passed from our personal and social traditions. There may be the occasional holiday gathering or family reunion, but for most people these are extraordinary events, not frequent or usual ones. Fast-changing social norms have pulled and stretched the fabric of our society's family life, and with books, cars and televisions, people can 'entertain' themselves.

Group activities are much reduced and more specialised. The youth culture and famous 'generation gap' of the sixties made a distinction between those over and under the age of thirty. That vivid polarisation has faded but the effect of the gap has actually broadened. Currently most activities are arranged according to age groupings. Adults have their own evenings in or out, teenagers their own discos and parties, children their own games and entertainments. Some activities are open to people of any age; nonetheless, those who attend are usually divided, with only slight variation, into the narrow groupings listed above. Spectators at a sporting event, for instance, will be groups of young men, teenage or university couples, young marrieds out with their in-laws for the afternoon, groups of children shepherded by one or two adults. An evening concert is distinguished by its preponderance of couples: adult men and women, pairs of students. The once-common sight of family or multi-age groupings, together for a good time and clearly having it, has all but disappeared.

The folk arts in festivity offer an alternative to our culture's entertainments and habits. As indicated in the first chapter, by festivity we mean occasions when people gather to enjoy themselves and each other. In this chapter we examine how the folk arts can contribute to such enjoyment, which in turn helps to build a genuine family and community life.

BUILDING FAMILY TRADITIONS

Festivity and festive customs are a vital factor in maintaining bonds between persons. Exploring the Passover in Jewish life, we saw the key role of its traditions and observances in preserving the Jews as a people. We also realised the significance of customs, handed from generation to generation, as they impart a sense of continuity to a people. In much of Western society such traditions are no longer observed; they survive mainly in the customs surrounding major holidays. But where they still exist, they do strengthen the bonds of unity and identity within nations and families. We experienced this forcibly during our first Christmas in Scotland. As our community then included families from England, Sweden, Canada and the United States, deciding how to celebrate Christmas as a community was not an easy task. Each nationality group had certain customs which were important to them. For our Swedish friends, a festive procession with candles, singing special songs, and giving away home-baked saffron rolls, heralded the coming of Christmas. For the English families Christmas wasn't Christmas without paper streamers and Christmas pudding. If our own customs were not observed, it was difficult to feel that Christmas was being properly celebrated. If some traditional food was omitted from the Christmas dinner through another's ignorance of our tradition, it was easy to feel personally slighted. We realised that customs were more than just habits; they were delicately intertwined with a sense of family, identity, and continuity. Discussing openly the importance of each nationality's traditions, we were able to blend the various customs together. The community's celebration then partook of the richness of diversity, as each group shared with the others their particular observances.

In addition to national customs, families develop their own traditions which are slight variations on the cultural theme. One family always makes their own tree decorations, another bakes certain kinds of Christmas biscuits or cakes, another goes Christmas carolling with their neighbours. These customs give a family a sense of solidarity, which sets them off slightly from other families: 'This is the way *our* family celebrates.' Thus the yearly observance of these customs reinforces the family's unity.

Church family traditions

The evolution of traditions and customs in the church family is crucial in the present renewal of the church. As a sense of family is restored to the church, people desire not only to pray, study, and worship together, but also to celebrate. Developing festive traditions within the church serves a similar function as traditions in families: they draw the church family into an experience of unity and solidarity. Traditions may develop around the usual holidays, or a church may introduce its own special occasions – such as a mid-winter festival, or a summer fete. Of course, these occasions are only the beginning; festivity should not be limited to particular events, but should become a regular part of a church family's life.

In some circles, festive activities may be dismissed as 'unspiritual' or 'just social' events, but churches and communities which are growing together as a family, are grasping the importance of the festive aspect of their life.

An American woman, raised in the Non-conformist tradition, has written this account of the formative effect of special events in the life of her church family:

> There were several children in our family, and our home always had an air of excitement and activity. Our parents were lively and loving, and we had many family traditions, rituals and occasions. We were close as a family, and this closeness was intensified by our church family's closeness. I have countless memories. . . .
>
> I remember the church suppers, held every five or six weeks. They had a strong sense of 'big family'. Everyone brought a big dish of food which was enough for themselves and the guests and new people. We all sat together at trestle tables; it was so exciting for three families to be at the same table, or to eat next to Peter and Julia, who had just got married, or to find that Frank, one of the single people, would be sitting with our family. After the meal we'd sing or play games; as the babies got tired, then some of the older children would go off to the nursery with a few of the young mothers or grandmothers.
>
> A yearly event was the Pancake Supper. On a Sunday afternoon, the children would play and the women set tables and chatted while the men of the church cooked pancakes and sausages. Draped in great white aprons or ridiculous flowered ones, they busily measured flour, beat eggs, heated syrup, worked at the griddle. Then, when it was all ready, the men would serve us. Everyone helped clean up, and usually there was singing as we worked. We'd go home about eight o'clock in the evening, tired and sticky and happy. Another highlight of the year was the Hallowe'en party. Everyone, from oldest to youngest, came in costume. We'd bob for apples and play hide and seek and blindman's buff, and drink apple juice and eat doughnuts.

There were other special events, suppers when the missionaries came home, evenings when people showed slides of their holidays, concerts with visiting choirs. When the church offered a sewing course, there was a style show at the end, with each person modelling something they'd made.

The Sunday morning service always seemed special. It was all so *familiar*: everyone singing together, the flowers on the dark wood of the communion table. Sometimes all three choirs would sing together, and that meant extra rehearsals and last minute attention to choir robes. Then there were the Sundays when something special, really special, was happening: baptisms, or the Youth Service, or joining-the-church day, or Children's Day, or communion days. Some weeks there would be an extra hymn after the sermon, which gave time for prayer and quiet thinking. But I anticipated going to church whether it was a regular Sunday or a special one. I knew I'd see friends from other parts of the city, and sometimes I'd just made a new friend, and we'd planned to sit together.

Anything we did at church, the suppers, the worship, the parties, was something we could take our friends to. It didn't matter if they were the same denomination or not, they always had a good time there. [The parents of one friend were divorced, and for a long time she had no church home. She went with me a lot, though.]

Then things changed . . .

Church suppers became much less frequent, only once or twice a year.

For some reason the Pancake Supper was cancelled one year, and then never started again.

Then there weren't any more Hallowe'en parties.

The Sunday services weren't really changed, we still sang the same hymns and said the same prayers and did everything in the same order, but something was different. It didn't seem that we were all one family anymore. If felt divided, as if a lot of different people had somehow all ended up in the same place at the same time. There was a sort of hollowness, emptiness.

Our friend's experience is a graphic example of the positive function of festivity in the church family. From a purely efficient or business point-of-view such activities may appear to be a luxury of time and effort; from a spiritual perspective they may seem like mere socialising. But the inclusion of festivity in the church's life has far-reaching implications. Clearly, in our friend's situation, when festive occasions were disregarded, even though the church's worship remained the same, the vitality of the church family was diminished.

In the present renewal, the observance of special occasions in the church's life is also being revitalised. The festive aspect of Christian life is again asking for expression as the church recognises that offering the whole of one's humanity to the Lord certainly includes one's capacity for spontaneity, enjoyment, and festivity.

Alternative celebrations

In many churches and communities where renewal has taken root, celebration has become an important part of life. However, celebrating together has often necessitated re-evaluation of the usual cultural observances of particular holidays. For instance, the celebration of Christmas often places undue emphasis on giving and receiving expensive material goods; what place does materialism have in the life of a church which is concerned for the poor? Or in England, the celebration of Guy Fawkes Day often results in serious accidents or senseless destruction; what does this observance contribute to the life of a church family? For many of our friends, evolving alternative celebrations has seemed a necessary step in their renewal.

One of the most glaring inconsistencies between Christian principles and the prevailing cultural observances concerns the customs surrounding Hallowe'en in the United States. A growing trend towards destructive mischief directly opposes the values upheld by Christians. To counteract this tendency, many churches have developed alternative approaches to Hallowe'en celebration, similar to the one described above.

Another approach to this celebration, developed recently at the Church of the Redeemer in Houston, focused on All Saints' Day rather than Hallowe'en. Working in small groups for several months, they studied the lives of saints – both ancient and modern. Combining music, drama, poetry and dance, they created a series of vignettes depicting the lives of dedicated men and women of God. The resulting presentation drew the church family into a deep awareness and appreciation of the faith of God's servants from the Apostle Paul to St. Francis to Mother Theresa.

For churches wishing to develop alternative celebrations, we suggest making this the task of a particular group. Their purpose would be to examine the underlying attitudes and values promoted in cultural observances, and to assess their relationship to Christian principles. From this discussion, they would explore alternatives for developing traditions consistent with their values as a church family.

Sharing in the church family

Imagine a family who only eat together once a week. During the rest of the week, they go their separate ways: they fix their own meals, they work on different schedules, they engage in separate leisure activities. One of the primary lacks they would soon feel would be the absence of spontaneous sharing: the dinner table conversation where the youngest chatters excitedly about her newly-discovered knowledge of volcanoes, or Dad regales the family with funny incidents from his work. They would miss the casual conversation during washing-up when the eldest describes his much-anticipated weekend away and the relaxed bedtime when Mum tells the story about when *she* was a little girl.

Family life without regular sharing of the little everyday things is unthinkable – but this is often what the church's family life is like! The family members meet together only once a week and worship doesn't offer opportunities to share everyday things. However, as a result of the present renewal, many groups are recognising their need for times of sharing within the church family. They are also discovering the value of the folk arts as media for casual sharing. People can grow in appreciation for each other as they share simple expressions. During a recent visit to the Post Green community we joined in the Folk Night – a perfect example of family sharing:

Hubbub is the only word to describe it. A busy, fairly organised hubbub, but hubbub nonetheless. The Folk Evening was being held in the cafe of the caravan park. In the small kitchen there was a multitude of activities. Several guitarists were tuning; people occupied with last minute skit preparation were tying on pig noses and checking to be sure they had the old bedstead, the wooden spoons and the straw hats; homemade punch was being served from the short counter. In the cafe itself a few high stools indicated the stage area. People were trailing back and forth and around, greeting each other, finding a place to sit, getting drinks, settling the children on huge cushions on the floor.

The lights dimmed, a hush ensued, the entertainment began. Stuart was the relaxed, humorous compere of the evening's stories, songs, poetry, skits, dances and recitations. Folk songs from several traditions, English, Irish, American country-western, African, were sung, with everyone joining in the choruses. Newly written songs were shared publicly for the first time, old favourites were repeated. Jon's 'Brer Rabbit' story from the American South was amusing and fascinating, with its simple homespun wisdom and cunning and Jon's amazing facility to reproduce the diverse folk dialects. When Maggie took the centre stool, she explained that the theme of her poetry that evening was 'people – because, I suppose, people are my "best thing".' Before each poem she described the relationship behind it: 'Tramp' came from her childhood memories of the old wanderer with two donkeys, a dog and a tent home; 'Susann' was a tribute to the charm and delicacy of a beloved child; 'poppies' reflected the fear and anxiety felt when she was first learning to trust others with her thoughts and feelings. Peter's poetry, shared later, was a contrast to Maggie's. His was based on experiences that had struck him with special force: the exhilaration and uncertainty of a sailing adventure, a sudden and profound perception of the Lord's supper.

The intermission gave people time to chat and refill their drinks, and take the younger ones home. Then participants were entranced by Stephen's original English folk ballad about young lovers, stirred by the plaintive and compelling 'Hava Nagila' played as a flute solo by one of the young adults, hilariously challenged by Stuart's counting song with ten verses and swift repetitions. One still wonders, though, how sixty people managed not only to learn but also to execute folk dances in a space measuring not more than 24 feet by 32 feet, and in about a quarter of an hour! Such a feat must be attributed not only to Andy and Dave's concertina and fiddle playing, but also to their clear instructions and enthusiastic optimism.

Soon the intended one and a half hours were stretching into two. The organisers whispered back and forth, making the difficult decision about what to leave out. Stuart's notice, 'I'm afraid there are several things we don't have time for, so they will form the basis of our next Folk Evening,' was received with approving applause and cries of 'When?!' Indeed, as people left, chatting and laughing, carrying now-weary older children, calling farewells to each other across the cold, starry night, more than one was thinking, 'Now, the next time *I* could . . .'

Expressing appreciation

The Folk Evening and similar events are effective in augmenting our appreciation of each other as persons. Hearing our friend's newly-composed song, or telling the favourite story of one of the children increases our awareness of them as unique individuals. Appreciation is a vital factor for those who live closely or interact frequently, as familiarity often causes us to take each other for granted. Therefore, in family life we provide special occasions, like birthdays and anniversaries, to focus our attention and affection on a particular individual. Similarly, in the church family, occasions for expressing our appreciation of each other are important.

These occasions may conclude a major effort like a children's summer programme, a parish weekend, or a spring fete in which many have worked hard. The folk arts can be effective in this setting as well. Amusing sketches can highlight the accomplishments of individuals or groups, and humorous poems may introduce the giving of awards. Everyone may be drawn into composing lyrics for a song commemorating funny incidents. Appreciation may also be stimulated by some regular way of recognising individual contributions to a church's or community's life. A friend from a monastery shared with us his community's custom of electing a 'Brother of the Week'. The nominations for this weekly honour gave a place to acknowledge special accomplishments or to recognise the many constant contributions of each brother.

Importance of anticipation

As family traditions develop, festive events become a regular and eagerly anticipated part of a church family's life. Such occasions supply a vital factor in our lives: they give us something to look forward to. The importance of anticipation is epitomised in an encounter with Stanton Denman, the youngest son of a family who joined our community in the summer of 1976. Though he was just four years old, Stanton was determined to join in the activities of his older brothers and sister. One evening we were dividing up into teams for a game. Going down the line each person counted off: 'One', 'Two', 'Three', 'Four', 'One' – but when the counting got to Stanton, ignoring the person who was counting, he shouted at the top of his voice, 'FIVE – IN MARCH!' His anticipation of attaining to the age of five was so great that his March birthday was never far from his consciousness. Looking forward to this event gave him the necessary assurance that he would soon be old enough to join the league of his elder siblings.

For Stanton, and for all of us, the significance of a special event is not limited to its actual duration. The planning, the preparation, the anticipation of the event are an integral part of our experience. This quality of expectancy buoys us up especially when we feel oppressed by the daily-ness of life. In our community's life, we discovered the importance of expectancy as we launched into our first summer season in our bakery. Almost half of the community were working long hours in both bakehouse and bake shops. Providing hospitality for a constant flow of visitors occupied others full-time, not to mention keeping up with cooking, cleaning, laundry, and the children! But, as we considered the demands before us, we decided it was still important to schedule a monthly festive evening. As the summer wore on, the planners of these evenings would often look around at the weary bakers or exhausted shop personnel and think, 'Let's just cancel the celebration and let everyone get an early night.' At this point, almost invariably someone would say: 'Even though I'm tired, I'm coming tonight. Looking forward to the evening has kept me going today.' We discovered that an evening of Scottish country dancing, or games, or a good film were much-needed oases in the busy-ness of the summer. And looking forward to these events sustained us as much as the events themselves.

BREAKING DOWN BARRIERS

A primary sign of renewal in the church today is the breaking down of barriers between people: barriers of age, role, self-consciousness, doctrine, culture. Many churches and communities are finding that festive occasions, more than any other, are effective catalysts in overcoming these obstacles.

Age barriers

As we stated at the outset of the chapter, age groupings have become a hallmark of our times. These divisions, while useful for some activities, often prevent necessary interaction between age groups. The lack of interaction further intensifies the generation gap, leaving each side muttering concerning the other: 'They just don't understand.'

If the church family is to be truly a family, rather than a series of age groupings with isolated activities, we must find occasions in which all members of the family interact freely. We must initiate events that involve everyone together.

In our own community, we have found festivity to be an indispensable arena for such age group interaction. One of our most successful ventures has been evenings of entertainment which offer several options: Scottish country dancing, disco, or quiet conversation areas with refreshments. The following description of one evening captures the easy mingling of age groups in various activities: entering the semi-darkened room, one of the first things one noticed was disparity. Disparity of age, disparity of size, disparity of dress. There was tall Don, in his late twenties, dancing with twelve year old Martha. She had recently sprung up in height but still did not really balance Don's 6′6″. Greeting Dave, one noticed that his usual muffler had been replaced by a suavely tied ascot. Alison, an elegant older woman nearing seventy, wore a flowing dress of Indian print, which was a sharp contrast to Phil's faded jeans. When the dance ended Martha rejoined Judith, a woman in her mid-twenties, at the turntable. Martha and Judith had spent most of the afternoon selecting and arranging the records for the evening. A slow dance was introduced, and Graham led Jane, his sixteen year old daughter, in graceful circles about the room. When the music changed again to a rock song, Bill appeared with Brendon Graham, his two year old son. Holding 'wee Graham' at chest height, Bill danced back and forth, up and down the room. Mimi, Bill's wife, was also dancing, claimed by nine year old David.

The room next door was equally active. A large central table and a sideboard were decorated with flowers from the garden and birds made of ribbon, and filled with special food and refreshing drinks planned and prepared by the teenagers. Clusters of people, seated or milling about chatted, made frequent trips to the buffets, left to dance, returned. Strains of the disco music faded, then another melody, familiar to all, was heard. 'Aha! It's time for the line dance!' The room was suddenly deserted as everyone rushed to join the simple stroll-kick-turn dance. Two great lines ran the length of the room; one took for one's partner the person immediately opposite. The dance's symmetry was occasionally interrupted by laughter or chatter, as those doing the dance for the first time kicked instead of turned, turned rather than strolled. No matter, just carry on and try again. . . . The song concluded, and some stayed to dance the next number. Others returned to the buffet room, or made their way downstairs to the 'Midnight Cafe', where soft classical music and candlelit tables offered a quieter conversation area. Still others, hearing Louise tuning her violin, Sandy her guitar and John his bass, went to another room where the country dancing sets were just forming.

Role barriers

As festive activities help to topple the age barrier, they also aid in overcoming barriers of role. In most situations, children and young people experience adults in well-defined roles: parents, teachers, advisers; adults experience children primarily as dependents, students, persons seeking advice. Roles are necessary to some extent, but if they impose too narrow limits on relationships, they may become stultifying. For instance, if adults expect children always to be demanding, noisy, and bothersome, they may dismiss a child's valuable insights, or discredit a child's idea as fanciful or impossible. Festive events can expand our expectations of children as they can enter into the planning and preparation. Roles can be reversed at times as adults listen to the suggestions of children and follow their lead. In our experience, following the ideas of children has led us into some of our most delightful family traditions.

Pooh Plays became part of our traditional festivities through four year old David's initiative. One morning in the midst of breakfast he had simply asked: 'When are we going to do a Pooh play?' Actually, we had never thought of doing a Pooh play! It's true that more than one of the Fisherfolk had become hoarse from reading aloud the stories of Winnie-the-Pooh in a voice that could reach all corners of our van as we travelled the highways and byways of England: it is also true that a birthday ritual had developed in which the birthday person chose the Pooh story to be read at their birthday celebration. But no-one had considered making a play from the stories – no-one until David. As soon as his idea was tossed into the midst of the breakfast conversation, the other children began to buzz with ideas:

'Carl, you could be Pooh – you just sort of – remind me of him.'

'Jane would be a wonderful Kanga – because she's mothery.'

'Rabbit always talks a lot – a good reader would have to do that part. Anna, you could do it!'

'What story are we going to do? I like the one about Pooh getting stuck in Rabbit's hole and they hang the washing on his feet. Can we do that one?'

Adults were enlisted to work out a script and to direct the rehearsals, but the primary motivation came from the children themselves. In a few days time David's idea had become a reality and the whole community was drawn into the excitement of the first performance:

'Oh Carl, where's the paper with my part on it? I had it just a little while ago! I'm sure I put it under that dressing gown on top of that pile of old books under the broken chair in the corner. And now it's not there! Have you seen it?'

'Jody, this lounge is not the place to practice your Tigger leaps. Try outside in the garden.'

'Sweetie, it really would be better if Roo just hopped alongside you, instead of trying to fit into the apron pocket. Yes, I agree it's a big pocket but Martha, who's playing Roo, weighs almost five stone and is nearly as tall as you. Just stand up as straight as you can, and we'll have Roo crouch beside you. That's right, put one hand protectively on Roo's shoulder. Yes that's good. . . .'

And this initial performance was only the first in a series. Every few months one of the children would say, 'When can we do another one?'. So the Pooh Play became firmly established simply because we had listened to David.

On one occasion, the Pooh Play tradition enabled us to break through the role barrier in the opposite direction. After our move to Yeldall Manor, we were joined by several families with young children. The combination of so many children unaccustomed to a community lifestyle and just so many people under one roof created its own unique problems. For children who'd never lived with adults other than their parents, the sheer number of adults was intimidating. Several of the new children were particularly awed by Graham Pulkingham, whose frequent travels lessened his opportunities to cultivate close relationships with them. Their estimation of Graham rose greatly, however, when his household decided to perform a Pooh Play with adults taking the children's usual parts. Graham's portrayal of the honey-loving, hum-composing Pooh, brought the house down. It also brought down some of the walls of unapproachability surrounding Graham. Anyone who can play good old Pooh Bear can't be all *that* scarey!

Performance barriers

The production of the Pooh Plays had other unexpected side benefits as well. We found that the children's performances were melting the barrier of self-consciousness and fear which we term the 'Performance Barrier'. Sharing in front of people became a normal part of life, rather than a rare, emotion-charged experience. The extent to which this had happened was evidenced by our involvement in a family camp shortly after the advent of the plays. The Fisherfolk had been asked to lead the worship at the camp, and our whole household, including the children, were invited to participate in all the camp activities. One afternoon we were asked to share our experiences as a household. As we discussed our approach to the session, the most recent play production came to our minds. The story 'In Which Kanga and Roo come to the Forest' seemed to exemplify the chief difficulties we had experienced: the problems of working out a family life with persons whose habits, traditions and customs were different from our own. The presentation of the play, the adults agreed, would be the perfect beginning for our session. But what would the children think of performing in front of sixty strangers? Half-expecting protests of stage-fright or complete refusal, we presented the idea to the children. 'Oh, sure,' they agreed almost off-handedly, 'Why not?' It was obvious to us that their experience of acceptance and encouragement in the arena of our sitting room, had helped them to overcome the performance barrier. Extending the sitting room to include sixty other people? Why not?

Barrier between humanity and spirituality

In our consideration of both worship and teaching, we've discussed the unfortunate separation of these activities from other human endeavours. Many of our materials are directed towards the breaking down of the false distinction between our humanity and our spirituality. Festive occasions incorporating the folk arts supply the ideal situation for the further integration of these seemingly-opposed aspects.

The Folk Evening described earlier is a vivid example of this integration. In the context of its relaxed atmosphere, the audience was led through a spectrum of experiences: from the foot-stomping enthusiasm of country-western songs, to the quiet appreciation of Stephen's ballad, to the awareness of relationships stirred by Maggie's poetry. The evening flowed from one expression to another, not separating worship from personal sharing or humorous story. But the feeling of the whole evening was one of worship as the audience recognised and appreciated the Lord's life in each other expressed in a myriad of ways.

Festivity may also serve as a necessary balance to worship and teaching in a parish weekend or week-long mission. The teaching in such events often stimulates people to look carefully at their lives, to apply the teaching to their experience and to make important changes. Because of the intensity of this process it must be balanced by intervals of relaxation and enjoyment, or it may become too introspective. In this context a festive evening incorporating the folk arts can offer the necessary balance. The relaxed humour of an evening of sketches, a talent show, or a folk song sing-along will refresh people and draw them together in a simple, but profound awareness of their humanity in the midst of their spiritual re-evaluation.

Barriers of culture and doctrine

We have primarily been dealing with the functions of festivity in the parish community or church family. For those involved in broader ministry, festivity also plays a key role. In situations where differences of culture or doctrine are present, misunderstandings or tensions may arise. A festive occasion which employs the folk arts may help to relax these tensions. Such an event can provide a neutral ground for persons to get to know each other as persons, rather than as proponents of a particular cultural or doctrinal point-of-view.

At one of our first Fisherfolk weekends in Scotland, we were slightly apprehensive about our reception in this unknown culture. Looking at the weekend programme given to us by our hosts didn't ease our apprehensions. We didn't even speak the language! What *was* a 'Cup of Tea and a Carry On'? Our host graciously informed us that it simply indicated a relaxed evening, chatting over tea, and joining in some Scottish dancing. Though the custom was an unfamiliar one, the warmth of the atmosphere and the vigour with which we were swept onto the dance floor, soon dissolved any self-consciousness or feeling of being aliens. And during the teaching sessions the next day, one had the feeling of being among friends – after all the man on the second row was my partner in the Eightsome-Reel!

Similarly in conference or large meetings where various churches and doctrinal positions are represented, festivity can offer times of refreshment. Intense discussions may be generated by divergences of opinion, and tensions may result. Though dialogue may be stimulating and lead to better understanding, it often proves wearying as well. In the midst of this intense involvement, a time of simply having fun together, even allowing oneself to appear silly, helps to knock down walls caused by disagreement and misunderstanding. Working together on funny sketches, sharing songs from one's particular background, just laughing together eases tensions and builds bridges of appreciation and respect between persons.

In conclusion, we believe it is important to appreciate festivity as an integral part of the present renewal in the church. A primary thrust of the renewal is the restoration of an experience of family within the church. Employing the folk arts in festive occasions draws the church family into experiences of sharing, appreciation and anticipation. Breaking down the barriers of age, role and performance festivity assists people to 'be themselves' with each other. In this atmosphere of participation and freedom, barriers between humanity and spirituality and barriers of culture and doctrine are more easily overcome. Through festivity, the church family is joined together in bonds woven of laughter, song and games as well as those fashioned by worship and teaching.

PART II Materials and Helps

Liturgy of the Manuscript Culture

The service is ordered in segments: it has start-stop, start again quality . . .

Many symbols, ideas and images compete for supremacy in the service. Sermon, scripture, anthem, hymns and printed pages all express different ideas . . .

Liturgy of the Body of Christ

The service has a style, a flow that gives dramatic energy to our life together.

One idea is developed with depth. The whole service builds around this stating it in various ways. The music, drama, dance, speaking words are integrated into the wholeness.

When you are preparing . . . avoid putting the service together in bits and pieces. In other words, don't just take a 'call to worship' from one source, a 'confession' from another and a prayer from still another, and stick them together. Avoid using the arts in this same kind of scrapbook way. The expressive arts must flow throughout the service and not just be stuck in the slot where the choir's anthem used to be. It will not work!

KENT E. SCHNEIDER
FROM *A Dancing People*

CHAPTER 8

A Word in Season

Effective Use of the Folk Arts

By selecting herbs and spices carefully, a chef brings out the flavour and enhances the quality of his special dish. But the anticipated response to this artistry is not 'What an excellent use of thyme and marjoram!' but rather 'What an exquisite meal!' Likewise, use of the folk arts should be motivated by a desire to enhance and accent, rather than one that calls attention to the art forms themselves. Effective use of folk art forms is a sparing and sensitive one.

The following is a fairly detailed description of such use. Primarily in the context of worship we consider Nurture, Reflection and Meditation, Enjoyment. This is only a partial listing: the Appendices have more suggestions, all based on materials in this book and the songbooks. Appendix 3 contains ideas and examples for Festivity.

NURTURE

At times our travelling ministry was so innundated with requests that we divided teams to fulfil two ministries simultaneously. Two members might teach at a parish weekend while the other four or five led worship at conferences. After several such experiences, we noticed a similarity in the teaching teams' evaluations. 'On the whole the teaching went well, but it seemed to take a while before the people were really with us. We kept wishing the whole team were there, to help people relax and to lead in worship. Then the stage would have been set for teaching.' Gradually, we became more aware and appreciative of the delicate inter-relationship between worship and teaching.

An expanded concept

This inter-relationship is more than just 'breaking the ice' with a new group or 'getting warmed up', although those are factors. Leading people into a deep experience of worship creates an atmosphere of receptivity for instruction. Communicating God's tender love through quiet worship songs imparts a sense of peace and well-being which prepares people to hear God's word. Inviting groups to join in simple choruses or children's songs with hand actions, rejoicing together in lively praise – these break down barriers between speaker and congregation. When people have been encouraged to participate actively in worship, rather than being spectators, and they have responded, they are then free to interact with a teacher, to ask questions when a point eludes them, to smile, laugh, enjoy themselves.

Other expressions than music create an atmosphere conducive to instruction. Drama, dance, mime, poetry – each contributes uniquely. We implement these forms to set the stage for teaching, to build a service theme, to enlarge upon a point, to illustrate a principle, to restate an idea in different terms. Integrating the spoken message with other messages, non-verbal and verbal, engages imaginations and emotions and stirs visual perception. This communicates on many levels, and the varied communications reinforce the message and improve people's retention.

These insights changed our whole concept of instruction, expanding and broadening it. We no longer thought of it as a short (or lengthy!) verbal monologue occurring at one set time during a service or meeting; it occurred many times, expressed in a different medium each time yet always balanced overall. A service with the teaching theme of forgiveness, for instance, in addition to the verbal message, would include several of the following:

1. Small group reading, Psalm 51, p. 144
   Purpose: Illustrates the need for forgiveness
   Use: Introduction to theme
2. Solo reading of a poem, 'Coventry Cathedral', p. 182
   Purpose: Illustrates the power of forgiveness
   Use: Focuses thoughts before the teaching
   Used during teaching for emphasis

   or Drama, 'The Unforgiving Servant', p. 233
   Purpose: Illustrates the effects of refusing to forgive
   Use: Precedes the teaching
   Stimulates thinking along lines of teaching
3. Solo song, 'Turn me, O God', FS 15
   Purpose: Responds positively to teaching
   Use: Provides response time and direction for response after teaching
4. Prayers, written for occasion or led spontaneously
   Purpose: Directs thoughts to relationships where we need to give or receive forgiveness
   Use: Reiterates teaching theme in prayer

Instruction then, became a series of repeated nurturing actions which used a diversity of media to reiterate and emphasise theme and teaching points.

Teaching aids: experiential

Planning actions or activities which give people a definite experience is a wise preparation for instruction. One might teach about worshipping the Lord joyfully and freely but, if the congregation has sung a song which leads them into doing so, they will then have a basis from which to understand the teaching. 'The instrument song', CH, is a good example: involvement is infectious and it's difficult to remain apathetic or merely cerebral whilst miming the vigorous pounding of a bass drum, the delicate bowing of a violin, the enthusiastic shaking of a tambourine! The concept of wholehearted worship will have been enfleshed by experience, and people will then listen and learn with a practical, rather than theoretical, reference point.

Congregational drama is also effective as an experiential aid. 'By Their Fruits Ye Shall Know Them', p. 243, transforms the congregation into the crowd at Jesus's trial before Pilate. Crying out 'We have no king but Caesar! . . . Crucify him!', one participates emotionally in the horror and reality of the events. The cruel, misguided power of Pilate and the crowd, the sense of responsibility for Jesus's death – these become real in personal experience. The teaching which follows strikes us with greater impact: our involvement in the trial scene, our realisation that we participate in our world's guilt, results in a deeper awareness of God's love and forgiveness.

Instruction which draws on experience is especially important when teaching children. Scriptural words or incidents may be remote to them, outside their experience; or their experience, when imposed on biblical stories, may give rise to humorous misconceptions. A church school teacher once told her six year olds the stories of Jesus's birth and early childhood, then asked them to draw pictures about the stories. Most children drew the traditional manger scenes but one worked diligently on an aeroplane with four persons aboard. When asked to talk about his drawing he proudly announced, 'This is the flight into Egypt. And that's Joseph, Mary, the baby Jesus and Pontius, the pilot!' What an apt interpretation for a child of the space age! Yet looking beneath the humour, we can see the weakness of relying on the Bible's stories and imagery to be comprehensible just on their own. Children who have witnessed or participated in a drama-game like The Obstacle Walk, p. 388, will have a definite understanding of Jesus as an ever-present guide, whilst those who have only heard the words, 'I am with you always,' may never perceive their practical meaning.

It's not just in church school classes or worship services that children misunderstand biblical or 'religious' words and ideas. School assemblies (as well as religious education classes, Christian youth clubs, and brigade and scout groups) frequently use ancient hymns with convoluted sentence structure and literary archaisms, or Bible quotes which are cryptic snippets from the Authorised Version. Again, the folk arts can bridge the gap between past and present: rhythmic songs with compelling words, forthright dramas in everyday language ('The Unforgiving Servant', p. 233, 'Peace! Be Still', p. 231), participation stories and puppet shows ('The Good Shepherd', p. 191, 'The Amazing Change', p. 219), relaxed prayers which reveal a comfortable and secure relationship with God, contemporary Bible translations (*The Good News Bible* or Phillips's) – all these impart a vision of Christian life as real, current and vital, all relate practically to experiences of contemporary children.

The need to cope with disparity between scriptural and contemporary meanings is not confined to children. As a British Council of Churches publication states:

> The modern reader of a parable is often in the position of a man who has to have a joke explained to him. The image which was meant to clarify has become for him something to be clarified. To remain true to the Bible and its method the nurturer ought often to abandon the Bible's own image or story and find an alternative which is *immediately* understood and which makes its own point without the necessity of explanation. It goes without saying that this puts a heavy responsibility on the nurturer to make sure that he, at least, thoroughly understands the original and what it means.[1]

Thus we must find illustrations, images and parables from our own lives and experiences which will communicate the Bible's principles. The 'Good Samaritan' story in Luke is one that has probably lost most of its original impact. To us, 'Samaritan' does not denote a group of despised people; in fact, as the name of a current group associated with deeds of kindness and mercy, it represents the very opposite! To regain the story's shock and meaning, we must set it in a contemporary situation with groups known to be antagonistic: Northern Ireland, perhaps, with the merchant as a Protestant and the Samaritan as a Roman Catholic.

Teaching aids: visual

Concepts requiring laborious verbal explanation may often be captured in visual illustrations. One of the most effective explanations of the Body of Christ that we've ever seen was accompanied by a series of transparencies shown on an overhead projector. The first transparency showed many different people scattered at random; so did the second. The addition of the third transparency, however, filled all the spaces between the figures and showed that together they formed the clear outline of a single human body. Not one of the people was outside the body, and each was necessary to complete the larger form. This graphic illustration said volumes at a single glance. Though we saw it more than six years ago, it has remained clearly in our minds.

Symbol, used in conjunction with drama, dance and mime, is another powerful visual aid. In 'The Hat Race' mime, p. 214, John and Richard's competition is represented by their ever-increasing hats, which dwarf them, separate them from their followers and ultimately cause their downfall. This symbol becomes a shorthand way to refer to the concept; in this case, the abuse of a leadership role. Following one performance, a leader's prayer was' 'Lord, help us to take off our hats, and just be friends to each other.'

REFLECTION AND MEDITATION

Services which include time for reflection or meditation reap the maximum benefit from folk art (and other) forms. To proceed immediately into a rousing hymn after a moving drama, pertinent sermon or thought-provoking poem is not only jarring, it also deprives people of the time they need to respond, to reflect, to apply the message to their lives. The following suggests ways of integrating theme, silence and reflection.

Prayers

During a worship conference with the theme of openness to change as regards traditions and habits of worship, we wrote the poetic meditation 'Wind of Spirit, Wind of Change', p. 165. It contrasts our natural desire for control and security with the Spirit's flexibility and mobility, and it was developed as a meditation to precede the confession. Additionally, we wrote our prayers in a special format which propelled thoughts in the same thematic direction. This combination of meditation and directed prayers is not difficult to implement, yet adds depth to worship.

Well-known prayers which tend to 'roll off the tongue' and lose meaning because of familiarity can occasionally be enhanced by a written meditation. 'Thy Kingdom Come', p. 163, based on The Lord's Prayer, expands each aspect of that prayer and provides a framework for specific concerns.

Graphic aids are also useful in guiding prayers. Newspapers with the names of troubled areas painted across them brightly, or photographic collages, if hung within people's sight lines, help quicken awareness and intercession for places and people of need.

Reflections on sermons, teachings, scripture readings

Use poetry for a directed meditation that follows a teaching or scripture reading. 'As Peter', p. 155, which draws parallels between the experiences of Peter and those of the writer, might be especially suitable subsequent to a teaching about trusting the Lord and obeying his call. Similarly, 'The Woman at the Well', p. 177, may amplify a teaching or personal testimony about acceptance and forgiveness.

Music helps establish a reflective atmosphere: instrumental music provides a background whilst solo songs direct thoughts.

Written meditations illuminate scripture passages rich in symbolism by exploring the meaning of each phrase. Between each section of 'I Stand and Knock', p. 141, based on Revelation 3:20, is an interval of silence which gives time for individual reflection. The reading was written as a preface to a service with the theme of receiving the Lord.

Lastly, when a conference or series of meetings has been organised around a single theme, the written meditation is singularly useful in summarising the points made throughout the sessions. Each section of the meditation reiterates the main emphasis of a particular teaching whilst relating it to the overall theme. Silence or instrumental music between the sections gives opportunity for further recollection and personal application. We do not include an example because all our meditations of this sort have been tailored to the needs of particular groups, but Chapter 16 gives suggestions for writing your own.

Symbol, mentioned above, is powerful in this context as well. A single image can summarise a teaching point or intensify perception of a scriptural theme (See Illustration I, p. 465). In like manner, a wall hanging with just a few words or a phrase, the letters cut out of fabric and glued onto hessian, gives focus for meditation and reflection and provides an alternative to spoken direction (See Illustration H, p. 465).

ENJOYMENT

Chapter 6 develops the idea of people enjoying themselves while they're learning; this same concept applies to worship. The old catechism reminds us 'the chief end of man is to worship God and . . .' what? . . . '*enjoy* him for ever'. If God does want us to enjoy him eternally, we may as well begin now, by enjoying our worship. We see worship as a family occasion, as a time when we meet with God and our sisters and brothers. We know God to be creator and sustainer of the universe, yet he has also revealed himself as 'Abba', the Jewish equivalent of our 'Daddy'. God is both awesome and approachable, and when we worship we do so in awareness of his majestic splendour as well as his intimate friendship. 'Morning Song', p. 134, is a call to worship that skilfully weaves these two aspects together.

A welcoming environment

It has been jokingly remarked that church renewal would be accelerated immeasurably if churches were heated enough to allow worshippers to remove their coats and feel 'at home'. Economic obstacles prevent this desired state, but the folk arts help create an atmosphere that at least looks and feels warm and homely. Art and graphic additions help make a building feel personal. Folk art well integrated into the surroundings aids visual enrichment, focuses and directs thoughts, strengthens ties of familiarity and friendship. 'Well integrated' is important: the child's drawing placed on exactly the same plane as the speaker's head will distract, not heighten, just as a crimson wall hanging next to an orange coloured window fashions visual discord, not harmony.

The occasional surprise also contributes to participants' enjoyment. A parade with banners and harvest gifts might commemorate the autumn festival, a special service order with a cover that matches the flower arrangements or newly made wall hanging will make Easter or a wedding more festive or reinforce the theme of a guest service.

Participation and anticipation

Dance and movement contribute greatly to enjoyment and participation. Barriers sometimes exist between different sections of a church, and fluid movement through the building's spaces, perhaps with an entrance or offertory dance, visually weaves the separated areas together. Simple movement in which the entire congregation can share, such as the graceful and dignified hand actions accompanying 'The Lord's Prayer' from El Shaddai communion music, CH, results in an experience of unity and 'at-home-ness'.

Dramatic timing is another tool. A few minutes of silence at the beginning prepares the congregation to hear the far-away, coming-closer strains of a procession beginning outside. By the time those parading enter the church, all are singing the entrance song fully. Alternatively, silence at the beginning may be broken by a reading such as 'Come, Lord', p. 135, which concentrates everyone's attention on the Lord's presence in their midst.

The younger members

'But how can we involve the children in our worship?' is one of our most-heard questions. Our simplest answer is: Make your worship enjoyable, give your children real, not gratuitous, opportunities to participate; and they will *want* to be involved.

Children are often disruptive in worship because of pent-up physical energy. Channel this energy into a lively dance, an active drama or a special task, such as giving out the song books. A dance like 'On Tiptoe', p. 262, in which children can join spontaneously, is best used prior to a time when children will be expected to sit still. The dance gives them a chance to release some of their energy constructively and also makes it easier for them to settle down. This teaches them that worship includes times of active participation and times of quiet. Maintaining a balance between these two is a cardinal factor when training children in how to participate in worship.

Plan the occasional surprise for children as well. Our family services are sometimes visited by a gentle clown, costumed in traditional garb. His amusing antics, all centred on the teaching theme, captivate the attention of children beyond their normal rather limited span. 'This is the first Sunday wee Alastair hasn't stayed on the floor playing with the heating vent,' an appreciative grandmother confided after one of our clown's appearances.

When children participate fully in worship, other members of the church family benefit. Children have a unique ability to draw others into their joy and delight. It's hard for anyone to be aloof whilst a tiny shepherd, the bath towel on his head slightly askew, earnestly searches for his lost sheep; it's next to impossible to remain uninvolved in the intense anticipation of the youthful triangle player awaiting the moment to triumphantly clang her precious instrument. The freedom of children is an impetus and catalyst to our own.

NOTE

1. British Council of Churches, *The Child in the Church*, Consultative Group on Ministry among Children, Report of Working Party on 'The Child in the Church', 1976, p. 30.

Introduction to Materials

As a great deal of Fisherfolk music is readily available through records, tapes and songbooks, this book includes only that music which is essential to an arrangement or performance and which has not been published elsewhere. Almost all song references pertain to Fisherfolk music, and the suggested songs are found in *Sound of Living Waters, Fresh Sounds* and *Cry Hosanna*, all published by Hodder and Stoughton; and *Hey Kids, Do You Love Jesus*, Celebration Records. Occasionally we suggest traditional or well-known songs from other sources. The songbooks are abbreviated SOLW, FS, CH and HK throughout, page numbers are not given for *Cry Hosanna* as they were not available at the time of publication.

Terms and Abbreviations Used in this Section

L: left
R: right
C: centre
U: upstage (area of stage furthest from audience)
D: downstage (area of stage closest to audience)
SL: stage left (from player's viewpoint, looking out to audience)
SR: stage right (from player's viewpoint, looking out to audience)
Cross: move to another part of playing area
Freeze: hold position without moving
Stylised: abstract; not meant to be realistic

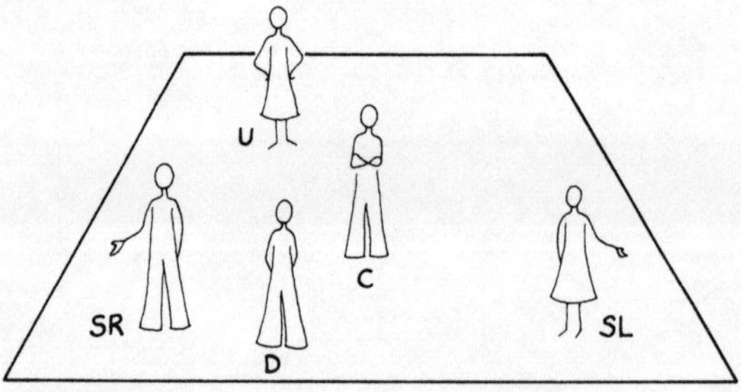

CHAPTER 9

Readings, Prayers and Poetry

READINGS

Readings, in one of their many forms, are a practical, diplomatic starting place for churches and groups just beginning to express themselves through the folk arts. Readings are different but not *too* different. Most readings are simple, which means they fit easily into the existing structure, and individuals or small groups can prepare them without lengthy rehearsals. Since people are already accustomed to scripture readings during worship, it's not a very radical departure for there to be other readings as well, perhaps poetry or meditation by a solo reader, perhaps a call to worship or a dramatic scripture reading by a small group. Worship readings generally are either based on scripture or use scriptural imagery, so the new is firmly escorted by the familiar. In other contexts, such as youth or coffee-bar groups, or home meetings, using readings is a practical way to lead into personal sharing, testimony teaching or group discussion. Finally, readings are easily accessible. Most people know how to read, and though they may not yet be liberated enough to dance or act, they are usually willing and eager to read. Similarly, people who doubt their ability to write a play or make up a mime often find the idea of writing a prayer, a dramatic reading or perhaps a poem for a special occasion much more attainable.

As people both construct and present readings, they become more relaxed as well as more adventurous. Those who began with only a two-voice reading may in future decide to experiment with sound effects, then add two or three more readers, then a vocal embellishment or two, then an interpretative dancer . . . the very ones who hesitated in dance, drama, mime are likely to find themselves striding ahead in those areas!

See Choral Reading and Music Exercises, Chapter 18, for full explanation of the abbreviated or specialised terms on the choral reading scripts.

Morning Song

Like dew upon the earth
like plants that grow
like wind that blows:

so is the gentle majesty of the almighty Lord

Once more welcome him
who always welcomes you

Louis Newton

Endless Rejoicing

Sing, O Israel, a new song.
Sing, O daughter of Zion, to the Lord your hope.
Rejoice and stand in gladness, O bride of God,
    for now has salvation wed you.

Sing to the nations, O city,
    for the world is bathed in your light.
Sing of the Lord of lords,
    for he has made all whole and new.

Dance the great dance.
In motion sing out what tongue alone can never tell.
Weave patterns of praise to the Word
    who is all that can ever be told.

Sing, dance, in utmost joy:
    all perfection is lost and found in love.
Sing, sing, and ever dance!
    There is no end of him!

Louis Newton

Come, Lord

(based on Psalm 27)

Come, Lord
be our God!

Be that mighty rock
    that towering fortress
that dwarfs other stones,
that crumbles other strengths

Be that pure light
    that steady lamp
that overpowers other lights,
that dims other flames

Be that strong shepherd
    that firm guide
that directs other leadings,
that obstructs other paths

Come, Lord
be our God!

Lead us into the land of the living
that land where death is life,
that land where love undoes strife

Come, Lord
be our God!

Patricia Beall

Psalm 24

(adapted from *Jerusalem Bible*)

arranged by Patricia Beall

GROUP 1: To the Lord belongs the earth and all it holds,
GROUP 2: The world, and all who live in it!

GROUP 1: He himself founded it on the ocean,
GROUP 2: Based it firmly on the nether sea.

GROUP 1: Who has the right to climb the mountain of the Lord?
GROUP 2: Who has the right to stand in his holy place?

GROUP 1: He whose hands are clean, whose heart is pure,
GROUP 2: He who doesn't delight in worthless things,
who doesn't swear to what is false.

GROUP 1: God's blessing belongs to him
GROUP 2: And he will save and vindicate him.

GROUP 1: Such are the people who seek him,
GROUP 2: Who seek your presence, God of Jacob!

GROUP 1: Gates, raise your arches!
GROUP 2: Rise, you ancient doors!
BOTH: Let the King of glory in!

GROUP 3: Who is this King of glory?
(Solo or small group)

GROUP 1: The Lord, strong and valiant!
GROUP 2: The Lord, mighty in battle!

GROUP 1: Gates, raise your arches!
GROUP 2: Rise, you ancient doors!
BOTH: Let the King of glory in!

GROUP 3: Who is this King of glory?

BOTH: He is the Lord God Almighty,
He is the King of glory!

Let Us Rejoice, Let Us Be Glad!

by Patricia Beall

READER: This is the day which the Lord has made
ALL: Let us rejoice and be glad in it!

READER: We are the people the Lord has made
ALL: Let us rejoice in him!

READER: God gave us his son in the fulness of time
ALL: Let us be glad in him!

READER: On earth Jesus lived, on earth he died
ALL: Let us rejoice in him!

READER: He returned from the dead and now reigns on high
ALL: Let us be glad in him!

READER: God gives his Spirit to live in our hearts
ALL: Let us rejoice in him!

READER: The Lord our God is three in one, Father, Spirit, and the Son
ALL: Let us be glad in him!

READER: This is the day which the Lord has made
ALL: Let us rejoice and be glad in it!

Thanksgiving

(response based on Psalm 107:21)

by Patricia Beall

Presentation style: A congregational thanksgiving for communion. Individual readers seated in the congregation take solo parts, or two readers alternate parts.
Note: This reading may be inserted after first sentence of paragraph 28 and before first sentence of paragraph 29 in Series III of the Anglican Liturgy. If using in this context, omit final congregational response.

SOLO: Thank you for your life, Lord Jesus, body and blood, given that we might be forgiven, given that we might forgive.

SOLO: Thank you for walls walked through, Lord Jesus, for barriers broken down.

WOMEN: Thank you, Lord, for your love
MEN: for your love
ALL: for your wonders to all!

SOLO: Thank you for your Word, living and present with us.

SOLO: Thank you for your Spirit, who drew us together today.

WOMEN: Thank you, Lord, for your love
MEN: for your love
ALL: for your wonders to all!

SOLO: Thank you that your love draws us, warms us, frees us. Thank you that love heals.

SOLO: Thank you for your grace, which makes it possible for us to trust each other.

WOMEN: Thank you, Lord, for your love
MEN: for your love
ALL: for your wonders to all!

SOLO: Thank you for your glory, given to your people that we may be one.

SOLO: Thank you for your peace which joins us, thank you for your presence now as we gather and share at your table.

WOMEN: Thank you, Lord, for your love
MEN: for your love
ALL: for your wonders to all!

The Tax Question

(Mark 12:13–17)

arranged by Patricia Beall

Presentation style: Dramatic scripture reading for use in worship or teaching

Characters: 5 or more

Narrator	Herodian
Pharisee I	Jesus
Pharisee II	Additional Pharisees and Herodians, if desired

Placement: Readers stand in a group visible to congregation

The Tax Question

NARRATOR: Later the church officials sent some Pharisees and Herodians to Jesus to catch him in his words.

PHARISEE I: Teacher, we know you are a man of integrity.

HERODIAN: You aren't swayed by men, because you pay no attention to who they are; but you teach the way of God in accordance with the truth.

PHARISEE II: Is it right to pay taxes to Caesar or not?

PHARISEES and HERODIANS: Should we pay or shouldn't we?

NARRATOR: But Jesus knew their hypocrisy.

JESUS: Why are you trying to trap me? Bring me a denarius and let me look at it.

NARRATOR: So they brought the coin, and Jesus said,

JESUS: Whose portrait is this? And whose inscription?

PHARISEES and HERODIANS: Caesar's!

JESUS: Then give to Caesar what is Caesar's and to God what is God's.

NARRATOR: And they were amazed at him.

Why Doesn't He Come?

(based on Luke 24:6–11)

by Maggie Durran

Presentation style: May be presented as a drama. If done as a drama, Peter exits first.

Characters: 2
Mary
Peter

MARY: (*convincingly*) Don't you believe me?

PETER: (*hesitantly*) Well, not really.

MARY: You know what that angel said?

PETER: I know he said that we knew Christ had to suffer and be crucified and rise again.

MARY: Well then, don't you believe it?

PETER: No, (*pause*) not yet. (*longer pause*) I think I have to see him myself to believe it.

MARY: (*frustrated*) But he is risen; you saw the empty tomb and then he spoke to me in the garden.

PETER: I think I need to see him myself, Mary.

MARY: (*affronted*) Do you mean you doubt my word?

PETER: (*doubtfully*) No, (*pause*) but I think you might be mistaken. Mary, I'm sorry, but I can't be that hopeful. You might just have imagined it.

MARY: But, I didn't! He stood and spoke to me and told me to tell you he has risen.

PETER: (*painfully*) I want to see him myself. You saw him, and he spoke to you. I want him to speak to me.

MARY: (*gently*) You miss him, don't you?

PETER: Don't we all!

MARY: Yes, (*slight pause*) but I know he's risen, Peter.

PETER: (*emphatically*) Then, why doesn't he come?

MARY: I don't know, but he said he was going to ascend to the Father.

PETER: I want him to come here first. Where could I find him? He has to come here.

MARY: I think he will.

PETER: The others asked me to go fishing with them. I think I will.

(*Exit, downcast.*)

'I Stand and Knock'

(based on Revelation 3:20)

by Patricia Beall, Lewis Paul, Jim Wilson

READER I: 'Listen! I stand at the door and knock. If anyone hears my voice and opens the door, I will come into his house and eat with him, and he will eat with me.'

(*silence*)

'Listen!'

READER II: Picture a group of people sitting, talking, while others move around. In the general hubbub of noise and activity, a mother suddenly picks out the cry of her child from the other side of the hall. Mother and child are on the same wavelength.

In the same way we can be aware of the presence of God. We can be receptive to him, to what he says to us. When Jesus spoke at the side of Lake Galilee he spoke to everyone by means of parables, saying, 'Listen then, if you have ears to hear.' Why did he say this? He clearly wasn't talking of the deaf. He wasn't saying, 'if you can't hear me at the back would you raise your hand.' No. He was saying, 'If you have ears to hear, if you have a mind to listen, if you come with an aim, an intention of receiving a message, if you are looking for something to change your lives – then here we go. LISTEN!'

(*silence*)

READER I: 'I stand at the door and knock.'

READER III: Can't you hear me – or won't you hear me? I am here, I want to come into your life. I am here, trying to come into your life. Are you trying to make me a part of yours? I want to be with you – will you accept me or will you refuse to hear my knocking? I am here, and I want to be with you.

(*silence*)

READER I: 'If anyone hears my voice . . .'

READER II: 'Hears his voice?' How do we hear Jesus?

READER IV: You can hear him: in your heart, as you search for peace,
in your mind, as you long for things to make sense,
in written words, which he spoke aloud thousands of years ago, which he speaks aloud to you now.
You can hear him: in others, as they care for you, guide you, help you,

in songs and music, in words
and dances, in thoughts and
prayers.

Listen! and you will hear the voice of Jesus everywhere!

(*silence*)

READER I: 'If anyone hears my voice and opens the door . . .'

READER II: 'The door?!' What door?

READER IV: The door of your life. This door is yours alone. Only you have the key, the power to open it. Only you can decide to unlock your life, to open it to him who stands waiting, knocking, speaking.

(*silence*)

READER I: 'I will come into his house.'

READER II: Yes, he is trying to attract our attention, he wants to speak to us, he wants to share with us. All he asks is that we open the door of our hearts to him when we hear him knocking. If we do this, we have his assurance that he will come in . . . come into our lives, make his dwelling place in our hearts.

(*silence*)

READER I: 'I will come into his house and eat with him, and he will eat with me.'

READER III: We will share our food together, we will share our lives together. I do not want to be apart, I want to be a part of you, be with you. I do not want to watch you working, I want to work with you. I do not want to watch you living, I want to live with you.

So many people accept me as their Lord, their Saviour, their master – but cannot accept me as their friend, as part of their lives. I'm not someone who is apart, or distant from you – we must be together.

(*silence*)

READER I: 'Listen! I stand at the door and knock. If anyone hears my voice and opens the door, I will come into his house and eat with him, and he will eat with me.'

Psalm 51

(paraphrase based on *Jerusalem Bible*)

by Patricia Beall

Presentation style: Three voice meditation or confession

1: In your goodness, Lord, have mercy on me;
in your great tenderness, wipe away my faults.
Wash me clean of my guilt, cleanse my sin.

2: I am well aware of my faults,
my sin is constantly in my mind.

3: And is it against you, Lord,
that I have sinned.

Chorus:

1: Create in me a clean heart, O Lord,
and put in me a new and right spirit.

2: Cast me not away from your presence,

3: do not take your Holy Spirit from me.

ALL: For you are the God of my salvation,
you are the king of love.

1: I am guilty, Lord guilty.

3: I was born guilty:

2: I inherited the curse of Adam's disobedience.

Chorus (*as above*)

3: You, Lord, love honesty:
you love trueness and sincerity of heart.

2: You, Lord, can purify me:
you can wash me whiter than snow.

1: You, Lord, can give me joy and gladness:
you can heal the bones which you have broken.

2: If you will be my saviour again, my joy will be renewed.

1: If you will open my lips, my mouth will show forth your praise.

3: If you will save me from death, I will sing aloud of your deliverance.

Chorus

2: There is no sacrifice, Lord

1: no sacrifice of burnt flesh

3: no sacrifice of animal blood

2: that could please you now.

1: So the offering I make,
the only one which I think you will not refuse,
is a broken spirit

3: a broken and crushed heart

2: a heart contrite and humbled.

Chorus

pause following chorus, then repeat final two lines:

ALL: You are the God of my salvation,
you are the king of love.

Renewing the World

(selected verses from Psalms 104, 105, 107, *Jerusalem Bible*)

arranged by Patricia Beall

ALL: Let us thank the Lord for his love
(*c.c.*)*

WOMEN: for his love

MEN: for his love

ALL: for his wonders to all!

SMALL GROUP: They de mand ed food
(*REST OF GROUP: scatter on 'food'*)

SOLO: He satisfied them with the bread of heaven!

SMALL GROUP: He opened the rock

ALL: The waters gushed like a river!
(*drawing out 'shhhhhh' sound in 'gushed'*)

ALL: Let us thank the Lord for his love
(*c.c.*)

WOMEN: for his love

MEN: for his love

ALL: for his wonders to all!

WOMEN: All creatures depend on him to feed them

MEN: With generous hand he satisfies their hunger.

WOMEN: Filling the starving with good things

MEN: He satisfies their hunger.

ALL: Let us thank the Lord for his love
(*c.c.*)

WOMEN: for his love

MEN: for his love

ALL: for his wonders to all!

ALL: For he gives his Spirit,
(*SM. GRP: 'whoosh'ing sound after 'Spirit'*)

(*Divide into three equal groups for next line, creating canon effect.*)

GROUP 1: (*softly*) fresh life begins

GROUP 2: (*growing louder*) fresh life begins

GROUP 3: (*louder still*) fresh life begins!

ALL: He keeps renewing the world!

* *For chance chords (c.c.) and other techniques in this reading, see Exercises, pp. 377, 380–81.*

Psalm 118

(verse 15–24)

arranged by Betty Pulkingham

CHANCE CHORD: Hark!

WOMEN: Glad songs of vic – tory in the tents of the righteous

MEN: The right hand of the Lord/does valiantly.

WOMEN: *(rising in pitch)*

The right hand of the Lord is exalted.

MEN: The right hand of the Lord/does valiantly!

Sung Duet (Alto and Tenor)

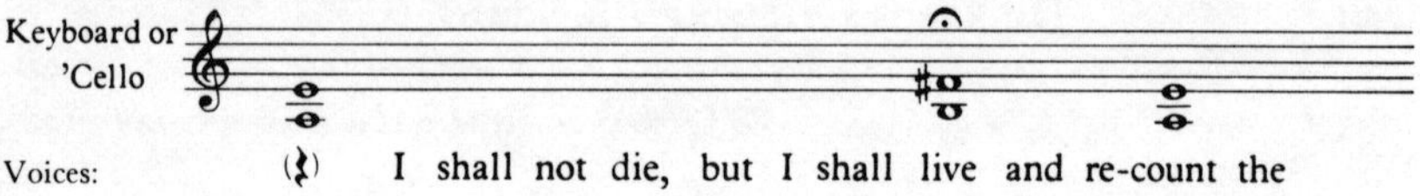

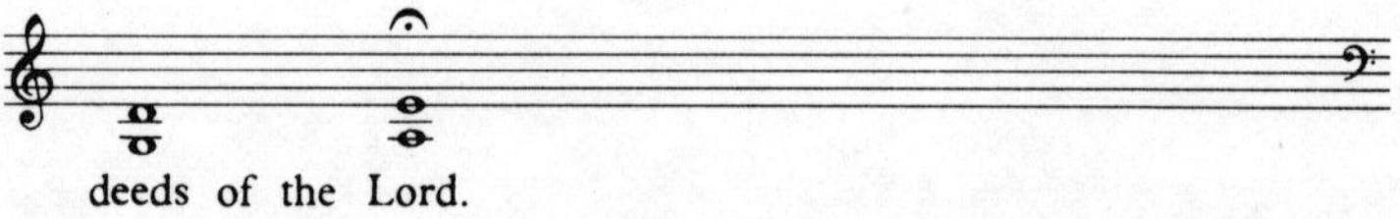

Keyboard or 'Cello

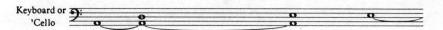

MEN *(spoken)*: The Lord has chastened me sorely, but he has not given me over to death.

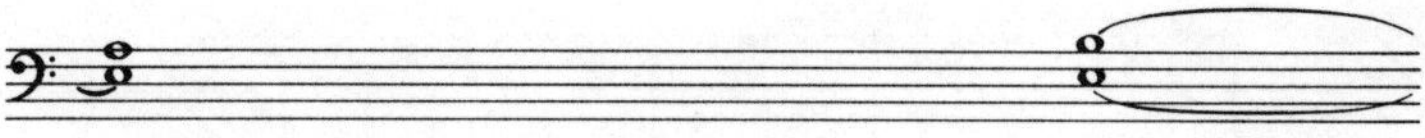

ALL: Open to me the gates of righteousness, that I may enter through

them and give thanks to the Lord.

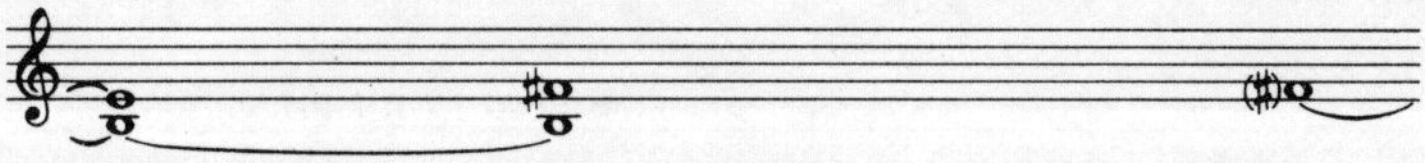

WOMEN: This is the gate of the Lord; the righteous shall enter through it.

MEN: I thank thee that thou hast answered me and hast become my salvation.

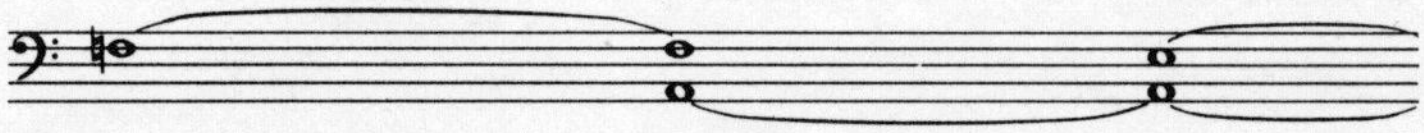

WOMEN: *(add men gradually)* The stone which the builders rejected has become the chief Cornerstone.

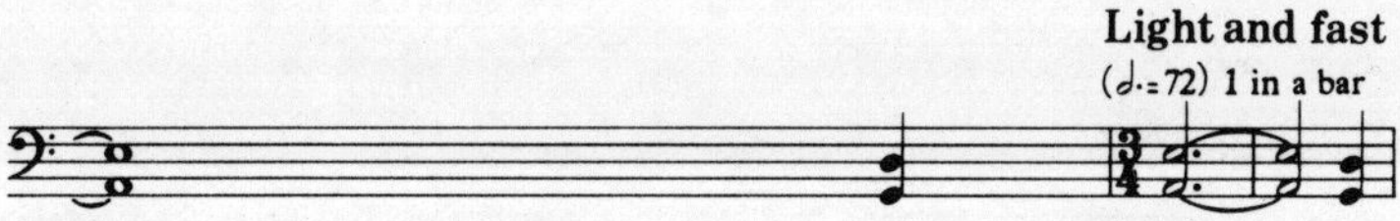

ALTOS & BASSES: This is the Lord's doing. ALL: It is marvellous in our eyes. *(segue)*

from 'Yeldall Carol' by Diane Davis Andrew.

Revelation

poem by Grace Krag

arranged by Patricia Beall

The solo reader for this should have a strong, expressive voice, and can be either a man or a woman. Soloist reads parts marked 'ALL' only in middle section.

WOMEN: *(soft but firm)* Blind.

SOLO: I do not see you.

MEN: *(building intensity)* Blind.

SOLO: I do not hear you.

ALL: *(peak of intensity)* Blind.

SOLO: I do not believe you.

(pause)

ALL: I weep
('weeeeeeeeeep'
*Soft, high pitched c.c., pitch sliding to low. Sound final 'p' gently but well.)**

because I know

only you

can keep the darkness
(WOMEN: echo on 'darkness')

from me.

SOLO: *(slowly, rounding o's)* I bow low

to find you.
(ALL: scatter on 'find you')

I sing
*(ALL: Soft 1–3–5 major chord, one or two people free-singing. Pitch of bottom note sounded by one person, others build chord. Fade out singing by *.)*

because you appear a person before me

because you speak to my understanding*

because now

WOMEN: I see

MEN: and hear

ALL: and believe you.

* *For chance chords (c.c.) and other techniques in this reading, see Exercises, pp. 377, 380–83.*

We Are His Witnesses

(based on Acts 2:1–4)

by Maggie Durran

Participants: 4
Three readers
Instrumentalist (violinist or cellist)

Instrumentalist's cues		*Reader*	
Make 'busy' sounds		1:	Heat.
giving the effect of		3:	Buzzing flies.
the hustle and bustle		2:	Distant hubbub of
of a market place			market sound.
		3:	A dog is barking
		2:	and a neighbour yells
			at her kids.
Stop.			
		1:	*(lazily)* And the buzz
			of lazy flies.
			(pause)
			Silence.
Begin to play	*reverent yet*	3:	Bread and wine,
softly, 'Seek ye	*joyful*	2:	eaten together;
first', SOLW, 58.		2,3:	peacefully.
Stop.			*(pause)*
	stage	1:	Silence.
	whisper	2:	The baby snuffled in
			her sleep.
			(pause)
		1:	Silence.
			(pause)
Make sound of	*intense*	2:	Listen!
stormy wind,		1:	What is it?
gradually build		2:	Listen!
	words almost	3:	Sound
	tumble over		
	each other;	2:	like a roar,
	begin with		
	stage	1:	like the wind,
	whisper;		
	speak fast	2:	in a storm,
	and close		
	together;	3:	filling the house,
	crescendo	1:	growing louder

	until very loud	1,2:	and louder
		1,2,3:	till our ears will burst.
Stop.			
Begin playing staccato notes to depict dancing flames.		2:	*(amazed whisper)* It stopped. *(Group 'sees' the flames on the heads of those in the audience and excitement builds as flames move around.)*
	without speeding up, use voice tone to show excitement	1:	Look!
		3:	Flames,
		2:	brilliant flames of dancing fire
		3:	dividing,
		2:	touching,
		1:	resting,
Change to legato and emphasise crescendo. Stop.	*crescendo, speak each word deliberately*	2:	anointing
		2,3:	with power,
		ALL:	power-filled sons of the Most High God. *(pause)*
	speak with slight pause between every two words		*(with realisation of what God has done)* And we are his witnesses.

As Peter

I

As Peter, water-walking
sank
when winds swelled, waves roared –
so cry I
'Lord!'

And you,
sea-striding, wind-riding
again
stretch your hand,
grasping mine, clasping me,
holding me fast
on water suddenly
firm as land.

But more the water swells and soars,
stronger it tosses.
Yet still you hold me,
not stopping the storm
not stopping the sea
yet not dropping me:
teaching me
it is your hand,
not the land,
that does not falter.

II

As Peter, God-finding
'Call me, Lord,' I said
and you did.
But now
my ears are deaf to hear your voice.

'Take me, Lord!' I cried
and you did,
stopping my sighs,
wiping dry my eyes.
But now
I am blind, unable to find the way ahead –
because I look behind.

'I'll follow, Lord!' I said
and I did.
But now
I hesitate, wanting to wait –
afraid to brave the way you lead.

As Peter, heart-speaking
'I love you, Lord,' I said
and I do.
So again I say
Call me, Lord
Take me, Lord
Lead me, Lord.
I am afraid, it is true
But hold me, keep me with you.

Patricia Beall

leaping

Your word, Lord

is what I long for
in this waiting place

this place between and
one frog leap of faith another

Your word
to strengthen the muscles

Your word
to light the path before me

Your word
to encourage my weak heart

boldly your faithfulness
I will leap remembering and steadfast love

Diane Davis Andrew

Jesus, keep me tender

Jesus, keep me tender.
I want to smooth over
the unclean wound,
smile bravely to the passers-by,
and say blithely:
'It's nothing really.'

Jesus, keep me tender.
I want to deny
the piercing pain,
present the facade
steel and grey,
and say blankly:
'You don't touch me.'

Jesus, keep me tender.
I want to hurt
my friend whose leaving
leaves me empty.
I want to hurt –
to be blasé
and say politely:
'It's been nice,
but I really can't remember
your name.'

Jesus, keep me tender.

Jesus, help me
to stay able to be hurt.

Jesus, help me
to be able not to hurt back.

Martha Keys Barker

a prayer

Holy Spirit
with the threads of my life
weave your glorious tapestry

with each breath I take
stretch the fibres ever finer

with each step I take
make the strands reach much farther

with each tear I weep
cut the ravelled edges even closer

with each love I risk
drape the stunning fabric more softly

Grace Krag

confession

oh Lord
we admit we have sinned against you
in thoughts
words
deeds
grievously
enough to kill you as you stood in our place
relentlessly
as we struck you dumb with our unknowing
coolly
as from the corner of our sins we watched you die

Grace Krag

Litany to the Father

Good Father
    Who dwells in heights unseen
    yet to our depths has leaned
Be merciful to us

Dear Father
    Who dispelled darkness with lightning word
    Who expelled sin with flaming sword
Be merciful to us

Kind Father
    Who sent from above
    redeeming Love
Be merciful to us

Gentle Father
    Who makes brothers of strangers
    disciples of wanderers
Be merciful to us

Loving Father
    Who breathed Your Breath of life
    empowering victory in the needful strife
Be merciful to us

O Father
Be merciful to us

Patricia Beall

Hands

I see, Lord, in my tightly clenched fists
a symbol of my self.
I grasp my life,
hiding all I don't want others to see.

I hold my pride:
    my desire to appear right,
    my desire to appear strong.

I hold my anxieties:
    my fear that I won't be accepted as I am,
    my inability to be who I am.

I hold my anger:
    my violence that protects me
    against anyone
    who comes too close to my secrets.

I ache with this tension,
with the immense energy required
to hide myself –
    from you, lest you change me,
    from them, lest they hurt me.

With these fists, I want to strike out –
    against you,
    against them,
    against all that threatens me.

(*pause*)

But I see,
in these whitened knuckles
and straining forearms,
what this is doing to me:
I am enslaved,
imprisoned within myself.
I am destroying myself and others.

(*pause*)

But I sense your presence, Lord,
your open hands
reaching out to me.

I slowly open my hands,
and release myself to you.
I offer all I have been grasping so tightly:
the fear of being known,
the anxiety of being alone,
the anger, the guilt, the pain.

Lord!
My arms no longer ache!
My hands can move again!
They can stretch and wiggle.
They are open and able to receive –
Fill them with your love!
Show them how to touch,
how to serve.

Freed from my own grasp,
I am suddenly aware of others.
I reach out to my sisters and brothers.
Let my hands be your hands
as I take their needs and cares
and lift them to you.
Give us your sustaining grace,
touch us with your healing love.
Take us and shape us together
into the body of your Son.

Let our hands be your hands
to reach out to the world you love.

original author unknown
adaptation by Martha Keys Barker
and Patricia Beall

Lord of the Gentle Hands

Hands, Lord: Your gift to us.

Hands: rough, calloused, smooth, rounded,
soap-scoured, ink-stained, tanned,
aesthetic.

We stretch them up to you, tentatively . . .
in worship: high, lifted
in joy: widespread, stretched open
in pain: gripped, tautly white
in despair: pleading, desolate, still, empty
And always you hold them.

Your gentle hands hold ours.

Your hands, which took beating, battering,
throbbed in head-tearing pain.
Your hands, scarred, became the sign
of your love no time can erase.

Your hands, which have us inscribed
upon their palms, pour down
blessing on the details of our days.

Your hands, steady and controlled, hold
our minds, re-create us in their design.

Your hands lovingly touch our deepest selves,
until we are complete in you.

Praise you, Lord, for your hands, which never let us go.

We reach our hands to you, thankfully.
Hold them, Lord, always.

Alison Allan

Prayer for Renewal

Burst the day
say honey-sweet words
that pour health and strength
into our dry, used-up bones.

Crack the brittleness
of stale, frail
windless night
hanging
not stirring
over our empty, blind souls.

Let the music
of your wind-Spirit
blow fresh and vital
over us
until
tuned together,
like old and seasoned instruments
we respond in rich, deep tones
filling the air with melody
stirring the listeners to dance.

Jodi Page Clark

Thy Kingdom Come

(based on the Lord's Prayer)

developed by Oxford workshop group

READER 1: Our Father, who art in heaven, hallowed be thy name.

READER 2: Let us praise God for his eternal being: his holiness, his mercy, his mysteries, his gentleness.
Let us thank God for his revelation to us in history: his son Jesus.

READER 1: Thy kingdom come, thy will be done on earth as it is in heaven.

READER 2: Let us pray for the unity of all those who serve the Lord:
for those on foreign mission fields
for those in isolated situations
for the Churches of *(local situation)*.

READER 1: Give us this day our daily bread.

READER 2: Let us offer our needs and concerns to the Lord:
(*spontaneous prayers*)

READER 1: And forgive us our trespasses.

READER 2: Let us offer the times we have offended through ignorance.
Let us offer the times we have known the Lord's will and rejected it.
Let us offer any other things that have separated us from God and each other.

READER 1: As we forgive those who trespass against us.

READER 2: Let us recall those we have not forgiven, and forgive them now.

READER 1: Lead us not into temptation, but deliver us from evil.

READER 2: Let us ask the Lord to strengthen us by his grace.
Let us expect miracles in our places of weakness.
Let us rejoice in our sufferings, knowing they will not be beyond our endurance.

READER 1: For thine is the kingdom, the power, and the glory for ever and ever. Amen.

Wind of Spirit, Wind of Change

When we think we know
the way to go
to be fully ourselves –
When we have things all arranged –
You come suddenly, wings of change,
erasing our order, displacing our plans.
Wind of Spirit, wind of change,
You move at will to rearrange
our thoughts, our longings, our lives.

When we think we know
positions into which others go
to please ourselves, to please them –
You come, weeping wounded,
shattering our limited lovelessness.
Wind of Spirit, wind of change,
You move at will to rearrange
our attitudes, our intentions, our plans.

When we think we know
the direction our lives should go
to bring your kingdom to man,
often we end with things arranged
to prevent change:
we become fixed, caught by the cares
that will get us there.
Then you come, sudden sweeping,
to lead us anew.
Wind of Spirit, wind of change,
You move at will to rearrange
our goals, our priorities, our vision.

Wind of Spirit, wind of change,
move at will to rearrange
our thoughts, our plans, our lives.
Help us to lead, help us to follow.
Break our hearts, bend our wills,
soften our words, temper our thoughts.
Use us to fulfil
your hope, your vision, your life.

Teach us to come as you,
suddenly, weeping,
bearing change to rearrange
your people, your church, your world.

Patricia Beall

'Wind of Spirit' Prayers

We confess that we are part of governments and economic systems that keep your world bound in poverty, injustice and ignorance. We ask that we may be changed by your love, that we may be an instrument of your Spirit to rearrange the power and resources of your world.

We pray for the world . . . (*spontaneous prayers*)

We confess that we are part of a church that has often been known for its rigidity, its lack of forgiveness, its resistance to change. We ask that here and in every place your church may be known as a people easily moved by your winds of change, as a people open to receive all persons.

We pray for your church . . . (*spontaneous prayers*)

We confess that as a family we are not always open to receive each other and our neighbours. When we experience opposition, we are tempted to be discouraged. When people don't meet our expectations, we become impatient. Renew in us your accepting love for each other and our neighbours.

We pray for our community, our neighbourhood, for those in need . . . (*spontaneous prayers*)

We give thanks for your Spirit moving among us and in all your world – changing and rearranging lives and priorities. We give thanks for all you are doing to bring new life, health, justice and peace.

We offer our thanksgivings . . . (*spontaneous thanksgivings*)

Martha Keys Barker

Litany of Resurrection

by Martha Keys Barker

We were buried with him by baptism into death
so that, as Christ was raised from the dead
by the glory of the Father, we too might walk in newness of life.

Romans 6:4

Dying and resurrected Lord,
as we were buried with you in baptism,
and walk with you in newness of life,
we pray for your resurrected life
to touch and heal the brokenness
for which you were broken.

You took upon yourself the brokenness of your people:

Those who were so tied to religious structures
that your life of change
threatened death to their security.

Those who were so fearful of death
that to preserve their lives,
they denied you.

Look upon the brokenness of your people:

May your church be clothed
in resurrection hope:
knowing death has been swallowed up in life.

May your church have grace
to enter into your sufferings
with our only security:
the certainty of resurrection.

May your church have courage
to stand against the forces of death,
especially in places
where this witness invites death.

We pray for your church . . . (*spontaneous prayer, if desired*)

Dying and resurrected Lord,
You took upon yourself the brokenness of your world:

The competition among nations
where instruments of death are valued
above the nurture of life.

The sickness of nations
where governments use torture and death
to preserve their own lives.

Look upon the brokenness of your world:

May your world know hope,
as your people live
your healing life
in the midst of its pain.

May your world know peace,
that life may flourish
and all humanity know your love.

We pray for your world . . . (*spontaneous prayer, if desired*)

Dying and resurrected Lord,
You took upon yourself the brokenness
of every family and community:

The despair of families
where the death of love
makes life meaningless.

The suffering of communities
where division and strife
make life joyless.

Look upon the brokenness of our families and community:

May your love put to death
anything among us that denies you,
your immense love for us,
your forgiveness,
your final victory over death and sin.

May the victory of your resurrection
give us hope and healing
in the broken places
of our lives and relationships.

May we in this church
become a family of love
gathering together
those who long to share your life.

May we as a family
become a sign of resurrection
in this community where we live.

We pray for our families, our community, the needs among us . . .
(*spontaneous prayer, if desired*)

Dying and resurrected Lord,

We give thanks for your death and resurrection.
We praise you for the certain hope you give us:

For, as you were buried in earth's grip
waiting for life to spring again,
So your Spirit,
implanted in us, earthen vessels,
endures death's grip
knowing your life will spring forth to reign.

In joy we offer our thanksgivings . . . (*spontaneous prayer, if desired*)

POETRY

Poetry is extremely versatile. It provides a superb form for personal and artistic expression; additionally, it can enhance other art forms. Throughout this book we give many examples of our use of poetry with movement and dance, mime, graphic and fine arts, and as the basis for readings. Workshop structures for each of these areas contain the use of poetry, and many poems are found in other Materials chapters.

Poetry can be used with great diversity in worship: a full listing of suggestions is in Appendix I. Other suggestions for the use of poetry are found in Chapters 16 and 19.

gooseberry pie

the enormous fat girl
could see herself in size 12
and so longed
for her image
to be real

the wandering gigolo
could see himself as eternally potent
and so built his body
daily
in a gym

the aging matron
could see herself as famously charitable
and so gave mightily,
according to her desire

the gnarled country man
could see himself as Farmer of the Year
and so gave his blood
to fertilise his dream

ah,
images, icons, idols –
    shining, lustrous
how subtly they become us

and we them

Patricia Beall

Bondage

Eels glide the water,
water heavy with oil and silt.
After years of waste, dredged sands no longer leaven.
Scavengers slide the thickness,
parasite and host confused.

Logs
    tossed in momentum
collide
    and recoil,
splintering.

Slouching frogs stare –
Silent birds, grey with soot,
stain the sky.

A sun rises somewhere
    lost in the untorn veil of smoke.
The trembling moon has vanished,
its flicker blackened by eclipse.

The destruction lives,
inhaling its sustenance
preserving its death
starving darkly for revelation:
'Creation still contains the hope of being freed
from its slavery to decadence.'

Patricia Beall

Depressed Area

by Maggie Durran

Presentation style: This poem, used also as a solo reading, is an effective stimulus for discussion.

Suggested discussion topics: As families are separated from friends, relatives and neighbours, due to urban development, they often experience loneliness. What community and family values are torn by such separation? How much does breakdown of local community life contribute to social problems? What part should Christians and the local church play in community development? Consider these in relation to your own locality.

Depressed Area

God, we're not depressed . . .
We're angry,
Fightin' bloody mad!
Man, you seen it;
Y'saw what it was;
Rotten wa'nt it? . . .
When yer 'ouse is 'eld together
By planks
'ammered on t' winders,
An'alf the 'ouses
'ave corrigated on t' doorways.
But it was 'ome,
And y'could see water
From y'winder.
An'ave y'seen t' cobbles in t' street?
Hell, why do they 'ave to take it away?

Some places
They moved 'ole lot out . . .
Put 'em wherever there were 'ouse empty,
All over city,
Then rolled place flat.
They left the boozers tho' . . .
Moved regulars,
But left the bloody boozers.
No-one knows anyone,
But they left the boozers.
Shook 'em up a bit too . . .
Got 'em done up wi' new paint.

Hey, did y'see what Charlie wrote
On t' wall of 'Stars 'n' Moon'?
'e wrote 'SHIT' in gre't, black paint . . .
Got caugh' too.
Get sloshed now 'n' y' find
Five thousand doors all look like your'n,
An' yer in trouble, mate.

Did y'ear th'mericans
Are buying stain'-glass from t' church?
They're building one like our'n.
An' we got a new one . . .
No winders, mind y',
So won't get smashed?
'ave y' seen them demolition gangs?
They 'ave a crane with a gre't iron ball,
An' it swings down t' row.
There's a roof gone
An' M's Brown's wallpaper
Peelin' in t' wind,
An' ball swings,
Knocks it clean off.
An' nex'-door's living room,
An' they left a picture on t' wall . . .
Looks like someone's granny.

Hell, can't y' stop it?
God Almighty, can't y' stop 'em?
So it were bad . . .
But it's better bad an' alive
Than dead in li'tle boxes.

David Danced

(based on II Samuel 6:16–20)

I

Startled
I saw you from my window
Naked
    clothed only in joy
you danced
tambourine hammering triumph's rapid rhythm

My anger trembled, flared
outraged
    by your abandon

King!
How dare you dance so!
How dare you move so!
King!
Do you not know that all watch:
servants, children, soldiers,
maids, grooms, dogs!
King!
How dare you show yourself!

II

I danced
    laughter pouring as cold springs,
    motions flashing as melted silver
I danced
    amazed,
    joy, power, victory dazed

God is the King! my heart cried
God is the one who shows Himself!
And we,
    servants:
    king, soldiers, grooms, dogs
have seen Him!

We watched as He revealed Himself!
We saw His naked arm, mighty in battle!
We saw His power, His victory,
giving us life in place of death!

I danced
    amazed, joy dazed
knowing the God who shows Himself

Patricia Beall

There Was a Man

There was a man whose flesh was like bread,
in whose body was all the fruit of the earth,
in whose bones were all the strivings of man.
Like bread he was beaten and bruised,
he was strained, he was stretched on wood,
his soft flesh conforming to the cross.
He hung there naked to the greed of the wind
and from his nailed-through hands
came blood flowing like wine.

Veronica Zundel

Friday

steel smashed and wood cracked
    the wind, moaning in grief,
    wept as a star burning in betrayal

voices shouted
    urging destruction
    dark as the sun

rain fell like thorns
henna rivers
corroded the earth

the strained man
pierced
moved torn hands,
fearful men
hearing psalms of anguish
stared silent

He sighed
sightless
and the ground split

Patricia Beall

Martha's Poem

I come to my heart
And I'm glad for Him

I'm glad that He told me
He would love me
And all the saints in light

Three men coming up the hill
He went down the hill to see them

Tell my heart what You have done

Martha Pulkingham
Age 3

The Woman at the Well

(based on Luke 4)

I had come to draw, the day was dry.
The sun seemed to sleep in the drowsy sky.
The marketplace, now motionless, stood.
From doorways, figures stared with eyes of wood,
    Fearing the motion that brings us only
    To the knowledge of our loneliness.

Small dust clouds, like sifted sawdust, rose and fell
Before my feet as I shuffled toward the well.
I should never have ventured out at all –
But there was within me a dryness deep,
    Driving me to seek at many wells
    Returning always more emptied and weak.

I had already drawn deeply from five lives,
Sapping them to fill my need,
Hoping always the next one would be
The one who could see and love all that was in me,
    And by a tender word, or a morning's song
    Could free me to be as I so longed.

I lived with one who sang songs of lovers;
His songs were no different from all the others.
He too was broken, grasping in need,
Longing and aching to be freed.
    We went through the motions of loving,
    Despairing of reality.

Your words, young Galilean, so startled me;
It was not until I had been so rude,
That I saw your eyes and understood.
Though you, a Jew, asked for water, I could see
    No thirst within you demanding of me,
    No desire for me to fill your need.

I gave – not water – but the frightened child inside.
You received and held me with your eyes:
You saw all there was to see –
The thirst, the shame, the need,
    The dryness driving me to empty wells,
    The torments of my private, silent hells.

Nothing within you judges me or rejects.
Your eyes – stilled waters – my broken life reflects:
I see my thirst was a gift from you
To draw me to your truth.
    In your face forgiveness blooms
    For all I have been and done in seeking you.

The husk of my heart splits and falls in pieces:
Washed in the warm, it opens and releases
A shower of seeds springing from me
Into fountains of flowers – fragrant and free
    Do you wonder that I ran singing, 'Come, come and see –
    The one I have always loved, He has always loved me!'

Martha Keys Barker

the self-giving God

the self-giving God
dressed in rags as a junkman
went about
collecting the hulls of rock hearts

the self-giving God
dressed in nothing as a slave
went about
serving the poor of the earth

the self-giving God
dressed in flesh as a man
went about
stripping from mortals their husk of Adam death

he clothed them with himself
giving them themselves
giving them each other

Patricia Beall

Wilderness Wanderers

(based on Exodus 16 and 17, John 6:1–15;25–58)

We are wilderness wanderers,
so soon forgetting
the miracle
of the sea's dividing,
the triumph
of the tambourine shimmering song,
so soon longing
for the pleasures
of the bondage
we have left behind.

We hunger.
We hunger.
What manna comes?

We are wilderness wanderers
in the void of alone.
Abandoning hope of the promised land,
we litter the desert with our bones.

Our hearts are rock –
we have ceased to trust you
to meet our need;
demanding accustomed comforts,
we grasp in greed.
Denying your tender care,
we turn and complain:

We thirst.
We thirst.
What Moses comes?

Who will strike the rock,
break the hard of our hearts,
unleashing sea songs
sending them flowing into our barren alone?

We hunger.
We hunger.
What manna comes?
We thirst.
We thirst.
What Moses comes?

There was a man
whose flesh became manna.
Into the wilderness of our wanderings
he walked.
Seizing the rotten crusts we clutched,
he gave us his own bread flesh.

We turned from our wandering
to see him –
nailed to the tree:
his soft heart
slowly knowing our hunger,
weighted with our complaint;
his fluid voice,
parched in our desert,
crying:

I thirst.
I thirst.
Father, why?

The shrieking sky struck.
His heart cracked.
Love's blood poured into our thirst.

'This is my blood shed for you.
This, my body broken.
You, though many, are one.'

Hearing his voice,
crying in the wilderness
of our isolation,
we turn
to see before us
the single loaf:
once grain scattered,
in this bread made one.
And we,
receiving this bread of life,

caressing it in our open hands,
are gathered together
into his outstretched arms.
We, though many, become one.

No longer wanderers,
we become the manna
to feed those reeling from thirst and heat,
those weary with wandering,
We become his body,
given to bind the wounds
of earth's jagged hunger.
We, though many, are one.

Martha Keys Barker

fitly joined

having taken the time
    to see ourselves
  as we are seen
    to know us
  as we are known

now
   we must see others
  as they are seen
    and know them
  as they are known

we must know others
     each other
   gently   lovingly   freely

the Lord has fashioned us
     to work together
   as time pieces:
as those who have read
    the signs of the times
He has given us watches
    and each has a place

we are able to run together
    wondrously   gracefully
        by His design

there are
        many shapes
    but one structure
        many ways
    but one plan
        many parts
    but one piece

there are
        springs of samson strength
    putting pressure into power
        careful cogs
    turning in eternities of going forth
        tender balances
    regulating the movements

many minute ministries
        each
    bringing closer
        the coming Kingdom
the Kingdom
        which has wound its Way
    in our hearts

Patricia Beall and
Cathleen Morris

Introduction to 'Coventry Cathedral'

This poem emerged from an afternoon in Coventry Cathedral. Some understanding of the various areas of the cathedral may be helpful, as they provide strong visual stimuli to thoughts concerning the power of love and forgiveness over the forces of destruction and death.

I. The old Coventry Cathedral, reduced to ruins in an air raid during World War II, is a powerful image of human destructiveness. Within the ruins are relics of the devastation: a charred cross formed from timbers of the burned roof, an altar made from stones that fell during the attack, on the altar a cross of nails fashioned by someone inspecting the ruins the morning after the holocaust. Behind all this are the words 'Father, forgive'.

II. Standing in the Porch, the passage between the old and the new, one can see both the stark beauty of the ruins and, through the screen of engraved glass, the splendour of the new cathedral. One has a sense of the unity of the two: the new creation has its roots in the spirit of forgiveness which is embodied in the old.

III. On the altar, the focal point of the new cathedral, stands a large gold cross which is sculpted to capture the feeling of a soaring bird – symbol of resurrection. Into this cross is incorporated the original nail cross of the ruins.

IV. The Gethsemane Chapel for private prayer and meditation is separated from the main cathedral by a screen whose basic motif is the crown of thorns. Even when the cathedral is bustling with visitors, this chapel maintains a sense of quiet. A relief mural depicts the three sleeping disciples and the Archangel bearing the cup of death. These focus one's attention on Christ's human struggle in choosing the cross.

Coventry Cathedral 1973

I. The Ruins

The charred cross stands
within the gutted hulk
beneath the words scrawled:

'Father, forgive'

It would have been easier
to cry 'Why?',
easier
to fall
into fashionable despair,
easier
to desire
desperate revenge,
But you scrawled

in the anguished timbers
the ancient message
of the first tortured tree:

'Father, forgive'

II. The Porch

Lord,
I stand before my brother
whose fire has left me
torn and blackened
eyes streaming
throat choked
in smoke confusion.

I want to cry,
'Why this again?'
I want to demand,
'When will you change?'

But, tempted to retaliate,
I see:
my unforgiving hardness
binds him in the prison
of the person
he has been,
never freeing him to change.

III. The Altar

The nail cross now stands
embedded in soaring golden wings
bathed in dancing coloured light

'Father, forgive'

Within the word
of forgiveness
grows the seed
of re-creation,
as death embraced
bears seed
of resurrection.

IV. Gethsemane Chapel

Lord,
I struggle
in this place
between
your will and mine.

I want to collapse
into despair,
to spare myself
the pain
of trying
to love again.

I want to hurt
as I've been hurt.

But
stronger than these fierce teeth
tearing my soul
twisting me
shaking me with rage,
stronger than them all:
your word to me –
a sudden blade
ice sharp
cuts through chaos of emotion
quenching the searing flames:

'Father, forgive'

Lord,
take the twisted limbs
of my scorched soul,
make of them
the cross-armed tree
bearing for my brother
the certainty
of the constant message
of your own torn tree:

'Father, forgive'

Martha Keys Barker

We Shall All Be Changed

I

Chasing fantasies, we labour
ceaselessly until we
drop
and gasp that all is
nothing.

Losing ourselves in our egos
and our needs,
we grasp each other
in the night
and we cling
until we are all near death.

We catch a glimmer of light
and scramble
calmly to pursue it.
But the light dims and fades,
Leaving us in darker darkness,
to remember only
the striving
of false rest.

We cannot bear
to face each other.
Each face quivers
as we watch
our world dissolve
into disillusionment.
We freeze with fear,
our pulses
stop.

II

We stir at a word,
dig deeper and find the vision,
alive and real.
We run and hide, then return
to find it waiting.

Moving from glory to glory
with the darkness
in between:
the eternal rhythm.
Halting, straying, delaying,
returning: we can follow
no other way.

We are crawling,
crawling
back to the
earth, the
life, the
source.

We are joining:
many who were separate
becoming one,
many far apart
forming one Body
of closeness.

We warm in the sun
and lifebeats
begin, yes,
slowly
begin
once again.

Grace Krag

CHAPTER 10

Story

Storytelling, an ancient folk art expression, probably rivals music in terms of frequence and familiarity. Stories are told through gesture, sound, movement and words, and combinations of all. The following stories are representative of those the Fisherfolk have used; secondly, they are all suitable for worship, teaching and festivity. These stories can be used in a variety of ways and told in a variety of styles. More specific suggestions and examples are given in Appendix 3 and Chapter 8.

The Sower and the Seed

(based on Matthew 13:1–8)

developed in Fisherfolk ministries
script by Martha Keys Barker

Characters: 2
Storyteller
Person 2 does the hand actions

Props: Chair
Large coat (optional)
Bible (optional)

Placement: Storyteller sits on Person 2's lap.

If coat is used: Coat is draped backwards over Storyteller. Person 2 puts hands through coat armholes.

If Bible is used: Person 2 holds Bible in one hand and leafs through it, 'looking' for the story. A marker should be placed in the correct place, so he can turn to it easily. Storyteller should memorise the story, however, so he doesn't actually need to refer to the Bible.

Diagram:

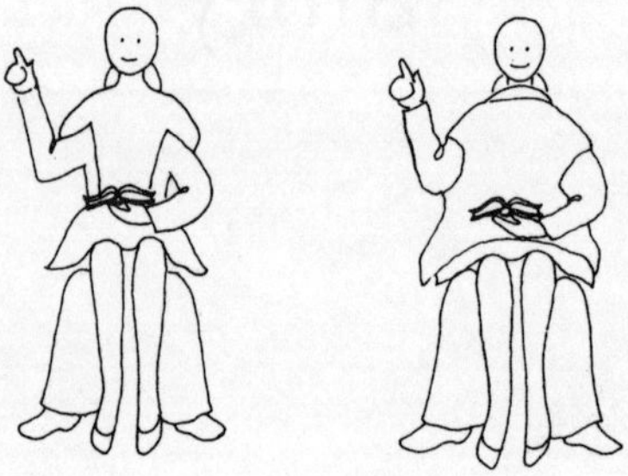

STORY	*ACTION*
A sower went out to sow. And as he sowed, some seed fell along the footpath;	*Fingers throw grain in all directions.*
and the birds came and ate it up.	*Fingers swoop down and pick up grain. Put it in mouth of STORYTELLER, then fly away.*
Some seed fell on rocky ground, where there was little soil, and it sprouted because there was no depth of earth;	*Hands in fists. Fingers begin to flicker, then extend straight up like stalks.*
but when the sun rose, the young corn was scorched, and as it had no root, it withered away.	*Fingers crumple and fall.*
Some seed fell among thistles; and the thistles shot up, and choked the corn.	*Fingers bent and gnarled.* *Fingers choke STORYTELLER.*
And some of the seed fell into good soil, where it bore fruit, yielding a hundred-fold or, it might be, sixty-fold or thirty-fold.	*Fingers come straight up like stalks waving in the sun. Flash fingers as if counting by tens: ten, twenty, etc.*
If you have ears, then hear.	*Cup hands behind ears of STORYTELLER.*

The Good Shepherd

by Patricia Beall

This may be presented as either a drama or a group participation story.

DRAMA

Characters: 4
Shepherd
2 Sheep
Narrator

Staging: Divide the area into two locations. The SHEEP wander to one; the SHEPHERD mimes in the other, until the point when he crosses to the SHEEP. The NARRATOR stands to one side.

STORY

Characters: 1 or 2
Storyteller
Assistant (optional)

Method: Use the script as the basis for a story: 'Once there were two little sheep, out for a walk. They had gone quite a way from the flock, when one of them said, "Do you really think it's all right for us to just wander about?" "Oh yes," said the second sheep back to him. "But . . ." said the first sheep, whose name was Woolly, ". . . actually, I didn't want to say anything earlier on . . ."' etc.

The middle section (NARRATOR's part) can be used for group participation. The STORYTELLER dramatises the narrative with hand actions and gestures, which the children imitate. Vocal effects are also useful. It's best to introduce the story as one with which you need assistance. This approach is likely to secure willing, rather than forced, participation: the children will feel their support has been enlisted.

If desired, an assistant can sit (stand) beside the STORYTELLER, leading the actions and sound effects while the story is told.

Examples of Actions and Sounds:

First, the shepherd went across the fields.	*With hands flat, strike palms alternately on lap, making hollow, 'walking' sound.*
They were filled with rocks: . . . hidden ones.	*Vary rhythm of walking, to show both care and speed.*
Then he came to a river . . .	*Make sounds of rushing waters; make waves with hands.*
. . . but he plunged in	*Diving gesture with arms and hands; 'Splash!' sound with voice*
Etc.	*Etc.*

Note: Use lots of imagination and facial expression: if you show the strain and risk encountered, the children will mirror it right back to you!

The Good Shepherd

(*Enter two SHEEP, chatting as they walk.*)

1: Do you really think it's all right for us to just wander about?

2: Oh yes!

1: But – actually, I didn't want to say anything earlier on, but I can't see very well. I'm not sure where we're going.

2: That's all right! I'm sure we'll be fine!

1: Maybe . . . I'm used to the shepherd leading us, though.

2: Don't worry, I'll lead the way!

1: Oh! Then you can see clearly, can you?

2: Well . . . no . . . but . . . I'm sure we'll be all right! What could happen to us here? Just follow me! I'm not – – – (*Both SHEEP suddenly stumble, then fall, caught in prickly bush. The more they try to get free the more entrapped they become.*) Oh! Oh! Oh my!

1: What happened? What is this?

2: I don't know! I've never seen this sort of thing before! Whatever it is, it's very strong!

1: And I can't move! I can't get out! I'm caught, I'm just caught! Oh, how ever will we get out! What can we do! If only the shepherd were here! I'm sure he could save us! (*freeze*)

(*Enter the SHEPHERD in another area of stage, searching.*)

SHEP: My sheep! They just wandered away! I must go find them! It was this way they went . . . (*For following section, SHEPHERD stays in place, miming as NARRATOR carries on. SHEPHERD faces directly front, so children can see his struggles and his facial expressions.*)

NARR: So the shepherd went to collect his sheep! But oh! what a job it was to get to them. They had wandered so far away, and through many dangerous places. First the shepherd went across the fields. They were filled with rocks: some were large and could be seen quite easily, but others were small and sharp, and tucked into the ground in unexpected places. So he had to be very careful not to cut his feet. He went at great speed, hoping he wouldn't trip over the hidden ones. Then he came to a river. The waters were rushing fast but he plunged in anyway, hoping he wouldn't be swept away by the currents. It was a hard fight, but pushing, fighting, straining against the water, he managed to get to the other side. Then it was up the mountain. As he climbed he saw that the only passage was on a narrow rock ledge. Flattening himself against the side of the mountain, very carefully, very slowly, he moved along. And just beyond, he saw the briers of a prickly bush, and his trapped sheep.

1: Ohhhhh! We're so far away from the flock! Why did we ever leave? The Shepherd will never find us here! Why, we went across a field, and through that river, and over the mountain, and –

2: It's hopeless, it's awful! We're just going to die here –

(*SHEPHERD moves towards SHEEP calling as he goes*)

SHEP: Ho, sheep! (*They look up, stunned.*)

2: Why, it's the shepherd! How did he ever get to us?

SHEP: Sheep! Sheep! I've come for you! (*reaching them, bending to unwind briers, cut away prickly bush, etc.*) And just look, you're completely caught in this prickly bush! Don't worry; it won't be long now. I'll get you out. Now, don't be afraid (*etc.*) . . . There! Now you're both free. Come along! And stay close, don't wander away from my protection! (*All exit.*)

The Faithful God of Daniel

by Patricia Beall

Presentation style: Group participation story, led by Storyteller.

Method: A warm, relaxed Storyteller teaches a series of responses which the audience makes at appropriate times. Introduce the idea of needing help to tell the story and secure the congregation/audience's willing participation. Explain and demonstrate responses, interspersing chat with the audience's trying them out. If people are a bit tentative or faint-hearted, encourage them verbally: 'Come now! Those lions didn't frighten me a *bit*!' etc.

Responses: Whenever the word '____________' is spoken,

'Daniel': people cross their hands over their hearts, tilt their heads to one side, say 'Ahhhh' gently, drawing it out a bit.

'the King': people put their hands on their hips, lean forward in their chairs, open eyes very wide and exclaim 'WOW!'

'the lions': people stiffen, shape their hands like claws, reach forward in severe scratching movement, growling ferociously 'Grrrrrrr!'

'the one true God': people clap their hands in the air or over their heads, cheering 'YAAAYYYY!'

The Faithful God of Daniel

There was a chap called Daniel who lived in ages gone:
He was faithful to Darius, the king of Babylon.
But he also served, as his greater Lord,
The one, true, living God.

Now, not many people in this far-away land
Knew the living God, who'd made earth and man.
So they worshipped other gods they believed they'd found
In rocks or trees or under the ground.
And they made shapes for these gods, out of stone and gold.
But there was no <u>life</u> in their statues, they were hard and cold.
Silent, they sat like towers on the plains,
Getting weatherbeaten and ruined by heavy spring rains!
And such people, who make idols to worship,
Are called pagans, for not knowing what's true:
That there's one living God,
Who made them, and me, and you!

Now Daniel was a prince and an excellent man,
And the other princes were jealous of his care for the land.
'There must be something,' they said, 'that we can do
To be finished with Daniel, who to his own God is true!
Yes! That's it! We'll make a plan
To get rid of him however we can!'
Then they talked to the king, who was mighty but unwise:
He didn't know they were telling him lies.
'King!' they cried, 'wouldn't it be lovely if you lived forever?
Though others die, you wouldn't, not ever!
That's what we hope for, that's what we pray!'
And then the princes went on to say,
'Everyone in the kingdom is completely agreed
You should be the only one to give what we need!
Make a law that makes you tops,
So no-one can ask anyone but <u>you</u> for <u>anything</u> –
All that must stop!
And if anyone dares to disobey – why then,
He must be taken to the lions' den!'
The king was so flattered, he didn't see this new plan
Meant death for Daniel, his favourite man.
He wrote the bill that very day;
And, signing his name, signed his friend's life away!

Daniel heard that the law was signed,
Yet still went to his house at the proper time
To kneel and pray and give thanks to his God.
And this fit perfectly the wicked plot!
The princes spied on him and saw him praying,
Then hurried to the palace, saying:
'Our mighty lord! Didn't you just make a new rule
That everyone must honour only you?'
'Yes, I did,' the king agreed,
'Everything must come from me!'
'Then Daniel has broken this new decree,
For today, we saw him pray to his own God.
He must be arrested, he mustn't go free!'
When the king heard this he was terribly dismayed!
He planned and schemed the entire day, trying to keep Daniel free.
But, though he talked and thought, and worked and fought,
He found no way to break his decree!
The setting sun put him to the test,
And he gave the command for his friend's arrest.

Captured by the royal men,
Daniel was taken to the lions' den.
The king himself said a blessing,
Asking the one true God to give protection.
The night was filled with mighty roars
As Daniel was shoved inside –
Then a heavy stone sealed the door,
Hiding everything from human eyes!

The king went home but couldn't sleep,
And then decided not to eat,
Hoping a fast would do some good.
He had no music, no wine, no entertainment, no food:
All he did was worry and brood:
'Is Daniel alive? Has he been eaten?
Is Daniel dead? Has his God been beaten?'
But he had no answers the long night through,
There was nothing left for the king to do
But wonder and suppose.
Then morning came, the pale sun rose –
And he ran again to the lions' den!

As he got there he cried out in pain,
'O, my dear friend! Have you been saved?'
And Daniel himself gave the reply:

'Yes! Here I am, safe and alive!
An angel of God came last night
And stopped the lions from even one bite!
Their mouths were closed the whole night long:
My God saved me, for I'd done no wrong!'
Then the king rejoiced and with a shout
Commanded that Daniel be let out!
Then he ordered the den filled again,
This time with the jealous men.
They and their children, along with their wives
Were the ones who ended up losing their lives.
Against the lions they were no match,
Though Daniel had been saved without a scratch.

Then the king wrote a message to be sent all 'round,
Proclaiming the power of the God he had found:
'If anyone in the world wants to know what's best,
He must listen to what I suggest!
There is one God, living and true,
With much more power than me or you.
Praise him, for he does live for ever!
And his kingdom destroyed? – No, never!
The things he does leave me amazed:
He delivers and rescues, he works wonders and saves!
He, who protected Daniel from the lions,
Is the one, true, living God!'

Samuel Merryweather

by Maggie Durran

Samuel Merryweather, sitting on the edge of the pavement with his feet in the gutter, had just decided to change his name to King Samuel I. This rainy day the gutter was a river with islands and barges pouring in torrents into a huge drain. It was cold though, and Samuel's toes were hurting. He wriggled them slowly, then decided to go somewhere else. He wandered along dreaming, perhaps he'd find something really delicious today. Once, but only once, he had found a bag of sandwiches filled with all sorts of scrumptious tastes. His tummy had felt good for hours afterwards.

He passed an open doorway, and a child, a boy bigger than Samuel, ran out almost knocking him over. The boy clutched a bag of roasted peanuts, hot and delicious. Noticing Samuel's stare, he grinned, took some nuts from the bag and dropped them on the ground. As a startled Samuel tried to salvage a few, the boy stamped on them, then ran away, laughing to himself.

The cafe dustbins hid in the corner by a jutting-out wall, in a backstreet that was a mixture of tumbledown walls, half-open doorways, derelict houses.

Samuel looked around carefully to make sure no-one was coming. People weren't too happy to have little boys poking in their dustbins.

Anyway, here were the bins. He lifted the first lid gently so as to be very quiet, only too aware of every tiny scrape of the lid as he eased it from the bin. Then he looked inside. Nothing but old and screwed-up newspapers, some splashed with paint; they must have been decorating. He gently put back the lid.

There was another one; perhaps, there'd be something better in it. He prised off the lid very carefully and sorted over the things at the top; no good. He reached further inside. Maybe amongst the older stuff there'd be a bit of something. His little fingers grasped and dropped several things; then, at last, something felt like bread. He drew it out . . . bread, stale with mould on one corner, but, otherwise, not bad. He'd eaten worse . . . mm . . . not bad for an evening meal.

Suddenly the cafe-man caught Samuel with a well-aimed kick. He hadn't heard anyone coming. He scrambled out of the yard, his hand on his side. It hurt a lot. It wasn't by any means the first time in his life that he'd been caught but that thought didn't stop the pain.

His bread was still clutched tightly in his hand.

Samuel Merryweather had no house or home; he had no friends or family. Probably no-one ever noticed him; well, maybe the tramp who slept in the station yard did. Samuel would see him sometimes shuffling through the same back alleys, and wondered if he got chased away, too.

Behind an old derelict house, at the bottom of the garden, two dustbins shut off a secret shady corner under a precariously overhanging wall. It was here that Samuel came now, climbing through a gap in the wall and sitting down on his ragged brown coat. He looked at his handful of dirty bread. The pain in his side felt worse; he didn't want the bread any more. He lay down and pulled his old coat round him, but the draught got in, and he felt sick. The bruised side throbbed and he tried to sleep but only dozed fitfully. The car lights woke him with their persistent bouncing shadows. His coat wasn't big enough, not for keeping the cold out.

Footsteps came slowly along the pavement on the other side of the wall. They stopped at the gap. Samuel listened, but was sure no-one knew of this hiding-place. There were grating sounds of someone climbing onto the rubble of the wall. He began to be a little worried.

He half-opened one eye to see a man standing, hesitating, just a shadowy dark outline against the light of the street. Samuel tensed in an effort not to move; it would hurt too much even to be seen. The man stepped down nearer to the boy and stood, watching and listening.

Samuel held his breath till he could hold it no longer; tensed his muscles till he could tense them no more. Then he moved his leg to ease the cramp, and in a rush he curled up his thin little body as protection against the blow he knew was coming. But it didn't come, and it didn't come . . . till he could bear it no longer, so again he took a sneaking look. The man was bending over him, half-kneeling, blocking out the already dim light. The expectation of being hurt was almost worse than the pain that was to come, and unable to bear it any longer the little boy, King Samuel I, dissolved into uncontrollable sobs.

Then, two strong arms went round him and grasped his shaking body, holding him close. Samuel could not remember ever having been held close by anyone before, but he knew that it was good. The old tramp smiled a little and moved, but only to reach into his pocket . . . he pulled out a sandwich. Cheese sandwich was new to Samuel. He loved the creamy taste, and he sighed with contentment as he chewed the last piece.

Wrapped up warmly in his new friend's man-sized coat, Samuel Merryweather gave a sleepy grin; life behind the dustbins is good when you have a friend.

The Lost and Found Kingdom

by Patricia Beall

Peter was a boy who was eight years old. He had brown hair with a little yellow in it, and very green eyes. He had a frog named Walter – that was also his grandfather's name – and a fish named Cat. He also had a brown box filled with earth things: a snail shell, a dried walking-stick, some crinkled leaves, and two or three smooth rocks.

Peter liked many things. He liked to play with his friends; he also liked to play by himself. He liked to sing: lots of times he made up songs, right as he went along. He liked to play outside. His house was near a wood, and in the summer he would leave early in the morning, taking his lunch in a brown bag, and go to the wood for the whole day. He would play in the stream that ran silver along the stones; he would sit in the yellow-green meadow and watch the grasshoppers;

he would climb the apple tree and work on his tree house; he would sit in the shady shadows of the damp wood, listening for flower songs or wind sighs or watching for beetles and chipmunks.

He spent a lot of time thinking, and he also talked out loud. 'I wonder,' he'd say, 'about the way stars are born?' 'I wonder,' he'd say, 'how cows make milk?' 'I wonder,' he'd say, 'about the Kingdom?'

The Kingdom was a very wonderful place that he had made up. But sometimes, he thought that he hadn't made it up. He felt, deep in his quiet places, that somewhere, there really was a Kingdom. But he didn't know where, and so until he found it, he just daydreamed about it. He would lie still, in the dark of the woods, and imagine the things of the Kingdom: great iron gates, and the gateman to let everyone in and out; enormous gardens, with red daffodils and bright butterflies; celebrations where everyone would dance and sing, full of joy and laughter.

Peter knew the Lord Jesus, and sometimes he'd talk to Him too. 'How did You put the roar in the waves?' he'd ask, 'and how did You give the mouse a squeak?' 'Where did You find the gold for the sun and the silver for the moon?' 'How was there enough wood for all the trees, and enough soft for all the moss?' He asked many questions, and the Lord answered. One day he decided to ask the Lord some questions he had been thinking for a long time. 'Who would I be,' he asked, 'if I weren't me? Who would I be, and what would I do?' 'Do you know?' asked the Lord back. 'Do you have any ideas?' 'Well,' said Peter, 'I have had a few thoughts about it.' 'All right,' said the Lord, 'tell me.' And this is what Peter told Him.

'If I were a butterfly, I'd thank you, Lord, for giving me wings.
And if I were a robin in a tree, I'd thank you, Lord, that I could sing.
And if I were a fish in the sea, I'd wiggle my tail and I'd giggle with glee.
But I just thank you, Father, for making me "me".

refrain: For you gave me a heart and you gave me a smile.
You gave me Jesus and you made me your child.
And I just thank you, Father, for making me "me".

If I were an elephant, I'd thank you, Lord, by raising my trunk.
And if I were a kangaroo, you know I'd hop right up to you.
And if I were an octopus, I'd thank you, Lord, for my fine looks.
But I just thank you, Father, for making me "me".

refrain

If I were a wiggily worm, I'd thank you, Lord, that I could squirm.
And if I were a crocodile, I'd thank you, Lord, for my big smile.
And if I were a fuzzy-wuzzy bear, I'd thank you, Lord, for my fuzzy-wuzzy hair.
But I just thank you, Father, for making me "me".'

refrain[1]

The Lord was pleased with Peter's song. When it was over, He said, 'Bless your heart! I like that song! But those are things you'd do if you were an animal, and you're not! Who are you, and what do you do since you're you?'

Peter had forgotten that he had started out by asking the Lord some questions, and he thought slowly and long about the Lord's questions to him. 'Who am I?' he asked himself, 'and what do I do?'

He thought about the games he played and the meals he ate and the tears he cried, but somehow they didn't seem to be the answer to who he was. He thought about the bugs he found and the leaves he saved and the fields he walked in, but those things didn't seem to be the answer either. 'Who am I?' he asked, 'and what do I do?' He thought about his father who loved him, and his mother who brought him ice and ginger ale when he was sick, and his sister Mara who was older than he, and his brother Sam who was younger. They didn't seem exactly the answer, but they were more than the others had been. Then he thought of his Gran, who lived alone in a house with pink flowers, and of his teacher who had a very deep, scratchy voice, and of his friends Michael and Anna and Josh. And the answer seemed to be closer in coming. 'My parents,' he thought. 'My brother and my sister, my teacher, my friends.' And then he thought about the Lord, Who was his Father and Brother and Friend all in one. 'That's an awful lot to be,' he thought. 'Why, someone would have to be a, a . . . King to be all of those at the same time.' And then he knew the answer! He knew who he was and what he did! 'I am a child of the King!' he said out loud. 'I am a child of the King, and I live in the Kingdom!'

And sure enough, that was the answer. He knew it in his very heart. The bugs and leaves and trees, the fields and sun and woods: they were all part of the Kingdom, and he was part of it too! The Kingdom was real, and he was already in it! But he wasn't the only one, there were lots of others; parents and relatives and friends and other people that were lovers; and together, they all made the Kingdom! The Kingdom wasn't somewhere else, it was right now, right here: in these very woods, in this very life! 'Lord,' he cried, 'I know who I am and what I do! And I know Who You are! You're the King, and I'm your son, and I live in the Kingdom!' And it was all true.

NOTE

1. 'The Butterfly Song', © *Celebration Services (International) Ltd., 1973, 1975. All rights reserved.*

Chapter 11

Mime and Drama

MIME

Traditionally Mime has been described as 'the art of silence'. The Mime artist relies completely on his own physical movements and postures to create the world around him and to express his relationship to it. In *The Mime Book* Claude Kipnis describes the task of the Mime artist in this way (*Note:* In this introduction only, 'Mime' indicates the art form; 'mime' indicates the artist):

> The mime re-creates the world around him as well as representing and expressing his own inner world for others to see. The 'outer world' contains objects, people, animals, organic life of all sorts, the sum and substance of his environment. The 'inner' world consists of his own feelings, his thoughts, his impulses, his dreams. The mime must make an outer world seem to exist; at the same time, he must express his inner world of imagination. The art of Mime begins where and when these two worlds meet.[1]

The effective mime employs careful observation, concentration, imagination and precise movement. He does not merely 'look like' someone who is drinking a glass of water; the audience must actually 'see' the glass and the water level. Thus, Mime focuses one's attention on subtle changes in posture, body positioning, and expression to indicate changes in mood, atmosphere, situation and relationships. Knowledge of Mime technique enhances both drama and dance. The use of Mime to establish a scene or convey a character provides the picture worth a thousand words of dramatic dialogue; the economy of movement required in Mime gives precision to dance movement.

Mime is an invaluable tool in worship and teaching situations. Because it requires a minimum of props, scenery, or costumes, it is easily adapted to any situation. Within the context of a worship service, a group or individual can easily mime without taking time to set a stage, change into costumes, or assemble props.

The material in this section has been selected to provide a cross-section of possible uses and to introduce various aspects of Mime technique. In addition to silent Mime, we also include narration, the use of music, percussion and sound effects. The material may be categorised as follows:

Title	*Style*	*Technique*
On Tiptoe	Mime with reading	Characterisation
Let Me In!	Silent Mime	Working with imaginary objects Expressing emotions
The Wise and Foolish Farmers	Narrated Mime	Representing inanimate objects For use with children
The Hat Race	Narrated Mime	Characterisation More advanced technique Group co-ordination

Material in other sections which provide a basis for Mime:

Poetry	
Hands	Conveying emotions and relationships
the self giving God	Characterisation
fitly joined	Group co-ordination
We Shall All Be Changed	Expressing relationships
Wind of Spirit	Characterisation
Arrangements	
gooseberry pie	Characterisation
Scriptural Development	
The Prodigal Son	Characterisation

Improvisation

Exercises and ideas for group improvisation

Suggestions for Mime and Drama

Instruction and improvisation suggestions for parables

On Tiptoe

by Patricia Beall and Jodi Page Clark

Characters: 8 or more
Man
Floor Sweeper
Woman
Child (can be played by adult)

Person walking imaginary dog
Two people (to be themselves)
Reader

Props: Broom for Floor Sweeper
A recognisable instrument case (guitar, violin, cello, etc.)
Sunglasses for Musician
Seven or more mirrors (one for each person in mime)

Placement: Reader stands to left and is in place at outset. Characters enter one by one, forming line across playing area.

MAN:
Enter slowly, look all around, move to centre of stage.
Look straight out toward audience.
'See' something.
Freeze in that position.

FLOOR SWEEPER:
Enter sweeping vigorously.
Slow down sweeping and begin to 'look' as well, facing audience, straining on tiptoe to 'see' something.
Freeze.

MUSICIAN:

Enter carrying instrument case, snapping fingers to imaginary tune.
See others 'looking'; do the same.
Freeze.

CHILD AND WOMAN:

Enter, Child with Woman in tow.
Suddenly see 'lookers'.
Woman: become intrigued and attempt to 'see'.
Child: squirm, etc., then become fascinated and peer out as well.
Freeze.

PERSON WALKING DOG:

Enter, walking imaginary dog.
Discover others; after looking at them in bewilderment and at audience in enquiry, join the line, peering intently at audience.
Freeze.

READER: (*stepping forward one pace*) 'All creation's straining on tiptoe to see the sons of God.' (*pause*) Where are the sons of God?

TWO PEOPLE:

Enter carrying mirrors, cross to the characters. Lift mirrors to the characters' faces, revealing to them that they are the sons and daughters of God.

After all characters have seen themselves, they go into audience/congregation with mirrors. Holding mirrors before people's faces, characters let people see their own reflections.

(Time or group size may make it impractical for players to go to everyone individually. If so, players should go to different parts of the room and select individuals randomly, holding the mirrors before them. Then players, regrouping at front, turn mirrors outward and revolve them slowly, obviously including the entire group.)

Note: This mime is effective prior to teaching. Because it often has a profound effect on both children and adults, the teaching section should be handled carefully, to allow people time to respond. Some suggestions for doing this:

1. Leave a couple of minutes for silence, so people can think through what they've just experienced.

2. Ask a few questions to draw out responses. Questions

may be rhetorical: Do we think of ourselves as children of God in everyday life? Was seeing ourselves in the mirrors surprising or embarrassing? Or the leader may ask direct questions to particular persons with the expectation of response.

3. Encourage people to share some of their thoughts and responses with those around them.

'On Tiptoe' mime is reprinted from Fisherfolk Kit 1, *'All Aboard the Ark'*.

Let Me In!

developed in Fisherfolk ministries
script by Martha Keys Barker

Theme: Acceptance and approval. This mime contrasts the complicated ways we try to win or buy approval with the simple way the Lord accepts us just as we are. The mime is most effective in the context of discussion and/or teaching about the Lord's love, which is not dependent upon our being beautiful, having the right things or being clever.

Presentation: The basic mime is geared towards teenagers; there are variations for children and adults. Notes about teaching suggestions accompany each variation.

Characters: 5 or more
Seeker
Enclosure (4 or more; 1 of these is the 'Door')

Props: All may be mimed.
Or may use: Article of stylish clothing
Sports equipment (tennis racquet, football, skateboard)
Variation 1: Sweets
Sports equipment
Variation 2: Article of fashionable clothing
Large book

Placement: Those forming Enclosure stand in circle, holding hands, facing the centre of the circle. The 'Door' stands facing outward; holding hands with person on his left, he bends right arm at elbow to form handle.

Diagram:

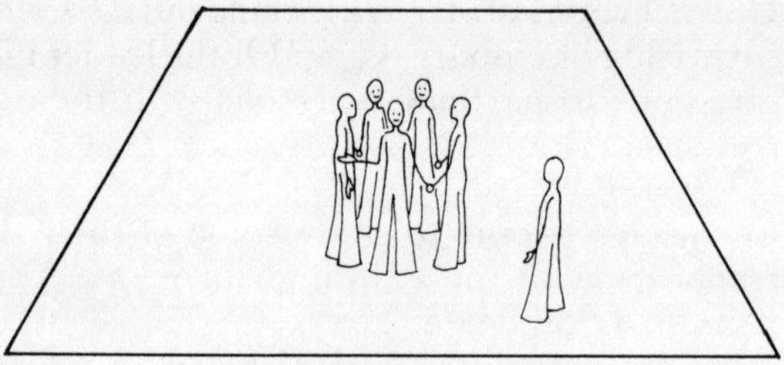

ACTION

a) SEEKER walks around outside of circle,
looks for way to get in.
Tries climbing over clasped hands,
tries crawling under them.

Pushes and shoves people,
tries to make them lose their grip.

Circle does not yield.

b) SEEKER crosses to one side,
puts on stylish clothing.
Attempts to impress others so they'll let him in.

They are not impressed.

c) If SEEKER is a girl, crosses to one side,
mimes putting on makeup.
Crosses to boy in circle,
tries to charm her way in.

If SEEKER is a boy, crosses to one side,
mimes combing hair.
Crosses to girl in circle,
attempts to charm his way in.

Attempt fails.

d) SEEKER crosses to other side,
picks up sports equipment.
Demonstrates athletic ability.

No response from circle.

e) SEEKER throws down sports equipment in disgust,
angrily strides to one side.
Stands with arms folded,
pretends disinterest.

f) After a short while SEEKER looks back at circle,
notices handle on the door.
Walks to door,
turns handle,
door opens and he goes in.

Notes: Preliminary discussion may be centred around ways youths try to win or buy acceptance. Use these as a basis for improvisation, rather than following the outline above. This mime can also be used as part of a study about people that society rejected yet Jesus accepted, using such scriptures as Luke 7:36–50; Luke 18:9–14; Matthew 9:10–13.

VARIATION 1: CHILDREN

a) Same action.

b) SEEKER brings sweets to children in circle,
tries to bribe way in.

It doesn't work.

c) SEEKER gets currently popular item
(e.g. skateboard, football, ice skates)
offers one child a turn if he lets him in.

This fails.

d) SEEKER throws himself onto the floor in front of the door, kicks and pounds the floor.

e) SEEKER looks up and notices door.
Rest of action same as f).

Notes: Children (or younger teenagers) may need to have some of the symbolism interpreted. Explain that the circle stands for acceptance and the 'door' to the circle which the seeker didn't see at first, stands for a friendship with Jesus. Another point may be that friendship with Jesus opens the way for us to experience approval and love just as we are, rather than needing to become better or like someone else.

VARIATION 2: ADULTS

a) Same action

b) SEEKER offers money for admittance.

c) SEEKER crosses to one side,
puts on expensive, fashionable clothing,
tries to win approval.

d) SEEKER crosses to other side,
picks up large book,
mimes delivering intellectual speech,
tries to impress circle.

e) SEEKER throws down book,
walks to one side angrily.
Rest of action same as e) and f).

Notes: As adults we are often more subtle in the ways we attempt to gain acceptance and approval. Discuss together what some of these hidden ways might be. Alternatively, consider the simplicity of Jesus' acceptance. Are we content for that to be the foundation of our self-acceptance, or do we still seek other reassurances?

The Wise and Foolish Farmers

(based on 2 Corinthians 9:6–8,10)

by Patricia Beall

Characters: 12 or more

Foolish Farmer	Wind
Wise Farmer	Sun
Narrator	Seeds: 6 or more
Bird(s)	

Note: Those playing Seeds for Foolish Farmer can double, if necessary, as Seeds for Wise Farmer. Seed, Bird and Wind parts can be expanded to include as many as desired.

Props: Sun made of heavy coloured card or foil
Wings made of flimsy paper or cloth, fastened to Bird's wrists or arms
Thin piece of fabric for Wind to shake

Action: Actions accompany narration as indicated in script.

NARRATION	*ACTION*
Once there was a farmer.	*Enter FARMER.*
It was spring, and time to plant. So he took a few seeds and went to his field, which he had already ploughed.	*Exit briefly, return with three SEEDS, which cling to his arms.*
He planted all his seeds. They nestled down, safe and warm within the ground.	*FARMER twirls each SEED which, spinning, falls into hunched position on floor.*
The Farmer hoped to have a good harvest!	*Looking hopeful, FARMER exits.*
Things went well for a while.	
Then suddenly!	*Enter BIRD, flapping wings.*
a hungry bird appeared, looking for lunch. He flew straight to the field, swooped down, and	*BIRD flies, swoops, and snatches,*
snatched away a seed!	*exiting with one SEED.*
Another day, the wind, which had calmly stayed away, suddenly blew in!	*Enter WIND, swirling fabric,*
All the seeds were shaken, stirred from their sleep.	*making 'WHOOOSH!'ing noises. WIND stirs SEEDS, then exits.*
Then the sun, which had risen hot and strong,	*With sweeping movement, SUN raises large circle to cover face.*
burned down into the soil.	*SUN shakes circle menacingly.*
One tiny seed could not survive: exposed to the air, terribly thirsty, he struggled, then died!	*SEED rises to knees, clutches throat and gasps, struggles, then collapses.*

Harvest time came soon thereafter, and the Farmer went to gather his crops.

Enter FARMER, who looks at the dead SEED, looks round at the field in despair, then picks the remaining SEED. Exit with SEED, shaking head sadly.

There was another farmer.

Enter FARMER.

It was spring, and time to plant.
So he took his seeds and went to his field, which he had already ploughed.

Exit briefly, return with at least six SEEDS, which cling to his arms.

He planted all his seeds. They nestled down, safe and warm within the ground.

FARMER twirls each SEED which, spinning, falls into hunched position on floor.

The Farmer hoped to have a good harvest!

Looking hopeful, FARMER exits.

Things went well for a while.
Then suddenly!

Enter BIRD, flapping wings.

a hungry bird appeared, looking for lunch. He flew straight to the field, swooped down, and snatched away a seed!

BIRD flies, swoops, and snatches,

exiting with one SEED.

Another day, the wind, which had calmly stayed away, suddenly blew in!

Enter WIND, swirling fabric, making 'WHOOOSH!'ing noises.

All the seeds were shaken, stirred from their sleep.

WIND stirs SEEDS, then exits.

Then the sun, which had risen hot and strong,

With sweeping movement, SUN raises large circle to cover face.

burned down into the soil.

SUN shakes circle menacingly.

Some of the seeds couldn't survive: exposed to the air, terribly thirsty, they struggled, then died!

Two SEEDS, several feet apart, rise to knees, clutch throats, struggle, then collapse.

NARRATION

Harvest time came soon thereafter, and the Farmer went to gather his crops.

ACTION

Enter FARMER, who looks sadly at the two dead SEEDS, then happily gathers the many remaining SEEDS. Exit carrying one or two SEEDS, other SEEDS clinging to FARMER's arms.

'The point is this: if you only plant a few seeds, you'll have only a small crop. But if you plant generously, you'll have a big harvest!'

Optional continuation of conclusion:

'Make up your mind how to give, and then do it, not holding back or just giving because someone tells you to. God loves a cheerful giver. And God, who gives seed to the sower, and bread for food, will supply and multiply what you have, and increase the harvest of your righteousness.'

(Paraphrase of 2 Corinthians 9:6–8,10)

The Hat Race

by Martha Keys Barker

Characters: 7 or more

Narrator	Richard
John	Followers (at least 4)

Props: All may be mimed. If props are desired:
A badge with 'prize' written on it
A medallion with 'honour' written on it
6 hats: 4 for John, ranging from small to very large and impressive
2 for Richard, equal to the largest of John's hats

Preparation time: You will need at least two rehearsals with a day or so between to give participants time to become familiar with the mime walk and the script.

NARRATION	*ACTION*
	Mime begins with JOHN, RICHARD and FOLLOWERS together in a close, friendly group. The basic movement throughout is the mime walk. Whenever JOHN begins walking, the whole group walks. When he stops, the whole group stops.
Once there was a group of friends. The leader of the group was a very good leader. His name was John. He was very close to all his friends and they thought he was wonderful.	*Group stands together in centre of stage, talking and smiling. JOHN is in centre of group, RICHARD is to John's left. JOHN looks around with pride at his followers. ALL look at him with admiration.*
They showered him with honours, they awarded him prizes.	*One pats him on back, another puts 'honour' around his neck, another pins 'prize' on his lapel. ALL clap silently.*

NARRATION	*ACTION*
They even gave him a hat that said 'Our Leader' on it. That made him feel very special. 'My!' John thought, 'being a good leader is the most important job one can perform.'	*FOLLOWER gives him small hat. JOHN stands taller, smiling broadly, looking very self-satisfied.*
	JOHN begins 'walking' and ALL follow.
One day as John was leading, a doubt nibbled at his mind. 'What if I am not leading the right way?' he thought. And	*JOHN looks doubtful.*
then, 'What if my followers overheard these doubts? What if they knew I was wondering whether I was leading the right way? They might stop giving	*JOHN looks around nervously at followers.*
me prizes. They might even take away my hat!'	*Looking very worried he puts hand over 'prize', holds onto hat.*
'Well, I know what I'll do! I won't let them get close enough to know what I'm thinking. I'll move up a few steps and walk by myself.'	*Looking satisfied and relieved by his solution, JOHN takes two large steps ahead of the others. Turns head to see followers' response.*
As John moved forward, the people cheered. They liked to see John walking ahead of	*FOLLOWERS clap silently.*
them. 'Such a good leader should have a special place,' they said. So they made a rule: 'No one may walk within three steps of John.'	*FOLLOWERS look at each other approvingly. One FOLLOWER puts arms out to stop others. Holds up one hand as if making rule. ALL agree.*
In honour of his new position, they gave him a new hat – larger and more impressive than the first. John felt very important walking three steps in front of everyone with his big new hat.	*FOLLOWER presents new hat. JOHN begins 'walking', looking very proud. ALL follow him.*

NARRATION	*ACTION*
Then one day, John realised he felt lonely. 'I shouldn't feel lonely,' he thought. 'I'm a strong leader.	*JOHN looks around as if he is alone. He begins to droop, then straightens in determined manner.*
I can succeed without help from anyone. I just need a little more recognition from my followers.'	*JOHN stops walking. ALL stop.*
So John got himself another hat – a very ornate hat. He walked ahead a few more steps so that everyone could see his new hat.	*JOHN tosses away hat and puts on larger one. He takes one large step ahead. ALL begin walking.*
All his followers thought this was wonderful – all except one, that is. Richard had been John's best friend before John became the leader of the group. He felt that John had become so busy and important that he no longer had time to be his friend.	*FOLLOWERS smile and nod. RICHARD, looking hurt, begins to turn away from JOHN to his left.* *Two FOLLOWERS notice his withdrawal and move toward him.*
So he decided to start his own group. He took a few of John's followers with him. He felt much better then.	*RICHARD invites the two followers to join him. They look at each other and nod. RICHARD leads them to his left.*
Things went well for awhile, but then Richard began to wonder if he was leading the right way.	*RICHARD smiling, walks along with his followers. He begins to look worried.*
He moved a few steps ahead of his followers so they wouldn't suspect that he wasn't sure.	*RICHARD moves ahead a few steps.*
They liked that. They felt more secure with Richard out in front. They wanted him to look just as important as John. They gave him an enormous hat – just like John's.	*FOLLOWERS watch him approvingly.* *RICHARD and FOLLOWERS stop walking for presentation of hat. FOLLOWER presents hat.* *ALL begin walking again.*
He looked just like John!	*JOHN notices RICHARD; he stops and in bragging manner, straightens hat. RICHARD straightens his hat in response.*

NARRATION	*ACTION*
From then on John and Richard competed to keep up with each other. If John moved up a step, Richard moved up too. When John got a more impressive hat, Richard got one too.	*JOHN and RICHARD begin to race. FOLLOWERS walk at original pace. JOHN moves up. RICHARD moves up. JOHN picks up a larger hat.* *RICHARD picks up hat. They stagger under the weight of the hats.*
Before long they were so far away their followers could barely see them. Only their colossal hats were visible.	*FOLLOWERS stop walking. Stretch necks, try to see a great distance.*
As they raced, John and Richard suddenly realised they were coming to the very edge.	*JOHN and RICHARD look worried.*
They raced on, not daring to admit they had made a mistake,	*Continue to race, determinedly.*
hoping that the other would be the first to retreat.	*Give each other sidelong glances.*
But one day, there it was: they were on the edge! They tried to stop.	*Both stop as if on edge of cliff: Bend forward to catch balance, bend backwards.*
But the weight of their great hats carried them over!	*Then, as if blown from behind, they fall to knees and then flat on faces.*
By the time their followers arrived at the edge, they saw there was nothing to be done. John and Richard were at the bottom – dead. Grieved, they summoned the doctor to determine the cause of death:	*FOLLOWERS begin walking, moving forward to the 'edge'. Stretch necks to peer over edge, focus at great distance.*
'It wasn't the fall,' the doctor concluded, 'but the weight of the hats that crushed old John and Richard.'	*On 'hats' FOLLOWERS look at each other amazed, then freeze.*

DRAMA

Dramatic presentations can be as simple or elaborate as desired. We often have extremely simple ones, with a minimum of props, costuming, staging. Alternatively, some groups will seek projects lasting several weeks or months, and in these instances making costumes, locating props, fashioning scenery, etc. intensifies and heightens the whole endeavour.

The following dramas can be presented in other ways than acting. Some would do well as dramatic readings, others as puppet plays, entertainments for festive evenings, improvisational guides.

It's Impossible!

by Patricia Beall

Characters: 7

Child	Young man
Older woman	Woman or man

Placement: Players are scattered about area and have no relationship to one another. Each says lines from place or moves forward a bit; each freezes when part is completed.

It's Impossible!

YOUNG CHILD: (*in posture of student: seated at imaginary or real desk*) Oh, this maths homework! I can't make any sense of it! What should I do with this sum! I just can't remember! It all looks like Chinese to me! I can't do it – it's impossible! (*freeze*)

OLDER WOMAN: Ah, my garden is lovely. (*wandering about, plucking leaves here and there, sprinkling with can*) Just look at my delphiniums! And at my tulips! They're better this year than ever before! And my – Oh! Oh! LOOK! These stalks are all broken! And this dirt is trampled! It was those dreadful school children! I'm sure they've been through my garden again! And I've told them so many times not to come through here on their way to school! Those children are absolutely impossible!!! (*freeze*)

YOUNG MAN: (*intensely*) The fighting in Ireland has been going on for ages. Not just this year, or last year, but years and years. Why, whole generations have grown up with war in their streets. And there have been talks, and council decisions, and laws, and international discussions, and threats from governments, and still it goes on. The fighting in Ireland is impossible. *(freeze)*

WOMAN: *(avidly)* Yes, it's going to be interesting to see what happens next! John and Robert have NEVER gotten along, not since they've known each other! Why, when they were only THIS high they were having at it with each other. And now they're both on the same committee, and they're supposed to take decisions! Hah! We'll see how it goes! Those two men working together? Impossible! *(freeze; then all exit.)*

The Amazing Change

original idea Fisherfolk training programme
script by Patricia Beall and Martha Keys Barker

Presentation style: A puppet play, combining a puppet character and a child.

Characters: 2
Peter, a school boy
A caterpillar puppet with puppeteer

Props: Sock puppet for caterpillar
Wings to fit onto caterpillar
Hat and scarf for Peter
Table (covered on front and sides) or upright piano to use for puppet stage

The Amazing Change

(CATERPILLAR appears over edge of piano or table, looking for food. Enter PETER.)

PETER: Say! I know you!

CATER: *(in much surprise)* Oh! *(peering at PETER)* Well, I don't know you.

PETER: You're a caterpillar, and I'm Peter! I learned all about you in school. You're going to make a cocoon soon, aren't you?

CATER: A cocoon?

PETER: Yes, sort of a little house, where you'll sleep for a long time.

CATER: I wouldn't mind that!

PETER: And then, after you've died, you'll –

CATER: (*interrupting*) What? What did you say? After I've what?!

PETER: Died! After you've died, you'll come out again, but you'll be different!

CATER: What do you mean, 'after I've died'! I don't think I like the sound of that! And if I did die, how could I come out again as anything?

PETER: Well, it's not exactly dying, it's like dying. When you go in you're a caterpillar but after it happens, you come out a new creature! You'll be changed.

CATER: I'm not sure about this. (*pause*) What if it . . . hurts?

PETER: Oh, I don't think it will hurt. But it's worth it, because you'll have beautiful colours, and wings, so you can fly!

CATER: Fly! Ha, this sounds stranger and stranger! I'm not sure I believe any of it! I don't think these things will happen! Goodbye! (*Exits under edge. PETER hesitates, then shrugs and exits opposite side he entered. A 10-second pause to indicate passage of time. Then PETER enters with hat and scarf on, same side he exited. CATERPILLAR, now a BUTTERFLY, flies happily, trying to attract his attention.*)

BTFLY: Hello, hello! (*PETER looks at him curiously.*) Don't you know me? (*PETER is puzzled.*) You don't recognise me, do you? It's me, your old friend the caterpillar! Oh, don't you remember?

PETER: (*delighted*) Oh! Oh, yes, I do know you! I do remember! And look, you have changed!

BTFLY: It was just as you said! When it first started happening, when I started getting sleepy in my cocoon, I was afraid. And then I remembered what you'd said, and that helped me. I remembered I wasn't really dying, I was just changing!

PETER: (*still amazed*) It really happened! (*exiting in excitement*) Hey, Colin! Guess what! Guess what happened! (*PETER exits, BUTTERFLY laughs happily then flies under edge of 'stage'.*)

Abraham and Sarah

original drama by Conway Barker
adapted by Patricia Beall

In Abraham and Sarah we have two great models of faith. But what if Abraham hadn't believed God's word? What if Sarah had been untrusting? The following drama is not meant as a character portrayal of Abraham and Sarah, nor as an historically accurate account of their lives. Rather, it puts into Abraham and Sarah's mouths questions or responses we ourselves might have, as we struggle with our own 'what if's'.

Characters: 2
Abraham
Sarah

Props: Two chairs or stools

Costumes: Shawl for Sarah
Robe for Abraham

Abraham and Sarah

(*Two chairs or stools, C.*)

SCENE 1

(*Enter SARAH, who crosses to chairs. She sits, knitting. Soon she falls asleep.*)

ABRAHAM: (*as he enters*) Sarah? (*crossing to her*)

SARAH: (*awaking*) What, love?

ABRAHAM: I've been thinking, Sarah. I'm a bit tired of this country. There's no adventure or excitement any more! I want to go out and do something! (*sitting down*) A man like me needs to move around!

SARAH: Move around? Why, Abraham, you've been here seventy-five years! You've never needed to move around before! Besides, don't you think you're a little old for gallivantin' around the world? What's made you think this way? Have you been talkin' to those wanderers that came in on yesterday's caravan? Have they stirred you up?

ABRAHAM: No . . . no, it's not them. (*not exactly sure how to tell her, just plunging in*) It's . . . well, it's that . . . that . . . the Lord has been talking to me.

SARAH: The Lord! Oh, Abraham! Were you sun-bathing at the oasis again? I told you too much sun isn't good for a man of your age!

ABRAHAM: (*adamantly*) I have been sun-bathing, but what happened wasn't a mirage, Sarah. The Lord himself spoke, telling me to leave my country, to leave my father's house –

SARAH: (*interrupting*) To leave your father's house! But Abraham! If this place was good enough for your father, why isn't it good enough for you?

ABRAHAM: It is, Sarah, it's just that . . . well, the Lord told me to leave, and to go to . . . ah, to go to . . .

SARAH: To go where, Abraham?

ABRAHAM: He didn't say where, he just said 'go'!

SARAH: Oh, if it wasn't the sun-bathing it must have been the vineyard! Have you been there today?

ABRAHAM: No, I haven't! I've not been drinking! God spoke to me, and said to go, and so we must!

SARAH: But my dear! Aren't you happy with our life here? We have so much! Our flocks and herds: sheep, cattle, camels. And our lovely home, and all the things we've collected over the years . . . Oh, I just can't bear to leave it all behind, to throw it all away. When we married, Abraham, we said it was for richer or poorer. What's wrong if it's richer? And our friends? How could we ever leave our family and friends? Why, they depend on us!

ABRAHAM: But the Lord is depending on us as well! He said that thousands – thousands, Sarah! – would be blessed through this.

SARAH: How?

ABRAHAM: 'How?'! Oh, questions, questions, Sarah! Always questions! I don't know how! All I know is what the Lord wants us to do, and that's leave!

SARAH: And mother! What will my mother say if we go traipsing off to some foreign country? You know how suspicious she's always been about you. This will confirm her worst fears! Taking her daughter only God knows where!

ABRAHAM: I'll handle your mother, Sarah. But we must obey God.

SARAH: Is it me, Abraham? You're not happy with me? I haven't been a good wife to you? You're saying all this so you can get away from me?

ABRAHAM: Sarah! Of course not. What does all that have to do with what the Lord said? Don't be so foolish!

SARAH: Foolish, am I? You think I'm foolish! I think you're the fool, Abraham ben Terah! First you don't care enough about my well-being to stay here, where things are safe and comfortable; and then you insult me, by calling me names! Well, I won't have it, Abraham! I'm going home to mother! (*She begins to exit.*)

ABRAHAM: Sarah!!! (*She stops, turns to look at him.*) Now Sarah, I don't understand this any more than you do! But going to your mother's won't help anything! Now. The Lord told us to go, and we will. Whether we feel like it or not. All right?

SARAH: (*after long, considering pause*) But we can't go now.

ABRAHAM: Why not?

SARAH: Because I'm not packed! There's all the clothes, and the linens, and the household goods . . . and what about the silver, and the new colour television?

ABRAHAM: What?!!

SARAH: And the servants, they'll all have to be told. And Lot! What will we do about Lot? He's your brother's son, you know. We'll just have to take him with us. He's only a baby.

ABRAHAM: A baby! He's forty-five years old, Sarah!

SARAH: But Abraham –

ABRAHAM: (*interrupting*) All right, all right! Do what you will about the silver and the servants and the television and anything else! But do it! (*SARAH exits hurriedly.*) We've got to get going! (*Exit.*)

SCENE II

(*Following pause after SCENE I. Enter SARAH, talking as (she walks. Cross to chair, where she sits and knits. She's the same as before but older and a bit slower.*)

SARAH: Oh, such a life. Those last caravanners that came through here, my, my, I just don't know what things are coming to. A body's too old for living, yes indeed. You know, Abraham thinks the Lord gave him this land for his inheritance. I'll tell you what I think: I think the Lord gave it to him because he was the only one who would have it! Oh . . .

ABRAHAM: (*entering, excited*) Sarah! Sarah! Sarah! Guess what!

SARAH: Yes, dear?

ABRAHAM: The Lord spoke to me! During my sun-bathe!

SARAH: Oh, no! I remember what happened the last time the Lord spoke during your sun-bathe twenty-four years ago! Where are we going this time?

ABRAHAM: (*laughing*) Nowhere, Sarah! This land is our home, we're settled here! The Lord's given it to us for our inheritance!

SARAH: What inheritance, Abraham?

ABRAHAM: That's exactly what the Lord spoke to me about! Our son! He said many nations would come through us!

SARAH: Through us? But Abraham, you know we have no children of our own. Do you mean through Ishmael, your son by my maid?

ABRAHAM: No,I don't! That's the same question I asked the Lord. And he said, 'No, Abraham, I mean a child born to you by Sarah your wife.' By you, Sarah!

SARAH: (*laughing*) Me?

ABRAHAM: That's what the Lord said! Isn't it wonderful! What do you think, Sarah?

SARAH: (*still laughing*) What do I think? Why, what could I think! It's – (*realising he's serious*) why, Abraham, do you believe it? (*pause, then rising, continuing before he can answer fully*) Abraham, this has gone far enough! Do you know how old we are?

ABRAHAM: We're . . . uh . . . well, let's see, when was that last party? Oh, that was a good one, Sarah! We had those red balloons, and those nice little party crackers, and –

SARAH: (*interrupting*) I'll tell you! You're one hundred years old, and that makes me ninety! Ninety years old, Abraham! I think that's a bit past it, don't you?! We're not like we used to be! (*softening*) Oh, Abraham, I wish you'd stop hearing voices! You should just relax and enjoy life, and settle down in your old age. Be content with what we have and stop dreaming about other things. Ishmael will be your heir, and maybe a great nation will come through him. He's not a bad sort. . . .

ABRAHAM: Sarah, I know what God said. You'll see. He'll do what he's promised.

SARAH: I'm losing patience with you, Abraham ben Terah! And

others will, too! You'll be the laughing stock of the world! A child born to us, at our age! (*recovering herself*) Oh, why am I getting so upset! You'll probab – (*in sudden pain, clutching her stomach*) Ohhhhh!

ABRAHAM: What is it, dear?

SARAH: I, I think (*sitting down in chair*) . . .

ABRAHAM: Can I get anything for you? Some water from the well? Your camel skin blanket?

SARAH: No, no . . .

ABRAHAM: What is it?!

SARAH: I'm not sure . . . It's the oddest feeling. I know I was too sick for breakfast this morning, but suddenly I fancy some ice cream and pickles!

ABRAHAM: Ice cream and pickles, Sarah? At ten o'clock in the morning?

SARAH: (*Looking at him in amazement*) Yes . . . isn't that odd?

ABRAHAM: (*Leading her out*) Why don't you rest for awhile, dear, and I'll see about your ice cream (*chuckling, winking at audience as they exit*).

Ruth and Naomi

(based on Ruth 1:1–18)

by Maggie Durran

Presentation style: Dialogue or drama. If done as drama, work out entrances and exits. Stage directions in this script pertain to presentation as a dialogue.

Characters: 3
Ruth Narrator
Naomi

Placement: All characters are on stage with Ruth and Naomi together in the centre and Narrator to one side.

Ruth and Naomi

NARRATOR: (*Read Ruth 1:1–5.*)

NAOMI: Love, I think I'll go back to Ireland. I'm tired of this land with its dirt and smog and busyness. I'm going back where I belong.

RUTH: Don't you belong here where we love you?

NAOMI: Not really. I'll go home to my kinsfolk, and maybe I'll get back my interest in life. (*pause*)

It's a terrible thing to bury your husband and your two sons in a foreign land.

No, I'm going back where I'm understood and I know the ways.

(*reminiscing*) There's lots of places I went when I was a kid that we used to walk over. I'd like to see 'em again.

(*returns to the present*) I think I'll pack and go fairly soon. It'll be good to be home.

RUTH: What will we do when we get there? (*pause*)

Tell me what it's like. Is it very different?

NAOMI: Oh, you won't be coming. You'll stay here. This is your country.

RUTH: But I'd rather stay with you than be here.

NAOMI: You'd not want to be a foreigner in Ireland now, 'specially a Protestant one. No, you stay here.

RUTH: Couldn't I become a Catholic and really get to be one of your people?

NAOMI: You wouldn't, not you. Now, if you were an atheist or something you might, but not you.

RUTH: I want to do it. I can't let you go back on your own.

NAOMI: Don't be stupid; no-one can do it. I'm Irish; you're American. You can't change your whole way of living. Everything about you is so American; you could never be Irish.

RUTH: I don't think it's true . . . I want to be with you enough that I can get used to things being different.

NAOMI: But, don't you see? You can't really do it; you'll always be American. You'll always like American food and the national anthem, and the colours and mountains you grew up with. It's not possible to change that much.

RUTH: Look, I'm not talking about going to Ireland to be Irish. What I want is to be in your family . . . you and me, together.

NAOMI: (*firmly*) That's what I'm saying, too. You can't be Irish and like our ways and our food and everything so much that it feels like home. You can't help loving all that you've grown up with, and that's all there is to it!

RUTH: What I am saying is that I love you.

A lot of my friends think it's strange that we're so close. They say they can't believe anyone can be friends with their mother-in-law. And maybe it is strange. But what I know is that even since John died, you still feel like the only real family I have. I'm much closer to you than I am to my own mother. So I want to go with you . . . wherever you go.

NAOMI: (*pause*) Do you realise you may never get to come back? Ireland's not the safest place, what with bombs and all. You'd best stay here, love.

RUTH: (*determinedly*) Well, you're going back, and if it wouldn't be safe for me it wouldn't be safe for you; it's all the same.

NAOMI: But it's not. They're my people; I grew up with them, played with them, went to dances with them. Now, I'll grow old with them. I don't mind it being dangerous as long as I'm with my own folks.

RUTH: If they're your people they're my people, and if you can grow old and die there, so can I. I belong with you, and I'm going where you go.

NARRATOR: So Naomi returned to Ireland, and Ruth went with her. They set up home together in Naomi's home-town in Co. Armagh.

RUTH: I did the shopping; couldn't get everything. They didn't have marmalade yet.

NAOMI: I'm sure we can manage without it for a bit longer.

Would you like a cup of tea?

RUTH: Mm . . . lovely. (*pause*) I saw a notice while I was out . . . about jobs, in that supermarket in Shannon Street.

NAOMI: Did you ask about it?

RUTH: Yes, they're interviewing on Monday. I said that I'd go.

NAOMI: Is it the place with black and grey tiles under the window? Supermart, I think they call it?

RUTH: Yes, d'you know it?

NAOMI: Oh . . . I do. The man who owns it, James O'Mahoney, is my cousin. He's a good man. I don't know if he knows I'm back. When you go on Monday tell him who you are; he'll be pleased to meet you.

(*long pause to denote time lapse*)

RUTH: Hello, I'm home. Hello, I'm here.

NAOMI: Hello. How did it go; did you get it?

RUTH: Yes, I did . . . but let me tell you all about it.

NAOMI: Then I'll make the tea afterwards; go on.

RUTH: Well, he asked me all sorts of questions about money and goods and so on.

NAOMI: (*looks surprised*) You mean, James O'Mahoney?

RUTH: Yes, and then he said, 'Fine, I'll let you know.'

Then he had another question. He asked, 'What's a pretty American girl doing over here in Ireland? Surely America has more jobs than Ireland, better paid, too?'

So I told him.

NAOMI: (*apprehensively*) What did you tell him?

RUTH: Oh, all about us, and how I came back with you and about us being one family and all.

NAOMI: Oh, you never did!

RUTH: I did too. And he said you were his family, so I was his family, and he was glad to meet me. And if I wanted to start tomorrow, the job was mine. He said he'd rather keep it in the family.

(*All exit.*)

Peace! Be Still

(based on Mark 4:35–41)

by Patricia Beall

Characters: 6 or more

Jesus
John
Peter
Waves: 2 or more
Storm leader

Props (optional): 3 chairs representing seats in boat
Scarves tied to wrists of Waves

Staging: Imaginary boat located centre stage. Storm leader stands downstage L or R.

Note: See p. 385 for explanation of Rain Clap.

Peace! Be Still

(*Enter WAVES to C S. Kneel, with body tucked together, arms over head. Sway gently. Enter JESUS, PETER and JOHN from L.*)

JESUS: What a day it's been!

JOHN: Thousands of people came to hear you today! You must be exhausted!

JESUS: (*stretching*) Oh, I am. Let's go for a boat ride across the lake. A change will be nice!

JOHN: Right! Just the thing!

PETER: (*simultaneously*) Yes, that's it! And I'll row!

(*Entering boat, JESUS moves to stern, PETER takes up oars, JOHN sits between them facing PETER. Soon JESUS falls asleep. Rain begins: Level 1.*)

JOHN: What do you think! It's raining!

PETER: Shouldn't last long. It's been clear all day.

(*RAIN CLAP: Level 2, Level 3. WAVES uncurl, stretching and swaying, becoming larger as storm grows. Add WIND sounds.*)

PETER: Is he still asleep then?

JOHN: (*looking over his shoulder at JESUS*) Yes. I don't see how, though, with all this water coming in! (*He attempts to bail water out with his hands.*)

(*Level 4 of RAIN CLAP, with WIND getting louder and WAVES getting larger. PETER and JOHN raise their voices above the noise of the storm as their boat rocks in the wind.*)

JOHN: Peter! I am getting a bit worried . . .

PETER: Worried, man! It's not getting any better, is it!!!

(*Level 5: Peak of STORM sounds and WAVE movement*)

PETER: I can hardly row! Can you help?!

JOHN: There's no more oars! But they wouldn't help anyway, it's too windy!

PETER: I don't think I can carry on . . .

JOHN: I'll wake him, I will! (*staggering to JESUS*) Jesus! Teacher! Jesus! (*shaking him*) Wake up now! There's a great storm, don't you know! We're perishing! Don't you even care, Jesus?!

JESUS: (*awaking, rising*) Winds! Stop! (*WIND noises cease*) Waves, sea, water: Peace! Be still! (*RAIN CLAP stops abruptly, WAVES collapse, again lapping gently. Silence! Then, to PETER and JOHN:*) I wonder why you were afraid. Don't you believe I can save you? (*Slight pause, then JESUS returns to his seat.*)

PETER: (*looking at JESUS, talking to JOHN*) Who is this man . . .

JOHN: (*still amazed*) He spoke to the wind . . . and the water . . . and they obeyed him! (*looking out at audience*) They obeyed him! (*Freeze, all exit.*)

The Unforgiving Servant

(based on Matthew 18:23–35)

by Patricia Beall

Characters: 6

Joseph Clark	Fourth Servant
Andrew Coatman	Fifth Servant
Third Servant	King

Props: Large book(s) as ledgers

Costumes (optional): Robes and crown for King, smocks or breeches, etc. for Servants

Staging: Playing area divided into 2 sections: imaginary courtyard occupies R one-third, King's house the other two-thirds. Imaginary door connects house and yard.

The Unforgiving Servant

(*Enter CLARK, COATMAN, THIRD and FOURTH SERVANTS, lolling about.*)

CLARK: I say, Coatman, I'll bet you two pounds you can't hit that wall (*gesturing to imaginary wall behind audience*) with a stone!

COATMAN: (*gazing directly out, looking at wall*) Fie! o' course I will!

THIRD SERV: I don't know, Andrew, it's quite a ways . . .

COATMAN: Here's my hand, it's a deal, Clark! (*They shake on bet, then COATMAN seizes imaginary stone, gathers self together, hurls stone forward. All watch as it hurtles through air, then CLARK speaks as COATMAN makes rough, disappointed gesture.*)

CLARK: Ho! What did I tell you! Now, my two pounds, please (*extending hand*)!

COATMAN: Oh, Joseph, I haven't it wi' me just now! I'm sorry . . . I'll pay ye soon.

CLARK: See that you do, Andrew! See that you do, then!

FOURTH SERV: It's time we were gone, the master will be wanting us!

THIRD SERV: Aye! We're off then! (*All exit R.*)

(*Pause, then enter KING from L.*)

KING: HO! Where are you now!

(*Enter THIRD, FOURTH, FIFTH SERVANTS, talking at same time, bowing.*)

THIRD SERV: Here, my Lord!

FOURTH SERV: Just coming, your Majesty!

FIFTH SERV: Yes, my Lord! Just here!

KING: Today is the day to sort my accounts. Where are the ledgers?

THIRD SERV: I'll just get them, Sire! (*Exit R, KING seats himself; other SERVANTS take positions U. THIRD SERVANT returns, carrying large book. Crosses to KING, opens book and reads aloud.*)

Malcolm Abernathy – he works in the stables, Sire – two horses and fifty pounds. He has sent word he will pay by next week.

Stephen Campbell, from the northern farms. One hundred and fifty bushels wheat. Payment will be made day after tomorrow.

Frederick Winning, from the gardens. Two hundred and fifty pounds, uh, no, that came in yesterday.

Joseph Clark, from the household, Sire, five thousand pounds. Uh, no word from him.

KING: Clark? Five thousand, is it? I think we must settle that account. How long has it been?

THIRD SERV: It's been . . . (*consulting book, then looking up wide-eyed*) it's been . . . ages, your Highness.

KING: I see. Well, go collect him. (*FOURTH SERVANT exits R, KING and THIRD SERVANT carry on softly. Loud knock, FOURTH SERVANT returns with JOSEPH CLARK. CLARK walks forward, falls before KING in low bow; SERVANT returns to former place.*)

KING: Joseph Clark.

CLARK: Yes, your Majesty.

KING: I am told you owe me five thousand pounds.

CLARK: Yes, my Lord. That I do, my Lord.

KING: Very well, Clark, pay me the debt.

CLARK: Oh my Lord, I can't.

KING: You can't, did you say?

CLARK: Aye. I have no money.

KING: You have none?

CLARK: No, Sire, none at all.

KING: But Clark, it's been years and years since you contracted this debt. And I pay you well. How do you not have any money?

CLARK: I, I have none, my Lord.

KING: The penalty for paupers, Clark, is prison! Steward! (*FOURTH SERVANT steps forward.*) Cast Clark and his entire family into prison. Go to their home, sell all they have, and bring the money to me as partial payment. The law is the law, Clark! You'll be released when you've paid your debt!

CLARK: Oh my Lord! (*throwing himself down, grasping KING's feet, wailing*) Have mercy, I beg you! Have mercy! If you give me time, I swear I'll pay the whole debt! Have mercy!

KING: Well . . . all right! I'll be kind to you. I forgive your debt! Yes, I do, I forgive it! (*CLARK collapses in gratitude.*) Now, now, man! (*to SERVANTS*) Show him out. (*SERVANTS take CLARK to 'door' on R, put him out. They shut door half-way, then re-open it as the following ensues.*)

(*Enter ANDREW COATMAN R, as CLARK is picking himself up off the ground. CLARK is brushing his clothes off and straightening them when he sees COATMAN.*)

CLARK: Coatman! Andrew Coatman! Come here, I say! (*Surprised, COATMAN crosses to CLARK, who rushes forward to meet him, grabbing, shaking, almost choking him.*) You owe me money, Coatman! You owe me two pounds! Pay it!!!

COATMAN: (*struggling*) Oh, I beg you! Have mercy! If you give me time, I swear I'll pay it! Have mercy, Clark!

CLARK: Mercy, fie! I'll have none! I want my money! You, your wife, your whole family will be imprisoned until you pay me! (*dragging him off R*) Constable! Constable! Arrest this man! (*They exit.*)

(*Aghast, the SERVANTS look at each other, then rush L to KING. In rapid succession:*)

THIRD SERV: Master! Master! Joseph Clark, whom you just forgave his debt! He's having Andrew Coatman – from the stables, Sire – put in prison!

FOURTH SERV: For indebtedness, my Lord! Coatman owed him two pounds, and he couldn't pay!

FIFTH SERV: The Constable's taken Coatman away, Master! He's taken him!

KING: What? Coatman imprisoned? For owing Clark? Find Clark! Bring him immediately! (*SERVANTS exit R, return with CLARK, who throws himself at KING's feet, truly frightened this time.*)

KING: (*outraged*) Joseph Clark, you are rotten! You owed me five thousand pounds and I forgave it because you asked me! But Andrew Coatman owed you two pounds, and you refused to forgive him! Oh, Clark! I was merciful to you for a great sum, you should have been merciful to him for such a small one! Now! (*to SERVANTS*) Cast him into prison, and let him stay there until he's paid all he owed me!!! (*SERVANTS drag CLARK off L. KING exits R, still fuming!*)

How Can the Body be Complete?

by Martha Keys Barker

Characters: 7

- Eye
- Ear
- Hand I
- Hand II
- Foot I (Woman)
- Foot II (Man)
- Musician

Props: Musical instrument (guitar, violin, cello, flute)
Chair, if needed by Musician

Costumes: (see drawing overleaf)

Eye: Mask with movable lid
Ear: Hat with large ears attached
Hands: Rubber gloves with painted nails
Feet: Brightly coloured, striped socks

Music: The Musician can play any lively music. The drama concludes with 'The Body Song', *Sound of Living Waters*, 111. The characters may sing solos on their particular lines.

Diagram:

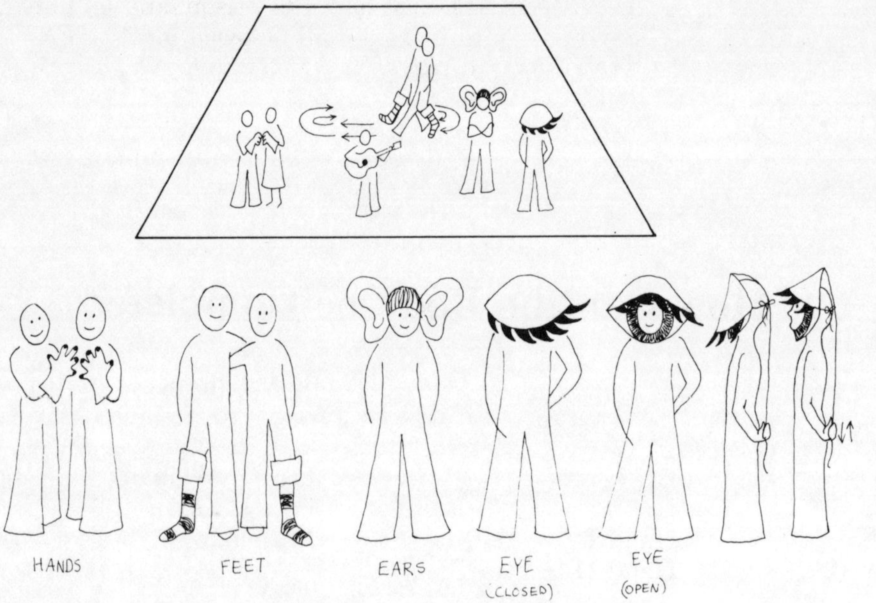

How Can the Body be Complete?

(*Characters enter and take places on stage. Each does characteristic action: HANDS knit or twiddle thumbs, FEET pace from left to right, EAR hums to himself, EYE is napping. All appear bored and uninvolved with each other. MUSICIAN enters with instrument and begins to play. Characters respond in delight: HANDS clap, FEET tap and dance, EAR perks up and nudges EYE who raises lid and watches intently. All look around and nod approvingly to each other. MUSICIAN finishes piece and exits. Characters turn to each other and respond.*)

EAR: I haven't heard anything like that for years! It makes me feel young again . . .

EYE: Did you see that? He was so vigorous as he played. A feast for the eye!

HAND I: I felt I could almost touch his music –

HAND II: (*interrupting*) I just wanted to clap and clap. I felt so invigorated watching the way his hands commanded the instrument.

HAND I: Yes, it's quite an example, quite an inspiration . . .

FOOT II: That was a real experience! (*mimes following actions*) I feel like I could climb a mountain, or run a mile, or jump higher than I've ever jumped!

FOOT I: (*singing and swaying from side to side*) 'I could have danced all night, I could have danced all night'. . .

EAR: I wish I could hear it all again. Where did that young man go? (*exits and returns with MUSICIAN*) Now, we want you to play for us again. We were all inspired and excited by your first concert and we want to hear it again.

ALL: (*at various times*) Oh, yes, please! Encore! Let's hear it again! Encore!

MUSICIAN: I could play it for you again, but if you like the music so much, I have an even better idea. You could learn to play the music yourselves.

ALL: (*surprised and dubious*) Us? We couldn't do that! You must be having us on (*etc.*).

MUSICIAN: (*cutting off debate*) Actually, you have everything you need among yourselves. If you just put all your abilities together, you could easily play it.

EYE: I'm afraid you can't count on me. I can't hear at all and when you get down to it, music is a matter of hearing, isn't it?

MUSICIAN: Hearing is an important part of music, but it is only one part. You don't need to hear, that's what the ear is for. But we need . . .

EYE: (*interrupting, realising the implications*) You mean I'd have to depend on Mr. Ear for hearing? Oh, no! I'm afraid I really must maintain my independence at any cost . . .

MUSICIAN: But you didn't let me finish . . .

EYE: (*interrupting*) I don't need to hear anymore. I have been taught never to depend on anyone! (*lowers lid with air of finality*)

HAND I: (*to EAR*) What did the Musician say?

EAR: He said that if we put ourselves together we could make music like he did.

HAND I: (*clapping with HAND II*) Isn't that exciting? He said we can make music!

HAND II: Oh, wonderful! Let's get started! (*They clap louder and faster.*)

EAR: (*shouting*) Quiet! (*in superior tone of voice*) You are confusing noise with music. (*to audience*) I really don't see how I can be expected to do the hearing for all this lot. Why, they have no ear for music at all! (*looks condescendingly at HANDS*) I'm afraid any co-operative venture is entirely out of the question. (*HANDS hold each other protectively.*)

FOOT I: (*to FOOT II*) What do you think about it?

FOOT II: I'm not certain yet. It was lovely dancing to his music. But getting involved with all these others to make music ourselves – I just don't know. I'm never one to jump into things. (*walks a few steps to one side of MUSICIAN*) I like to walk around and look at things from all sides. (*walks to other side*) I like to consider all the angles. (*He looks carefully at the instrument, pauses, then recognises major objection.*) You know, this could be dangerous! If the hands weren't careful, and this instrument slipped – who would feel the blow? That's right – the feet!

FOOT I: (*to audience*) Oh dear, I was so excited about it, but it doesn't look as though he wants to get involved. And, of course, we always do everything together . . . (*wistfully, to FOOT II*) What do you think, dear?

FOOT II: I've decided. It is definitely too dangerous for us! Come on, let's go for a walk. (*begins to exit with FOOT I*)

MUSICIAN: Just a minute – I thought you wanted to hear the music again. Don't you want to stay and learn to play it?

FOOT II: I'm afraid we've just gotten cold feet about the whole idea. We're going for a walk. (*They exit*)

HAND I: Well, can't we carry on without them?

HAND II: (*clapping softly*) Yes, let's do. We want to make music. (*to EAR*) Mr. Ear, will you help us? We know we can't hear what our clapping sounds like to your sensitive ear, but we want you to hear for us.

HAND I: We'll do whatever you think best.

EAR: You mean you are willing to change what you are doing?

HAND II: Yes, we'll do anything to make that wonderful music.

EAR: Well, if you're willing to change, that's a different matter. I think we can arrange something. I can hear the music and tell you when to clap. (*He demonstrates several possibilities while humming different tunes.*) You see, sometimes you should clap on the beat, and sometimes you should clap on the offbeat, or in different rhythms.

HAND I: (*following his example, HANDS practise clapping different rhythms*) Oh yes, this is much more interesting!

HAND II: Now can we make music?

MUSICIAN: There are still a few elements which we lack. You need someone to read the music score. Let me see . . . (*He looks around for someone.*)

EYE: (*Attracted by the music, he opens lid and moves over to see what the EAR and HANDS are doing, then speaks to audience.*) I must see what is happening over here.

MUSICIAN: Aha! You are just the person I was looking for.

EYE: (*surprised*) I am? But you said I would need to depend on the ear, and I told you I could never depend on anyone!

MUSICIAN: You didn't give me the opportunity to finish my statement. I was going to say that in making this music, everyone has an essential part to play. No-one is more important than anyone else. Each has his own unique contribution which no other part can offer. So, though you must depend on the ear for hearing, all the other parts must depend upon you to read the score.

EYE: Oh, I see! Well, why didn't you say that at the beginning? That makes quite a bit of difference! I'd like to read this music, so the others can play.

HAND I: Hurray! Now we can play!

MUSICIAN: (*to the EYE*) Try this score.

EAR: Right! Here we go.

(*EYE moves slightly from side to side as if reading, EAR begins humming and directing HANDS, HANDS clap softly and rhythmically.*)

EAR: It sounds better, but it still isn't quite right. Something is still missing. (*to MUSICIAN*) What do you suggest?

MUSICIAN: You lack the support of the feet. As I said before, you need all the parts working together to make music like mine.

HAND II: But what can we do? They've gone away.

MUSICIAN: Just keep playing together. Perhaps the feet will hear the music and come and join you. Try another song.

(*As they begin to sing 'The Body Song' the FEET come tiptoeing back to observe. On the line 'How can the body be complete without feet?' the group turns to them invitingly. They exchange glances and agree to join. At end of song all freeze for a few seconds, then exit.*)

By Their Fruits Ye Shall Know Them

(John 19:1–42, *Jerusalem Bible*)

arranged by Max Dyer
script by Martha Keys Barker

Presentation style: This congregational dramatic reading may be presented in two styles: a) as a reading only, or b) as a dramatised reading.

Characters: a) 14 or more b) 16 or more

Solo speaking/Drama parts

Narrator	Jew 1
Pilate	Jew 2
Jesus	Soldier

Crowd: Choral Reading Group
4 or more men
4 or more women

Drama only
Joseph of Arimathaea
Nicodemus

Note: Throughout the script the Choral Reading Group's part is designated by 'MEN', 'WOMEN', or 'ALL'.

Props: (For drama only) Large chair for Pilate

Costumes: (For drama only)
Purple robe or cloak and a crown of thorns for Jesus
Impressive robe or cloak for Pilate

Staging: Varies according to presentation style.

a) The Choral Reading Group is arranged in the centre of the stage area, with women on one side and men on the other.

b) The Choral Reading group is SR. Pilate's chair is DL.

Congregational participation: The congregation joins the Choral Reading Group in the part of the Crowd. If the reading is performed effectively, it draws the congregation into the emotions of the crowd demanding Jesus's crucifixion. The script for the congregation should be distributed before the service begins. Give a brief explanation of the reading and lead the congregation through the part of the Crowd with the Choral Reading Group at least once, giving particular attention to the chanted portion.

Music: The reading may be introduced by the song, 'By their fruits ye shall know them', *Fresh Sounds*, 54. 'Were you there?', *Sound of Living Waters*, 126, may be incorporated into the reading or may be used to conclude it.

By Their Fruits Ye Shall Know Them

NARRATOR: Pilate then had Jesus taken away and scourged; and after this, the soldiers twisted some thorns into a crown and put it on his head, and dressed him in a purple robe. They kept coming up to him and saying,

MEN: (*chanting in jeering fashion*) Hail, King of the Jews!

NARR: . . . and they slapped him in the face. (*Several men clap hands to make slapping sounds.*)

NARR: (*PILATE strides to centre stage*) Pilate came outside again and said to them:

PILATE: Look, I am going to bring him out to you to let you see that I find no case.

NARR: Jesus then came out wearing the crown of thorns and the purple robe. (*JESUS walks slowly to right of PILATE.*)

PILATE: (*gesturing toward JESUS, but still facing crowd*) Here is the man.

MEN: Crucify him!

WOMEN: Crucify him!

ALL: Crucify him!

PILATE: Take him yourselves and crucify him: I can find no case against him.

(The next two lines may be chanted in canon, accenting the underlined words. The MEN begin; when they reach 'die', the WOMEN begin. Repeat three times, constantly increasing volume and intensity. May be accompanied by drum beats. If canon is not used, ALL read loudly and with intensity.)

MEN: We have a law and according to that law he ought to die,

WOMEN: because he has claimed to be the Son of God.

NARR: When Pilate heard them say this, his fears increased. Re-entering the Praetorium, he said to Jesus:

PILATE: *(turns and faces JESUS)* Where do you come from? *(pauses expectantly)*

NARR: But Jesus made no answer.

PILATE: Are you refusing to speak to me? Surely you know I have power to release you and I have power to crucify you?

JESUS: You would have no power over me if it had not been given you from above; that is why the one who handed me over to you has the greater guilt. *(JESUS and PILATE freeze.)*

NARR: From that moment Pilate was anxious to set him free, but the Jews shouted:

JEW I: If you set him free you are no friend of Caesar's.

JEW II: Anyone who makes himself King is defying:

ALL MEN: Caesar!

(PILATE turns and seats self on large chair with JESUS standing on right.)

NARR: Hearing these words, Pilate had Jesus brought out, and seated himself on the chair of judgement at a place called the Pavement, in Hebrew, Gabbatha. It was Passover Preparation Day, about the sixth hour.

PILATE: Here is your King.

MEN: (*whispered*) Crucify him! Crucify him!

WOMEN: (*spoken intensely*) Crucify him! Crucify him!

ALL: (*spoken louder*) Crucify him! Crucify him!

ALL: (*shouted*) CRUCIFY HIM!

PILATE: Do you want me to crucify your King?

ALL: We <u>have</u> no King but Caesar!

(*PILATE throws up hands in despair and exits to his left. Chair is removed. JESUS remains in freeze.*)

NARR: So in the end Pilate handed him over to them to be crucified. (*JESUS mimes walking with cross on his back.*) They then took charge of Jesus and carrying his own cross he went out of the city to the place of the skull or, as it was called in Hebrew, Golgotha, where they crucified him with two others, one on either side with Jesus in the middle. (*JESUS stretches out arms, assumes crucifixion posture.*) Pilate wrote out a notice and had it fixed to the cross. It ran, 'Jesus the Nazarene, King of the Jews'. This notice was read by many Jews because the place where Jesus was crucified was not far from the city, and the writing was in Hebrew, Latin and Greek. So the Jewish chief priests said to Pilate, 'You should not write "King of the Jews", but "This man said: I am King of the Jews."' Pilate answered, 'What I have written, I have written.'

When the soldiers had finished crucifying Jesus they took his clothing and divided it into four shares, one for each soldier. His undergarment was seamless, woven in one piece from neck to hem; so they said to one another,

SOLDIER: Instead of tearing it, let's throw dice to decide who is to have it.

NARR: In this way the words of scripture were fulfilled:

'They shared out my clothing among them.
They cast lots for my clothes.'

This is exactly what the soldiers did.

Near the cross of Jesus stood his mother and his mother's sister, Mary the wife of Clopas, and Mary of Magdala. Seeing his mother and the disciple he loved standing near her, Jesus said to his mother:

JESUS: Woman, this is your son.

NARR: Then to the disciple he said,

JESUS: This is your mother.

NARR: And from that moment the disciple made a place for her in his home.

After this, Jesus knew that everything had now been completed, and to fulfil the scripture perfectly he said:

JESUS: I am thirsty.

NARR: A jar full of vinegar stood there, so putting a sponge soaked in vinegar on a hyssop stick they held it up to his mouth. (*SOLDIER mimes holding stick up to JESUS*.) After Jesus had taken the vinegar he said:

JESUS: It is accomplished.

NARR: . . . and bowing his head he gave up the spirit.

(*Optional song: 'Were you there?'*)

NARR: It was Preparation Day, and to prevent the bodies remaining on the cross during the Sabbath – since that Sabbath was a day of special solemnity – the Jews asked Pilate to have the legs broken and the bodies taken away. Consequently the soldiers came and broke the legs of the first man who had been crucified with him and then of the other.

(*SOLDIER mimes piercing JESUS's side*.)

When they came to Jesus, they found he was already dead, and so instead of breaking his legs one of the soldiers pierced his side with a lance; and immediately there came out blood and water. This is the evidence of one who saw it – trustworthy evidence, and he knows he speaks the truth – and he gives it so that you may believe as well. Because all this happened to fulfil the words of scripture:

> 'Not one bone of his will be broken,'

and again, in another place scripture says,

> 'They will look on the one whom they have pierced.'

After this Joseph of Arimathaea, who was a disciple of Jesus – though a secret one because he was afraid of the Jews – asked Pilate to let him remove the body of Jesus. Pilate gave permission, so they came and took it away. Nicodemus came as well – the same one who had first come to Jesus at night-time – and he brought a mixture of myrrh and aloes, weighing about a hundred pounds. They took the body of Jesus and wrapped it with the spices in linen cloths, following the Jewish burial custom. *(Two men go to either side of JESUS, placing his arms on their shoulders, they carry him off.)* At the place where he had been crucified there was a garden, and in this garden a new tomb in which no-one had yet been buried. Since it was the Jewish Day of Preparation and the tomb was near at hand, they laid Jesus there.

By Their Fruits Ye Shall Know Them

Script for Congregation

(The congregation joins the Choral Reading Group in the following responses of the CROWD.)

PART I

NARRATOR: Jesus then came out wearing the crown of thorns and the purple robe.

PILATE: Here is the man!

MEN: Crucify him!

WOMEN: Crucify him!

ALL: Crucify him!

PILATE: Take him yourselves and crucify him: I can find no case against him.

(The next two lines may be chanted in canon, accenting underlined words. The MEN begin; when they reach 'die', the WOMEN begin. Repeat three times, constantly increasing volume and intensity. May be accompanied by drum beat. If canon is not used, ALL read loudly and with intensity.)

MEN: We have a law and according to that law he ought to die,

WOMEN: because he has claimed to be the Son of God.

PART II

NARR: . . . It was Passover Preparation Day, about the sixth hour.

PILATE: Here is your King.

MEN: *(whispered)* Crucify him! Crucify him!

WOMEN: *(spoken softly, but intensely)* Crucify him! Crucify him!

ALL: (*spoken louder*) Crucify him! Crucify him!

ALL: (*shouted*) CRUCIFY HIM!

PILATE: Do you want me to crucify your King?

ALL: We <u>have</u> no King but Caesar!

NOTES

1. Claude Kipnis, *The Mime Book* (Harper and Row, London, 1974), p. 5.

Chapter 12

Dance

Movement and dance are basic human abilities. From our earliest moments we express our responses to the world around us through movement: we draw back from a loud noise, we flail our arms and feet to express discomfort, or dissatisfaction. As soon as we can propel ourselves, we crawl towards a desired object and back away from a frightening one. Movement is also a basic form of communication. When we're sad, we walk slowly and move lethargically, seemingly weighed down by the heaviness of our feelings; when we're happy, we skip, leap, jump, or dance for joy.

Everyone, unless severely handicapped, has the ability to express himself or herself in basic movement, and therefore can learn to dance. By this we do not mean that everyone has the potential to be a ballet dancer, as there are limitations of physique and co-ordination. But everyone can develop his or her natural ability to communicate in expressive movement and gestures. In our use of dance as a folk art we seek to stir up this potential in each person.

In considering dance as a 'folk art' we do not mean to limit it to 'folk' or 'national' dance. Rather, we include any dance form which enables non-professionals to develop their natural capacity for expressive movement. This may encompass folk or national dance, interpretative dance and movement, jazz and modern dance, and even elementary ballet.

The use of dance in worship takes this basic human capacity for movement and offers it to the Lord. Dance provides a vehicle for persons to present their entire selves to the Lord, as they offer their bodies and all that they hold – mind, emotions, will, strength, energy. Because it is such a total experience, dance can be a symbol or a picture of the whole of life. All parts of the body and all kinds of movement are needed to express this picture. Often liturgical dance is characterised by uplifted hands and faces turned heaven-ward. While such movement expresses one attitude of praise, the full gamut of physical expression is required to portray a more complete picture of man's relationship to God. The fuller picture embodies movements which are strong, pulsating, angular, and painful, as well as those which are graceful, flowing, and smooth.

With this in mind, the material in this section includes a variety of dance expressions: the dances to 'God has spoken', 'This is the day of the Lord', and 'Come go with me to that land' use folk dance steps from several nationalities; the 'On tiptoe' dance, arranged for use with children, and the 'If I could get through' dance (in the Arrangements chapter), incorporate interpretative movements; the dance to 'Once no people' combines the two styles, employing folk dance steps in the chorus and interpretative movement on verses. Suggestions for further development of interpretative movement are also found in the Dance Workshops.

GOD HAS SPOKEN

Adapted Israeli Folk Dance

The dance is done with 4 – 6 people, in a circle.
Hands are held unless otherwise stated.
The dance is a simple one and is centred around these three basic steps:

Figure is drawn with back to reader.

A. Grapevine:

cross R foot over L (FRONT)

step to the side with L (SIDE)

step behind with R (BEHIND)

step to side with L (SIDE)

B. Step-slide:

step with R (STEP)
or step with L

slide L up to R , (slightly bending knees on slide) (SLIDE)
or slide R up to L

C. Turning 180°:

swing L over and around R foot turning 180° (TURN)
or swing R over and around L foot
turning 180°

NOTE: On the end of last chorus of song, lift held hands high.

'GOD HAS SPOKEN' DANCE

grapevine
Figure is drawn with back to reader.
R L R L R L R L
Grapevine: Front side behind side Front side behind side
Chorus: God has spo - ken to his peo - ple,
-clap-
R L R L R L R L
in in out out Front side behind side
hal - le - lu - jah! And his words are
-clap-
R L R L R L R L
Front side behind side in in out out
words of wis - dom, hal - le - lu - jah!
L R R R R L R L
Hop touch touch brush-turn step slide step slide
Verses: O - pen your ears, o Christ - ian peo - ple,
He who has ears to hear his mes - sage,
Is - ra - el comes to greet the Sa - viour,

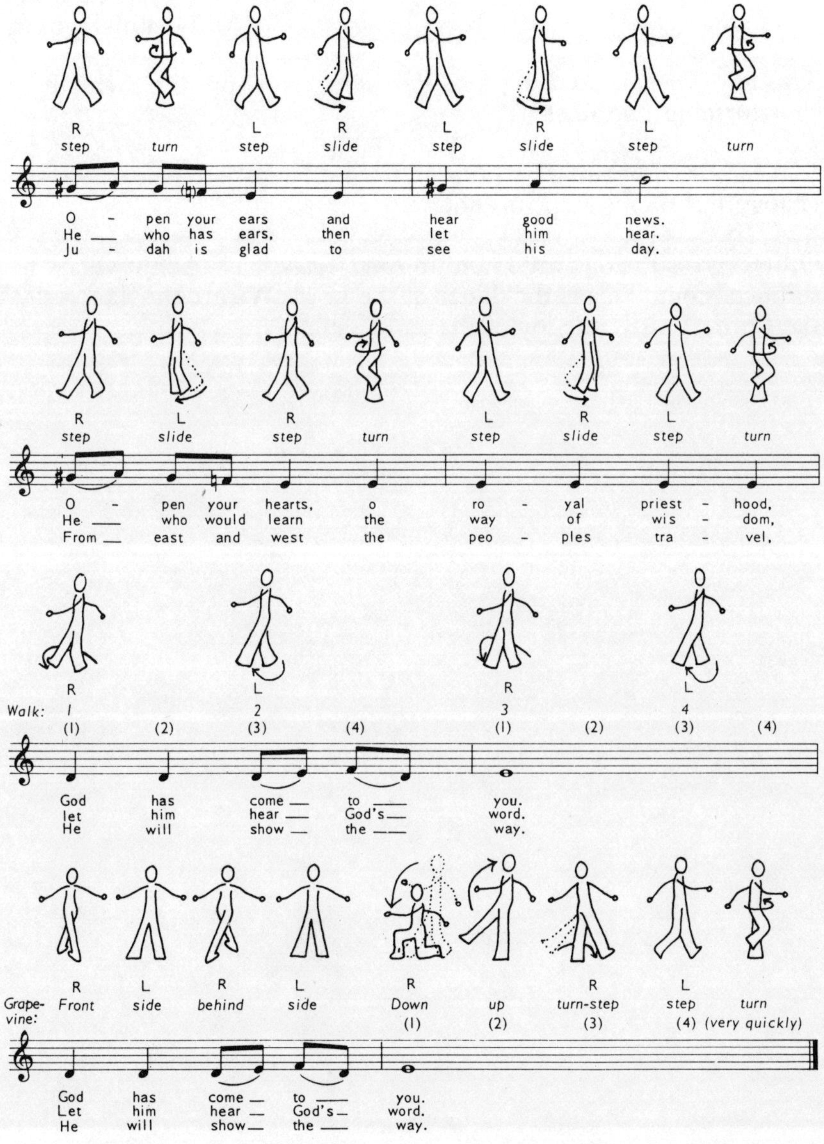
R L R L R L
step turn step slide step slide step turn
O - pen your ears and hear good news.
He — who has ears, then let him hear.
Ju - dah is glad to see his day.
R L R L R L
step slide step turn step slide step turn
O - pen your hearts, o ro - yal priest - hood,
He — who would learn the way of wis - dom,
From — east and west the peo - ples tra - vel,
R L R L
Walk: 1 2 3 4
(1) (2) (3) (4) (1) (2) (3) (4)
God has come — to — you.
let him hear — God's — word.
He will show — the — way.
R L R L R R L
Grape-vine: Front side behind side Down up turn-step step turn
(1) (2) (3) (4) (very quickly)
God has come — to — you.
Let him hear — God's — word.
He will show — the — way.

This is the day of the Lord

choreography by Jeff Cothran
Margi Pulkingham

This line dance is done in pairs. Partners stand opposite each other, thus forming two lines.

Join hands to begin. The same pattern of steps is repeated: verses change but dance steps do not.

Other verses to song are found in *Fresh Sounds*, 14. Adapt verses to suit occasion: 'This is the dance of the Lord, We are the dancers of the Lord, This is the joy of the Lord', etc.

A B
R L R R L R L L
step (1) step (2) step (3) hop (4) step (1) step (2) step (3) hop (4)
This is the day__ of the Lord.
R L R R L R L L
step (1) step (2) step (3) hop (4) step (1) step (2) step (3) hop (4)
This is the day__ of the Lord.
Lines A and B release hands;
each line steps to their right, turning clockwise;
-clap- B A -clap-
then to their left, turning anti-clockwise, returning to original position.
B -clap- A -clap-
A R L R -clap- L R L -clap-
step side (1) turn (2) turn (3) bend (4) step side (1) turn (2) turn (3) bend (4)
This is the day__ of the Lord.______ Al - le -
A B
R L R L R L
step in (1) bend (2) step back (3) step back (4) step in (1) bend (2) step back (3) step back (4)
lu,___ al - le - lu.

Come go with me to that land

adapted English folk dance

by Maggie Durran

This dance requires four couples, arranged in a square; the man on the left, the woman on the right.

All steps are done with a simple running step as in English folk dances.

Music for the dance is found in *Fresh Sounds*, 78.

First Phrase:
(Men/Women)

(Men begin the first verse; women begin the second. Continue the alternation throughout.) Join right hands in centre of square to form a star. With running step, circle in clockwise direction. Partner stands in original position, claps in time to music.

'Well, come go with me to that land,
come go with me to that land,'

Second Phrase:
(Men/Women)

Drop right hands, turn. Form star with left hands. Circle in anti-clockwise direction.

'Come go with me to that land
where I'm bound.'

Third Phrase:

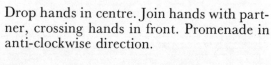

Drop hands in centre. Join hands with partner, crossing hands in front. Promenade in anti-clockwise direction.

'Come go with me to that land,
come go with me to that land,'

Fourth Phrase:

Link right elbows with partner and turn in place. On last bar stop turning and form square again, ready to begin next verse.

'to that land, to that land,
where I'm bound.'

Alternative Suggestions
Experiment with setting English folk dance steps to the following songs:

Alleluia! sons of God arise!, SOLW 86
Ho! Everyone that thirsteth, SOLW 88
Jesus Christ is alive today, SOLW 16
The Lord has put a new song, SOLW 100
The dancing heart, FS 8
I'm not alone, FS 92
Jubilate Deo, CH
This – this is the day, CH
Clap your hands, CH

Scottish folk dance steps may be set to:

Give me oil in my lamp, SOLW 4
I will sing, I will sing, SOLW 7
Allelu, FS 34

Once no people

choreography by Conway Barker
Margi Pulkingham

This circle dance is done with five or more people. Circle moves in clockwise direction at start. Hands are held during choruses and dropped during verses.

The chorus is repeated twice at the beginning and end, with a concluding musical coda. The same dance steps are used each time the chorus is sung. On end of final chorus, lift held hands high.

The verses are interpreted by a soloist or by all dancers.

If a soloist: during choruses, soloist kneels in centre of circle.
during verses, dancers kneel and soloist rises.

If all dancers: verse 1 interpreted by one dancer.
verse 2 interpreted by two dancers.
verses 3 and 4 interpreted by all dancers.

Complete song is found in *Fresh Sounds*, 68.

This chorus contains two basic steps: the grapevine and the rock step.

The grapevine is explained on p. 253. The rock step is as follows:

Beat 1: Step to L side with L foot, weight on ball of L foot.
2: Shift weight to ball of R foot.
3: Shift weight to ball of L foot.
4: With R foot, step behind L foot.

Note: The first four figures in dance illustrations demonstrate this step. Figure is drawn with back to reader.

ONCE NO PEOPLE (CHORUS)

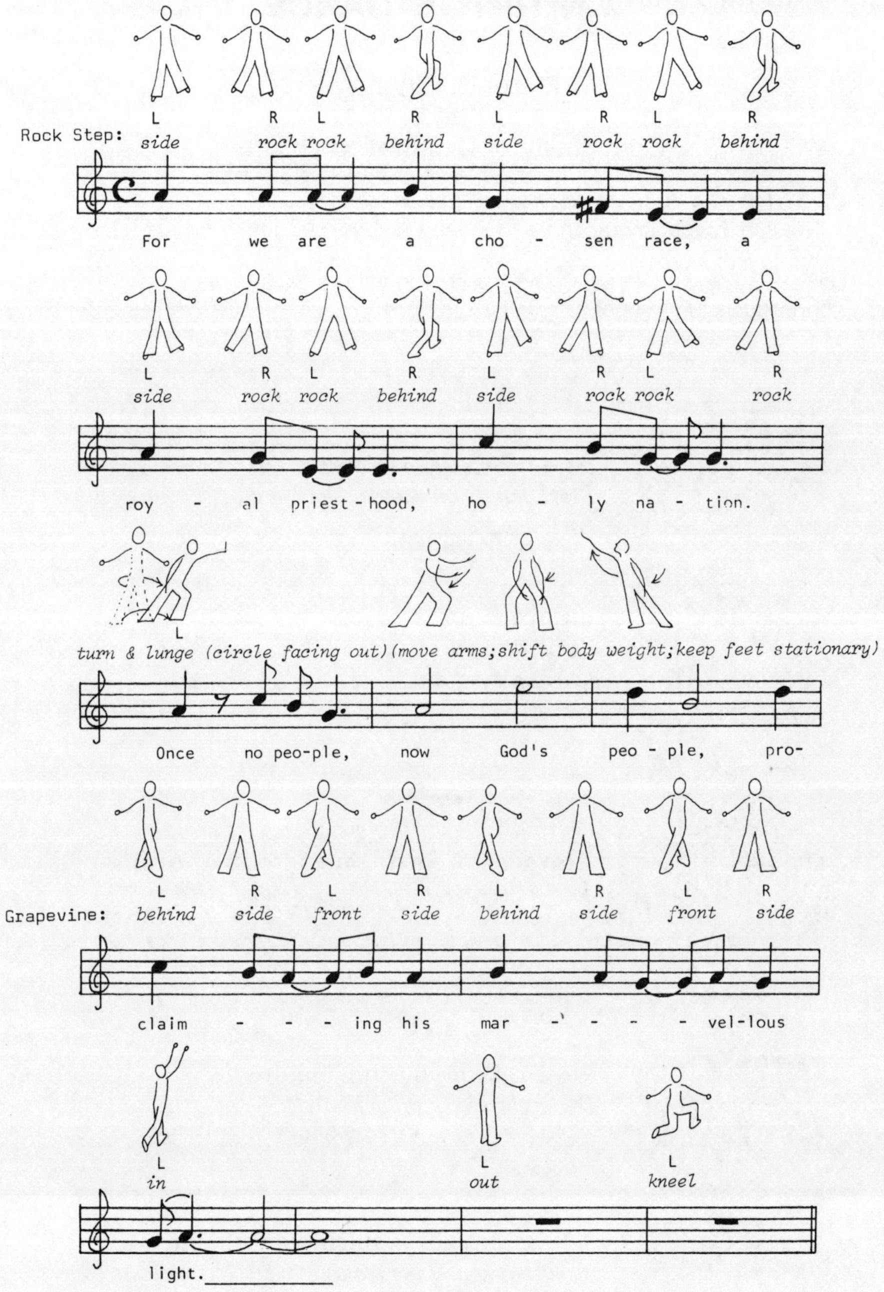

'ON TIPTOE' DANCE

by
Margi Pulkingham
and
Community of Celebration children

Circle dance: 4–8 dancers (children and one leader)
The 'On Tiptoe' song can be found in the music edition of FS, 84.

Dance begins with verse 1, and the chorus follows each verse.
Abbreviations: R = right, L = left.

CHORUS:

And all creation's straining
Place hands on knees: walk with bent knees around circle clockwise.

on tiptoe just to see
Stand upright on tiptoes, shading eyes by placing R hand on forehead. Peer to left and right.

The sons of God come into their own
Join hands, skip clockwise around circle.

VERSE 1:

I walk with you, my children
Walk clockwise around circle.

Through valleys filled with gloom;
Continue walking, making a dip on 'valleys' by bending low and straightening up again.

In echoes of the starlight
Standing still, all lean to the R and cup R hand over R ear, listening.

And shadows of the moon
Swing R arm downwards in sweeping motion, gesturing to indicate shadows on ground.

In the whispers of the nightwind/Are gentle words for you
Turn to face centre of circle, bend slightly at waist. Sway upper body from L to R and make soft whistling sounds.

To touch you and assure you/It's my world you're walking through.
Turn 180°, gesturing with gentle sweep of R arm, to include audience. Continue turning, completing a full circle.

VERSE 2:

I made the mottled stickleback to hide in crystal streams.
Wide-eyed, bend from waist and point R hand toward an imaginary fish in centre of circle.

The staring owl to scan the night,
Hands on hips, and 'hooooot!'

The candle's gentle beams;
Stand, with hands above head, palms together to form a candle flame.

I made the silly camel/To roam the desert sand,
Turn to L, place hands on waist of person in front, all bend at waist and walk, swaying.

But you I made, my children, to walk and hold my hand(s).
Join hands, walk around circle clockwise.

VERSE 3:

If life were filled with bubbles,
Stand still, holding R hand up in air, joining thumb and forefinger together to form 'bubbles'.

They'd glisten and they'd burst;
On 'glisten' spread fingers wide; on 'burst' pop an imaginary bubble with forefinger.

(Note: Drawing of leader only is for clarity, but children follow leader as before.)

If life were filled with jewels/They'd line a rich man's purse.
With both hands, open an imaginary money bag. Peer inside with wide eyes and wide mouth.

But life is filled with water/That flows from depths of love.
Raise R hand high and slowly move arm in flowing figure-8 fashion.

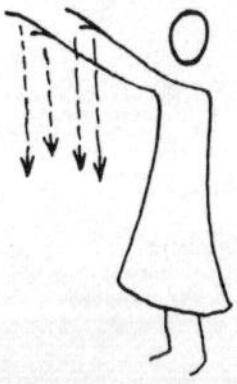

It flows to fill your weariness/With blessings from above.
Continue figure-8 motion: on 'blessings' raise both arms above head and then slowly lower them to sides, wiggling fingers to suggest falling rain.

VERSE 4:

My love for you, my children, puts rainbows in your hand.
On 'rainbows' each extend arms above head, forming arc with hands.

Born of clouded sorrows/In a sunburst morning land;
Droop upper body to left, arms still circled above head. On 'sunburst' thrust arms apart while quickly standing upright, bright-faced.

They arch above the smiling eyes
Bend over at waist, rest chin on hands linked together at fingers, palms down.

Where tears can still be seen,
On 'tears' tilt head R pointing with forefinger of R hand to R eye.

And adorn with gentle trembling touch/The bride who is my own.
Turn 180°, gesturing with gentle sweep of both arms, to include audience. Continue turning, completing a full circle.

Chapter 13

Scriptural Development

Developing one scriptural passage in a variety of ways brings out diverse aspects of its truth and application. In this chapter we include five interpretations of the parable of the prodigal son as an example of this multi-faceted approach to scripture. Each portrayal of the story sheds light on various dimensions of the original account. Its humorous elements are drawn out in the foot mime and the balloon improvisation. Contemporary applications are emphasised in the 'Family' version through its use of local dialect and current jargon. This version has wider usefulness than in its particular locale; it may be adapted to any situation by using a different dialect. A full length dramatisation in a contemporary setting, of which the last script is an excerpt, provides scope for in-depth development of character, conflict, tension and resolution (for full improvisation structure of this drama see p. 394). Though we've not included them here, arrangements of dance, music and poetry would reveal other facets of the characters and interaction. Other approaches to scripture may be found in Chapter 16 in the Writing from Scripture section.

The Prodigal Son

(based on Luke 15:11–32, Phillips translation)

dramatic action by Swedish workshop group
script by Patricia Beall

Presentation style: This is a foot mime, which means some sort of screen hides all but feet and lower legs of players. The audience never sees players' bodies, arms or faces. All conversations, emotions, responses are conveyed by foot gesture and action.

Characters: 7 or more

Father	3 or more: multiple roles
Elder Son	Merry makers
Younger Son	Pigs
Narrator	Servants

Props: Large blanket or screen to cover most of the playing area. A space of one and one-half to two feet should be left above floor level, so lower legs and feet of players will be visible.

Costumes: A pair of sandals for Father; legs bare. All other players have both feet and legs bare.

Placement: Players mime behind screen; Narrator is visible to R or L of playing area.

Diagrams:

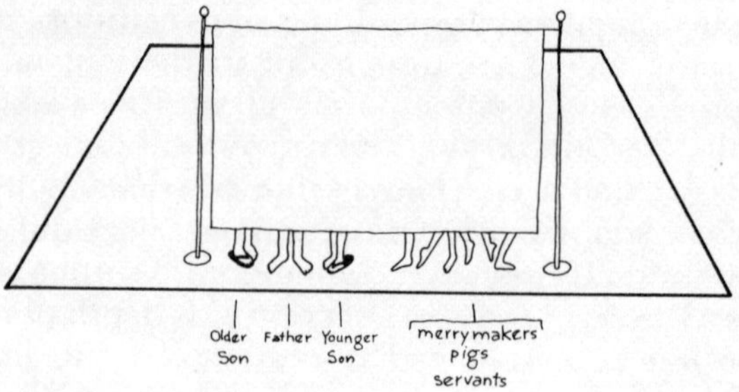

NARRATION	*ACTION*
Once there was a man	*Enter FATHER, wearing sandals.*
who had two sons.	*Enter YOUNGER SON L, ELDER SON R. Cross, stand either side of FATHER.*
The younger one said to his father, 'Father, give me my share of the property that will come to me.'	*YOUNGER SON talks to FATHER.*
So he divided his property between the two of them.	*FATHER gives one sandal to each SON.*
	FATHER and ELDER SON exit R; YOUNGER SON remains, admiring fortune.
Before very long, the younger son collected all his belongings and went off to a foreign land.	*YOUNGER SON exits L.*
	Enter MERRYMAKERS R, laughing loudly, singing raucously. They dance in haphazard circle. Enter YOUNGER SON L. Offering his sandal, he joins dance. Sandal is tossed from foot to foot and finally kicked out of sight. MERRYMAKERS exit R, SON remains.
And when he had run through all his money, a terrible famine arose in that country, and he began to feel the pinch. Then he went and hired himself out to one of the citizens of that country, who sent him out into the fields to feed the pigs.	*SON exits L, alone and dejected.*
	Enter PIGS R, snorting, grunting, making many quick, darting, 'sniffing' movements. Enter

NARRATION	*ACTION*
	YOUNGER SON L; PIGS surround him SON becomes noisy, greedy, piggish.
He got to the point of longing to stuff himself with the food the pigs were eating, and not a soul gave him anything.	
Then he came to his senses, and cried aloud, 'Why, dozens of my father's hired men have got more food than they can eat, and here am I dying of hunger! I will get up and go back to my father, and I will say, 'Father, I have done wrong in the sight of Heaven and in your eyes. I don't deserve to be called your son any more. Please take me on as one of your hired men.' So he got up and went to his father.	*SON suddenly freezes, PIGS carry on.*
	SON EXITS L, then PIGS exit R.
	Enter FATHER.
But when he was still some distance off, his father saw him and his heart went out to him and he ran and fell on his neck and kissed him.	*Enter SON L, walks in place.* *FATHER sees SON, excitement grows!* *FATHER runs to SON, 'falls on his neck' etc. by touching and caressing SON's foot with his own.*
But his son said: 'Father, I have done wrong in the sight of Heaven and in your eyes. I don't deserve to be called your son any more . . .'	*SON resists, abashed and ashamed; but FATHER continues.* *SON relaxes . . .*
'Hurry!' called out his father to the servants, 'fetch the best clothes and put them on him! Put a ring on his finger and shoes on his feet, and get that calf we've fattened and kill it, and we will have a feast and a celebration! For this is my son –	*SERVANTS enter R and L, dashing about. Some exit and re-enter, obeying the commands; others dance a happy jig.*

NARRATION	*ACTION*
I thought he was dead, and he's alive again. I thought I had lost him, and he's found!' And they began to get the festivities going.	
But his elder son was out in the fields, and as he came near the house, he heard music and dancing.	*Enter ELDER SON R, sandal on one foot.* *Stops abruptly after two or three paces.*
So he called one of the servants across to him and inquired what was the meaning of it all.	*ELDER SON stamps foot once, a SERVANT crosses to him.*
'Your brother has arrived and your father has killed the calf we fattened because he has got him home again safe and sound,' was the reply. But he was furious and refused to go	*ELDER SON's increasing anger is shown as he taps one foot, first measuredly, then faster and faster.*
inside the house. So his father came outside and called him.	*FATHER crosses to ELDER SON.*
Then he burst out: 'Look, how many years have I slaved for you and never disobeyed a single order of yours, and yet you have never given me as much as a young goat, so that I could give my friends a dinner! But when that son of yours arrives, who has spent all your money on prostitutes, for him	*They talk:*
you kill the calf we've fattened!' But the father replied: 'My dear son, you have been with me all the time and everything I have is yours. But we had to celebrate and show our joy.	*FATHER leads ELDER SON across to YOUNGER SON.* *Conclude with SERVANTS U to men, and FATHER between two sons, one foot next to each.*
For this is your brother; I thought he was dead and he's alive. I thought he was lost – and he's found!'	*YOUNGER SON is L, a bit U, ELDER SON R, a bit D.* *Both SONS face FATHER, who faces out.*

Family

(based on Luke 15:11–32)

by Maggie Durran

Characters: 2

Young Man — All others are imaginary.

Narrator

Props: Imaginary

Costumes: Jacket, leather if possible, and jeans for Young Man

Placement: Young Man and Narrator are both onstage at outset. Young Man mimes as Narrator reads.

NARRATION	*ACTION*
Life's funny y'know.	*Shrugs nonchalantly.*
It's not so long since I found out something.	
See, I realised that when you get an inheritance it's when your old man pop's off an' you collect the cash.	*Nods confidentially to audience.*
Easy really.	*Swaggers a little proudly.*
Well, I didn't wish the old man would pop off, but I just needed the cash; just a little deal here and there I could get into, so I asked for me inheritance before he died.	*Looks sideways to be sure he is not being overheard; nods to agree on a shady deal.*
And he gave it me. Boy, was it good.	*Surprised; open-mouthed, receives money.*
Cash in hand, and I made some real good deals . . . I mean real good . . .	*Hands ticket to 'bookie', receives wad of notes.*

NARRATION	*ACTION*
though some bad 'uns too, and got in debt a bit,	*Dejectedly flicks away a losing ticket.*
but I was ready to make it real big.	*Looks at 'dealer' hopefully.*
Then some guy got nasty about his money and I was wiped out; had to get a job.	*Fearfully looks over shoulder, turns pockets inside out searching for more money.*
Only one going was for flipping pighand; but I had to get cash	*Looks at job advertisement in evening paper.*
fast or I'd be in clink.	*Turns sideways, walks, kicks empty can angrily.*
Somehow, luck never quite got 'round my corner, and I was so	*Stops. Looks at audience over shoulder.*
darned hungry: I used to nibble on the pig food.	*Puzzled, he shrugs.*
Not a bad taste if you've ever tried it.	*Picks nut from food bin, tastes it. It's not too bad, so takes another.*
Well, I got sick of it . . . not sick of it . . . but a bit fed up.	*Faces audience, hands in pockets, a bit dejected.*
Then I thought of me old man.	*Brightens; looks up.*
He's not such a bad guy, and I figured he might help me out, like get me set up again.	*Shrugs; gives it a thought; nods once: it's a good idea.*
So I headed home.	*Turns; walks positively.*
You wouldn't believe what happened.	*Stops.*
He was that glad to see me that he ran up a right feast.	*Looks at table spread for a feast.*
Got me some real good gear to wear . . .	*Thumbs under lapels, shows off smart clothes.*
you don't look so good, or smell it, if you've spent your time round pig whatsit for a while.	*Takes trouserleg, near knee, between finger to thumb and gives it a shake.*

NARRATION	*ACTION*
Boy, but it was a real spread, I felt like . . . uh . . . a real star.	*Looks at feast again, appreciatively, then rocks forward onto toes to emphasise his importance.*
(*stage whisper*) But you should have seen me brovver, he was so mad 'cos I was the no good, and I got the feast.	*Indicates over right shoulder to brother. On 'mad' bangs fist on palm.*
(*resuming normal voice*) Boy, is that luck.	*Looks at the audience smugly.*
I dunno what I'll do now.	*Turns; walks slowly, confidently.*
I reckon me old man might give me a job, maybe, even the odd feast.	*Gives a little swagger, still walking.*
I guess it's not so bad to be in a family.	*Exit with smile to audience.*

The Prodigal Son

developed by Swedish workshop groups
script by Patricia Beall

This stylised mime uses a symbolic motif of circles. The son leaves the acceptance and security of his family circle to go alone into the world. Devastated by his experiences, he returns home.

Read as a narrative, Luke 16:11–32 is interpreted by players in one of two circles. Another player moves between them. A heightened effect is achieved when the reader is accompanied by a single instrument, such as flute, violin, cello, or piano. Movement parallels story line.

Movement suggestions are listed below. Movement should be kept simple and stylised.

The Family: Symbolised by several players, including Father and Elder Son characters. All stand with arms encircling each other. The son is part of this group in the beginning, then leaves. Movement in this circle should be strong and graceful. Players sway, stretch to hold son and then release him, reach out to receive him when he returns. Circle stiffens, contracts, showing tensions of Elder Son's dialogue with Father.

The World: Symbolised by several players. This circle is semi-connected: some players are interlinked, with arms and hands grasping each other's; other players have no contact with those next to them. Movement in this circle is rough and irregular. As the son approaches some players reach eagerly for him, clutching and grasping.

At appropriate point, players in this circle drop the their knees and become pigs.

The Son: His solo movements, when he is not in either circle, carry out the circle motif. He may spin rapidly to show his relief at leaving home, smoothly to show his wilfulness, haphazardly to show his confusion, slowly to show his despair.

The Prodigal Son

developed by workshop group
script by Martha Keys Barker

Balloon Device

When the son leaves home he is given four large bright balloons on strings as his 'inheritance'. During his adventures in 'a far country' his balloons are broken one-by-one as a symbol of the loss of both his money and his illusions. The group may create their own dramatic situations or use some of these:

1) He encounters a group of merrymakers who dance and drink with him. As they drunkenly stagger off, one pops a balloon with a straight pin.

2) A woman approaches the son suggestively and attempts to seduce him. As he embraces her, she pops one of his balloons, looks disappointed or bored, and saunters off.

3) A street vendor sells the son a beautiful red apple. When he turns and bites into it, he finds it is rotten. As he turns, the vendor quickly pops a balloon and hurries off.

4) Left with only one balloon, the son flops down dejectedly, places balloon beside him and covers it with his large hat for protection. A large hat pin sticking through the hat pops his last balloon.

The Prodigal Son

improvised by workshop group
script by Marty Pearsall and Patricia Beall

(The dining room of a middle class home, tastefully and unostentatiously appointed. At rise GEORGE and ROBERT are seated at table. GEORGE, a dynamic man in his mid-fifties, is dressed casually in slacks, shirt and cardigan. His tremendous energies are tempered with wisdom and patience. ROBERT, a nervously confident man in his mid-twenties, is meticulously dressed in a conservative grey suit, a white shirt, a subdued tie. His briefcase is nearby. Coffee and juice are already set at GEORGE's and ROBERT's places; juice at a third place which is conspicuously vacant. GEORGE is drinking his juice, ROBERT emerges periodically from the financial pages of the morning paper to give a report.)

ROBERT: Oh Father, I see our mutual profits have climbed. (*He returns to paper as GEORGE gazes at him speculatively.*) And our latest overseas investments are slowly stabilising. And I think . . . I believe (*as he reads silently*) . . . yes, our transatlantic stock is still rising. (*returning to paper*)

GEORGE: Tell me, son, how you're finding your studies this term.

ROBERT: Fine, Father, fine. Absolutely nothing to worry about. I'm still top-rated in my section.

GEORGE: But do you find the courses are what you'd hoped?

ROBERT: Ah, I do have reservations about –

(*DAVID enters, interrupting ROBERT. DAVID is 19, imma-*

ture and casual, dressed in jeans and a work shirt. Unlike ROBERT, who has been working in the management of the family firm and taking advanced degrees, DAVID is uncertain of his future. Currently working as a stockboy in one of their warehouses, he is lackadaisical about his direction in life. The brothers don't know each other very well, and there's not a great deal of affection between them.)

DAVID: (*brightly*) Good morning, good morning!

GEORGE: (*pleasantly*) Good morning.

ROBERT: (*coldly*) Good morning, David. (*continuing as before interruption*) It's the accounting course that –

DAVID: (*interrupting*) I really didn't mean to be late!

GEORGE: That's all right, David. Did you have a late night?

DAVID: (*laughing*) Yes! But it was super, well worth it!

ROBERT: As I was saying about my accounting course –

DAVID: (*looking around table*) Say, where's breakfast?

GEORGE: (*with sympathetic glance at ROBERT*) We've been waiting for you, son, before going –

ROBERT: (*interrupting GEORGE*) Really, David! If you'd get up on time, then breakfast could be served on time! The entire household wouldn't have to be conditioned by your habits, rather, the lack of them!

GEORGE: (*to DAVID*) Go ahead with your juice, Sarah will be along in a few minutes with the rest of the meal. I'd just asked her to hold it back.

ROBERT: (*still continuing*) And if you were on time, then important conversations wouldn't be interrupted!

DAVID: Oh, I see. 'Important conversations' again.

ROBERT: (*formally*) I do consider them as such.

DAVID: Right! Business, accounting, economics, the stock market . . .

ROBERT: Yes, David. Someone has to accept a certain amount of responsibility, you know! The world does not run itself. Economic and financial considerations are the heart of our society.

DAVID: 'The heart of our society'! Where'd you get that! Dad never taught us that sort of thing. Responsibility is one thing, Robert, and I admit that I'm not the most responsible, but you've gone way overboard! When's the last time you thought about football? Or . . . about the trees? Do you ever think about trees, Robert?

ROBERT: Football . . . ah, well, yes . . . football is a good example of increased managerial skills resulting in rising returns. And trees . . . the market for lumber is always increasing! (*looking at DAVID with new respect*) Maybe you're not as isolated from reality as I thought, David. Either of those areas could be significant investments!

DAVID: (*hopelessly*) That's not what I mean, Robert. We're not communicating at all.

ROBERT: (*irritated*) Really, David, I can't follow your line of reasoning! One moment you raise issues, and the next you abandon them! It's impossible to continue a conversation with you!

CHAPTER 14

Arrangements

Arrangements combine various media to develop a theme. The 'Image' and 'Identity' arrangements use poetry, music, dance, mime and scripture passages to address the problems of self-image and confused identity. The production 'Tableaux of Faith' focuses on the theme of faith through music, dance, drama, and choral reading, portraying biblical events.

These arrangements may serve as models for those who wish to experiment with a variety of media. A group may draw together existing resources, write new material, or combine the two approaches. For the 'Tableaux of Faith', for instance, we gathered resources already available: three songs, a dance, and a drama. To complete our journey of faith, we wrote a dramatic reading; to weave these elements into a cohesive statement, we supplied a narrative reading chorus. For the 'Image' and 'Identity' arrangements we used existing poetry, songs, and scripture passages, but added a mimed interpretation of a poem and a paraphrase of a scripture passage to emphasise important points.

The preparation of arrangements is an excellent long-term group project. The productions' diversity requires a broad spectrum of talents; gifts in music, drama, choral reading, dance, poetry and graphics can all be employed. A group may design arrangements to highlight its strong points and to encourage its weaker aspects. For example, a group with an accomplished flute soloist may feature a flute solo while also including a brief but challenging drama to stimulate its nascent drama group. A large group can divide into smaller units to rehearse the components of arrangements. The large group then reassembles to rehearse the whole production. Preparing an arrangement thus gives impetus both to individual and small group creativity and to large group co-ordination.

All material for the arrangements is included in this chapter, with the exception of music available in the songbooks.

Identity

developed by Patricia Beall

Participants: 7 or more

Elements

Reading: Excerpts from Psalm 139, paraphrased *Jerusalem Bible*, p. 282

Songs: 'If I could get through', p. 286

'Fear not, for I have redeemed you', CH

Dance: 'If I could get through', p. 288

Arrangement suggestions

1. Song: 'If I could get through'

   Solo or small group presentation
   Accompanied by dance

2. Song: 'Fear not, for I have redeemed you'

   Solo verses, with small group or congregation on refrain

Presentation pattern

Song and dance: 'If I could get through'

Reading: Excerpts from Psalm 139

Song: 'Fear not, for I have redeemed you'

Images

developed by Patricia Beall

Participants: 6 or more

Elements

Narrated mime: 'gooseberry pie', p. 284

Scripture readings: I Corinthians 13:12
I John 3:1–2
Romans 8:14–17a

Songs: 'If I could get through', p. 286
'Do you know?', p. 285

Dance: 'If I could get through', p. 288

Arrangement suggestions

1. Song: 'If I could get through'

   Solo or small group
   Accompanied by dance

2. Song: 'Do you know?'

   Solo verses, with small group or congregation on refrains

3. Scripture readings

   Select one or more to use as reading following mime presentation
   Use as basis for discussion or teaching

Presentation patterns

I

Song: 'If I could get through' alternated with narrated mime: 'gooseberry pie'

song
1 and 2 stanzas
song
3 and 4 stanzas

song
5 stanza
song (culminating in minor key)
Reading: Selected scripture(s)
Song: 'Do you know?'
Optional Talk

II

Song and dance: 'If I could get through' leading into
Narrated mime: 'gooseberry pie'
Talk based on one of the scripture readings
Song: 'Do you know?'

Reading for 'Identity'

(paraphrase of Psalm 139:1–6, 13, 15–16, *Jerusalem Bible*)

by Patricia Beall

The Lord looks closely at you, he knows you.

He knows when you sit down, when you stand up.

He may be far from you, but he knows all you think.

He carefully plans what happens to you; he knows when you're tired, when you've had enough.

You needn't even speak: before the words are out of your mouth, the Lord knows everything you were going to say.

The Lord is in front of you and behind you, his hand forms a shield around you.

These things are amazing, they're impossible to comprehend! Our minds and imaginations are too limited, too stiff, to stretch to such understanding.

The Lord himself planned you, shaping you inside your mother.

He knew you well: nothing was hidden from him, even before your birth. You grew quietly, secretly, hidden in the heart of the earth; yet he saw you, he knew you.

And even before that he saw you: before you were even formed he began thinking about your life, about your days to come.

And remember, all this was happening before you were even born!

The Lord has gotten through: he knows where he is. He's seen you, he knows what he sees. He knows who he is, and who you are. This Lord, this God of all creation, loves you. Do you know?

Scripture readings for 'Images'

paraphrase by Patricia Beall

Now we see in a mirror dimly, but later we will see face to face. Now we know in part; then we shall know fully, even as we have been fully known.

I Corinthians 13:12

See what love the Father has given us, that we should be called children of God; and so we are. The reason why the world doesn't know us is that it did not know him. Beloved, we are God's children now; it does not yet appear what we shall be, but we know that when he appears we shall be like him, for we shall see him as he is.

I John 3:1–2

All who are led by the Spirit of God are sons of God. For you did not receive the spirit of slavery to fall back into fear, but you have received the spirit of sonship. When we cry, 'Abba, Father!' it is the Spirit himself bearing witness with our spirit that we are children of God, and if children, then heirs, heirs of God and fellow heirs with Christ, provided we suffer with him in order that we may also be glorified with him.

Romans 8:14–17

'gooseberry pie' Mime for 'Images'

Characters: 5

Two women — Reader

Two men

Structure: Each stanza is interpreted by a different player. Player enters,mimes for ten – fifteen seconds, then freezes in mime posture as Narrator reads. Each player remains onstage as others enter, creating a tableau effect for the final stanza. All props are imaginary except for chair. ('gooseberry pie' poem on p. 170.)

Characterisation suggestions

Stanza 1: Woman enters, walking heavily as if her body is too massive to move. She carries a tray of food and drink, which she places on a table beside her chair. Moving forward to turn on the television, she then settles into an evening of serious, unconsciously repulsive, eating.

Stanza 2: Man enters, with springy walk, excellent posture. Does a routine of gym exercises.

Stanza 3: Woman enters, walking slowly, smiling and nodding, as if surrounded by admirers. Halts, posing with artificial smile.

Stanza 4: Country man enters, walking stiffly. He appraises land, stoops to sift soil, labours with heavy machine such as tractor or plough.

Stanza 5: All resume actions, freezing as Narrator says 'and we them'.

Transition note for Arrangement II

Dancers stay in circle, frozen in place. One by one, as stanzas occur in turn, they leave dance circle, moving forward in mime character. If there are more dancers than poem characters, they stay in same position throughout narration, repeating some of the struggle movements during Stanza 5.

Do you know?

Jodi Page Clark

If I could get through

Capo 4 (C)

Brian Howard

A9

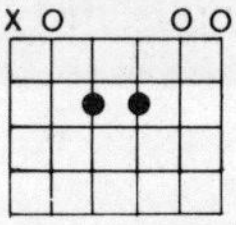

Em
(Can be played in this inversion)

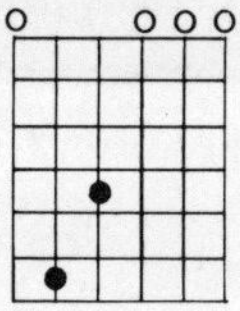

'If I could get through' Dance

by Margi Pulkingham

Presentation: Interpretative circle dance for 5 or more, including centre figure

Theme: Isolation and conflict

The central figure, trapped within the circle, is menaced by the other dancers. This figure tries to escape but attempts are futile, frustrated by those encircling him. As dance continues, the harassed figure becomes increasingly desperate, the other dancers increasingly rigid and malevolent. Dance movements are thrusting and angular, mechanical rather than graceful.

Structure: Five steps, each in a group of eight beats

Steps can be arranged in any order; a suggestion is listed below. Alternatively, work out your own dance, using theme and music or suggested steps as a springboard.

Circle dancers move clockwise, hands held through entire dance.

Central figure moves in opposition to circle dancers. When they're going clockwise, central figure moves counter-clockwise, confused and searching for a way out. Escape attempts are always frustrated by the structure: if central figure stoops, trying to get out between two dancers, it's one beat before the dancers thrust their legs, blocking the opening. Similarly, when central figure appears to consider thrusting body over the held hands, again it's too late: the way is blocked when the circle dancers raise their arms.

Suggested pattern

Each step takes eight beats, or two bars of music. Following a four beat introduction, the first step begins immediately.

Repeat this pattern as many times as song is repeated:

Steps: Circle, Guard, Rock, Intimidation
Circle, Guard, Rock, Intimidation

For final stanza:

Steps: Circle (counter-clockwise)
Circle
Guard, Rock, Intimidation, Attack (with transition)
Guard, Rock, Intimidation, Attack

'If I could get through' Dance Steps

	BEAT	MOVEMENT
Circle Step		
	1–8	Beginning on R, dancers walk around circle eight steps, one step per beat.
Guard Step		
	1–4	Beginning on R, dancers walk four steps
	5	Stop, drawing R foot up to L knee
	6	Hold position
	7	Swing R leg to side, extending it with toe pointed. L leg is bent slightly at knee; overall position is semi-lunge.
	8	Hold position
Rock Step		
	1–4	Beginning on R, dancers walk four steps
	5–6	Turning to face centre, swinging R leg slightly and planting R foot with finality. Hold.
	7	Rock to R, lifting L foot slightly
	8	Settle weight, planting L foot solidly. Feet should be shoulder-width apart.

	BEAT	MOVEMENT
Intimidation Step		
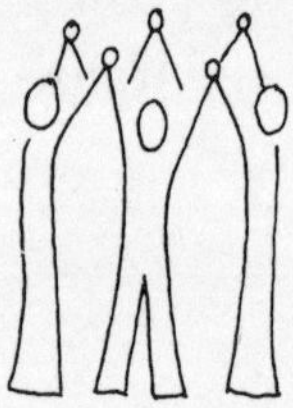	½–2	Raise held hands above heads
	3–4	Lower hands to shoulder level
	5–6	Thrust held hands down and back, simultaneously bending forward at waist, keeping back straight and head rigid, eyes staring at figure.
	7–8	Straighten to upright, return hands to waist level.
Attack Step		
	½–2	Thrust hands forward at waist level, clenched fists pointing into circle.
 by beat 8	3–8	With heads rigid and eyes staring directly at figure, move forward into centre, 'aiming' for figure. As circumference diminishes, raise arms until over heads, trapping figure still further and seeming to smother figure with sheer body weight.

Transition: Circle, Guard or Rock Steps can begin from this position: dancers merely widen circle while walking clockwise during first four beats.

For final stanza: Lead figure raises arms up, flailing, then sinks to floor, disappearing from sight.

Tableaux of Faith

by Martha Keys Barker and Patricia Beall

Presentation style: The tableaux depict biblical events through a variety of media. The entire presentation is an ideal project for workshop groups in music, choral reading, drama, and dance. Each group prepares one tableau. In addition, the Choral Reading Group also learns the narrative choruses which weave the sections together. Preparation for the production may be completed in a weekend of intensive workshops; alternatively, it may be rehearsed as a long-term project. Since each workshop prepares a different tableau, the production information for each group is given separately, following the script of the entire presentation.

Characters: 37 or more for the entire production, if no parts are duplicated. In groups with fewer participants, the same group may prepare both dance and drama.

Narrator	Drama Group: 12 or more
Narrative Chorus: 8 or more	Dance Group: 6 or more
Music Group: At least 10	

Note: If rehearsal time permits, the same person can play the part of the Narrator for the production and the Storyteller for the Drama Group.

Staging: The Choral Reading Group should be placed on one side of the playing area. The Narrator is part of this group. The Music Group should be placed on the opposite side. The centre playing area should be open for the Drama and Dance Groups.

Tableaux of Faith

CHORUS: The Lord spoke to Abraham,
The Lord spoke to Abraham,
The Lord spoke to Abraham,
He said, 'Come and go out of this land.
Through you I'll make a mighty nation
To bless and save the whole creation.'

NARRATOR: God said, 'Abraham, if you put your faith in me,
More than the stars will your descendants be!
More than the sands washed by the seas:
The salvation of all nations will come from these!'

SONG: *Abraham, father of the faithful*

CHORUS: At first we thought, 'How can this be!
Such a promise is an impossibility!'
But he whose word formed sea and land
Had spoken again, given the command.
Abraham believed, and now we see
That he who promised is faithful –
For the son came.

NARRATOR: The first born one, the first born son,
The first fruit of many to come.
But the salvation of nations –
How could that be?
The people of Israel had a lot to learn:
Just freed from slavery they weren't quick to turn
From rebellious ways. A wilful lot, a stubborn band.
Yet God wanted to give them the Promised Land.
It would be a home of their own, a land of peace.
They could live freely and worship as they pleased.
But the place where God took them was occupied
By fierce pagan people, filled with pride.
'Don't be afraid,' they heard God say,
'I'll fight your battles if you'll just obey!'
Then God empowered a faithful man
To lead his people, to fulfil his plan.

CHORUS: To Joshua the Lord did call,
To Joshua the Lord did call,
To Joshua the Lord did call.
He said, 'I will cause these walls to fall.
Just march around old Jericho town.
When the trumpet blows – the walls fall down.'

NARRATOR: People may scoff, they may shout
But God's word always wins out!
Marching in circles is odd, it's true,
And perhaps God's people felt like fools.
But that's what he'd told them they should do,
And when God speaks, his word rules!

DRAMA: *Triumph at Jericho*

CHORUS: At first we thought, 'How can this be!
That's no way to conquer a city!'
But he whose word divided the sea
Had spoken again, said, 'This shall be.'
Joshua believed, and now we see
That he who promised is faithful –
For the victory came.

NARRATOR: But the people of Israel had a lot to learn!
They were so quick to turn
Back to their ways of idolatry.
This proud people would not believe
Even if one returned from the dead.

READING: *I am the Resurrection (printed directly below)*

CHORUS: Lazarus, whom you love, is ill.
Lazarus, whom you love, is ill.
Lazarus, whom you love, is ill.
You can heal him if you will.
'Come quickly, Lord,' his sisters cried,
'Or our brother will surely die.'

NARRATOR: But Jesus didn't go in time
While Lazarus was still alive.
They'd put the dead man in his grave
Four days before Jesus came.

MARTHA: Jesus, Jesus,
If you had been here,
My brother would not have died.

JESUS: Martha, I tell you, your brother will rise.
In him God will be glorified.

MARTHA: Ah, yes, I know that he will rise
when death, our enemy, dies
on the last day.
Or in the past day,
before death came,
then I believed your life would reign.
In the future, or in the past,
your promise may be true.
But my present holds death, stone and cold,
it cannot hold your promise, too.

JESUS: Martha, Martha,
I am the resurrection.
I am the life.
He who believes in me,
even though he dies,
he will live.
And whoever lives and believes in me
will never die.

If you believe, you will see God's glory –
not only in the last day, or the past day –
but in the morning of today.
On the wings of faith,
you will see God's promise rise.

CHORUS: At first we thought, 'How can this be!
Life from death is a mystery!'
But he whose word became human life
Had spoken again, said, 'This is he.'
Jesus believed, and now we see
That he who promised is faithful –
For life came.

NARRATOR: 'The Christ Jesus proclaimed among you . . .
Was never Yes and No: with him it was always Yes.
All the promises of God are fulfilled in him.'

He is not bound in yesterday's wishes,
Not fettered by vague hopes of someday,
His resurrection is in the shock of now!
He stands definitely at the intersection
Of history and eternity.
He is the eternal word
Spoken in a human voice
Proclaiming Yes to all God's promises.

CHORUS: Yes! The promise will come to you.
Yes! The promise will come to you.
Yes! The promise will come to you.

Gather together and don't leave,
God's own life you will receive!

NARRATOR: The day of Pentecost came at last
God's long spoken word came to pass.
In wind and flame the promise came:

God's people were filled to overflowing,
They spoke in words beyond their knowing!
People may laugh, people may scorn
But in such foolishness the church was born!

SONG: *He will fill your hearts today*

CHORUS: We thought, 'How can this be!
They've had too much wine, if you ask me!'
But he whose word holds all things
Had spoken again, said, 'My power receive.'
The disciples believed, and now we see
That he who promised is faithful –
For the Spirit came.

NARRATOR: The promise given, the word received:
Now we are the ones who believe.
We join the family first begun
So long ago in Jerusalem.
We are God's new creation,
Gathered together from every nation.
To us the promise he gives,
In us the Spirit lives.
'Once no people, now we are God's people,
Proclaiming his marvellous light.'

SONG with DANCE: *Once no people*
or
God has spoken

MUSIC GROUP

Objective: To prepare the music for 'Abraham, father of the faithful', 'He will fill your hearts today', *Sound of Living Waters*, 131, and either 'Once no people', *Fresh Sounds*, 68, or 'God has spoken', *Sound of Living Waters*, 95. Time should be allowed to rehearse with the Dance Group.

Abraham, father of the faithful

This song may simply be sung by the group, or it may be dramatised by dividing the verses among various solo voices. If the song is dramatised, the following information applies.

Characters: 8 or more

Narrative Chorus:	Singers, snapping fingers during choruses
Solo Narrator:	Person with ability to 'song-talk' much of this part in dialect
Abraham:	Male soloist
Isaac:	Children's group or five light voices

Song structure: Choruses are sung between each verse except 6 and 7.

Opening chorus
Verses 1,2: Narrative Chorus
Verse 3: Solo Narrator
Verse 4: Narrative Chorus
Verse 5: Solo Narrator
Verse 6: Abraham
Verse 7: Isaac
Verse 8: Abraham
Verse 9: Solo Narrator
Verse 10: Narrative Chorus

Abraham, father of the faithful

Betty Pulkingham

Finger snapping (off-beat) is suggested on the refrain only.

Verses 1-4
Bm(Am)
1. Thank him for a - go-in' to a land so far a -
2. Thank him for a - leav-in' all the comforts of home be -
3. (spoken) An old man was A - bra-ham; Sa-ra was an old woman, too.
4. 'Long came lit-tle I - saac jus' like it was fore -
F♯(E)
Bm(Am)
(1) way, (♪) leav-in' home and kin-folk 'cause
(2) hind, (♪) go-in' where God told him, didn't know
(3) They did-n't have no chil-lun but God
(4) told. His pap-py was one hun-dred and his
F♯(E)
Bm(Am)
D.S.
(1) that's what he heard God say.
(2) what God had in mind.
(3) said, 'You're a gwy - en to.'
(4) mammy was ninety years old.
D.S.

Verses 5-6
Bm(Am)
5. God said, 'Take that boy of yours and offer him up to
6. A - bra - ham told I - saac, said, 'Son, come take this
F♯(E)
Bm (Am)
(5) me. He wouldn't ever have been here at all ex-cept to
(6) wood. We gonna climb up yon - der hill be-cause
F♯(E)
Bm(Am)
D.S.
(5) add to my glo - ry.'
D.S.
(6) God has said we should.'
D.S.

Verses 7-10
Bm(Am)
7. (Isaac) 'Fa - ther, dear fa-ther, there's something I don't un - der-
8. (Abraham) 'O, my son, a lamb God will pro-
9. Out of hea-ven an an - gel spoke. A-bra-ham gave a
10. Behind him was a thick - et, in it a lit - tle
F#(E)
Bm(Am)
(7) stand. Here is the fire and here is the wood, but
(8) vide.' Then he took his knife in his hand. On the
(9) start. 'You don't have to kill your son for God
(10) ram. Oh, what a beau-ti-ful of - fer - ing God pro-
F#(E)
Bm(Am)
(7) where is the lit - tle lamb?' (to vs. 8)
(8) altar little Isaac lay tied. (to vs. 9)
D.S.
(9) sees what's in your heart.'
(10) vi - ded for A - bra - ham.
to final refrain

Descant
Bm(Am)
F♯(E)
A - - - bra - ham, he be-lieved God
A - bra-ham, fa - - ther of the faith-ful, he be-lieved God
Bm(Am)
spoke to him. A - - bra - ham:
spoke to him. A - bra-ham, fa - - ther of the faith-ful:
F♯(E)
Bm(Am)
some day we're a - gonna' thank him.
some day we're a - gonna' thank him.
FINE

READING GROUP

Objective: To learn the dramatic reading, 'I am the Resurrection' and the narrative reading choruses which occur throughout the production.

I am the Resurrection

Characters: 2
Martha
Jesus
Note: Narrative Chorus and Narrator are the same as in complete production.
Script: Printed on pp. 293–94.

Narrative Choruses

Presentation style: The Chorus sections are read with a rhythmic swing to a steady beat from wood sticks or finger snaps (Tempo: ♩ = 60). The columns show where the beats fall. Words written across the line are syncopated. Rests are only approximate in duration. Set rhythm of each chorus with four clicks or snaps before speaking part begins.

Note: If a group prefers to present the reading without the rhythmic arrangement, the repetition of the first line of the choruses should be eliminated.

Wood sticks or fingersnaps = *

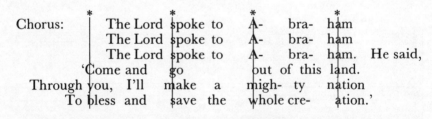

Chorus: The Lord spoke to A- bra- ham
The Lord spoke to A- bra- ham
The Lord spoke to A- bra- ham. He said,
'Come and go out of this land.
Through you, I'll make a migh- ty nation
To bless and save the whole cre- ation.'

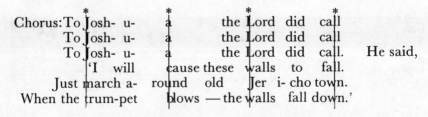

Chorus: To Josh- u- a the Lord did call
To Josh- u- a the Lord did call
To Josh- u- a the Lord did call. He said,
'I will cause these walls to fall.
Just march a- round old Jer i- cho town.
When the trum-pet blows — the walls fall down.'

Chorus: —Lazarus whom you love is ill.
(softly and Lazarus whom you love is ill.
lyrically) Lazarus whom you love is ill.
You can heal him if you will. 'Come
Quickly Lord,' his sisters cried,
'Or our brother will surely die.'

Chorus: Yes! The promise will come to you
Yes! The promise will come to you
Yes! The promise will come to you
Gather together and don't leave
God's own life you will re- ceive.

DRAMA GROUP

Objective: To prepare drama of the battle of Jericho, using either 'The Triumph of Jericho', printed below, or Arch Book *The Walls Came Tumbling Down.*

Triumph at Jericho

(based on Joshua 6:1–12)

by Patricia Beall

The story line for this drama is taken particularly from Joshua 6:8–16, 20. To avoid extending the larger presentation, the action for this drama begins on the imaginary fifth day of the Israelites' march.

Characters: 12 or more

Storyteller	Israelites: 7 or 8
Joshua	Jericho soldiers: 3 or 4

Note: Number of Israelites and soldiers can be expanded

Props: Cardboard boxes painted as wall of Jericho, at least three and one-half feet in height and five feet in length.

Costumes: Sashes, tied in two different ways to indicate which 'side' players represent. More elaborate costuming, i.e., robes, head-dresses, if desired.

Staging: Jericho's wall located L; Israelite's camp R.
Suggestions for collapsing walls:

In limited playing area: One of the Jericho soldiers, from position behind wall, shoves boxes forward and up.
In large playing area: Attach heavy twine or wire to several of the boxes. An off-stage, unseen person pulls strings at the appropriate time, causing wall to collapse 'miraculously'.

Placement: Storyteller to R and L of playing area; Joshua and Israelites sleeping in camp; Jericho soldiers behind Jericho's wall, guarding it.

Triumph at Jericho

(*Enter all players. STORYTELLER's opening lines establish scene.*)

STORYTELLER: (*looking at playing area, then audience*) It's Joshua, and the children of Israel! Asleep! What are they doing here?

JOSHUA: (*rising, yawning, stretching*) Wake up, men! This is the fifth day! Around the town of Jericho we go! (*ISRAELITES rise, stretch, etc., then fall into line behind JOSHUA, who leads them in a full circle around the walls and SOLDIERS of Jericho. This time, and each successive time, the SOLDIERS make derogatory comments: 'It's those silly Jews again! Marching 'round our town!' 'Tea break, lads!' 'Will you have a game of cards, then?' 'At ease, men!' 'Away, home!' etc. JOSHUA and ISRAELITES return to their camp, where they sleep again.*)

STORYTELLER: And now they've gone back to their camp! They said it was the fifth time they'd marched around that town! They must be daft, acting like that! What are they on about?

JOSHUA: (*rising, etc. as before*) All right, men! Up! This is the sixth day! (*same action as before*)

STORYTELLER: Right! And now they've stopped again! Well, I think I've figured them out. Every day they get up and march <u>once</u> around the town. They'll probably carry on for ever! Tomorrow it'll be the same: once around the town, then they'll settle down!

JOSHUA: (*rising as before*) Wake up, men! This is the most important day! Today the Lord will give us this city! Follow me carefully! And watch carefully for the signals. When I raise one arm, we'll blow the trumpets; and when I raise both arms, we'll give the shout! (*They march round the town. After completing one circuit, JOSHUA cries out 'ONE!' From this point on, whenever he completes a circuit, JOSHUA leads all, ISRAELITES, STORYTELLER, audience, in the count. The ISRAELITES complete seven circuits, to the growing uneasiness of the JERICHO SOLDIERS. Their taunts have continued: 'Getting dizzy, now!', but begin to ring hollow as their bafflement increases. After the seventh time around, JOSHUA halts, cries 'All right,men!' and raises one arm. All the ISRAELITES, making trumpets by cupping their hands round their mouth, 'blow' vigorously: 'DOO DOO DOO DOOT DOO DOO!' Then JOSHUA raises both arms, and all shout 'Ho!' The walls collapse; the JERICHO SOLDIERS desert their posts: JOSHUA, the ISRAELITES, and the audience all cheer mightily! During this cheer of triumph, and the applause that usually accompanies the success of the ISRAELITES, the players exit, clearing away the redundant wall as they go.*)

DANCE GROUP

Objective: To learn the dance to either 'Once no people', or 'God has spoken'. If time permits, the group may also wish to develop a dance to 'He will fill your hearts today' illustrating the Pentecost narrative.

Full dance instructions for 'Once no people' are found on p. 260. Those for 'God has spoken' are found on p. 253.

Time should be allowed to rehearse the dance or dances with the Music Group.

'Did you make that song up?' said Rabbit to Pooh.

'Well, I sort of made it up,' said Pooh. 'It isn't Brain,' he went on humbly, 'because You Know Why, Rabbit; but it comes to me sometimes.'

'Ah!' said Rabbit, who never let things come to him, but always went and fetched them.

A. A. Milne
from 'Rabbit has a Busy Day'
The House at Pooh Corner

CHAPTER 15

Uncovering the Word

Stirring Up Creativity

Creativity in the arts is often thought to be a mysterious quality which 'comes to one sometimes'. Indeed, anyone who has engaged in creative pursuits will attest to the difficulty of simply sitting down and writing a poem, composing a song, painting a picture on demand. One often does need an inspiration. At the same time, without exactly 'going out and fetching it', we have discovered several ways in which creativity can be stimulated and released.

In Chapter 3 we've outlined some basic principles to encourage creativity; in Chapter 17 we consider the leadership and structures which facilitate fruitful experiment. In this section we share specific practical suggestions for stirring up the dormant creativity of any group.

Break out of old roles

As Fisherfolk we travelled in small teams. The requirements of a particular situation would often challenge us to new ventures. A guitarist would be needed to take a lead role in a drama, a dancer would be the only person available to lead an art workshop. At first we were concerned about our lack of expertise, then we began to see the positive results of these challenges. We found that a novice often brought a refreshing perspective; we also discovered abilities we didn't know we possessed. Rather than being limited to roles – Max the musician, Ruth the artist, David the singer – we had our own expectations broadened and our potential drawn forth.

From these experiences we learned the importance of experimentation and exploration in encouraging creativity. Thus we advise others, as they employ the arts, to think of ways to challenge individuals beyond their accomplishments. Don't just rely on the same group of five young people to do all the drama. Perhaps the woman who writes so well for the parish newsletter would love to try her hand at producing a play for the Christmas party, if anyone thought to ask her. One of the sidesmen might be delighted to participate in a choral reading group. Also, leaders in one area will gain a new perspective by occasional involvement as a participant in other areas. The organist may be refreshed by joining in a dance workshop, the youth leader might unearth useful gifts through involvement in a song-writing session.

Combine different perspectives

When considering persons for teaching or worship planning, we often limit ourselves to those who are verbally adept. However, persons who tend to think visually have an invaluable contribution to make. A church may find it a useful exercise to ask a small group to carefully assess members' potential in the visual/illustrational area. They will find promise in unlikely places; the engineer who doesn't think of himself as artistic may have a facility for diagrams and illustrations to make complicated ideas clear, or the teenager who always dramatises her conversation may channel her dramatic ability to enhance teachings. Combine persons with visual/illustrational abilities with those with verbal skill in planning groups for teaching and worship.

- Preparation for teaching
  Include at least one person who can logically think through the progression of a teaching and one who is able to provide illustrations and dramatic ideas. Though one person sometimes does think in both these ways, the combination of two or more persons often strikes the spark that ignites a dynamic teaching.

- Preparation for worship
  Include persons from the various artistic fields. Given a particular theme and scriptures, a diversified group will think of many possible ways to develop a service. One person's ideas will elicit ideas from others. A dancer's idea for interpretative movement to a scripture passage, for instance, may prompt a musician to improvise an accompaniment.

Create opportunities to develop material

Which assignment would you find easier to fulfil?

1) Write a story about anything.

2) Write a story of 2,000 words about two boys, a deserted farmhouse and a fast, black horse.

Probably most of us would find it easier to fulfil the second assignment. The presence of some specifics provides a framework on which to hang our ideas, a seed for creativity.

We found this principle to hold true in our travel as we encountered many new situations with particular limitations: create a drama for a coffee-bar situation with a stage measuring eight feet by three feet; work out a dance for an entrance procession in a cathedral; write a story for four-to-six year olds about God's protection. Such specific needs were a constant challenge to our imagination, and creativity flowed freely to meet the challenges.

If such specific needs or demands are not in evidence, devise opportunities that require the development of new material:

– Projects

a. Give a small group the task of creating a dramatic illustration for a monthly Sunday sermon, Sunday school lesson or youth programme. Having a regular requirement will give an impetus to formulate ideas and will enable the group to develop a rhythm of preparation.

b. Give several groups the assignment of designing a presentation which develops a particular theme and uses a combination of three media. For example:

Group 1: theme – creation
media – music/dance/poetry

Group 2: theme – Christ's ministry to outcasts
media – drama/readings/graphic/illustration

Group 3: theme – forgiveness
media – music/mime/choral speaking

Give each group a month or six weeks to work out their presentations. Share with the entire fellowship at a special evening or incorporate into worship services.

– Special contests

Sponsor a contest for a specific type of material: children's stories, youth dramas, songs for Sunday worship. Or, the contest could solicit various contributions on a particular subject, such as material for Easter worship, for a conference on prayer, for a study group on John's gospel. At the conclusion of the contest provide an opportunity for prize-giving and for sharing the new materials.

– Special occasions

Use special occasions such as Christmas, Pentecost, harvest, as a time for organising special entertainment and creating new material. Or, plan your own special events:

a. Talent show: Ask several people or groups to prepare contributions.

b. Pantomime or humorous play: Ask one person or a small group to write and produce. Many others can be involved in props, costuming, scenery, if desired.

c. Folk evening: Arrange a time for casual, low-key sharing of songs, poetry, readings, stories. Include both humorous and serious contributions. (See Chapter 7, p. 112.)

d. Family festival: Ask each family to bring something to share: a song, a story, drawing or crafts, family heirlooms, a dance, home movies.

– Caring and outreach
Some fellowships have programmes geared to particular needs within the church or local community, such as preschools, daycare centres, senior citizens' clubs, service organisations, youth clubs. Entertainments or materials may be developed for these specialised groups. Occasionally a church or fellowship may be looking for ways to become more involved in such activities: using the folk arts may give the encouragement or direction needed.

Engage in brainstorm sessions

The constant demands of regular instruction, Christian education, sermons, often press us into ruts. Like Pooh, we're so busy bumping down the stairs on our head that we don't have time to stop and think of another way to do things. Periodically we need a 'spring cleaning' session, where we open all the windows and let in the fresh air of new possibilities. Some examples:

– Christian education teachers
Discuss needs of each age group. Consider new ways of presenting ideas. Don't be limited by considering practicality of suggestions at this point: think as broadly and as far as your imagination will take you. Don't attempt to make decisions, but appoint small teams to look into implementing at least two suggestions.

– Worship group
Gather together people representing various aspects of the church's life: children, youth, older persons, outreach. Brain-

storm about possibilities for enhancing Sunday morning worship and instruction. Explore new ways of communicating and teaching. Set aside small groups, of just two or three people, to pursue several suggestions.

Develop on-going resource groups

The development of creative resources shouldn't be left to just the ordained person. Groups which meet regularly can serve as a fertile ground for the growth of new expressions and communicating techniques.

– Creative resources study group
The group would study books on communication and creative expression. It should be a representative cross-section of the church. The study would be a basis for initiating changes in approach to sermons and Christian education.

– Workshop groups
Groups meeting weekly or bi-weekly to experiment in the arts. They follow a regular discipline of exercise, working on material, creating new material. (See Chapter 17, Structure I.)

Offer discovery sessions

Even if creative groups are formed, and various opportunities for creativity presented, some people will respond, 'I'm not creative . . .' 'I couldn't possibly do dance or drama, I'll stay home with the children.' It's important, therefore, to occasionally structure activities which will woo even the most hesitant. Emphasise that the session requires no previous experience, explain that it is especially designed to discover and bring out hidden abilities.

One excellent resource in a discovery session is the cinquain poetic form included in both the Writing and Graphics Workshops. The simple poetic structure enables anyone to write a poem. The results are often striking and produce a response of surprised satisfaction from the 'non-writer': 'I can't believe I actually wrote a poem . . . and I like it!' Such positive experience spurs one on to further exploration. Also, the cinquain itself can form a basis for other projects: a banner, a mime, a song or a more developed poem.

Workshop Structure I, applied in any area, is a good one for discovery sessions. It gently leads participants from exercises, to following simple instructions, to creating material. Each practical section in this book contains workshop structures which are effective in these sessions.

Share initially in house groups

'I'd like to share my poetry, but I don't think I could do it in church in front of all those people.'

'I have a new song, but I'm a bit nervous about it. I don't know if it's really a song for worship. If there were a smaller group, I could try it out and see what people think.'

It is rather daunting to think about sharing one's personal feelings as expressed in a song or poem in a large group, particularly if the group includes unfamiliar people. So, much good poetry stays in notebooks in bottom drawers, and many fine songs are never heard. Creativity, however, may be encouraged to come into the open in the context of smaller groups, like a house group which meets regularly. The more intimate and welcoming house group atmosphere draws out the timid and offers affirmation.

At times we are reticent to share things we've composed because they express doubt, fear or conflict, whereas we feel we *should* express only faith, hope and love. Sharing such expressions in a small group provides an arena for others to respond, to relate their similar feelings, to discuss how the Lord helped them in comparable experiences. The poem 'Jesus, keep me tender', p. 157 was originally written as a personal expression of emptiness. When it was shared in a group it became a stimuli for a discussion about the importance of fellowship. People who are becoming more familiar with each other through prayer, Bible study and fellowship find that sharing such expressions is another means of forming bonds between them.

Small groups can draw out creativity which may be useful in the worship or teaching of the larger fellowship. A small group is usually more capable of assessing the value of original material than the one for whom it is a personal expression. If persons in the group see the potential of a song, for instance, they may ask the composer to share it in a worship service. And the composer, encouraged by a warm reception in the smaller group, may then feel able to share in the larger context. In this way, the small groups enrich the worship life of the church as a whole.

Encourage children's creativity

Creativity in children flourishes in a comfortable, non-pressured family atmosphere. Barriers of self-consciousness and fear are minimised in low-key gatherings where children and adults are performing for each other, rather than children performing on their own. Particularly valuable in this connection are times of music sharing in which both children and adults who are studying (or have studied) musical instruments or voice entertain each other. In this context children gain performance experience in an accepting environment. They also see adults performing and perhaps making mistakes. In this environment adults who have had difficult experiences in performances also have their fear of failure diminished. Both adults and children experience the arts as a normal and enjoyable part of life rather than an event permeated by competition and fear of making mistakes.

In summary, we see that creativity comes where she is invited and made to feel at home. Creating opportunities which call forth undiscovered potential, constantly challenging ourselves and others in new areas, thinking widely and deeply about our needs, and setting a receptive atmosphere, all summon creativity to come and make her home with us.

All of us are artists. For all of us perceive; all of us enter into some kind of relationship to that which we perceive; and all of us tend to express to some extent at least our reactions to our experiences and relationships. Furthermore all of us make our expressions in different ways. No two people would describe a house, a view, a cow, a person, an event, God, in just the same manner. Therefore we are all creative.

Richard H. Ritter
from *The Arts of the Church*

Chapter 16

The Word Within

Writing Your Own Materials

> What I am commanding you today is not too difficult for you or beyond your reach. It is not up in heaven, so that you have to ask, 'Who will ascend into heaven to get it and proclaim it to us so that we may obey it?' Nor is it beyond the sea, so that you have to ask, 'Who will cross the sea to get it and proclaim it to us so that we may obey it?' No, the word is very near you; it is in your mouth and in your heart so that you may obey it.
>
> Deuteronomy 30:11–14 NIV

As we have stressed, a primary aspect of Fisherfolk ministry is encouraging individuals to believe that God's word is indeed 'in *your* mouth and in *your* heart'. In our experience communicating God's word is not solely the responsibility of the trained theologian or the ordained minister. Every Christian has some experience and understanding of God's love. Therefore we are eager to motivate individuals to share their experience and to articulate their understanding through writing their own materials.

In this chapter we consider ways to stimulate original writing and to encourage the creation of worship and teaching materials which reflect the life of a local group. We direct aspiring writers to three primary sources of inspiration: their own thoughts, observations and prayers, the scriptures, their church or group's need for material.

Prayers from life

We are creatures of dialogue. Throughout the day we constantly think in dialogue. We address statements and questions to an 'other' even when no-one else is present 'Look at that! . . . My, it's cold today . . . I wonder where I put that book . . . Doesn't he look well?' We pose questions, make observations . . . but to whom? Directing our inner conversation to the Lord is a basic form of prayer. This dialogue may seem trivial, but often through seemingly insignificant thoughts the Lord speaks to us. The prophecies of Jeremiah were frequently stimulated by his observations of common objects: the branch of an almond tree, a boiling pot, the work of a potter. Michel Quoist in *Prayers* begins his dialogues with God with careful observations of the objects, people and events that he encounters daily: green blackboards, a wire fence, a football game, his friend. For him everyday things are signs that point to God:

> The Father has put us into the world, not to walk through it with lowered eyes, but to search for him through things, events, people . . . We must learn to be still before him and talk over our lives fully with him – like a child who has been away for a while and returns to tell his father in detail of all that has happened. Some of our prayers describe this intimate sharing with our Father; they begin with an object, a person, an event, and throw the light of faith on some part of our everyday life.[1]

Quoist takes the simple experiences of life and describes them sharply and accurately. Reading his descriptions, one is able to see what he sees, to feel what he feels. These clear observations lead to fresh insight, to awareness of a fresh word from the Lord. One's response to these prayers is often a flash of recognition: 'I think like that – but I never think to write it down. I never think of it as prayer.' Capturing these everyday dialogues with our heavenly Father by writing them down may assist us in becoming aware of the many ways he does speak to us. The following suggestions are designed to develop the habit of recording these dialogues which may serve as resource for various kinds of writing:

1. Begin a writing journal. Establish a discipline of recording at least one event or observation every day or every other day. Concentrate on describing the actual situation vividly and accurately. Note your own responses to it.

2. In your journal, regularly record dialogues between your thoughts/feelings and the Lord. Ask the Lord to speak to you, and write what you feel he is saying. These dialogues do not need to be resolved. The Lord may simply be saying, 'Wait' or 'Listen', or 'I understand'.

   Example: 'Jesus, keep me tender', p. 157, 'leaping', p. 156, a prayer, p. 158.

3. Observe an object, person, or event carefully. Write your observations clearly. Relate them to some aspect of the Lord's life.

   Example: 'Lord of the Gentle Hands', p. 162
   This poem is a schoolteacher's observation of hands which led to a reflection on the Lord's hands, a sign of his love.

Writing from Scripture

As developed in Chapter 4, the Bible offers a fertile ground for writing inspiration. Considering persons in scripture and their relationship to God, we understand more deeply our own relationship to him, and his to us. The following ideas for writing original material based on biblical accounts provide excellent opportunity to study scripture, to 'get inside' scriptural characters and events. The results of these exercises may be effectively used in Bible studies, in teaching, and with scripture reading in worship.

1. Character Development

   Select one biblical character. Read all passages referring to him or her. From the passages write down any information concerning the character's physical, emotional, mental characteristics. If the scriptures do not give this information, use your imagination to complete the character. Refer to Building Characterisation Exercises, p. 374. Choose one incident from this person's life which reveals an important facet of his character, or his relationship to God. Write this incident from the character's point-of-view, incorporating as much information about the character as possible.

   Example: 'The Woman at the Well', p. 177, 'David Danced', p. 174.

   Variation: Develop a character as in exercise 1. Write an account of his or her experience and relate it to an experience in your own life. Show parallels between their experience and your own.

   Example: 'As Peter', p. 155.

2. You Are There

   a. Select a biblical account with several characters.
   Suggestions: The feeding of the five thousand (Matthew 14:15–21)
   The woman who washed Jesus's feet (Luke 7:36–50)
   The day of Pentecost (Acts 2:1–13)

   Example: We selected the parable of workers in the vineyard (Matthew 20:1–16) and traced it through each step.

   b. Read the account once. Select one character or a by-stander who witnessed the event. Read the account again, thinking of this character's sensory perceptions during the event. *Note*: If a group is studying the passage together, each may select a different character.

   c. List these perceptions under the appropriate headings.

   Example: Perceptions from the point-of-view of Simon, a worker hired in the middle of the day.

   Sound: haggle of market place, women's shrill voices bargaining, merchants' shouts, children's laughter and crying, buzz of flies around decaying fruit

   Sight: colourful array of stalls, baskets of fruit, grains, bread, jostling crowds in multi-coloured garments, children's thin brown bodies darting amongst the stalls

   Taste: dryness of dust and grit in mouth, sweet taste of water, foul taste of hunger

   Smell: closeness of warm bodies, sweat, animal smells, pungent overripe fruit, fragrance of spices

   Touch: heat of the sun, warmth of earth on feet, roughness of the wooden stalls

   d. Write a cinquain using these perceptions (see p. 386 for cinquain form). Don't try to interpret the scene, just describe it, using the most significant information from your list.

Example: Market place
bustling, haggling, sweating
noisily, uncomfortably
hides
idleness

e. Consider your character carefully. Write answers to these questions: What are his/her feelings? What associations does he/she have with the event? What are other's responses to the character?

Example:

Feelings: anxiety about not having work, worry about family, uneasiness at women's gossip, boredom, dullness

Associations: other years with bad crops and little work, impoverished childhood

Others' responses: women – criticising me for not working
children – too absorbed in games to notice me, carefree
men – some also without work, bored, on edge
working men – condescending

f. Write a cinquain describing this person's situation from his/her point-of-view.

Example: Simon
sweltering, anxious, unwelcome
hopelessly, uselessly
dreads
night

g. Write a paragraph or two describing the incident from the character's perspective, using information from perceptions list.

Example:
The heat is unbearable. All day standing in the market place again, watching the rough women haggle, watching them watch me as they gossip: 'Why isn't Simon working again?' Their quick tongues slash me to pieces. And here I stand, not really thinking I'll find work, but unable to go home and face my Anna another day with no wages, and the children staring at me with

vacant eyes and holding their empty stomachs. How long will I be idle, nothing to do but watch the children darting in and out amongst the stalls, playing their games while their mothers bargain? Laughing, crying, shouting, they knock over the fruit baskets. The juice oozes in sticky pools over the street and the flies feast. The buzz of flies and the buzz in my head are slurred together by the merciless heat. But a voice slices through the dullness. What's he saying? It's the vineyard owner! He's calling for workers! 'Wait, here I am! I'm coming!' . . .

h. If a group is working together on this exercise, share poems/paragraphs with each other. You may wish to incorporate the paragraphs in worship or teaching as a multi-faceted account of the event.

3. Change the Context

Re-tell a scriptural story or parable in a contemporary context. Read the biblical account thoroughly and research any particulars helpful to understanding the story in its original context: the historical setting, the social customs, the meaning of key words.

Example: Study the story of the woman at the well (John 4:1–42). Find the answers to the questions raised by the story: What was the relationship between the Jews and the Samaritans? How did their views on worship differ? What was the woman's position in her society? Why were Jesus's disciples surprised that he talked with her? After answering these questions, think of a comparable social situation in a contemporary setting. Re-tell the story in this context.

4. Experiment with Forms

a. Cinquains (see p. 386)

Read a biblical story or passage. Write a cinquain in response to passage. This is particularly useful in teaching children to draw out the important points in a story. (*Note:* for another example of children's poetry, see p. 176)

Example: After studying Mark 1:16–34 a group of 9–11 year olds wrote the following cinquains:

Jesus
strong, steadfast, willing
helpfully, patiently
heals
others

Jesus
bold, miracle-maker
early, faithfully, freely
calls
Saviour

An adult workshop group in Cowley, Oxfordshire wrote these in response to Luke 1:26–38:

Message
shocking
real
strong
searingly
tenderly
telling
word

God
creating
cleansing
lovingly
ceaselessly
irresistibly
gives
power

b. Haiku

The three-line, seventeen-syllable Japanese form may be arranged in a myriad of ways. In the most common, the first line has five syllables, the second has seven syllables and the third line has five. These examples demonstrate several alternatives. Haiku usually focus on nature, the beauty of creation, or subtleties of relationships. They may also be used to capture the essential detail of scriptural passages.

Example:
1) Nature/Relationships

ruffled
the dandelions broke:
seeds flew for a million seconds[2]

from the bay's bend
i can see the islands
as they curl into the sea[2]

Today, suddenly as the wind,
a butterfly
appears between us.[3]

Minuscule clenched fists
graze a squinting pigmy face.
The first hours are hardest.[3]

2) Reflections on Matthew 20

The Day

Night whispers and sighs
above the prowling of thieves.
Then the trumpet blares.[3]

Pray that it is not winter:
a day groaning
with bare branches and ice.[3]

5. Select a familiar Bible story and re-tell it in couplets. Writing in this format will challenge your understanding and your ability to maintain the integrity of the story while working within the confines of rhyme.

   Example: 'The Faithful God of Daniel', p. 194

Writing for worship

New material written specifically for worship may develop a particular theme or highlight a special occasion. Especially at the close of a conference, weekend retreat, or parish study series, a group may wish to articulate their experiences, insights, and conclusions in writing new material. Allowing time for the group to reflect and write together will help crystallise individuals' thoughts, and to unify the group. Possibilities in group writing for worship include:

1. Thematic Prayers

   Each person states two or three significant points from the discussion and teaching. Formulate these into prayers. The group may then organise the prayers under general headings: confessions, intercessions, thanksgivings. These may be structured to allow for spontaneous prayers.

   Example: 'Thy Kingdom Come', p. 163, 'Litany of Resurrection', p. 167, 'Wind of Spirit Prayers', p. 166.

2. Thanksgivings

   The group reflects and shares insights, events, relationships for which they are thankful. One person organises these into a form which can be incorporated into the worship service. Or the leader may write a specific format on a large sheet of paper. Everyone offers their thanksgivings according to the format.

   Example: 'Thanksgiving', p. 137

   a. Use this pattern: You have given us ______________.
      We offer you ____________________.

      Possible responses: You have given us your creation.
      We offer you our faithful stewardship of its resources.

      You have given us your love.
      We offer you our hearts. Fill them with love for each other.

b. With children, the leader may write the beginning of the verse to 'Thank you, Lord', SOLW 113, adding blanks to complete the line. Children fill in the blanks with their thanksgivings. Then sing the song using the children's verses.

3. Poetry

The group discusses the theme, readings and music for the service.
One person writes a poem which weaves these together.

Example: 'There Was a Man', p. 175
This poem was written by a participant in a ten-day series of workshops on the folk arts in worship. The eucharist which concluded the workshops centred on Christ's giving his life to sustain us as God gave manna to sustain the Israelites in their wanderings. The poem summarised the theme and drew out important points from the readings. Also used in this service were 'Wilderness Wanderers', p. 179, 'Thy Kingdom Come', p. 163, and 'I am the bread of life', SOLW 63.

4. Psalms

One psalm may have particular relevance to the group's experience. Arrange the psalm as a choral reading, a responsive reading or a congregational reading. Select verses which are especially meaningful or paraphrase the full psalm.

Example: 'Renewing the World', p. 146 (choral reading)
'Let Us Rejoice, Let Us be Glad', p. 137 (responsive reading)
'Psalm 51', p. 144 (paraphrased group reading)

5. Scriptural Meditation

Write a meditation based on a familiar scripture passage. Suggestions: 'The Spirit of the Lord is upon me' (Isaiah 61), 'How lovely is your dwelling-place' (Psalm 84), The Lord's Prayer, The Beatitudes (Matthew 5), 'I am the resurrection' (John 11:25). Consider each phrase or primary statement in the passage. Ask questions about them: What did these words mean to the people who first heard them? What do they mean now? How can this idea be expressed in contemporary terms? How can this point be illustrated? Write your responses to these questions. Decide on a format for the meditation. Work your thoughts into the format.

Variation: For a group meditation each person takes one phrase or idea in the passage and develops it. Combine these in a meditation format.

Example: 'I Stand and Knock', p. 141
The format for this meditation is as follows:
Reading of entire passage
Line of scripture
Questions about the meaning of the scripture/Elaboration on meaning of particular words or ideas
Silence
Entire passage is read again to conclude meditation

6. Songs

Write a) lyrics for a new song, or b) new lyrics to a familiar tune. The song may express a theme, or meet a specific need – a song to lead into a confession, a song for dancing, a song to respond to a teaching.

a. The group should have a clear understanding of the theme. Decide on a metre and rhythm for the lyrics. One person may write the theme and some ideas on a large sheet of paper, then ask group for contributions. One person arranges the ideas into stanzas.

Example: The overall theme is 'Our Understanding of the church'. Contributions from the group include: God's family, a home in which everyone feels welcome, the expression of God's love and care in the world, the body of Christ.
First stanza: God's people are gathering to build a home
That all God's children call their own.
We know his love and know we're free.
Let's gather together, to be his family.

b. New words to a familiar song
Children enjoy writing new words to songs they know. The leader writes part of a line on a large sheet of paper or blackboard, leaving blanks to indicate words or syllables necessary to complete line. Children offer their suggestions and leader fits them into the metre.

Example: New words to 'The butterfly song', SOLW 106

Leader writes this form: If I were a ____ ____ ____
(Or ___ ___ ___ ___)
I'd thank you, Lord,
for ____ ____ ____

Verses written by children at a family camp:

If I were a monkey in a tree
I'd thank you, Lord, that I could swing.

If I were a little green frog
I'd thank you, Lord, for my wet bog.

Guidelines for writing

Good writing is a combination of seeing accurately, thinking imaginatively, communicating faithfully and sparking another's imagination to see accurately. This section suggests disciplines to develop good writing habits. Grace Krag, a contributor of material to this book, shared with us guidelines which she applies to her writing and uses to encourage fledgling writers:

My eyes can't see what your eyes see.
Tell me. Let me see it, too.

My ears can't hear what your ears hear.
Tell me. Let me hear it, too.

My nose can't smell what your nose smells.
Tell me. Let me smell it, too.

My tongue can't taste what your tongue tastes.
Tell me. Let me taste it, too.

My body can't touch what your body touches.
Tell me. Let me touch it, too.

My heart can't feel what your heart feels.
Tell me. Let me feel it, too.

1. Develop a habit of observing persons, events and objects with an eye for small, sharp, dramatic detail. Use your senses, your emotions, your awareness of movement and rhythm. Write these descriptions regularly in a notebook.

2. Words are your raw material. Pay attention to them. Ask yourself about the qualities of specific words: How do they sound? Do they flow rhythmically? How do they feel on your tongue? Are they enjoyable or difficult to say? What images or associations do they bring to your mind?

3. Choose words that create a picture. Many words are too vague to communicate anything specific. Words such as 'mercy', 'truth', 'faith', 'hope', are elusive. Try to relate these intangible ideas to specific images, objects and daily experiences. When you think of mercy, does anything move? Does mercy have a colour? Describe a situation in which you experienced mercy.

4. Energetic, specific verbs create concrete pictures. Make your subjects act, hear, and see as vividly as possible. Use verbs that etch a sharp picture in your mind. For instance, rather than saying, 'The wind blew through the forest', which conveys a vague impression, say, 'Leaves shuffled across the forest floor', which presents a definite picture.

5. Visualise while you write as though you have a three-dimensional, stereophonic, technicolour film playing in your mind. Are your words clear and precise enough to create the scenario you see in your imagination?

6. Set realistic goals. Begin with a single idea and an uncomplicated format. In writing poetry, start with cinquains or haiku to focus your ideas, then expand to more complicated forms. In writing prose, set yourself a three-paragraph description of a character or scene, rather than a full story or drama. Determine a regular writing goal: one poem or one page of prose per week, or one story a month. Stick to it. Setting more ambitious goals may result in disappointment.

7. Revision or rewriting is important. Materials written in the 'flash of inspiration' usually need to be re-evaluated more critically when one is more objective. Check for unnecessary words, awkward constructions, clear and precise descriptions, grammatical errors.

The following pointers apply specifically to writing poetry:

8. Experiment with different forms. Find a book on poetic forms and practise writing in each form.

9. Experiment with spacing and format. Put one poem in several

formats and note differences. (*Note:* See format of 'leaping', p. 156)

10. Read a variety of poets and imitate their styles. Note each poet's use of rhythm and metre, imagery, format. Discover the styles that feel comfortable for you.

11. Gather impressions and observations about your friends. On birthdays or special occasions write poems for greeting cards, or as gifts in themselves.

12. Write as naturally as possible. Composing awkward sentences with inverted word order for the sake of rhyme is rarely justified. Metre is generally more important than rhyme and half-rhymes are perfectly acceptable.

13. Check carefully to see if what you've written makes sense, or if it just seems a 'poetic' way to say it. Clear communication is the purpose of writing, and obscurity is not a mark of good poetry.

Writing Exercises

1. Concentration Game

Collect an assortment of magazine pictures or photographs with people, activities, scenes. Give one picture to each small group of four or five persons. Tell each group to observe the picture for two minutes while thinking of the sensory perceptions inherent in the picture. Pictures are then taken away and each person lists his sensory perceptions. Allow about five minutes for this. Then, either stay in small groups and share lists, or re-assemble into large group. Each group shows their picture to the other groups and reads their observations. The differences within each group demonstrate the uniqueness of each person's perceptions. This exercise motivates concrete, physical observations rather than vague generalities.

2. Blindfold Exercise

Leader prepares a variety of sensory stimuli for each category:

Sound: (may be recorded) crunching leaves, bells, buzzers, rumpling paper, pouring water, snapping twigs, bird calls, screeching brakes, a flute melody

Smell: burning match, scented candle, vanilla extract, a cut lemon, vinegar, cloves, fresh coffee, perfume, incense

Touch: smooth stones, a furry toy, firm fruit, rough bark, silky fabric, soft petals, hand lotion

Taste: salty peanuts, lemon, peppermint, chocolate, hot or cold drink

(Leader keeps object hidden until Partner 1 is blindfolded.)

Divide group into partners.
Partner 1 is blindfolded. Partner 2 assists Leader who brings out half of objects in each category.
Leader plays half of the sounds. Partner 1 gives verbal response or descriptions. Partner 2 writes them down.
Partner 2 gives Partner 1 objects from other categories, one at a time. Writes down Partner 1's responses.
Partners exchange blindfolds. Leader brings out other objects.
Partner 1 gives these to Partner 2 and records his responses.
Remove blindfolds. Each person writes two cinquains or two haiku from their perception lists.

3. Colours

Leader brings several items of each colour and arranges them around the room. Ask each person to select a colour and to list sensory perceptions associated with it under appropriate headings. Also ask: How does it move? Of what does it remind you? How do you feel? Using these lists, compose a short poem or cinquain on the colour.

4. Free Association Poem

Leader writes one word on a large sheet of paper or a blackboard. Ask each person to say another word, an object, or an event which they associate with that word. Leader writes these on sheet. When everyone has contributed something, each person writes a poem on the word, drawing from the words on the sheet and adding others, if necessary.
Suggestions: tomorrow, fire, breath, delight, pain, loneliness, peace, childhood, forgiveness, family, spirit.

NOTES

1. Michel Quoist, *Prayers* (Gill and MacMillan, Dublin, 1965), pp. 17, ix.

2. by Patricia Beall. © *Celebration Services (International) Ltd., 1972, 1975.*

3. by Grace Krag. © *Celebration Services (International) Ltd., 1971, 1975.*

Part III Workshops

Groups, as distinct from meetings and committees, encourage sharing of experience, and throw emphasis upon people for their own sake . . . Groups break down, more or less, people's fear about loving and communicating. Because people find new inter-personal freedom, they begin to realise the supremacy of people over things. Because they talk about new things and reveal new anxieties they learn the values of intuition, laughter, instinct, imaginative sympathy and mutual help, while still giving reason and calculation their proper due. Because they enjoy meeting people at a new informal level they become less interested in the customary glut of material possessions or in the lonely exercise of power. They also become more critical of a world which, they increasingly perceive, does not encourage communication of the type they are enjoying. In other words, groups help people to become persons rather than remain person-machines.

Roy Stevens
from *Education and the Death of Love*

CHAPTER 17

Workshops

Leadership, Planning and Preparation, Structure

'A workshop? One of those little sheds in the back, where gardening tools are kept?!'

We've heard this question more than once! 'Workshop' has now acquired another everyday meaning: a period of time set aside for intensive work or study by a small group. Dance workshops, writing workshops, even gardening workshops have become common. Workshop groups are usually small, about ten to twenty people, and meetings are limited in time, from about one and one-half to three hours. Another characteristic is active involvement: people expect – and are expected! – to participate fully.

Workshops are sometimes one-off gatherings, the result of a special occasion: a touring mime troupe may be in the locality and offer open sessions, a choir may want to develop a particular skill more fully, such as sight-reading or listening sensitivity. A series of workshops is also frequent: a local community action group may sponsor a weekend of workshops, a church offer one meeting a week for several weeks, youth leaders arrange a special holiday programme, teachers structure an after-hours skills course. Still another type is the cumulative series, which establishes a regular time for an on-going group to explore or rehearse in a specified area, such as music or drama.

People getting to know and enjoy each other is an important part of the workshop experience. A healthy small group situation is conducive to people learning to trust each other and share openly together. Warm relationships and deepened friendships usually accompany the knowledge acquired and projects completed.

There are two basic types of workshops, discovery-oriented ones and task-oriented ones. Frequently, because each type serves the other, workshops will combine both interests to greater or lesser degree.

Discovery (exploratory/experimental) orientation

Motivated by interest in a common area, people attend workshops in order to learn more. Often there is no pre-structured programme: group participants decide. Intentions such as hoping to encourage people in writing their own songs, or an eagerness to develop dance as a communicating medium, or deciding to set aside time for a group of people to deepen their relationships together, could lead to establishing this type of workshop.

If someone in the group has professional knowledge or expertise, that person will probably arrange the details of each programme. Some groups have no experts, which means that participants will talk and explore together. They may read books, listen to tapes or invite guest speakers, in order to augment their knowledge. Usually the group leaders arrange the programmes or delegate the task to different members.

Task orientation

These workshops are geared to accomplishing a pre-determined goal. There may be a date for the end product; frequently group meetings allow just enough time to complete the project. Likely goals for this type of workshop group would be preparing a musical performance for a seasonal supper, rehearsing a drama improvised by children for a family service, developing new techniques for outreach ministry.

LEADERSHIP

Leadership is of cardinal importance. Its functions include preparing the agenda, being familiar with materials or exercises to be used, careful time planning, being sensitive to group members. Additionally, there are always a number of on-the-spot considerations and decisions: has a discussion run the course of its usefulness?, should one divert from the planned programme?, is the group overtired so that further effort will not be productive? If such leadership functions are not exercised, the group may collapse from apathy, anxiety or discouragement. Some groups have one leader, others may have several. Throughout this chapter we generally use the plural form, 'leaders' or 'leadership', since it encompasses both situations.

Why is specified leadership necessary?

Generally, when a group of people decide that all members will share preparation and responsibility equally, 'everyone's concern becomes no-one's business'. The first few meetings may be profitable but after that energies wane. People go to meetings unprepared or fabricate excuses for non-attendance. The truth is, without direction even enthusiasts have nowhere to go! Even when all the members have faithfully prepared a contribution to the evening's programme, the result is likely to be disjunctive and unco-ordinated. Endless free-wheeling experimentation is often frustrating as well as unproductive. Groups which have begun with the best intentions have disintegrated from lack of structure, from lack of co-ordinated preparation and direction.

How do groups get their leadership?

Most groups find their leadership in one of three ways:

Pre-structured leadership: An external person or group, such as clergy, governing body or another leadership group, selects the group's leadership prior to the group's first meeting.

Happenstance leadership: This is the result of coincidence or concern, rather than careful planning. Those who want to experiment in a certain area or those eager to accomplish certain goals within a small group setting may end up as group leaders. One may have become a youth leader, for example, because of concern for young people; another person may have ended up as the drama group leader because of administrative ability in organising group members, arranging meetings, securing scripts.

Natural leadership: Occasionally a group will decide they want no structured leadership, preferring to explore together. If the group carries on beyond a few weeks, it is usually because natural leadership has emerged. If this leadership is sanctioned either explicitly or implicitly by all group members, progress results and the anticipated purposes are achieved. If the leadership has not been accepted and approved, group time will be dissipated by conflict, division and power struggles.

Leadership which has evolved naturally or inadvertently will almost always have to be reconsidered at some point in the group's life. Pre-structured leadership should also be re-evaluated from time to time, but when leadership has come about informally or haphazardly, groups sometimes experience difficulties without knowing the source of their dilemmas.

Often the person with the original idea or impetus may not be the one to be the main or only group leader. A person gifted with ideas may be singularly undiplomatic in personal relationships. To insure the health and stability of the group, that person either would need another person to take the main leadership or could step entirely out of a leadership role, offering the needed and helpful suggestions in planning meetings or during the group meetings. Similarly, someone with limited creative imagination but warm sensitivity to others might be the person to initiate a series of exploratory workshops. This person would also need at least one other leader or assistant, to help plan the programmes.

Attitudes and actions

If you are a leader, or aspire to be one, the following questions may help you recognise and clarify your attitudes towards leadership, groups and the process of group work.

> Do you regard meetings and rehearsals as times allotted for you to 'tell them what do do' and 'get things done'?
>
> Do you see yourself exclusively as director or instructor?
>
> Do you anticipate that group meetings, particularly when completing a specific task or preparing a performance will include contributions from members?
>
> Does the role of facilitator challenge you as much as that of director or teacher? Do you find it an appealing role?
>
> Does being a facilitator/encourager colour your thinking? Does it bear itself out in your actions during group meetings?

If your answers to the first two questions were an unqualified 'No' and to the others an unqualified 'Yes', you score 100% in positive, outgoing, other-centred leadership. But what if you didn't score that high? Most of us probably won't, at least not initially and just on our own. Graceful, perceptive leadership is a natural gift for some, an acquired skill for many others. People who know themselves to be overbearing and impatient or unassertive and hesitant may have already crossed themselves off the leaders' list. Yet both sorts are potential leaders, if they are willing to work closely with others.

Leadership can be learned through openness, patience, perseverance and prayer. Openness to others, as one receives correction from someone more mature or is confronted by critical responses; patience with oneself, as one slowly changes long-standing personality habits; perseverance, as one makes mistakes and fails, perhaps time and again; prayer, individually and with others, as one learns more about oneself and one's attitudes which are then borne out in actions. These characteristics are relevant to the obviously gifted as well, for natural abilities also need refining.

Like any other skill, leadership improves and matures with practice. The small group context is ideal for growth in leadership capability. A relatively small number of people is less threatening than a large number, and in such a limited setting one can see clearly the impact of one's actions. One recognises the effects of rigidity rather than flexibility, of a dampening response rather than an encouraging one, of control motivated by insecurity instead of direction stemming from confidence. Yet how does one actually change one's leadership or personality habits? Earlier on we said that openness, patience, perseverance and prayer were helpful aids to becoming a good leader. In the next section we give further practical applications of these.

Shared leadership

As we have seen, some groups must have more than one leader in order to function productively. Other reasons than necessity however, substantiate the advantages of shared leadership. It does require extra sensitivity and preparation time, at least in the beginning, but the benefits are multiplied far beyond these initial investments.

Shared leadership is first of all an attitude. It means surrendering the individual 'leader as hero' image so pervasive in our culture. For the confident or extrovert, zealous to speak their opinions, sharing leadership requires whole-hearted willingness to seek out and listen to others. For the shy or uncertain, it signifies determined commitment to speak out one's thoughts and feelings.

This attitude means openness, even eagerness, to hear what others think about how one presents oneself, how one directs meetings or rehearsals, how one relates to others. Balancing this is the commitment to communicate these things, when they are critical, carefully and sensitively, not just 'honestly'. This latter commitment includes an equal readiness to affirm the others' good points, pointing out and emphasising positive aspects of their actions and relationships.

To genuinely share leadership one must truly let go, entrusting others with responsibility; at the same time, one must continue to hold oneself and all other leaders involved fully accountable. Sharing responsibility in this fashion means full acceptance for everything that happens, regardless of whether, in the actual group meetings, one says or does any of it. Shared leadership, then, is not simply task division, with various people accepting responsibility for 'their' part. Division of leadership and labour however, will certainly be a practical outworking. Everyone can't do everything, and attempting to 'lead together', Siamese-twin style, when it would clearly be simpler and more workable for just one person to be actively leading, parodies the concept.

Sharing leadership may require more preparation time than if one were doing it all on one's own. Sometimes though, when two or three are contributing, planning time is reduced because the task is shared. Leadership meetings should include the following: time to review the last group meeting in terms of group dynamics, leadership effectiveness and amount of work accomplished; and time to plan the next meeting, in terms of goals and leadership. Specific content may or may not be planned during this meeting: people sharing leadership develop their own patterns according to personnel, gifts and time.

The practice of sharing leadership facilitates development in leadership skills. People inexperienced or immature in any leadership area, whether it be group dynamics, interpersonal relationships, time balancing or task skills, find that being able to share leadership with others helps build confidence and develops expertise. Along these same lines, inexperienced people can benefit greatly from working with an experienced leader whose example and counsel provide both model and direct guidance. Finally, individual leaders sometimes end up feeling or actually being isolated from those they lead. When more than one person is genuinely responsible, the pressures of leadership are minimised because they are shared. Observations and evaluations are able to be more balanced and less subjective. Those who lead are then more likely to experience a deeper, more satisfying personal involvement with group members and group work.

Leaders are not the only ones to gain from shared leadership. For group members, it can reveal a dimension of relationship and encounter hitherto unknown. This dimension lies chiefly in the relationship between the leaders. When that relationship is relaxed and comfortable, group members find themselves more relaxed, more comfortable.

Secondly, leaders who undisguisedly respect and enjoy each other are an example of caring and friendship. Workshop participants become freer to express their own feelings of openness and tenderness.

Thirdly, well-shared leadership demonstrates flexibility and openness to change, qualities that teachers and leaders often lack. When a true relationship of trust and familiarity exists between leaders, there is room for one of them to have a sudden new idea, for another to revise the programme on the spot, without threatening or unnerving the other(s). Participating in an atmosphere unfettered by competition and marked by give and take, change and compromise can be liberating and horizon-expanding for group members.

Conversely, shared leadership without a basis in actual relationships is usually strained and discomfiting. The workshop atmosphere tends to be hollow and uneasy, and there can be a ring of insincerity and tension in the leaders' tones. The positive benefits detailed above do not accrue; in fact, the opposites occur, and group members feel strangely deceived. Relationships characterised by ease, caring and flexibility cannot be manufactured artificially. They are dynamic and organic, the product of active personal commitments, demanding dedication, sincerely shared concern and, for Christians, persevering prayer and willing forgiveness.

PLANNING AND PREPARATION

Leaders should consider participants, administrative details, time, content and goals for each small group meeting.

Participants

When planning workshops, find out as much as possible about those likely to attend. If it's a one-off affair, this may be hard to project, which is all the more reason to think workshop plans through as carefully as possible. If children are likely to turn up, say for a drama workshop, a sophisticated excerpt from one of T. S. Eliot's plays would certainly be inappropriate. A better choice would be a dramatised Old Testament story, such as Joshua and the Battle of Jericho or the II Chronicles story of the choir that led the army into battle; or a Dr. Suess book, such as *Have You Ever Thought How Lucky You Are?*, *The 500 Hats of Bartholomew Cubbins* or *The Lorax*. Any of these alternatives would capture both young and old. Or, if youth have been invited but may not attend, plan a programme that will appeal to them without being so juvenile or specialised that adults feel offended or excluded. When possible, find out if any disabled people are likely to attend, and think your programme through accordingly.

Administrative details

Poor administration can seriously hinder group work. Be sure that facts concerning time, location and attire have been communicated clearly. Be sure that you have sorted out any particulars well in advance of your workshops, so there is not last minute confusion or disorder.

Leaders should always be familiar with any exercises or materials they intend to use or have others use. Introductions and explanations to workshop sections or activities should be short, clear and practised beforehand, so no group time is wasted. If scores, books or scripts will be used, be sure there are enough copies, similar copies (a play, for instance, may have been revised, and your file contain both versions, or a book may be printed in several editions), and readable copies. If using visual aids, props, instruments or mechanical equipment of any sort, organise everything well before meeting time, being sure of power supplies, points, lighting, etc.

Time

Work out in advance a time estimate of the various activities you intend to use. Groups may be more or less responsive, imaginative, creative than you thought, so cultivate the principle of flexibility.

For your own sake it's better to overplan than underplan: it's easier to remove activities than to add them. In thinking about warm-up exercises, for instance, plan five and be able to omit two, rather than planning just three and then discovering that although the group has completed them, it is still not relaxed enough to go on to the next section.

Be as realistic as possible in your time projections, but don't cut yourself short. In the actual workshop an exercise or discussion may take more time than you imagined. Plan options, so you'll be able to extend an activity if you want to, without having to eliminate another one that you had considered important.

As you gain experience, your time estimates will become more accurate and easier to project. Your ability to improvise without pre-planning will also improve. Careful preparation, however, will always increase your security. That in turn will free you to direct a larger proportion of your mental and emotional energies to the participants and their needs.

Although group members may be aware of what they hope to accomplish, it is the leaders who ensure that it happens. Time balancing holds in tension the necessity of moving forward and the importance of flexibility and useful diversion. In the workshop itself, keep in mind the passage of time, which seems to go faster during small group work. In an exploration group, leaders must regulate activities, ensuring that the group accomplishes the bulk of its intentions. In a task or rehearsal group, leaders must keep things progressing, watching that the limited time isn't frittered away.

Content and goals

As we have stressed throughout this book, sensitive leadership seeks to draw people out of themselves and their preconceptions. It helps them discover unsuspected abilities, forgotten gifts. Particularly if working with a regular group, it won't take long for you to sense abilities and potentials. You will develop an astute awareness of what are challenges to some, seeming impossibilities to others.

When planning content, include some activities within easy reach of all, others which require a bit of effort, still others which are beyond reach, demanding mental, physical, emotional stretching. Intersperse these various activities, so that if one is beyond some, the next won't be. The entire group will not accomplish everything at first, but they will, sooner or later. And usually, it's sooner!

Always stay one step ahead of the group in your planning, looking for new challenges that will stretch them further. Take people beyond what they thought they could do: they are almost always able to achieve much more than they – or others! – imagine. Patricia shares: 'On one occasion we visited a church in the Midlands, offering a series of worship-oriented workshops in dance, drama, music and group reading. The drama workshop was going to produce a play as the sermon for Sunday's main service. In the initial part of the workshop we spent about forty five minutes doing warm-up, vocal, movement and imagination exercises. Then we cast for the play, which had been written prior to the workshop, and began reading through the parts. The man selected for the lead was a slender, quiet person whose brown eyes danced with excitement behind his thick glasses. He was gentle and willing, and I thought he would convey with clarity the careful sensitivity of the lead role. Sure enough, he did! His own admission was that he had never acted before, but he spoke the lines clearly and expressively, moved gracefully among the other characters, handled his script well. Other activities followed immediately on the workshop's conclusion. Except for a brief reassurance to the minister and the other Fisherfolk that the sermon was well in hand, there was no time for discussion. Imagine my surprise the next day, when I discovered that the entire congregation had been stunned to see that man taking the lead role. It turned out that he was possessed of a stutter, and that he had never before done anything more outstanding than collecting the service books and sweeping up after the church was empty!'

People's potential is like hidden treasure: all they need is someone to find the field and unbury it!

STRUCTURING WELL-BALANCED WORKSHOPS

We have developed two basic workshop structures applicable in almost any situation. The first we use most widely, the second is for groups with a specialised and limited purpose. Either structure works with any folk art form, such as music, reading, drama, dance, mime, art; or with any other small group meeting, such as communications awareness, group dynamics study, times set aside for people to develop closer personal relationships.

We give explanations of each structure here; other chapters in the book list exercises, techniques, teaching examples, etc. for each folk art form.

Structure I

Three complementary elements: 1) exercises and experimentation, 2) instruction, and 3) application or creativity, comprise this structure. The first element helps people relax, the second gives them a successful learning experience, the third allows them to apply what they have learned by developing their own project.

Exercises and experimentation

Purpose: to enable participants to settle in and relax
with themselves
with each other
with the group's leadership
with the art form or purpose of gathering
with concept of potential audience (if any)

Helping participants become comfortable in the workshop situation is the leaders' first concern. Many different reasons can motivate people to join workshop groups: opportunity for a new experience, desire to learn more about an unknown area, hope and eagerness for friendship and fellowship, discovery of an arena in which lapsed abilities will again be stirred, anticipation of new means for communicating or teaching. Prompted by such a diversity of motives, people have to be drawn out individually and drawn together corporately. New people, new events, new techniques, new situations: these are potential threats which a warm, relaxed atmosphere, established by comfortable, secure leaders, helps dispel.

A reassuring introduction will answer unspoken questions or fears. Describe what will happen in the time together, what they should expect. If working with a particular art form, you may include a brief explanation of what it is or why it is being emphasised. (Much of this sort of teaching, though, can be incorporated into the workshop activities: as you introduce exercises, you can also explain what they are intended to do and how they relate overall.) Solicit willing participation: people have an easier time trying new things when they've verbally acknowledged their willingness. This also releases leaders to gently and sometimes humorously, at a later point, exhort participants into making more effort or exerting more energy.

Some introductions may include a time for discussion, ascertaining hopes, intents and previous experience, but it's best to time this carefully. If people are apprehensive or uncertain, they tend to spend time theorising and talking, to avoid actually working! Finally, if the workshop is meant to produce an item for a large group demonstration, worship service or entertainment, the group's awareness of this goal should be confirmed during the introduction.

Exercises used during this section of the workshop should be casual and attainable. Leaders should be conversational and encouraging, helping people become more at ease, telling the occasional joke, sometimes doing a few foolish things so that people don't feel awkward or foolish about what they're doing. Leaders should, on the whole, do the exercises with the group, first demonstrating them if necessary. The activities during this period fulfil several purposes. They help people relax, they provide fun and enjoyable experiences, they begin the development of personal and group awareness.

Exercises also form 'building blocks' to be used later in more intensive work. This relaxation time is significant, particularly if the group has a goal which involves presentation or performance. When executed before a group, even such simple movements as walking, standing, sitting, are magnified immensely. Learning to relax in a small group environment is the first step to relaxing in front of a larger group, such as an audience or congregation.

Example: A series of exercises for a group reading workshop might include rhythmic sounds, vocal expression experiments, phrase repetition, corporate reading. These exercises stimulate first self-awareness, as people become conscious of their voices and how they use them in regard to pitch, expression and breathing. Gradually, they stimulate group awareness, as people listen to and recognise these same factors overall.

Later, the principles of some exercises, such as rhythmic word plays or pitch and volume variations, will be used in the readings themselves. What began as exercises will eventually evolve into techniques. This is the 'building block' principle.

Instruction

Purpose: to give participants a successful, unstressed learning experience.

The second section of the workshop employs pre-developed material similar to the project the group will work out later. Supplied by the leaders, the material is complete within itself and implements techniques taught in the first section. The group should be able to master it with limited explanation and brief rehearsal.

To understand the effectiveness of this section, let's review what has happened so far in the group. During the introduction your people committed themselves to attempting whatever came their way. Then they learned exercises and techniques, which proved them adept at following directions and responding to leadership. Since the material they will now work with is fully developed and since they have already learned most of the techniques, participants need only continue with what they have already been doing: participating actively, responding to direction. This makes responsibility for the 'success' of the material before them obviously the leader's, not theirs. Dynamically, the group are enabled to have a successful learning experience unpressured by fear of failure. This section is also an appropriate time to explain more fully the mechanics and application of the techniques being learned.

Example: Our group readers have just received a script. It is printed out in an easily readable format and carefully marked with volume, pacing and techniques. The group follows along as the leader takes them through the script. Occasionally, following the leader's secure directions, the group practises isolated bits aloud or learns additional techniques. One or two members have queries; after they've been answered, the group reads aloud the entire script. The leader makes critical comments and gives suggestions, then the group repeats the reading.

This section reinforces techniques already learned, ensuring that they're understood in practice and application, and teaches a few new ones. It also solidifies group experience, intensifies familiarity and deepens feelings of personal acceptance and positive group accomplishment. Additionally, it foreshadows the type of project group members will work on next.

Our willing readers group, for example, may have agreed that by the end of the time together they would have created their own group reading; but actually, members may not have had a clue as to how they would accomplish such a feat. Several probably had no idea what a group reading is! To do a few exercises, hear that they could be applied as techniques, and then be told to get on with developing a reading would be an impossibility for most. Even if they had a fair idea of what it could be, it's likely that the group would not have the confidence to undertake it. But once participants have seen and learned a well-constructed reading, the step to producing one of their own is not such a big one.

Application or creativity

Purpose: to provide participants with the opportunity of recognising, relying on and using their own abilities.

This final section is the most apparently rewarding. The goal is to improvise or develop a project, using ideas engendered in the two previous sections. Armed with newly-acquired techniques and fortified by a successful learning experience, workshop participants are usually ready for the challenge and release of this third stage. Endeavours that only an hour or so earlier might have seemed unattainable are now within reach.

Structure and content for this section depends upon several variables:

type of workshop
type and number of projects desired
group size

time
leadership
future intention for project(s)
group familiarity

Some general guidelines apply to most situations. The workshop remains a whole or subdivides into smaller groups. Workshop leaders may continue to direct the large group or, if there is more than one leader divide themselves among smaller groups. Alternatively, the leaders may appoint someone in each small group to assume responsibility, or request volunteers for that purpose. In some cases, such as groups that meet regularly, it may be that no directly appointed leadership is necessary for this section.

If the workshop stays together as one group, the leaders will usually have prepared material or planned ideas for development. If the large group has broken into smaller ones, the leaders may have given each group material to use as a springboard or to develop as a project: alternatively, making decisions about the content of their projects may be a significant part of each small group's work.

On the whole, those who lead the large group should not simply observe small group activity. Leaders in an observation-only capacity tend to intimidate group initiative or unsettle its sense of security. Such leaders should participate directly by leading, drop in briefly to see if their assistance is needed or not be present at all. An exception to this generalisation is in the case of groups which work together regularly. A person who has led one section of the workshop, such as the exercises or instruction part, may be able to participate in this third section, doing improvisatory or small group work, without any real difficulty. This is due to familiarity among group members, which often results in flexibility concerning roles.

Example: Reading group breaks into two smaller groups. Each group will work out a reading based on their workshop experience. One group has been asked to select a psalm as the basis of their reading; another group has been given four poems, and asked to select one.

or

The workshop remains together. The leader has an undeveloped script, with only the basic reading printed on it; this is given to the participants. By pointing out key words or likely sentences, or making occasional suggestions, the leader draws out of group members their ideas about techniques and dynamics which will enhance and develop the reading. There is much experimentation and change before all is agreed, and members mark their scripts as decisions are made.

This third section gives participants the chance not only to apply what they've been learning but also to go beyond it, implementing their own ideas. It provides an arena for them to express initiative and confirms that they can trust their own abilities and potential. Many people think that without a specialist they can't do anything at all: this section dispels that notion!

Developing a project further unifies the group. If the larger workshop sub-divides, each small group is usually very keen to see what the other group's worked out. It's of great benefit to plan a time when the groups re-assemble, so they can present their projects for each other. At such times there is a sense of inter-dependence and shared accomplishment. A further unifying is experienced, as a satisfying feeling of 'Look what we've done!' pervades, even about projects in which one's group was not directly involved.

This 'sharing together' principle has wider application. Perhaps there were several workshop groups, each exploring a different area. Plan a large group meeting, where members of the dance group, the music group, the design group, the reading group all share together. This can take many forms: perhaps a worship service, with each group contributing at an appropriate place, perhaps an entire evening of festivity, which allows time for all the sub-groups to present their projects; perhaps a session at the end of the day, just after a break for tea. The large group will experience the same satisfaction and awareness of interdependency, the same amazement at the group's productivity, that marked the smaller groups' sharings.

Sectional timing

A well-paced workshop with these three elements should be about two hours long. A general time breakdown is:

Exercises and experimentation:	25 – 40 minutes
Instruction:	15 – 25 minutes
Application/creativity:	45 – 60 minutes

Variable factors to consider are:

Administration time: to divide into smaller groups
Transit time: to move from one location and possibly back again
Culmination time: to share projects together

A workshop can fit into one and one-half hours, but with the variables it means a push and rush near the end, especially if re-grouping for the 'show and tell' culmination time. We have squeezed workshops into one hour, but very little would have been accomplished during the third sections had we not been directly involved in leading them. Even then, it was rather too pressured. With few exceptions, we do not recommend one hour workshops.

This basic, three-part programme may be abridged or counter-structured. Generally however, applying these three principles of exercises and experimentation, instruction, application or creativity, will result in satisfying, productive workshop experiences.

Structure II

Two elements, 1) warm-up and 2) task accomplishment, comprise this plan. It is useful for groups which regularly develop projects, like a church drama group or a travelling outreach group; and for groups which are familiar with techniques and have already acquired the confidence necessary to achieve specific goals.

Warm-up

Relaxation and warm-up are necessary for any group, no matter how experienced. It's a bit much to jump straight into improvisation, script or score work. People need to relax, to shift their focus from other activities of the day, to get comfortable together, to settle into the idea or concept of their project. Preliminary exercises chosen to focus the project at hand will help people to loosen up. They also direct concentration and energies to the content of the project. Drama, mime, movement or dance groups might use imagination, concentration, movement and characterisation exercises; music or singing groups might use breathing, movement and rhythm exercises.

Task accomplishment

Once people are relaxed together, work on the actual project can begin. A bridge between the two sections may be some discussion, to help make decisions about the project's content or development.

Groups which meet regularly and implement this Structure II may occasionally want to work with Structure I. It will prevent the group work going 'stale' and help diminish the pressure that builds up when a group must consistently produce a project.

ADDITIONAL POINTERS FOR WORKSHOP LEADERS

1. Language: Use everyday words to explain exercises and concepts. If you must use professional terms, be sure your manner doesn't assume or indicate that people should already know their meaning. If employing specialised terms as devices for instruction, use the word or phrase, then tell its meaning in simple, descriptive words. Repeat the terms once or twice during the workshop, to ensure they are understood in practice.

2. Humour: Build moments of comic relief or humour into the programme through exercises, explanation, demonstration, personal storytelling. They will help people relax.
3. Simplicity: As often as possible, teach people tools and building blocks, rather than concentrating on just one complicated endeavour. This is especially true in exploratory workshops, or workshops where the leadership is regarded as specialist. In these situations the emphasis should be on drawing people out and helping them to trust their own abilities.
4. Variety: A fair amount is necessary and profitable, but not so much that people are overwhelmed. Again, the building-block principle comes into play. It's of much more lasting value if people can acquire tools to work with and apply than if they have 'a super experience' or '*great* leadership!'.
5. Group involvement: A few exercises and activities can be geared towards individuals but, generally, most should be group exercises, with the whole group working together or dividing into several simultaneous small groups of two, three, or four, or combinations of small groups.
6. Facial expression: Art forms are used to communicate, but a double message is received when people don't allow their faces to express what they intend to convey through the art form. Exercises involving facial expression and blankness will help people realise the importance of facial communication in drama, dance, music and other performing arts.
7. Personal responses: Some workshop experiences may provoke deep and strongly negative reactions of fear, anger, insecurity, resentment, as painful experiences are recalled or people are threatened by fear of exposure or failure. This area requires special sensitivity and awareness. It may be wise to structure 'response' times into your workshop programme, or be sure that such times will be available after the group meeting or in the next few days. This is particularly true with groups that work together regularly. Prayer may also be an essential element in small group relationships and work. In *Praise Him in the Dance*, Anne Long makes several excellent observations and suggestions concerning prayer, commitment and small group work.
8. Positioning: Sitting in a circle, concentric circles, half-circles or a horseshoe shape draws people into a closer experience than if they are removed from each other in pew-like rows. It also helps break down the 'formal learning situation' barrier.

CHAPTER 18

Exercises and Techniques

PHYSICAL WARM UPS

Select a variety of exercises to include every part of the body, choosing one or two from each area. These exercises are important to begin a workshop involving dance, drama, or mime, as they increase the blood flow to the muscles and prepare them for activity. Physical exercises may also serve as a good loosening up tool in other workshops, particularly if people have been sitting for a long time. If the workshop is a one-off occasion, repeat each exercise four or five times; if the group meets regularly, gradually increase the number of repetitions.

1. Neck

   a. Rotate neck several times slowly, both clockwise and anti-clockwise. Stretch the neck to make as large a circle as possible.

   b. Drop head down to chest and bounce it gently four times. Drop head back and gently bounce four times. Repeat on each side four times.

2. Shoulders and arms

   a. Rotate shoulders, forward and backward, one at a time and together.

   b. Lift shoulders up as high as possible. Let them drop. Repeat several times.

   c. Place one arm straight up in the air next to your ear. Keep the other arm down straight by your side. Keeping arms straight, pull them backward as far as possible. Reverse arm positions and repeat.

d. Raise arms to shoulder level, extending them to each side. Rotate in small circles, clockwise and anti-clockwise. Repeat in large circles.

3. Wrists and hands

a. With arms straight out in front of you, bend hands back as far as possible and bounce gently four times. Then drop hands and bend them under as far as possible, bounce gently four times.

b. Rotate hands in small circles.

c. Shake hands and wrists as if trying to shake off water.

d. Tightly clench hands into fists. Then fling out fingers vigorously. Repeat rapidly at least ten times.

4. Torso

a. Stand with feet apart, stretch arms as high above head as possible. Balance on toes. Collapse into loose humped-over position, bending at waist and knees, with heels on floor, head down, arms limp and swinging. Rock up and down by slightly flexing knees, and swinging arms.

b. From standing upright position with hands on hips, bend forward at waist and bounce four times. Lean backwards as far as you can, placing hands behind knees, if necessary, to keep balance. Bounce four times. Repeat from side to side four times.

c. From standing upright position, drop down sideways, reaching as far down your leg as possible. Do not twist from the middle. Repeat on other side.

5. Back

Note: *The more vigorous exercises should not be attempted by those with back difficulties. Exercises a–c are adequate to loosen up the back without strain.*

a. Lie flat on back. Bend knees so feet are flat on floor. Firmly push the small of the back into the floor. Hold for five counts and release.

b. Begin as in exercise a. When small of back is pushed into the floor, slightly lift buttocks from the floor just until back is flat, not arched. Return flat back to floor and relax.

c. From standing upright position, bend forward from the waist, knees slightly bent. Allow arms to swing freely. Then, beginning with base of spine, very slowly uncurl back, feeling each muscle as it straightens until you return to erect posture.

d. Get on all fours. Swing one leg up behind you until your back is arched. Lift head upward and backward at the same time. Repeat with the other leg.

e. Lie flat on floor on your stomach, with your arms stretched out straight in front of you. Lift your legs up behind you at the same time as you lift your arms up, so only your stomach is touching the floor. Hold a few seconds and relax.

6. Hamstrings

a. Bend forward from the waist with knees straight, bounce gently until you touch your toes. (If this requires strain, just reach down as far as possible without touching toes.)

b. Lie flat on back on floor. Raise torso to sitting position and reach towards toes. (Again, do not strain to actually touch toes.) Return to original position and repeat.

c. From sitting position on floor, open legs as wide as possible while remaining in upright position. Lean forward and stretch arms towards feet, bounce four times with back straight, then repeat with rounded back. Bend towards left foot, stretching to touch foot. Bring head as close to left knee as possible. Repeat to right.

d. Start in same position as exercise c. Keeping right knee on floor, bend right leg behind you. Balance weight evenly. Then bend towards left foot, stretching to touch foot. Repeat with left leg bent, and stretch toward right foot.

7. Knees

   a. Keeping back straight, bend knees, sink down to the floor and up again.

   b. With knees bent slightly, bounce gently up and down.

8. Ankles and Feet

   a. Standing on one foot, lift opposite foot slightly. Stretch foot by pointing toe up and down. Rotate foot in circular motion. Repeat with other foot.

   b. Jump in place for ten counts.

   c. Standing on one foot, shake opposite foot. Repeat with other foot.

   d. Run in place.

ISOLATION

These exercises increase our awareness of the independent functioning of each part. Particularly vital in mime, they develop the potential for communicating changes in attitude and activity through subtle changes in position and posture.

1. Head and neck

   a. With a minimum of neck movement, move head forward, backward, left and right. Keep face forward and don't tilt chin or move shoulders. At first, movement from side to side will be difficult, but with practice it will develop. It is helpful to practise this exercise in front of the mirror or to place one's hands in oriental dancer fashion, with arms at shoulder height, elbows bent to form a right angle and finger tips toward ears.

2. Shoulders

   a. Lift shoulders up as far as possible and return to normal position. Then push shoulders down as far as possible, return to normal position.

b. Thrust shoulders forward as far as possible, return to normal position. Thrust shoulders back as far as possible, return to normal position.

3. Ribcage

a. Take a deep breath and expand chest fully. Place hands on ribcage and move it forward, backward, left and right. Do not move at waist or hips.

b. Rotate ribcage in full circle. This will be difficult initially, but muscle co-ordination will develop with practice.

4. Arms

a. Raise one arm straight up in the air next to your ear. Swing backwards in full circle several times. Place other arm in the same position and swing forwards in a full circle several times. Then beginning in same position with both arms, swing in opposite directions at the same time.

b. Let arms hang limply at sides. Shake vigorously and relax. Think of your hands as filled with a gas that is lighter than air. Let them slowly rise of their own accord until they reach a natural resting place.

5. Elbows

a. Lift arm to shoulder height and stretch out straight to side. Let lower arm flop at elbow and swing freely while keeping upper part of arm stiff. Repeat with other arm, and with both arms together. This conveys the impression of being a puppet attached by strings.

b. With arm bent in same position as exercise a, lift elbow as high as possible, return to normal position. Then lower elbow as far as possible while keeping elbow bent. Repeat with other arm, and with both arms together.

6. Hands

a. To prepare hands for practice with imaginary objects it is important to get the blood circulating and the muscles warmed up. Raise one arm straight up in air next to ear. With hands open, swing arm forward in vigorous circles. Feel the tingling in the palm of your hand. Repeat with other arm.

b. Independently lift each finger up and down, as if playing scales on a piano. Try to keep other fingers still.

c. Keeping fingers together and as straight as possible, draw them towards the palm until they touch. Slowly uncurl them, moving fingertips up the palm until in original position.

d. With a flat palm reach out to grasp an imaginary pole. Curl hand around pole. Release pole, flatten hand and return to original position.

7. Hips

a. Place hands on hips and move pelvis forward, backward, right and left. Keep upper torso still and straight.

b. Rotate pelvis in complete circle.

8. Legs and feet

a. Stand with feet slightly apart. Lift one knee slowly and lower without moving torso or head. Pretend there is a string through the knee. Hold end of the string in one hand, raise and lower knee as you pull string up and lower it.

b. In same position as exercise a, with one knee lifted, pretend string is through toes of foot. Raise and lower foot while raising and lowering string. Do not move knee while moving foot.

FOR CHILDREN

Through imaginative play children can do similar warm up and isolation exercises. Give them one from each section before moving into other exercises.

1. Head and neck

   a. Walk as though you have a string through the top of your head which holds it up and pulls you along. Someone cuts the string.

   b. Put on several imaginary hats: cowboy hat, large brimmed flowered hat, turban, policeman's hat. Walk around room as you would in each hat.

2. Torso

   a. Move like a wiggly worm.

   b. Move like a floppy rag doll.

   c. Walk with your back along a wall.

3. Arms and hands

   a. Try to catch a butterfly.

   b. Pick apples from a tree, put them in a basket.

   c. Pretend your hands are birds. They pick you up and carry you off.

4. Legs and feet

   a. Jump like frogs.

   b. Walk like cats.

   c. March like soldiers.

5. Overall isolations

   a. Your whole body is a puppet on a string. Move each part by pulling a string: head, shoulders, wrists, hands, arms, legs and feet.

   b. Your whole body has frozen. It thaws one part at a time. Move head without moving the rest of your body. Go through entire body in this way.

RELAXATION AND BREATHING

These exercises increase awareness of different parts of the body and release tensions. Soft music in the background may enhance their soothing effect. Particularly if workshops follow a day's work, these exercises are helpful in preparing for physical activity in drama, mime, dance, movement, music.

1. Relaxation

a. Tense and relax. Lie flat on back on the floor.	Instruct participants to imagine a stronger force of gravity which makes their bodies heavier and pulls them into the floor.
Stretch limbs in every direction. Hold, and release.	Hold stretch out as long as possible.
Tense feet by pointing toe firmly, while keeping rest of body relaxed. Relax feet.	
Work through entire body tensing and relaxing: calves, thighs, stomach, buttocks, lower back, shoulders, arms, hands, neck, head and facial muscles.	Instruct participants to push the body part into the floor. Remind them to keep other parts relaxed while tensing one part.
Repeat entire progression. Occasionally intersperse deep breathing and slow exhaling.	
Lie perfectly relaxed for a few minutes.	May walk quietly among people and gently move heads from side to side, to help them become aware of any tension remaining in neck and shoulders.

b. Freeze and Thaw:
Lie flat on back on the floor. Imagine you are frozen to the ground. Make your entire body rigid. Then bring one part of your body alive at a time.

Use words to help participants to imagine being frozen: wind, ice, sleet, etc. Then suggest ways to move as parts are thawed: in circles, flexing, bouncing.

c. Relax and listen: Lie flat on back on floor. With eyes closed listen to readings and scriptures concerning the goodness of creation, the positive nature of our bodies, offering our bodies to the Lord in worship. Peaceful instrumental music may be played as a background to readings, or as prelude or conclusion to them.

Read slowly to allow words to sink in. Leave silences between readings for personal reflection.

Appropriate readings include:
The creation narrative (Genesis 1 and 2)
Psalms 139, 149, 150
David dancing before the Lord (II Samuel 6:12–14)
'We are God's work of art' (Ephesians 2:10 *The Jerusalem Bible*)
Zephaniah 3:14–18
'i thank You God for most this amazing' by e. e. cummings.

2. Breathing

a. Take three short, sharp breaths that completely fill lungs.
Hold for ten counts.
Exhale in three short, sharp breaths.

Count out loud for the ten counts.
If this is too strenuous for a group at first, limit to five or seven counts.

Repeat four times initially and gradually increase.

b. Take in a long, sustained breath for five counts. Hold for ten counts. Exhale through teeth, creating a hissing sound, until lungs are completely deflated.
Repeat four times initially and gradually increase.

Explain the use of the diaphragm in breathing properly. The lungs are filled by dropping the diaphragm and inflating the lower lungs, rather than lifting the chest and shoulders. Ask participants to place one hand on their upper chest. The hand should remain stationary during exercise.

BASIC MOVEMENT

These exercises introduce a group to simple, directed movement. They explore the potential for dance and movement in other parts of the body than just the feet and arms. Music is helpful in encouraging easy flow and graceful movement.

1. Circles

Begin lying flat on back on the floor. Make circles with one hand, then the other, then both together. Standing up, make circles in the air with only one part of the body at a time: hands, feet, elbows, head, back.

Constantly ask questions that stimulate variations: how slowly can you make circles? How fast? In what rhythms? How high can you make them? How low?

2. Exploration

Lying flat on back, explore the air around you with one body part at a time. Stand up and continue exploration. Begin with easy ones: hands, feet, arms; then try more difficult ones: elbows, ankles, back of the neck.

Direct which part of the body to begin with and progress through other parts. Participants concentrate on one part at a time, which enables them to experience the maximum potential for movement in each area.

3. Four-Beat Rhythms

The leader performs a series of movements with the arms through four different positions. Workshop participants follow. Leader does series of four movements with feet while participants follow. Leader then combines hand and feet movements, and participants follow. Do several variations of these to music with 4/4 rhythm or drum beat.

This exercise develops the ability to follow simple movement sequences. It forms a basis for learning dance steps in 4/4 rhythm.

4. Emotion 'Freezes'

Participants walk freely around room. As leader names particular emotions, participants respond with movements and postures that express the emotion. When leader rings bell, all freeze in position.

Possible emotions: joy, fear, wonder, apathy, anger, puzzlement. After participants freeze instruct them to remove any expression from their faces and to observe others' postures without facial expression. Are they effective?

Variation: Do in pairs. One freezes, the other observes freeze and tries to imitate it as nearly as possible.

5. Sculptures

In groups of four to six, one person plays the sculptor while others are the clay. The sculptor forms the others into arrangements that express emotions or themes. Show other groups. Change sculptor and repeat several times.

Suggestions: confusion, peace, insecurity, reconciliation, tension, expectation, creation.

Develops economy of movement and heightens the effect of simple gestures.

Variation: One person takes a pose, others arrange selves around him to express an emotion or theme.	
6. Three Movement Freezes In groups of four to six, decide on three or four group movements to depict a theme or emotion.	Focuses on essential movements. Develops group co-ordination.

OBSERVATION and CONCENTRATION

1. How Do You Do It?

This helps people realise the movement complexity of many fairly common activities. Participants should select or be assigned an activity from those listed below and then work with it in the following ways:

a) Seated with eyes closed, think through every part of the activity. Then watch a mental picture of yourself as you do it.

b) Mime the activity, using only gesture and no props, words, etc.

c) Perform the actual activity, using the real objects if possible.

d) Mime the activity again.

Part a) requires focused concentration and stimulates imagination; part b) extends these abilities into movement. Part c) allows participants to experience the activity itself, and thus to gauge the accuracy of their thought and miming: part d) transfers the actual experience into the mime process. There is no time limit for any of the parts, and participants may stay with or repeat a given part until it has been completed to their satisfaction.

Select from the following:	pack a suitcase unfold an ironing board dress a one and one-half year old child

catch a frisky cat
set up a folding chair
collect cleaning equipment
arrange books on a shelf
wash up from a meal for two
repot a plant
make a pot of tea
put on hat, coat, boots
open window
pick up milk bottles from front door
sweep floor

2. What Did You See?

This party game is also a useful exercise for developing concentration. Place no fewer than twenty objects (tin-opener, glass, nail file, fruit, etc.) on a tray. Unveil the tray in front of the entire group for fifteen seconds, then re-cover it. Give participants thirty/sixty seconds to write down everything they remember seeing on the tray.

Variation I: Have participants walk through a garden or room for one minute. Then seat them and have them describe, with their eyes closed, the mental image they have of the place in which they were. Have some tell the description with their eyes open.

Variation II: Have seated participants close their eyes, then ask questions based on observations they have made unawares, such as 'Steve, what does Kevin have on today?' 'Marianne, does Karen have on any jewellery? If so what kind?' 'Are there designs on the ceiling of this room?' 'How many windows are there in the sitting room?' etc. Repeat this exercise in other group meetings, as a way of training people to become more observant and aware.

IMAGINATION

In these exercises participants encounter imaginary objects, unexpected obstacles, and changing substances and spaces. Through these experiences participants' thinking is stimulated concerning the effect of these factors on balance, posture, and movement.

1. The Walk About

Without talking, all participants walk randomly about the room. Cover as much space as possible, going into corners and through the middle of the room. Avoid running into other people.

If participants are not venturing out of certain areas, encourage them to explore entire room.

Vary the pace from slow to moderate to very rapid. Give verbal signals to stop and explore imaginary obstacles.

At verbal cue from leader, stop to examine a large pane of glass.

Direct participants to press hands flat against glass. Explore the size of the pane. How wide is it? How tall?

Continue to walk about freely at increased pace with slightly reduced space until verbal cue to stop and examine wall.

Instruct participants to feel the texture of the wall with flat hand. Determine size of the wall, and feel around ends of it. Push on wall. Turn around and move down the wall with back flat against it.

Resume walking at a faster pace and in more reduced space, taking care not to run into others.
Walk until cue to run into a wall of ice.

Direct participants to flatten hand against ice, but pull back quickly because of cold. Repeat several times. The hand sticks to the ice and more force must be used in removing it. May include more obstacles (door, window, large rock) or conclude exercise here.

2. Inside/Outside

Walk from open spaces into closed spaces. Begin walking as if in completely open space. Convey this through freedom of movement, sense of space and

Continually feed participants with words which convey the feeling of unconfined and open spaces: air, sun, freedom, large movement.

lack of confinement. Walk into a cave.

Instruct to walk around cave bent over, or on knees. Feel things bump your head, shoulders, and legs. Feel rough surfaces and jagged rocks.

Walk out of cave into open space again. Explore space freely.

Suddenly find you are in a cage.

Direct participants to establish size of cage by touching all four sides. Grasp bars. Look for a way out, find key and escape. May continue with other closed spaces: small room, glass container, cylindrical enclosure.

3. Walking through Substances

At leader's direction walk through a variety of substances: hot sand, mud, ice, over pointed rocks; walk with the wind blowing from behind, walk facing the wind, walk with someone pushing you from behind.

Direct participants to walk the full length of the room for each substance. If the room is small, double the length. May elaborate on substances. Encourage participants to think of the qualities of substances and to establish the balance necessary to navigate through them. Suggest use of arms to compensate and maintain balance.

4. The Ever-Changing Object

First person 'creates' an imaginary object, indicating its shape, length, width, and weight, and demonstrating its use. Others guess the object. Next person takes the object and changes it into something else.

For example: the first person plays a flute, the next person stretches it out into a skipping rope and skips with it a few times, the next person coils the rope and makes it into a hat.

5. Imaginary Catch

The leader establishes a ball, indicating its size, shape and weight. He throws it to someone across the circle. The person catches the ball and throws it to someone else.

Suggest changes in the size and weight of the ball: a football, a beach ball, a balloon or a rock. Encourage people to imagine the arc in which different sized balls travel.

6. Shopping Mime Game

Leader begins with line, 'Yesterday I went shopping and I bought . . .' and mimes an object. Everyone guesses the object. The next person repeats the line and the first mime, then adds another mime. Continue around the circle.

Good introduction to basic mime techniques. Encourages observation and memory of movements.

7. Moving an Imaginary Object

Each person thinks of a large object. Without speaking, they must establish its size, shape and weight. Then move the object across the room.

Develops consistency in dealing with imaginary objects and group interaction. Stimulates thinking about balance and force.

Enlist the help of another person (without talking) to move object back to starting position.

If necessary, remind participants to convey size, weight and shape of object through gesture and movement rather than speaking.

In groups of four, move objects across the room again.

Variation: Each person thinks of an animal. Must

then move animal across the room, individually, with partner and in groups of four.

8. Tug-of-War

Divide group into two teams. Play a game of tug-of-war with an imaginary rope.

Establishes group work in dealing with imaginary objects, and group co-ordination of balance.

9. The Runaway Balloon

Group imagines a large, hot air balloon hovering just above their heads. Pull on ropes attached to sides to bring balloon down to earth. While holding balloon down, all climb into the basket beneath the balloon. Balloon rises and floats, then returns to earth.

Stimulate thinking about sensations as balloon rises, creating illusion of movement, looking at scenery below. Develops group work in creating an imaginary scene, and group co-ordination in movement.

GAMES AND GROUP WARM UPS

At the beginning of a workshop, games and group warm up exercises help participants to get to know each other and to become comfortable working together. These exercises are designed to stimulate interaction between group members and to draw them into spontaneous use of basic mime, drama, movement and dance techniques.

1. Name Game

The group sits in a circle. The leader establishes a rhythm to the count of six, as follows: 1–2 Slap knees with both hands on each beat, 3–4 Clap hands together on each beat, 5–6 Snap fingers, right first and then left. All join in the rhythm. When rhythm is secure, go around the circle with each person saying his or her name in rhythm on the snaps. Repeat. Then, while keeping the rhythm going, one person says his or her name on the first snap and calls the name of another person on the second snap. Without missing a beat, the named person carries on with his or her name and calls another name on the second snap.

2. Name Catch

Group stands in a circle. Go around circle with each person saying his or her name. The leader begins by saying his or her name and tossing a ball – real or imaginary – to someone across the circle while calling his or her name. The person catching the ball says his or her name, then tosses the ball to someone else while calling his or her name. Continue until everyone has caught the ball at least twice.

3. What are you doing?

Player 1 stands in the centre of the room and mimes some activity, e.g. washing up. Player 2 walks up to Player 1 and enquires, 'What are you doing?' Player 1 responds by naming an activity which he is *not* doing, e.g. picking flowers. Player 2 must then mime 'picking flowers' until Player 1 enquires, 'What are you doing?'. Player 2 must then respond with an activity other than 'picking flowers'. They must continue in this way until: 1) one player cannot think of an immediate response to the question, 2) one player answers with an activity which is too close to what he actually is doing, e.g. he is brushing his teeth and responds, 'brushing my hair', or 3) one player repeats an activity already mentioned in the game. The player who makes a mistake sits down and another person challenges the first player. This develops concentration and also introduces basic mime techniques.

4. Guess the Title

Divide into two teams. Each team writes on small pieces of paper the titles of several books, films, songs, television shows, or famous quotations. The number of titles should equal the members of the opposite team. One person from the opposite team then chooses a piece of paper from the hat and acts out the title for his own team to guess. Allow two minutes for each player. Keep track of how long each team takes to guess the titles. The team with the lowest time wins. If a player can't think of a way to act out the title, the leader may assist him.

5. The Stick Game

Pass a stick around the room. Each person mimes some action using the stick, e.g. rowing a boat, smoking a cigar, playing golf, walking with a cane. Then go around the circle again with each person using the stick to communicate something about himself.

Variation: One person uses the stick as a certain object, another person responds to his use and then transforms it into something else. For example: Player 1 plays the stick as a guitar serenading Player 2. Player 2 comes out on the balcony and waves, goes to Player 1, takes stick and rides away on it as a horse. Stimulates more involved improvisation.

6. The Animal Game

Each participant chooses an animal and expresses it through movement, without any sound. Encourages the use of subtle characteristic movements, rather than easily recognised noises.

Variation: As an introductory exercise, each participant selects an animal which expresses an aspect of his or her personality. Then share reasons for selecting particular animal.

7. Machines

Divide into small groups and create machines with interlocking parts. The machines may either be well-known (lock, tin opener, cuckoo clock, washing machine) or imaginary (instant hair-cutting machine, shoe shine machine, bubble-making machine). Each machine part can make a different noise.

Variation I: One person begins machine by doing a repetitive action and making a repetitive sound. The next person, doing a different action and making a different noise, attaches self to first person in some way. All participants attach themselves one by one, forming a large imaginary machine.

Variation II: Each individual creates a machine, others guess.

8. Follow the Leader

The following exercises develop group sensitivity to following one person, group co-ordination, and non-verbal communication.

a. Movement Exercise
The leader initiates a variety of movements: walking slowly, skipping, jumping, dragging one foot. Everyone follows.
Variation: Leader is at the end of a single line. Instead of watching the leader, each person watches the person directly in front of him and does exactly what he does. Since there will be a slight time-lag in changing from one activity to the next, at times those at the front of the line will be doing something different from those at the end. Concentration is required to change only when person directly in front of you changes.

b. Hand-Clapping Exercise
The leader begins a hand-clapping rhythm, emphasising light clapping on the palm of one hand by the fingers of the other hand. Everyone follows exactly. Leader varies dynamics, speed, and intricacy of rhythms. Without speaking, leader nods or winks at someone who then becomes leader. This exercise develops sensitivity to subtle changes and flexibility in clapping to songs.

c. Group Sensitivity Exercise
Group sits in a circle. Leader slowly lifts hand up and down. Everyone follows this movement exactly. The leader makes other simple movements and all follow. The leader passes the leadership to someoneelse in the circle, simply by looking at them. Everyone then follows the new leader. This develops sensitivity to non-verbal communication, and requires the use of eye-contact to be aware of the change in leaders.

d. Two Person Mirrors
Divide group into pairs. One person leads, making movements with hands which the person mirrors exactly. Without talking, leadership moves from one partner to the other. Develops concentration and stimulates thinking about variations in familiar movements. Encourages co-ordination between persons.
Variation I: Player 1 leads, Player 2 mirrors movement with a different part of the body, e.g. Player 1 makes a circle with his hand, Player 2 makes a circle with his elbow.
Variation II: Player 1 makes a large movement. Player 2 mirrors with a small movement using the same part of the body.

Variation III: Player 1 makes a movement and Player 2 reacts to it, e.g. Player 1 lunges forward, Player 2 leans back.

CHARACTERISATION

Character is conveyed through posture, physical movement, mannerisms and actions, speaking voice, speech habits and content of speeches, and clothing, accessories and props. Generally, there are three sources to which one can refer in order to develop characterisation:

1. Text or improvisational structure
   Look for specific information or limitations, as well as general characteristics.

2. Players
   Those taking the parts should draw from imagination, experiences in life, projection of self, others or character into situations, education and whatever research facilities are available.

3. Others
   Casual dialogue, intentional discussion, improvisations all provide ideas, insights and raw material.

Encourage people to explore all of these areas as they discover and develop their character.

The following exercises are in three groupings. The first, Experimenting with Characterisation, focuses on establishing a character and expressing that character through movement, gesture and 'body language'. The second grouping, Exploring Characterisation, continues in this direction yet adds psychological and motivational factors. The third grouping, Building Characterisation, guides the way to still more in-depth character development and suggests use of external aids.

People who have experimented with and developed characterisation will have more confidence in performance situations than those who have just read over and learned a part. Some drama or mime parts, such as the inanimate objects like the Feet or the Ear in 'How Can the Body be Complete?', p. 237, or the non-speaking parts like the Farmers in 'The Wise and Foolish Farmers', p. 210, may seem unlikely subjects for characterisation exercises. Players however, will benefit greatly from working out as full a development as possible. Other parts, such as the characters in the teaching aid, 'It's Impossible!', p. 218, may seem too small to warrant development; again, such development is not only an excellent exercise but it also helps players mature in their imaginative and performance abilities. Intensive characterisation work is not a necessity, but it is useful and can be employed in an on-going way. These exercises can be used in conjunction with Improvisation suggestions, Chapter 19, as well as dance, movement and mime suggestions throughout the book. Additionally, they can be applied to speakers or characters in poems or readings.

1. Experimenting with characterisation

a. Character Walks
Group walks around room normally. The leader calls out various characters and participants adapt a walk that conveys the character.

Suggestions include: a large person, a timid person, a proud man, a happy child, an old woman, someone who is lost, someone who doesn't want to go where he is going.

b. Character Turns
Participants stand in straight line with backs to leader. The leader calls out a character and all turn to face leader, adopting movement that expresses the character. Resume original position and repeat.

Encourage participants to avoid stereotypes (a cane for an old person, skipping for a child). Ideal for children as it provides a limited time span in which to maintain a character and focuses on essential characteristics.

c. Character Questions
Each person develops one character fully in imagination. Answer questions about the character: Are you a man or woman, boy or girl? How old are you? How much do you weigh? What is your basic

May need to ask more questions to help define character. May also suggest imitating a friend. Challenge participants to express personality in subtle movement and gesture based on observation of actual people, rather than resorting to stereotypes.

attitude toward life? How do you feel today? Do you have any characteristic mannerisms? Are you timid or aggressive? Are you relaxed or tense? Walk around room in your character.

d. Characters in Action

After participants establish characters in exercise 3, leader gives pairs simple situations in which they interact. Pairs may interact spontaneously or may take about five minutes to work out interaction, and then present to group.

Possible situations: a) One loses a wallet, the other finds it. b) One is trapped in a room, the other discovers him. c) Both characters want the same thing. d) Characters are drawn together by something then separated by it.

Remind participants to think about their character's responses rather than their own responses to the situation.

2. Exploring Characterisation

The following exercises focus on four primary elements which convey personal characteristics, attitudes and mood: 1) Pressure 2) Tendency 3) Tension and 4) Rhythm and Speed. Though developed primarily in Mime technique, they are valuable in both drama and dance. (For thorough treatment of these elements, we recommend Claude Kipnis's *The Mime Book*.)

a. Pressure

This refers to the expression of psychological pressures through the bodily stance and posture. In a state of *positive pressure* a sense of confidence radiates from the centre of the body outward, creating an open posture. The shoulders are back, the head is up, the chest is held high, the arms, hands, and feet are slightly turned out from the body in a welcoming position. In a condition of *negative pressure*, the opposite is true. The pressure from within the body lessens, and the pressures from without seem to crush the body. The posture turns inward with the shoulders slumping, the head drooping, the chest collapsing, the arms, hands and feet turning inward. The whole body reflects withdrawal, melancholy, depression.

Exercise: Begin in state of positive pressure with open posture. Without altering any other part, lower head. How does this change one's presentation of one's self? Slowly curve shoulders forward and let stomach sag. Again, note change in self-presentation. Gradually turn hands, arms and feet inward. How does this affect one's feelings? Now, reverse the process. Begin from the negative pressure position and move slowly to the positive. Discuss changes.

b. Tendency

This refers to the basic tilt of the body, either forward or backward or to the side. Positive tendency which tilts the body forward is motivated by desire, aggressiveness, boldness, readiness. Negative tendency, which tilts the body backward, indicates hesitation, doubt or if exaggerated, fear or cowardice. If the body tilts from side to side, it indicates questioning rather than hesitation.

Exercise: To practise the use of tendency, imagine this scene and then mime it: You are on holiday. As you hurry toward your favourite beach, the positive tendency of your body indicates your eagerness to plunge into the clear beautiful water. As you get closer and closer you begin to notice bits of rubbish and oily patches floating on the surface of the water. By the time you reach the water's edge you see the full extent of the pollution. You draw back in disgust and the negative tendency of your body registers your horror and disappointment.

c. Tension

This refers to the general state of muscle tension or relaxation in a character. The presence of tension in the body conveys the difference between sauntering along on a pleasant spring day and walking through a dark passageway. The presence of tension gives the impression of a character who is anxious, nervous or expecting the worst. The body is unconsciously braced against the feared attack or anticipated unpleasant response. An absence of tension is reflected in a relaxed posture: hands hanging freely at sides and a bounce in the step. The change in tension in the body can convey sudden changes in environment – the beginning of a rainstorm, for instance.

Exercise: Perform a simple task with loose fluid movements, muscles relaxed and easy: thread a needle, pick up a piece of paper, smooth back one's hair, get dishes out of a cupboard. Repeat the same actions with muscles tensed. Notice the difference in the feeling of the action and the emotional message it conveys.

d. Rhythm and speed

This refers to a person's internal tempo which is communicated through his gestures, his walk, his acts. The speed and rhythm of an action reveals the character of a person. Small, quick gestures communicate something very different from languid or casual mannerisms. As with tension, the same action performed at different speeds and rhythms has a completely different meaning.

Exercise: This develops control over speed of action and awareness of changes in rhythm and speed. Choose several simple actions: waving at a friend, crossing a street, drinking a glass of water. Perform at a speed and rhythm that feels comfortable for you. Then repeat several times very quickly and several times very slowly. Now perform the same action going through a complete sequence from very slow to normal to very fast. Discuss how varying tempos effect the meaning of the action.

When developing a character, consider the above elements and ask these questions: What is the normal pressure of the character – positive or negative? Is he or she confident or retiring? Adopt a body posture that conveys this. What is the normal body tendency – positive or negative? Is the character generally eager and ready to move into a new situation, or more tentative and retiring? Tilt the body accordingly. What is the normal tension of the body? Are muscles generally relaxed or slightly tensed? At what speed and rhythm does this character normally perform actions? Establishing a normal presence of these factors enables one to use changes in pressure, tension, tendency, speed and rhythm to indicate changes in environment, circumstance, and emotional state.

3. Building Characterisation
These exercises can be used in both basic improvisation and in characterisation work based on a text. Some are appropriate for initial character development, others work better after character is fairly well established.

a. Physical Characteristics

1) Work out the following for the character, writing down what you decide and discover.

race gender age height weight physical build
abilities or disabilities posture hair colour
eye colour physical stamina

2) Build these characteristics into character during improvisations and rehearsals.

b. External aids

1) Find clothing, accessories and props that will convey character.

2) Work with the above in several ways. Sometimes use them all, appearing at rehearsals in full costume with all props, other times wear the costume but mime the props, other times wear only street clothes but act as if you were fully costumed and had all accessories and props. Learn to express character whether or not you have the external aids that clarify his identity.

3) Find three different sets of aids that would suit character, each set a different style. Use imagination, not elaboration, and think about your character in terms of symbol.

c. Psychological development

1) Write two paragraphs about character's family and background.

2) Write an employment history for character, including comments from employers and co-workers.

3) Motivation: Ask the following, and similar, questions:

What role does character play in the overall production? Why does character make the specific decisions or say the specific things he does, in light of what happens as a result? Does character tend to have his actions worked out regardless of other people or situations, does character act according to other characters' actions, does character tend to act spontaneously?

4) Relationships: Ask the following, and similar, questions:

Is the character honest or deceptive in relationships? Does character know himself well? Does character have any close relationships? If so, are they healthy or unhealthy?

MIME

1. Basic Techniques

a. Mime Walk

Starting position: The body is straight, heels together, toes slightly apart.

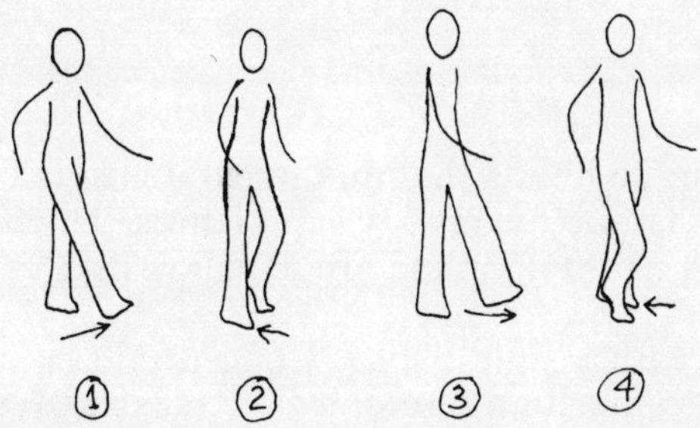

1) With weight on left foot, extend the right foot to take a normal-size walking step. As the right leg straightens, the right foot is flat on the floor. Weight remains on left foot.

2) Raise onto toe of left foot. As heel goes up, knee naturally bends and the right foot is drawn back to starting position.

3) Left foot, in continuous motion, is extended forward as in 1).

4) Raise onto toe of right foot, and draw left foot back as in 2).

Arms move in natural walking rhythm – the right arm moves with the left leg, the left moves with the right leg.

b. The neck

The neck may be used to create an illusion of closeness or distance.

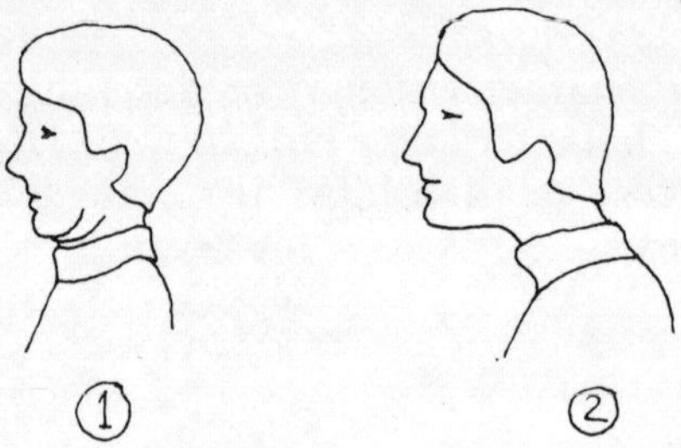

1) The neck pulled back creates the illusion of an object or person which is very close.

2) The neck stretched forward, with eyes focused on 'something' in the distance, creates the illusion of distance.

2. Everyday Mimes

This technique builds the fundamental elements of creating a mime from familiar everyday experiences. The basic principles for creating a simple mime are as follows:

a) Begin with a simple idea. Concentrate on interaction between yourself and an object or person. Action should be simple to allow attention to maintaining the position of objects and clarity of movement.

b) Set the stage. Establish in your mind the location of objects, doors, props or persons.

c) Imagine the interaction between yourself and objects or person. May give the action a humorous twist.

Example:

a) The idea: Looking for a pair of shoes before going to a dance.

b) The stage: A bedroom with a bed on one side, a wardrobe on the other, and a chair in the middle. Walk through this scene, establishing location of these objects.

c) Imagine the interaction: In your mind walk into the room, move from one object to the other looking for the shoes. Imagine your response: frustration, anger, puzzlement. Give the action a humorous twist e.g. someone else walks in wearing the shoes, or one decides to wear heavy boots instead of dancing shoes.

Suggestions:

Walking a dog	Picking a bouquet of flowers	Slicing bread
Sewing on a patch	Eating an apple	Crossing a busy street

CHORAL READING and MUSIC

These exercises help people use their voices flexibly, imaginatively and freely. Most of them can be applied as or translated into group and choral reading techniques.

1. Chance chords (or, how to make a joyful *noise*!)

At leader's signal, everyone sings any note desired.

This is superb for freeing people who may be afraid to use their voices. Since there are no 'right' or 'wrong' notes, it's impossible for anyone to make a mistake! The contributions of even tone deaf people are perfect.

Chance chords allow people to use their voices in an entirely new way, and they stimulate sensitivity and develop listening awareness. They are also useful as a means of release, helping people to relax and enjoy themselves.

a. Basic

Sing several chance chords.	Give a signal, and indicate the chord should be held until you signal its release. This is espe-

	cially important initially, as people are usually startled and sometimes embarrassed at the strange sound they're making together. Alternatively people are often timid and don't make much of a sound at all, so need to be heartily encouraged until they're familiar with the idea and the sound. Holding the chords will help people get used to the odd sounds.
b. Volume changes	Direct changes, indicating loud and soft.
Sing loud and then soft chance chords; then vary the volume without breaking the tone.	People should take breaths as needed.
c. Pitch changes	
All sing together on low notes, then high. Then vary the pitch, moving up and down without breaking the tone.	Indicate pitch by raising and lowering your hands.
d. Combinations	
Combine pitch and volume changes, without breaking the tone.	These pitch and volume exercises move along fairly quickly: don't belabour them, just let people have a good time.
e. Resolving	Give signal for chord, then signal people to begin changing their notes.
All sing initial chance chord, then begin changing notes to make it sound 'better'. It usually will resolve into a major triad.	

Note: Chance chords are abbreviated *c.c.* on scripts.

2. Sounds — To develop listening awareness and group sensitivity

a. Signals

Each person makes up a rhythmic pattern of beeps, such as 'beep beep beep' or 'beep-beep beep, beep-beep beep'. Patterns may include pitch variations as well. At leader's direction, all say patterns simultaneously. Then leader directs volume and pacing changes. At various times leader encourages participants to listen to overall sound and pattern, rather than concentrating just on their own contribution. When people are listening and participating with overall sensitivity, the group sound almost invariably decreases in volume and internal stress, then stabilises.

b. The Farm or Zoo

Similar to Signals, above, but using the sounds of animals, such as cows, ducks, pigs, chickens. Leader encourages people to make genuine animal sounds, rather than the common, humorous 'mooo' or 'quack, quack' which parodies animal sounds. Let entire group experiment with same sound; divide group into three or four, giving each group a sound, then add each sound progressively; let people select any sounds they choose. Encourage the same volume and pacing changes as suggested above.

c. Whistling

Follow same pattern as suggested for Signals, above. This exercise isn't always successful, as some people can't whistle and others can't help laughing, but it's fun!

d. Human response sounds

Following leader's directions, entire group experiments with groaning, moaning, sharply indrawn breaths indicating surprise, shock, horror, sounds indicating disgust, dismay, disappointment, disapproval.

3. Words — To develop expressiveness

a. Onomatopoeia

The following words sound like their meaning. Select several and lead group in experimenting with them, drawing out the expressive qualities of the meanings. Concentrate on the words one by one, the entire group saying it several times.

whirling shimmering enchanting rippling overflowing
crackle balloon hush crunch whisper broken creak

b. Emotive

Invest the following words with the emotional qualities they seem to elicit. Encourage people to express the emotion facially as well. Repeat each a few times, as above.

hurry fear maybe pain wait frown

heavy praise no wonders stop prolong

4. Phrases

Teach simple and possibly familiar phrases which have been embellished. Do each phrase two or three times. (See below for embellishing techniques.)

a. Glory to you, Lord Christ

Glory	to	you,	Lord Christ!
(*word canon*)		(*chance chord*)	

b. Come, follow me

Come,	come	follow	follow, follow, follow,	me.
(Solo voice)	*(scatter, by group)*	*(solo)*	*(echo, by group)*	*(solo)*

5. Embellishing Techniques

a. Scatter

One person says a word, usually as part of a sentence or text, and group members randomly repeat word several times, in a variety of pitches, volumes, tempos. Entire technique takes no more than three seconds.

b. Echo

One person says a word, as above, and group or portion of group repeats word together, two – four times, fading until volume is just a whisper.

c. Canon

Repetition of a word or phrase, one repetition sometimes overlapping others.

1) Word canon, two parts
Part 1: (*awed whisper*) Glory . . .

Part 2: (*softly spoken*) glory

Part 1: (*building volume and pace*) glory
Part 2: (*coming in on Part 1's final syllable; still building*) glory

Parts 1 and 2: (*without pause, uninhibited*) GLORY!

2) Phrase canon, three parts ('darkness' always spoken on 'not')

Voice 1: A light that shines in the darkness;

Voice 2: a light that darkness could not overpower.

Voice 3: (*medium volume*) Darkness could not overpower

Voice 1: (*volume fading to whisper*) Darkness could not overpower.

d. Group whisper

One person says a word at normal volume, all others whisper word.

6. Percussion

Let group experiment with bells, triangles, finger cymbals, wood blocks, wood sticks, etc. Any of these percussion instruments can add sparkle or emphasis to readings and certain songs.

MUSIC

1. Major and minor harmonies

Explain that the triad is the basic building block of Western music, and that songs are written in major or minor keys.

a. Sing bits of familiar songs in both major and minor keys.
   Major: 'Give me oil in my lamp', SOLW 4
   Minor: 'Fear not, rejoice and be glad', SOLW 59

Talk a bit about the differences in sound and tone colour in the examples the group is considering.

Divide the group into three groups, with both men and women in each.

For these exercises, hold up one, three or five fingers, to indicate to each group which tone should be sung next.

b. Singing major triads
   Entire group sings 'one', with Group 1 sustaining tone
   Group 2 moves to 'three'
   Group 3 moves to 'five'
   and/or
   Group 1 sings 'one'
   Group 2 comes in on 'three'
   Group 3 comes in on 'five'

c. Singing words with triads
   Group sings a low triad, then slowly moves up the scale, singing 'Alleluia' or 'Jesus, Jesus' or another word of praise.

Pitch the triad for the group.

d. Singing minor triads
   Repeat the above exercises, using minor triads.

Explain that the middle note ('three') is a semi-tone lower in a minor triad.

2. Free-singing

a. Experimentation

People with low voices sing on a medium to low note like 'D', those with higher voices sing a fifth above, on 'A'. All should sing the syllable 'ah'.

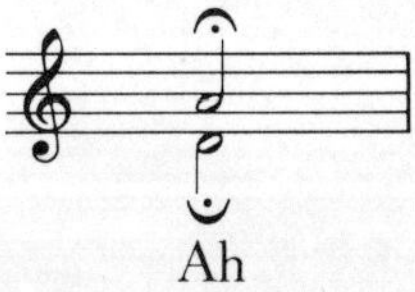

Explain that these two notes are the 'tone centres'. Demonstrate that simple melodies can be improvised around either note. Perhaps your demonstrations would sound like these:

Some people may only sing two or three notes around the tone centres, whilst others will be more experimental. Reassure the group that either is fine.

All sing the tone centres, then free-sing around them on 'alleluia'.

Indicate when to sing, when to begin the free-singing.

b. With reading

Choose someone to read a pre-selected scripture or poem, whilst the group supplies a free-singing background.

The background can vary in volume and intensity, enhancing and amplifying the words of the reading. Help people to be aware and sensitive as they sing.

Short and perhaps familiar passages are best. Try Psalm 23, Psalm 148, Isaiah 42, I Corinthians 13:1–17, or some of the poetry in Section II of this book.

Variation: To accompany reading during worship or as a background for a section of choral reading. Begin with lower tone centre. Add higher one. Free-sing softly in the minor key. Increase volume according to sense of words, resolve in major triad.

3. Listening

The leader sings a note or plays it on the piano or guitar, and the group tries to sing exactly the same note. The tone should be held, people breathing when necessary, until the pitch is achieved. Re-sounding the note may be helpful.

If some have difficulty, the leader should suggest they sing a bit higher or lower, as appropriate. Don't linger too long with this exercise, as some may find it a bit intimidating initially. It's a good one to repeat, either later in the same workshop or in successive workshops.

4. Vocalising

Within these exercises, cover from notes 'A' below middle 'C' to high 'G'. Encourage people not to strain their voices: sopranos and tenors may join in at a comfortable pitch, and altos and basses may drop out at the higher parts. Climb up a semitone at a time.

a. To help people learn to open their mouths whilst singing

Mouth should be opened enough for the person to insert the width of two fingers.

b. To develop flexibility

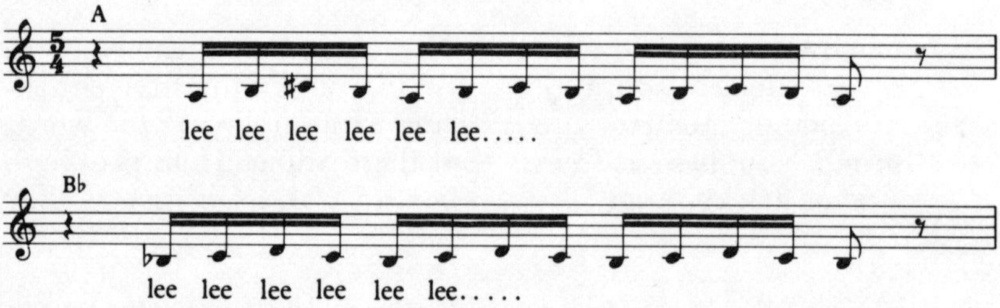

c. To develop smooth (legato) singing

Continue this exercise to 'A'. If you want to go higher, change vowel to 'ah'.

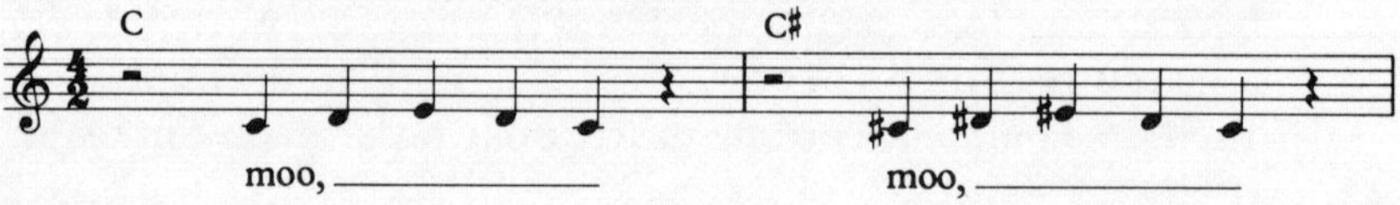

5. Music machines (variation of 'Machines', p. 367)

Divide into small groups, three to six people each. Each group makes a machine with a definite sound pattern, such as calliope, record player, etc. Each part of the machine should have a particular tune or rhythmic and repeated noise.

TECHNIQUES

1. The Lion Hunt

Many people may be familiar with the gesture-sound stories about the adventures of two lion hunters. While relating the tale, the storyteller leads participants through a multitude of natural situations, all of which are dramatised by gesture and sound. Thus the entire group rustles through tall grass (rubbing hands together and making 'shhhh, shhhh' noises), climbs up and down trees (placing fists one atop the other, building higher each time, and making a clacking sound with tongue), endures thick mud (jerking hands up and down, making a slurping sound with each jerk), etc. The climax comes when a hunter, entering a dark lair, carelessly awakens the lion. The wild chase back to the camp furiously retraces the approach. Once again grasses, lakes, trees, bogs etc. are encountered, but now at breakneck pace. Breathless when the camp's safety is finally reached, the leader of the two then tries to convince the other that he had never been afraid of the lion at all.

This technique of using gesture and sound to accompany storytelling is effective not only as a game but also as a teaching device. 'The Good Shepherd', p. 191, can easily be used in this way, and 'The Faithful God of Daniel', p. 194 is a variation of the technique.

2. The Rain Clap

This is an easy and quick way to produce the sound of a rainstorm. One person, clearly visible to entire audience or congregation, leads the group in the actions.

Leader begins by raising left hand, extending palm, and right hand, extending index finger; audience does the same. Leader taps palm with finger, which makes a light sound; audience follows suit. The storm is built by following the leader, who taps two, then three, then four fingers against the opposite palm. By the time everyone is tapping with four fingers, there are often people looking around for umbrellas! Leaders and/or others can also make sounds of thunder and wind, if desired.

We use the Rain Clap to introduce songs, such as 'Here comes Jesus', SOLW 49 or as a congregational participation tool with drama and mime, such as 'Peace! Be Still' p. 231.

3. Cinquain
This French word meaning 'five lines' is also the name of a poetic form. We use a variation of the form, assigning parts of speech rather than syllable numbers to certain lines. Such cinquains have a simple structure and are easily written. Below is an example, as well as an explanation of the form.

Example: bells

bright, brass, brilliant

clearly, cheefully

ring

bells

	Part of Speech	*Explanation*	*Example*
First line:	noun	the name of someone or something	bells
Second line:	3 adjectives	three words describing first word	bright brass brilliant
Third line:	2 adverbs	two words answering 'how?' 'when?' or 'where?'	clearly cheerfully
Fourth line:	verb	word telling some action of first word	ring
Fifth line:	noun	repetition of first word; another word with same meaning as first word; another word which intensifies or links meaning to first word	bells

After people understand the basic structure, they may want to experiment with variable spacing, punctuation, capitalisation. Below are some examples, and still others are in the Materials and Workshop sections.

red
pulsing
poignant
spiced
impudently
impetuously
BURSTS:
POPPIES!

by Martha Keys Barker

Ointment
cooling
healing

soothingly
lovingly
sacrificially

poured
balm

from workshop group in Cowley

We use cinquains in the following ways:

- get-acquainted exercise introductory or relaxation exercise
- Writing workshop exercise
- basis for improvisation, dance and movement
- tool for Art and Graphics workshops
- tool for youth ministry
- tool for Christian education and Sunday school classes

4. Obstacle Walk

Exercise

Arrange an obstacle course. If inside, use several chairs, one or two tables, boxes, perhaps one or two people making strange noises or striking percussion instruments at odd intervals. If outside, use natural 'obstacles' as well: trees, slopes, stones, water, flowerbeds, bushes.

One person is blindfolded, another leads that person through the walk. The guide holds person firmly, either by linking inside arms and holding hands or by placing one arm around the person's waist and holding the other hand. The guide must find other ways than verbal communication to lead and help the blindfolded person. Silence must be maintained throughout.

Note: The course may be more complex for older youth, including a flight of stairs (but not steep or poorly-lit ones), people needing to crawl under objects, to go through narrow places, to walk in a stooped position, etc.

Application

a. With children

A leader or older child who hasn't seen the course is blindfolded and led through by another leader or older child. The rest of the children watch.

Leader interviews person:	Did you feel afraid or uncertain? How did your guide help you? How would you feel if your guide were blindfolded?
Leader interviews guide:	How did you feel guiding the person? Was the person nervous or afraid? How could you tell? How did you reassure the person?

b. With older children and youth

Divide group into pairs: blindfold one and have the other lead through the course. Change roles and go through course again.

Discussion: The differences between leading and being led
Include some of the questions above

CHAPTER 19

Improvisation

Improvisation is a word for spontaneous action. Most commonly associated with music or drama, it is a valuable activity to use with any performing art. Initially the idea of 'doing whatever comes along' may seem intimidating, but as people become familiar and experienced with improvising, they find themselves more confident in their own abilities, more relaxed with others and more secure in performances. Improvisation is useful for groups as it gives members the opportunity not only to create together but also to respond spontaneously to each other. It is often the basis for a finished product or performance, as stories, music, dramas, dances, mimes which originally began as exercises are developed, refined and polished. Improvisation is a versatile and flexible tool. Depending on the leader's intention, improvisational projects can be widely unstructured or narrowly limited.

The scope of this book does not include extensive development of improvisation, but we do explain a basic working principle and pattern, and list a cross-section of exercises and suggestions. *Improvisation*, by John Hodgson and Ernest Richards (Eyre Methuen Ltd.) is a fine book which covers comprehensively the diverse aspects of its topic. Although basically a drama book, many of its principles are applicable to other forms, and its activities and projects are generally useful for improvisation in dance, mime, writing, group reading, workshops with children or young people, and, with adaptation, instrumental or vocal music.

Units of action

If you want to improvise specific scriptures or stories, divide them into basic units of action. Do this by reducing the story line to simple, inclusive statements. Each unit may have sub-sections but the entire story should be understandable from only the units of action. These divisions operate as an outline, allowing the material to be broken into manageable portions and making clear the interrelatedness of the various elements. Dividing the material into units of action can be done prior to rehearsals or as part of them.

Listed below are two examples of this sort of breakdown. The first, based on I Kings 17:8–24, is fairly simple. It is followed by an explanation of how one group worked with the scripture. The second, based on the familiar story of the prodigal son, is a more complex construction, including development of characterisation. An hour-long drama was improvised around this breakdown, and an excerpt is on p. 276.

Example: I Kings 17:8–24 – Elijah and the widow of Zarephath

1. Units of action

    a. God sends Elijah to Zarephath

    b. Elijah meets the widow

        Elijah asks for drink, then food
        The widow demurs at the latter
        Elijah assures her God will provide

    c. Elijah lives in the widow's home

        God miraculously provides food

    d. The widow's son dies

        The boy sickens and dies
        The widow accuses Elijah

    e. God answers Elijah's prayers

        Elijah takes the boy to his room
        Elijah cries out to the Lord
        Elijah lies upon the boy and prays – three times
        God restores the boy's life
        Elijah returns the boy to the widow, who praises God

2. I Kings 17:8–24: Group process

Four of us met together, two men and two women. We read the story in two versions of the Bible, then discussed it. We shared our thoughts about the events, actions and people, and talked about specific words that seemed significant. Then we broke the story into units of action. Each of us, one by one, retold the story, attempting to use as few words as possible yet not miss out any of it. We had each done it about twice before we could remember everything that happened as well as not be too wordy. Finally we could go right round the circle, each person adding the next action concisely. Working out these units of action helped us to really learn the story, so later we never had struggles trying to remember 'what happened next'.

Next we mimed the story, acting it out without using any words at all. As there were four of us and just three characters, one sat out each time. We mimed several times, changing parts each time so everyone could play each part once. Then we repeated this process, adding words. We intended to have a narrator for the drama, so the person sitting out each time improvised the narrator's part. We chose parts and went through the drama once more. Then we began to refine it, establishing definite actions and movements and using those words which we wanted in the actual play. All together this rehearsal took about an hour and a quarter, and it was two or three days before the service in which we wanted to use the drama.

We had one more rehearsal just before the service. We talked through the units of action and went through the drama once. Then we talked about things we'd missed out or forgotten, and went through it one final time. This rehearsal was about thirty minutes long.

3. Summary

This group's working pattern was as follows:

reading story
discussing thoughts and responses
unit of action breakdown
miming story
acting story with words
choosing parts and solidifying drama
final rehearsal

Example: Luke 15:11–32 – The Prodigal Son

An excerpt from the drama developed from the following units of action is on p. 276.

The Prodigal Son

Unit of action	*Development of characterisation and plot*
1. Younger of two sons asks father for his share of inheritance	Introduce father and elder son, establish relationship
	Younger son enters: develop personality and values conflict between the two brothers. Elder son departs
	Younger son asks father for money
2. Younger son leaves home	Two brothers talking and arguing as younger son packs to leave
	Departure of younger son
spends all his money in wild living	Son and several friends: they're living on his money
	Son and girlfriend, living together in a 'no commitment, no demands' relationship
	Son and drugs dealer or horse betting agent Son and friends buying expensive stereo equipment or taking spontaneous holiday Flashback to father at home: longing for his son
	Son and girl, who leaves him
	Son and friends, who mock him because most of his money is gone
runs out of money as famine hits	Son, desperate and alone, decides to get job

Unit of action	*Development of characterisation and plot*
gets job feeding pigs	Son works in restaurant. Wealthy, decadent clientele, eating luxurious meal, abuse son, waste food, become pigs in their table manners, actions, noises. Son is underpaid and starving
3. Son returns home	
decides to return: ask father for forgiveness, for a job	Son, suddenly aware of his debased and crooked life, decides to return to father: not as privileged son, but as poor and sinful man seeking employment
reconciliation with father	Father has waited eagerly, looking daily for his son's possible return. Runs to meet him, embraces him; accepts, almost disclaims his words of confession
	Commands servants to celebrate: bring clothes to replace rags of son, prepare extravagant food, etc. Much bustle, festivity, music
4. Encounter between elder son and father	Elder son enters, talks with a servant who tells him what's happened. Elder son infuriated
	Elder son and Father talk
	Elder son goes with father to celebration

Exercises

1. Three element improvs

   Divide players into groups of 3 or 4. Give each group a paper which has three elements, e.g., a telephone, a cellar, a dog, written on it. Allow the groups 10–15 minutes to work up an improv using the three elements; then regroup and present the results to each other.

   Variation: Unknown to the groups, have the same three elements written on all papers.

2. Two person improvs

   Divide group into pairs. Give all pairs the same topic for a one-to-two minute conversation. These may include:

   a. Disagree about something

   b. One tries to sell something to the other

   c. Both talk at the same time, ignoring what other is saying

3. Three person improvs

   Divide group into threes. Give group the following topics for conversations:

   a. One person communicates good news to the other two

   b. Two persons exclude the third person from their conversation

   c. One person tries to explain how to do something to the other two

   Note: These exercises develop the ability to create dialogue spontaneously, to respond to unexpected statements from others, and to keep a conversation going. They may also be used to develop street or group scenes where excitement, confusion or simultaneous activity is necessary.

4. Continuing Action improvs (Use no words, costumes or props)

One player establishes an activity, character or scene, then freezes. Another player 'replaces' the first, carrying on whatever was established.

Example: First player puts on hat, collects umbrella, picks up paper and walks toward door, then freezes. Second player steps in front of first, walks out the door to bus stop, waits for bus, then freezes. Or perhaps second player returns to house for something left behind, then freezes. Another player takes second player's place; etc.

5. Response improvs (Use only action, then words)

One player establishes a character or activity; another encounters the first, responding however is desired.

6. The Scarves

(For Mime and Drama, use in conjunction with characterisation exercise, p. 369+.) Bring a large collection of different scarves to the workshop. Each person selects a scarf and establishes a character using that scarf. The scarves will suggest certain characteristics: one may be very fashionable, another may be rather tattered and old: bright colours suit some characters while subdued colours complement others. After individual characters have been established, interact in pairs and then in the larger group. After spontaneous interaction, sit down and discuss possibilities for building into a single scene involving all the characters. Work out finished scene.

7. The Balloon Man

Divide a large group into smaller groups. Each group becomes one part of a park scene: one group may be children playing, another group may be the crowd listening to a soap-box orator, another group may be vagabonds who frequent the park, etc. The balloon man walks on and begins to blow up balloons, using his hands to indicate the size and shape of the inflated balloons. He offers the balloons to the various groups. Each group responds in a different way to the balloon man: the children may clamour for more, the old men may laugh at him, or a group of older boys may try to burst the balloons. Let each group decide how they will respond.

A more advanced group may develop this idea into a contemporary parable. The balloon man gives away all the balloons, but many children still want one. The balloon man reaches into his breast pocket and pulls out a balloon that represents his own heart. He blows this up and gives it to one child. Then the balloon man dies, to the shock of the on-lookers. Suddenly the heart balloon bursts showering them all in balloons, and they realise the meaning of his death. Several people now take his place blowing up balloons and giving them away.

8. The Carnival

Divide into small groups of four or five. Each group is one act at a carnival or circus. Possibilities: high-wire balancing act, animal trainers and animals, a weightlifter, acrobats, jugglers, clowns. Each small group decides on its act, and spends about twenty minutes working on it. The entire group then reassembles and performs for each other. One person may act as the ringmaster or the master of ceremonies and introduce the various acts. Taped circus music can provide a good background for this improvisation.

9. War and Peace

Divide into two groups. Each represents a group of people, or a tribe. They must determine what sort of people they are: In what country do they live? What do they do for their living – hunting, fishing, farming, gathering? What sort of houses do they live in? What are their daily activities? How do they care for their children? Are they generally peaceful or aggressive? Each group works out a series of three scenes that depict their lives and performs them for the other group. Group A then initiates some action to provoke Group B to war. Group B responds and a situation of conflict is developed. Each group must then decide some way to end the war and communicate this to the other group. Leave the conclusion for the groups to work out.

10. Life Cycle

The different stages of the life cycle provide the basis of several improvisations, in movement, mime and drama.

Basic Exercise

Participants begin on floor in tightly curled position. The leader names each stage of the life cycle: birth, infancy, childhood, adolescence, young adulthood, middle age, maturity, old age. Participants remain in the same place. By changing positions and walking in place, they go through each stage. The entire exercise should be done in one minute.

a. Movement

Play music which suggests the different stages of the cycle. Participants begin on floor in tightly curled position, gradually uncurl and respond to the music, moving freely throughout the room. Leader may give verbal cues when stages change, if necessary. Music suggestions:

Birth/Infancy: 'Morning' from *Peer Gynt* by Grieg

Childhood: 'Fossils' from *Carnival of the Animals* Saint-Saens

Adolescence: 'Lucy in the Sky with Diamonds' by the Beatles

Adulthood: 'Autumn' from *The Four Seasons* by Vivaldi

Old Age: 'The Swan' from *Carnival of the Animals* by Saint-Saens

b. Mime

Using only movement, walking and gestures, participants express characteristics of each stage. The leader may stimulate action by reading particular words relevant to each age:

Birth/Infancy: shock, breath, unfolding, stretching, discovering hands and feet, crawling, growing, security, warmth.

Childhood: exploring, discovering, wonder, energy, excitement, climbing, swinging, running, learning.

Adolescence:	awkwardness, shyness, embarrassment, enjoyment, awakening concerns and desires, friends, rhythm, music, unfolding potential, independence, freedom.
Young Adult:	choices, confusion, trying one's wings, risks, deepening relationships, love.
Middle Age:	security, confidence, experience, satisfaction, nurturing others, sudden questions, regrets, anxieties about the future.
Maturity:	fulfilment, accomplishment, respect, sadness, 'empty nest', perspective.
Old Age:	completion, aging, failing sight and hearing, impaired movement, wisdom, understanding humour.

c. Drama

Begin as in other exercises, using only movement and sound for birth and infancy. Then participants move at random throughout the room, relating spontaneously to others. At cue from leader, improvise dialogue and dramatic situations which express characteristics of each stage.

11. Parables

Biblical parables are ideal for mime improvisation. Discuss the parable so that its meaning is clear to everyone. Consider the characters and their responses. If the parable would be more relevant in a contemporary setting, determine a setting. Improvise in several of the following styles. A group may go through these in sequence, beginning with style a and progressing through style d, or may select one or two styles.

a. One person reads the parable while others mime. Encourage participants to portray ideas and characters, rather than simply miming words.

b. The parable is mimed silently with no reading or with just the last sentence or two of the original parable read as a conclusion.

Example: The parable of the good Samaritan may be concluded with the lines: 'Which of these three, do you think, proved neighbour to the man who fell among the robbers?'

c. The parable is mimed with sound effects.

d. The parable is read while participants mime the emotions of characters using only facial expression, hand gestures and postures.
Example: The wedding feast (Matthew 22) Participants stand in line. Two people portray the master's feelings, two depict the servants inviting the guests, two express the unwillingness of the first guests and two convey the happiness of the later guests.

Note: See Scripture Ideas at end of chapter for parables suitable for improvisation.

12. Eli and Samuel: I Samuel 3

This scripture story is ideal for improvisation with beginners or children. The action is easy to learn because it's repetitive, yet the personalities of Eli, Samuel and the Lord give scope for expressive and imaginative characterisation.

a. Read and talk about story.

b. Work out units of action.

c. Improvise story in several ways:

Mime: Use only movement, no words

Finger play: Small groups of three or four, using flat surfaces such as tables or game boards as a mini-stage, act out story with only fingers, hands, narration and sound effects.

Puppet show

The song 'Samuel' from *Hey Kids, Do You Love Jesus?* (suggested below) is an excellent storytelling aid: mimes or puppet shows can be worked out to the music. Alternatively, part of the group can learn the song while the others work out an improvisation, and then both groups can join to make a combined presentation.

13. See Games, p. 365, for additional ideas.

14. See Characterisation exercises, p. 369, for additional ideas.

Suggestions

1. Scripture ideas: improvise with mime/dance/drama/music or sound effects/writing

   Genesis 1–2:3 – – – Creation

   Ezekiel 37:1–14 – – – Valley of dry bones

   Mark 1 and 2 (excerpts) – – – Calling of the disciples

   Luke 10 – – – The good Samaritan

   Matthew 6:25–34 – – – Lilies of the field

   Matthew 13:24–30 – – – Parable of the weeds

   Matthew 22:14–30 – – – Wedding feast

   Matthew 25:1–13 – – – The ten bridesmaids

   Matthew 25:14–30 – – – Parable of the talents

   John 13:1–17 – – – The foot-washing

   Acts – – – Paul's adventures

2. Material in Section II which provides improvisational basis for drama, mime, movement, instrumental music and combinations

Poetry and Readings	*Story*
fitly joined	The Good Shepherd
Wilderness Wanderers	The Faithful God of Daniel
self-giving God	The Sower and the Seed
Bondage	Samuel Merryweather

gooseberry pie	*Mime and Drama*
Wind of Spirit	Hands
Revelation	On Tiptoe
We Shall All Be Changed	The Wise and Foolish Farmers
	Prodigal son suggestions
	The Amazing Change
	It's Impossible!
	How Can the Body be Complete?
	Identity
	Images

3. Songs from *Sound of Living Waters*, *Fresh Sounds*, *Cry Hosanna*, and *Hey Kids, Do You Love Jesus?*

   a. Useful for improvising hand actions, mimes, dramas, puppetry to music

      The body song, SOLW 111

      Wake up!, SOLW 116

      Drop everything and go, FS 99

      Hosanna, Lord, CH

      The 'seed' song, CH

      Samuel, HK 7

      I'm not alone, HK 14

      The whole armour, HK 18

      Jeremiah, HK 24

b. Useful for improvising dances

Alleluia No. 1, SOLW 1

Let us give thanks, SOLW 8

Morning has broken, SOLW 9

Fear not, rejoice and be glad, SOLW 59

He will fill your hearts today, SOLW 131

David danced before the Lord, FS 8

Israel is my vineyard, FS 56

For you are my God, CH

Harvest of righteousness, CH

The Lord is present in his sanctuary, CH

Lu-ia, lu-ia, CH

Introduction to Workshop Structures

Essential principles and directions which apply to all workshops are listed in Chapter 17, Workshops. Because we do not repeat these in the following chapters, we suggest a thorough reading of Chapter 17.

All workshops are suitable for adults and youth unless otherwise noted. Workshop and activity suggestions for children are in Chapter 27.

Information and suggestions concerning one workshop may be useful for others. Even if the art form or purpose of particular workshops doesn't parallel your intentions, perusing the various structures will give you additional ideas. The exercises and activities in all workshops are based on the 'building block' principle, which means they are easily and usefully interchanged or substituted.

By supplementing or changing the exercises, you can repeat any structure time and again.

The left column contains workshop structure, the right column leader's notes and additional information. Notes and information listed in another part of the book, such as the Exercises and Techniques chapter, are not repeated in the right column of these chapters.

Some exercises and projects suggest small group work. If your group is too small to sub-divide productively, complete the work as one group or abridge suggestions to fit your group.

Time estimations are approximate and will vary with each group.

When we intend particular exercises to be done in a workshop, they are listed specifically. Otherwise we indicate a general category or topic and follow it with suggestions from which to choose.

Chapter 20

Group Reading Workshops

Pointers

– Good posture is important for effective readings. Whether people are seated or standing, they should have their shoulders back and their heads lifted. Emphasise good posture during workshops and rehearsals, to develop the habit for presentations. Whenever possible, seat people in straight backed chairs rather than easy chairs.

– Sensitivity is increased when people are close to each other. People should stand with shoulders touching, or, if seated, have their chairs as close together as possible. Additionally, group should be in rows, rather than strung out in one long row.

– Group readings usually have a director during preparations but frequently not during presentation. As a director is oftentimes distracting, the decision on whether or not one is necessary should be based on context of presentation, the group and the reading's complexity. At any rate, after the initial rehearsals the director should work at a distance from the group. This will train members to project the reading the length of the building or room, rather than focusing on the area just in front of them.

– Undirected readings should have one group member as cue-giver. Located centrally in the group, this person takes a deep breath, quietly, to alert group members the reading is about to begin. All speak with the cue-giver however, so that the first syllable or word isn't said by just one voice.

– The use of scripts during presentation is optional. If used, they should be in uniform card folders or binders. Hold scripts at chest height, so eyes can drop easily to words without head having to be lowered. Always raise script up, never move head down, or words will be lost. At the same time, be sure that script does not block face, or much of the reading's expressiveness will be lost.

– Group readings have a tendency to lose their pacing and flow, bogging down into a monotonous drone. Be particularly aware of this danger and speak directly to it in workshops or rehearsals.

– Suggestions in Music Workshops may prove useful in Reading Workshops. Also, see particularly 'Structuring a Well-balanced Workshop' in Chapter 17, as the example given is a reading group.

READING WORKSHOP I: Introductory *Time: 1½–2 hours*

Purpose: To acquaint people with various types of readings; to develop sensitive group reading

Section I: Exercises and experimentation *25–30 minutes*

1. Physical Warm Ups, p. 349+
   Select two or three from Neck, Shoulders and arms, Torso categories.

   Breathing Exercises, p. 357
   Select one or two

   or

   Play one of the following games:
   Name Game, p. 365
   Name Catch, p. 366
   The Stick Game, p. 367

2. Sounds Exercises, p. 379
   Select two.

3. Words Exercises, p. 380
   Select three or four each:
   Onomatopoeia
   Emotive

4. Free-singing Exercises, p. 383

Section II: Instruction	*20–25 minutes*
	Introduce each reading in this section by noting particular characteristics and uses. See Readings and Appendices for additional information.
	Give out copies of readings.
1. Responsive reading 'Let Us Rejoice', p. 137	Draws out corporate response; led by one person or small group.
2. Two-part reading 'Psalm 24', p. 136	Encourages participation; each part builds in response to other.
3. Dramatic scripture reading 'The Tax Question', p. 139	Presents scripture in compelling manner; develops drama inherent in scripture.

Section III: Application/Creativity *45–75 minutes, depending on project*

Select from the following:

a. Give out copies of a variety of readings. Sub-divide, and let individuals or small groups disperse. Allow enough time for people to read their parts silently, then aloud; and enough time for groups to practise together. Then re-group, and present the readings, discussing after each the type and its usefulness.

'David Danced', p. 174 – solo, narrative, scripture based

'Psalm 51', p. 144 – three-part, confession

'I Stand and Knock', p. 141 – four-part, meditative

'Ruth and Naomi', p. 227 – dialogue, dramatic, scripture based

'Endless Rejoicing', p. 134 – solo, proclamatory

'Revelation', p. 151 – group, choral (Leader should work with this group, since some techniques were not taught during the workshop.)

'Prayer for Renewal', p. 163 – solo, prayer poem

'We Are His Witnesses', p. 153 – group, dramatic, scripture based

b. Divide into small groups, assigning each a type of reading to develop. Allow 45–60 minutes, depending on participants, then re-group to share results.

Groups may choose text, or leader can pre-plan theme and give out scripture references, poetry or ideas. Readings developed may later prove useful in worship; alternatively, if humorous topics or themes were given, the readings may be used for an entertainment.

READING WORKSHOP II: Exploratory *Time: $1\frac{3}{4}$ hours*

Purpose: To teach basic techniques of choral reading

Section I: Exercises and experimentation *50 minutes*

1. Sounds Exercises, p. 379
   Select two or three.

2. Word Exercises, p. 380
   Select six or seven each:
   Onomatopoeia
   Emotive.

3. Chance Chords, p. 377.

4. Physical Warm Ups, p. 349+
   Select one each; Neck, Shoulders and arms, Torso categories.

   Choose warm ups which don't require strenuous exertion or floor work.

5. Embellished Phrases Teach two, selecting from p. 380 and/or using your own.	Develop phrases before workshop, if intending to use your own.
6. Read a psalm or poem in unison. 'Come Lord', p. 135 Psalm under twelve verses, such as Psalm 15, 47 or 121.	Initially the reading will be rough and awkward, but objective is a smooth unified sound. After first reading, and as group goes along, encourage participants to listen overall, to pause together, to sense a common expression for key words. Help them achieve these; stop group at certain points during the reading, to work out trouble spots. A group will probably go through reading three times, possibly four; but don't belabour it.
7. Two part reading 'Psalm 24', p. 136.	Keep working on the smooth sound, and also emphasise both vocal and facial expressiveness. Encourage readers to respond to each other's parts, building in volume and accent according to word content.

Section II: Instruction — *15 minutes*

Teach a choral reading.

'Renewing the World', p. 146
'Revelation', p. 151.

Section III: Application/ Creativity	*20–45 minutes, depending on project*
Select from the following: a. Work out group reading to poem or scripture. 'Wilderness Wanderers', p. 179 excerpts from Isaiah 55 selected verses from Psalm 107.	Select text prior to workshop, have copies for all. Lead group in developing reading.
b. Divide into groups of four or five; select text and develop reading, using techniques learned. Re-group and present readings for each other	Give suggestions of topic, theme or content; supply Bibles or poetry books, if necessary.
or	
Leader gives each group a text to develop into reading. 'fitly joined', p. 181 'confession', p. 158 'Hands', p. 160 Psalm 100 Isaiah 52:7–10.	Copies of text should be printed out so participants can write on them.
c. Teach choral readings from selections in Part II.	

READING WORKSHOP III: Exploratory *Time: 1½–2 hours*

Purpose: To discover ways of linking readings and music. *Note:* People who play instruments should bring them; leaders should work instrumental experimentation into the exercises and/or third section.

Section I: Exercises and experimentation *45–50 minutes*

1. Follow the Leader
   Hand Clapping Exercise, p. 368.

2. Physical Warm Ups, p. 349+
   Select three or four from Shoulders and arms, Torso, Back categories.

3. Breathing Exercises, p. 357
   Select one or two.

   Vocalisation Exercises, p. 384
   Select one or two

   and/or

   Sing 'The Bell Song', SOLW 94, with participants playing various instruments (See Percussion Exercise, p. 381).

4. Sounds Exercises, p. 379
   Select one or two.

5. Chance Chords, p. 377.

6. Words Exercises, p. 380
   Select three or four each:
   Onomatopoeia
   Emotive.

7. Free-singing Exercises, a) and b), p. 383.

Section II: Instruction *15–20 minutes*

1. Teach a choral reading.
   'Revelation', p. 151
   'We Are His Witnesses', p. 153.

2. Teach music/choral reading 'Psalm 118', p. 148.	Work out instrumentation according to your participants.
Section III: Application/Creativity	*30–60 minutes, depending on project*
Select from the following:	
a. Continue work on 'Psalm 118', preparing it for use in worship.	
b. Develop a scripture reading similar to 'Psalm 118'. Use a psalm for a choral reading base, a gospel narrative for a dramatic reading base.	Select reading prior to workshop.
c. Divide into small groups and have each work out a reading with choral techniques, sound effects, musical background, or any combination. Re-group and present readings for each other. 'Friday', p. 175 'David Danced', p. 174 'Prayer for Renewal', p. 163 'Bondage', p. 171.	Give each group copies of text; one for each participant.

CHAPTER 21

Mime Workshops

Pointers

– If the use of mime is unfamiliar to the group, begin workshop with a brief description of mime, similar to the introduction to the mime section of the Mime and Drama chapter. Then move quickly into exercises and games involving mime technique.

– The workshops concentrate on several basic mime techniques: working with imaginary objects, characterisation, group improvisation and group co-ordination. See chart on p. 204 for listing of materials which develop these techniques.

— For those interested in further work in mime, we recommend the books listed in the bibliography. Observation of trained mime artists will also greatly expand one's ideas of the potential uses of mime.

MIME WORKSHOP I: Introductory *Time: 2 hours*

Purpose: To introduce basic mime techniques for working with imaginary objects.

Section I: Exercises and experimentation — *25–30 minutes*

1. Brief introduction and explanation of workshop's purpose.

2. Physical Warm Ups, p. 349+
   Select a variety of exercises

from exercise chapter to warm up each area of the body.	
3. Isolation Exercises, p. 352.	These are particularly helpful in developing mime technique. Include each area of the body. Particularly emphasise arms and hands in preparation for use in object manipulation.
4. Imagination Exercises, p. 361+.	Incorporate both the walk-about and object manipulation exercises. If the group does these easily, shorten the time allowed. If these are new and challenging, allow more time.
Section II Instruction	*35–40 minutes*
1. Present the principles of developing Everyday Mimes, p. 376.	
2. Demonstrate an example of an Everyday Mime.	Suggestions: hammering a nail, watering plants, meeting a friend, raking leaves, looking for a lost coin.
3. Introduce one Everyday Mime idea which all participants act out on their own at the same time.	Ask necessary questions to stimulate thinking about setting the stage, establishing a character, imagining interaction.
4. Divide into small groups to create own mime situation on same pattern.	You may give each group a simple idea, involving an object but leave development to them. Suggestions: collecting clothes for a jumble sale, dressing for a party, painting a wall, opening an old cupboard in a deserted house.

5. Present mimes for each other

Section III: Application/Creativity — *45 minutes*

1. Divide into small groups or keep same groups from above exercise if they worked well together. Give each group a different group mime selected from improvisation suggestions, p. 397+. Limit length of mime to five minutes.

   Allow each group between twenty and twenty-five minutes to work out their mime. Be sure each group actually works out mime in gestures and actions, rather than just talking through it. Each group should go through their mime at least once before presenting it.

2. Groups present mimes for each other.

3. Briefly respond to mimes, comment on good points and make suggestions for changes.

   Encourage positive comments first, then ask for suggestions for changes.

MIME WORKSHOP II: Exploratory *Time: 2 hours*

Purpose: To experiment with mime techniques in characterisation.

Equipment: Several small hand mirrors for 'On Tiptoe' mime
Hats and costumes, if desired.

Section I: Exercises and experimentation — *25–30 minutes*

1. Brief introduction and explanation of workshop's purpose.

2. Physical Warm Ups, p. 349+. Select a variety of exercises from exercise chapter which will warm up each area of the body.

3. Isolation exercises, p. 352.	The ability to isolate various parts of the body is important in characterisation.
4. Relaxation exercise, p. 356.	This assures that group begins with minimum of tension, and bodies are relaxed and supple.
Section II: Instruction	*45 minutes*
1. Discuss elements under Exploring Characterisation, p. 371+. Go through exercises for each element.	Familiarise yourself with these elements and practise explaining them in your own words. If desired, think up your exercises.
2. Using these elements and any questions from Character Questions, p. 370, create a character.	
3. Participants may select hats or costumes, if available, to suit character.	
4. Characters in Action, p. 371 *or* Use the 'On Tiptoe' mime script as a basis for a group exercise in characterisation.	Use the characters that have been developed in 2. above rather than those described in the script. Suggested procedures: Give participants several situations to respond to in character. e.g. looking for something which is lost and finding it, hurrying to catch a coach, arguing with a friend. Present situation of looking for something in the distance

	and ask for response in character.
	Walk through action of mime in sequence with different persons arriving at different times, looking into distance.
	Give mirrors to two persons to show to others. Encourage them to respond in character.
5. May want to allow some time for discussion, evaluation, response to these exercises.	Encourage participants to share any insights into characters they have created, and to evaluate interactions between characters. Did they seem realistic? What gestures and mannerisms most effectively conveyed the character? What could improve them? Encourage positive comments before corrective ones.
Section III: Application/ Creativity	*45 minutes*
1. Divide into small groups to work on particular improvisational ideas. See suggestions on p. 397+	Suggest working on those which emphasise characterisation, i.e. The Scarves, The Balloon Man, Parables.
or	
Give each group a poem to interpret in mime, employing characterisation techniques.	Suggestions for use: 'Hands', p. 160, 'gooseberry pie', p. 170, 'the self-giving God', p. 178.
3. Groups present improvisations to each other. Others may wish to respond, comment.	

MIME WORKSHOP III: Developmental/Project Oriented

Time: 2 hours

Purpose: To develop particular mime techniques and group co-ordination while working on a specific project.

Section I: Exercises and experimentation	*25 minutes*
1. Physical Warm Ups, p. 349+ Select a variety of exercises for all areas of the body.	
2. Isolation exercises, p. 352.	Particularly concentrate on the special effects which can be created with the neck, p. 376.
3. Relaxation exercise, p. 356+ Tense and Relax Freeze and Thaw.	
Section II: Instruction	*25 minutes*
1. Teach the Mime Walk, p. 375, and allow time for individuals to practise.	If participants don't pick up walk easily, encourage them to watch others and allow plenty of time so that all feel comfortable with the walk.
2. Group Co-ordination Exercise Group stands in a line or two lines, with participants one behind the other. At verbal cue from leader, all begin to walk together. When leader says to stop, all stop. Leader varies commands and group responds.	

Repeat exercise with leader walking in front of lines. Group follows his movements rather than verbal cues.

Section III: Application/ Creativity — *45–60 minutes*

1. Work out action to 'The Hat Race', p. 214.

This involves the Mime Walk, creating an illusion of distance with the neck, characterisation, and group co-ordination.

Suggested procedure:

Read through the script together.

Decide on characters and a reader.

All look at scripts as reader reads story, walk through actions. Repeat.

Outline basic units of action (p. 391) as they appear in script and review cues for stopping.

First stop: 'So they made a rule:'

Second: 'I just need a little more recognition from my followers.'

Third: (Richard's followers) 'They wanted him to look just as important as John.'

Walk through action without scripts, except for reader.

Review order of action and repeat.

If 'The Hat Race' is to be performed following the workshop, it is necessary to have another rehearsal to perfect timing and group co-ordination.

2. After working on script, relax together. Discuss any feelings about the script, or suggestions for making the mime more effective.

3. Finish with relaxation exercise.

MIME WORKSHOP IV: Introductory, for children 6–12

Time: 1½ hours

Purpose: To introduce basic mime techniques in characterisation and storytelling.

Equipment: Hats, costumes for characters, if desired.
Several small hand mirrors if using 'On Tiptoe' exercise.

Section I: Exercises and experimentation — *25–30 minutes*

With children, an introduction is generally not necessary. Launch into activities immediately.

1. Children's physical warm up exercises, p. 354+.

These engage children's imaginations as they warm up and become comfortable with movement.

2. The Walk-About, p. 362.

This involves the participants in basic mime technique, moving in space, imagining obstacles and responding to them.

3. Play at least two games. One should involve imaginary objects.
   Imaginary Catch, p. 364
   The Ever-Changing Object, p. 363
   Shopping Mime Game, p. 364.

Keep the pace moving. Have more games in mind than you need. If one game doesn't catch on, move to another one.

4. Group imagination exercise
   The Lion Hunt, p. 385
   The Runaway Balloon, p. 365.

This draws children into group work.

5. Write simple improvisation ideas on pieces of paper. Each child chooses one and mimes the action described. The others guess what each child is doing.

Suggestions:
  Act out one thing that happens in your house everyday.

  Act out your favourite activity.

  Act out what you want to be when you grow up.

  Act out something that happened at school this week.

Section II: Instruction

25–30 minutes

1. Introduce the idea of character. Demonstrate different personalities through walking, ask children to describe the person you are demonstrating.

May work out simplified version of characterisation elements in Exploring Characterisation, p. 371+. Demonstrate these elements, rather than just talking about them. Work out simplified exercises for children.

2. Children do Character Turns, p. 370.

This stimulates thinking about conveying character through simple movement and gesture.

3. Ask each child to decide on a character. Use Character

Questions, p. 370, to provoke thinking. Walk around room in this character.

4. Give children time to select appropriate hats or costumes for their characters.

5. Work out the 'On Tiptoe' mime, p. 205, using characters they've developed.

Section III: Application/Creativity — *25–30 minutes*

1. Select one of the following:

Work on 'The Balloon Man', p. 397. The leader may be the balloon man. Children may either be the same character as developed in Section II:3, or may select a new character and costume. If desired, names of characters may be written on pieces of paper which children draw from a hat

Suggestions for characters: a large, happy man, a little girl who is lost, a mother hurrying home, a brother and sister who are arguing.

or

Divide into small groups and give each group a fairy tale or familiar story to work out in mime, using whatever costumes and hats they need.

Suggested procedure:

Talk through basic units of action (p. 391), until all are familiar with story.

Possible stories: Cinderella, Jack and the Beanstalk, Joseph and his Many-coloured Coat,

Select characters.

Establish locations for places and objects.

David and Goliath. Ask the children for their suggestions.

Walk through basic units of action.

Perform entire story, with or without story being read.

2. If working in small groups, share mimes with others.

CHAPTER 22

Drama Workshops

Pointers

- Memorising parts in folk art drama is optional. Some people haven't time, others experience unnecessary strain in 'trying to remember'. Yet scripts aren't distracting if people learn how to handle them. If scripts will be used, work with people during rehearsals, helping them to treat their scripts as part of the character instead of an external mechanical aid. Emphasise that scripts should be raised to chest height rather than heads lowered, and that they must not block face.
- If not rehearsing in the presentation location, rough out the dimensions of the playing area in your rehearsal room. Use chairs, benches, chalk or tape marks to indicate boundaries. This will help people to become familiar with the actual amount of space they will have available.
- If participants are relatively inexperienced, or time at a premium, group leader or director should pre-cast parts, assigning them at the group meeting or in advance. With experienced people or as a workshop exercise, allowing people to experiment with parts and to select their own is generally productive and 'stretching'.
- When possible, build a collection of hats, scarves, jewellery, feathers, stoles, coats and other clothing, as well as props. Use them for exercises, improvisations and occasionally as costuming.

DRAMA WORKSHOP I: Introductory — *Time: About 2 hours*

Purpose: To acquaint people with basic dramatic techniques

Section I: Exercises and experimentation	*30–35 minutes*
1. Physical Warm Ups, p. 349+ Select five or six.	Choose exercises which are not strenuous; include floor exercises only if you previously told people to dress accordingly.
2. Do the following Imagination Exercises: Walking through Substances, p. 363 Imaginary Catch, p. 364 Moving an Imaginary Object, p. 364 Tug of War, p. 365 *or* The Runaway Balloon, p. 365	These flow easily from one to another.
3. The Stick Game, p. 367	Each mimes general action; after all have done so, each mimes action representing self.
4. Characterisation Exercises, p. 370 Character Walks *or* Character Turns Character Questions	These focus on a specific aspect of dramatic technique and also involve imagination, movement and improvisation.
Section II: Instruction	*10–15 minutes*
1. Tell a group participation story. 'The Faithful God of Daniel', p. 194 'The Good Shepherd', p. 191	This requires facial expression, vocal response and limited movement; it also stimulates imagination.

Section III: Application/ Creativity	*45–70 minutes, depending on project*
Select one of the following, depending upon group and time.	
a. Work out mime. 'On Tiptoe', p. 205 'The Wise and Foolish Farmers', p. 210	All read mime. Characters selected or assigned, more added if necessary. Repeat Character Questions, participants perhaps writing out thoughts, or do Physical characteristics, 1), p. 374 Costumes and props selected from ones you have supplied; or people work out their own, from whatever may be at hand. Go through mime once, then talk through any questions; go through mime a final time.
b. Work out drama. 'How Can the Body be Complete?', p. 237 'The Unforgiving Servant', p. 233	Assign characters, let all read scripts silently. Repeat Character Questions, participants perhaps writing out thoughts or do Physical characteristics, 1), p. 374. Seated in a circle, participants read through script. Discuss any questions about characters, plot, intent, etc. Walk through script, practising character order, entrances and exits, imaginary objects or locations, etc. Act entire drama, using scripts. If time, take a break, then repeat drama.
c. Develop one or more of the ideas suggested in Improvisation chapter.	

DRAMA WORKSHOP II: Exploratory *Time: 1½ hours*

Purpose: To provide a sample structure for groups which want to work together regularly

Section I: Exercises and experimentation *35 minutes*

1. Physical Warm Ups, p. 349+
   Select six or seven.

2. Isolation Exercises, p. 352
   Select five or six
   or
   Relaxation Exercises, p. 356+
   Select two.

3. Imagination Exercises, p. 362+
   Select two.

4. What are you Doing?, p. 366
   or
   The Stick Game, Variation, p. 367

5. Machines, p. 367
   or
   Sculptures, p. 359

Section II: Instruction *15 minutes*

1. Character Walks, p. 370
   or
   Character Turns, p. 370

2. Character Questions, p. 370

3. Characters in Action, p. 371
   or

1. Life Cycle, Basic, p. 399

2. Life Cycle, Mime, p. 399

Section III: Application/ Creativity

40 minutes (extend this section if desired)

Select one of the following.

a. Develop characterisation aspects of a drama.

Pre-select drama and have copies for all.

Repeat Section II progression; and see Drama Workshop Structure I, Section III, 1 and 2 for additional ideas about dramatic development.

Characterisation work in future meetings would draw from Exploring Characterisation and Building Characterisation, Exercises chapter.

b. Carry on with Life Cycle theme, using Drama variation, p. 400; work improvisations into a drama with set action and characters.

Follow a pattern of improvisation, group discussion, improvisation.

c. Three Element Improvs, p. 396, or develop another idea from Improvisation chapter, p. 391

d. Continue a project already begun, such as drama for worship, teaching, outreach or children's group.

CHAPTER 23

Dance Workshops

Pointers

- Leaders of dance workshops should know their material well. Practise explaining exercises and teaching specific dance steps with short, clear instructions to avoid spending workshop time figuring them out. Try out your explanations on a friend prior to the workshop, if possible.

- Many people have been put off dance at an early age because too much was expected of them in classical or ballroom dance where the primary emphasis was on learning the right steps. They will become discouraged if they can't pick up the steps immediately. Therefore, it is very important to set people at ease, to experiment with various types of free movement before concentrating on specific steps. Emphasis throughout workshops should be on exploring possibilities in movement, rather than just learning steps.

- Some people are intimidated by the word 'dance'. If this is the case, introducing the workshop as a 'movement' workshop may prove more inviting.

- Suggest that people wear clothes that are not restrictive. High-heeled shoes, tights, and tight fitting clothes will pose a problem to freedom of movement. Taking off shoes (if temperature permits!) is often desirable for dance.

- Think ahead about workshop space. A large area is needed for whole group exercises and instruction. For small group work, the large space may be divided by room dividers or smaller rooms may be used. Particularly if music is used, several groups in one room may prove confusing.

- To begin a dance/movement workshop, it is often helpful to use the Relax and Listen exercise, p. 357, as it gives a new perspective on fears and taboos about the body and dance. The readings affirm the goodness of creation, our ability to praise the Lord with our bodies, and encourage participants to offer themselves in dance.

- Stress that dance is a means of communication by picture rather than by word. Stimulate the imaginations of participants. Dance requires mental agility as well as physical co-ordination. Also, stress that dance comes from within. Those unfamiliar with dance will probably try to 'look' like dancers using ballet-like gestures and poses. The leaders' responsibility is to help people loosen up and 'feel' like dancers, and to enable them to find a movement style comfortable for them.

- In exercise and experimentation sections, as much as possible, rather than telling participants how to do movements, ask questions that help them discover new ways of moving. For example: 'How many different kinds of circles can you make? How many variations can you think of for a four beat rhythm?'

- When teaching dance steps, stand with back to group, so that participants do not have to 'mirror' your steps. When teaching circle dances, arrange group in a line or lines, so that those across the circle from the leader do not have to 'mirror' steps. When group has mastered the steps in lines, move into a circle. Arrange circle so that those who pick up steps more slowly are next to the leader and can follow the leader as the circle moves around.

- The following materials may enhance dance workshops:

  a. A drum is useful for rhythmic beat during exercises and interpretative explorations. Other percussion instruments – wood/sticks, triangles, finger cymbals, tambourines – also add rhythmic flavour and interest.

  b. Tapes or records of music for dances are helpful for teaching. It is especially effective to have a recording of dance songs at two tempos: one slower than normal and one normal. The slower tempo is used while teaching the dance and the normal tempo is introduced when the group becomes secure with the dance.

  c. If small groups are working with songs, have enough tape recorders and cassettes, or record players and recordings for each group to have access to one.

d. Props add variety and interest to dance. Begin a collection of these: scarves, canes, hats, tambourines, finger cymbals, wrist bells . . . let your imagination go.

– If dances are to be used in worship, remind participants that dance in worship is not solely communication between the dancer and God. Communication with other worshippers is also a primary focus. This is expressed through looking directly at people, smiling, offering encouragement to others as one dances.

– In a group that works together on a regular basis, it is helpful if someone in the group has had some dance training or experience. Or send one or two members to a modern dance class for a few lessons. Go to performances to get ideas. If a group continues to work together without outside influence, its style may become stale. The influence of other groups will open new vocabularies of movement.

DANCE WORKSHOP I: Introductory *Time: 1½ hours*

Purpose: To introduce basic folk dance steps and techniques, and to create new dances for use in worship.

Section I: Exercises and experimentation	*30 minutes*
1. Brief introduction and explanation of the purpose of the workshop.	May discuss role of folk dance in maintaining traditions of peoples. If possible, bring pictures of national dances from several cultures and discuss their function.
2. Physical Warm Ups. Select a variety of exercises from the exercise chapter, p. 349+, to warm up each area of the body.	Exercising to music will ease group into further combination of music and movement.
3. Play one game to loosen people up. Name Game, p. 365 Follow the Leader, p. 368 a. Movement Exercise.	If participants don't know each other, use Name Game to get acquainted and to introduce basic rhythm awareness. Follow the Leader introduces idea of duplicating movements which is developed throughout workshop.

Section II: Instruction	*30–40 minutes*
1. Four-Beat Rhythms, p. 359 Begin with basic movements, as described in exercise. Then lead through following progression, using Israeli Music or other folk music in 4/4 time:	Prepare a good repertoire of these movements, some easy and some more complicated. If group catches on quickly, use the more difficult movements.
Walk in a clockwise circle to the rhythm.	Prepares group for learning folk dance steps. Builds confidence in combining hand and foot movements.
While walking, clap hands on the beat.	
Still walking, snap fingers above head on the off beat.	
Walk three steps forward, one step backward. Then add hand clap on off beat.	
2. Teach the basic Grapevine Step, p. 253 *or* Teach a basic step for another dance which you'll be teaching later.	This step is the backbone of many Israeli folk dances.
3. Teach an easy folk dance. 'This is the day of the Lord', p. 256 'Come go with me to that land', p. 258.	This is most effective if you have a recording of the music at two tempos as described in workshop introduction.
Section III: Application/ Creativity	*30–45 minutes*
1. Teach a more complicated folk dance. 'God has spoken', p. 253 *or*	Remember to teach in lines rather than in circle.

Teach chorus of 'Once no people', p. 260
Divide into small groups to work out verses. Give each group one verse to work out.

Reassemble to put together entire dance.

or

Create a new dance.
Use any song with a verse chorus structure:
'O magnify the Lord', FS 36
'The King of glory', SOLW 124
'Sing, sing alleluia', FS 11
'Canticle of the gift', SOLW 2.

Divide into small groups, equalling the number of verses plus the chorus.

Group 1 make up chorus using the Grapevine step.

Each other group make up one verse.

Each group select one member to teach verse to the whole group.

Reassemble groups to teach verses.

Go through dance twice.

2. Conclude with relaxation exercise, p. 356 and a time of sharing, prayer.

DANCE WORKSHOP II: Exploratory *Time: 2 hours*

Purpose: To discover possibilities for interpretative movement, and to encourage freedom in offering dance in worship.

Section I: Exercises and experimentation	*45 minutes*
1. Brief discussion about the purpose of dance in worship.	
2. Physical Warm Ups, p. 349+ Select a variety of exercises from exercise chapter, to loosen up entire body. Do exercises to music.	
3. Do two relaxation exercises, p. 356+ Tense and Relax, or Freeze and Thaw. Then move into Relax and Listen.	Allow plenty of time for this section, so participants can feel free to relax. Encourages positive attitude toward the body and develops the idea of using the body in worship.
4. Still lying flat on floor, begin Circles exercise, p. 358.	Should flow smoothly from Relax and Listen. Ask questions to stimulate group: 'How many levels can you use? Can you make circles with one part while holding other parts still? Can circles convey feeling?'
5. Move without break from Circles into Two Person Mirrors, p. 368.	
Section II: Instruction	*15–20 minutes*
1. Leader uses simple movements to interpret The Lord's Prayer, as it is read or sung. All follow leader's movements. (For example,	Adjust movements to the ability of the group. If group has never danced before, use very basic and repetitive, easy-to-follow movements. For a more

see 'The Lord's Prayer' from the *El Shaddai* setting, CH).

advanced group, challenge with more variation.

2. All stand in circle. Using simple movements, interpret a song with verse/chorus structure.

   Chorus: Leader works out basic movement, all follow.

   Verse: In pairs, use circle movements and other flowing gestures to interpret.

   Possible songs include:
   'Alleluia no. 1', SOLW 1
   'All of my life', SOLW 31
   'This is the Feast', FS 59
   'Fear not, for I have redeemed you', CH
   'You are my witnesses', CH.

Have several of these songs on record or tape to play during this section. If group is very responsive to this experience, may use more than one.

Section III: Application/Creativity

45–50 minutes

1. Divide into small groups to do Sculptures exercise, p. 359.

2. In same groups, select a short expressive passage from the psalms. Decide on three or four group movements to express the passage. Use instrumental music, drumbeats, or other percussion instruments as background while reading and interpreting the passage

This will be facilitated if leader selects several passages and gives a choice of two to each group.
If preparing material for worship, may introduce theme or scriptures for the service as subjects for sculptures.

or

Give each small group a poem to express in movement. May use stylised movement, with only three or four changes in limited space. Or may interpret in more flowing style.
Use instrumental music, drumbeats, or other percussion instruments, if desired.

Possible poems include:
'the self-giving God', p. 178
'We Shall All Be Changed', p. 186
'David Danced', p. 174
'Revelation', p. 151
'Prayer for Renewal', p. 163

or

In small groups, write two cinquains, p. 386, one on an emotion, one on an object.

If preparing for worship, write one on a scripture for the service, and one relating the theme to our lives.

With group close together, interpret the cinquains in stylised movement, using limited space.

Interpret the same cinquain with larger, more flowing movement, covering more space.

Group may write cinquains together or each person may write one. Allow enough time for group to discuss scriptures and theme and to carefully consider cinquains. An example of using cinquains in this way is as follows. Scripture: Matthew 4:18–22 Jesus calling his disciples.
Cinquain on the scripture:

Jesus,
striding, sand-in-sandals
magnetically, compellingly, urgently
summons
fishers-of-men

Cinquain relating theme to our lives:

We,
believing, doubting
suddenly, clearly,
undeniably
hear:
'Come!'

3. Gather small groups together, to present sculptures, poetic interpretations, or cinquains for each other. Allow time for responses and sharing of feelings, insights, prayer.

Chapter 24

Music Workshops

Introduction

Sound is one of our most basic means of communication. We express our earliest responses through sound as we cry, gasp, sigh, gurgle. These simple expressions become more sophisticated as we grow, and soon we are shaping sounds into words, phrases and sentences. We also have the capacity to make music. It may feel 'natural' to hum as we work, whistle while we walk, tap a rhythm as we wait. And we fashion instruments, which also produce sound. Our ability to make music derives from our ability to make, recognise and shape sound. Music, whether instrumental or vocal, is very likely the most commonly experienced folk art of all.

Music is a powerful tool, capable of creating an atmosphere, of unifying a diverse group, of touching and stirring the human soul. We don't have to understand music technically or intellectually to be deeply affected by it, and sometimes we may express ourselves better through music than words. But there are some types of music, classical or jazz, for instance, which are available as personal expressions only after intensive training and practice, and many people never have such opportunities. Some people enjoy listening to music even though they themselves do not produce it, and still others don't like music much at all, perhaps feeling shut out of the musical world or self-conscious or doubtful about their musical abilities.

Folk music is often the ideal introduction or bridge to musical participation or growth. It is not dependent upon a great deal of knowledge and expertise, and its usually written by everyday people for everyday people. Folk music is easily learned which encourages those who despair of their abilities, and it gives those who may not have time or means to study music in-depth the chance to learn instruments and experiment. Folk music is effective in worship because it draws people together in a simple, common expression; it is useful in teaching because people are often better able to remember a song than words; and it's a great tool for festivity, not only because of its solo and group possibilities but also because of its ability to set a mood.

Pointers

- Whenever possible, ensure that the room for the workshop is large enough for people to move around. This is especially important for some of the exercises.
- It's easier for people to sing well if they're seated on straight backed chairs, rather than easy chairs or benches.
- A piano, though not essential, may be helpful.
- If you are teaching songs involving rhythmic gesture or dance, you may want to have a record or tape of the music.

General helps towards good singing

- Leaders may want to instruct groups in the following:

1. Singing preparation

   Prepare mouth: flatten tongue, lightly resting tip behind lower teeth. Without parting lips, 'yawn' throat open at the back.

   Place tone: imagine the note you want to sing travelling in an arc from your throat. It goes to the crown of head, then to top of forehead. Mentally pitch note there.

   Now you're ready to sing!

2. Expressive eyes

   Dead eyes make for a dull, lifeless tone. Sing with expression in your eyes and the tone will be vibrant and colourful. For bright tones, raise eyebrows and think 'surprise!'.

3. Volume and blend

   Learn to listen to the entire group, being careful to blend your voice with all the others. Roughly speaking, in a large group of about fifty people singing in unison, one would not be able to hear one's own voice if its volume was well-blended with the overall volume. In a small group, one should blend by listening carefully to those on either side.

MUSIC WORKSHOP I: Introductory *Time: $1\frac{1}{2}$ hours*

Purpose: To teach people more about music, to heighten participation in worship.

Section I: Exercises and experimentation	*35–40 minutes*
1. Sing three or four easy songs which people already know, one of the last being an action song. 'Peter and James and John in a sailboat', CH.	Pre-select songs that are simple yet interesting. They should be rhythmic and fun to sing. (See list at end of chapter for suggestions.)
2. Physical Warm Ups, p. 349+ Select two or three from Neck, Shoulders and arms, Torso categories.	The stretch exercises loosen up the whole body. Stress the importance of being relaxed whilst singing, emphasising that the whole body, not just the mouth and throat, is involved.
3. Breathing Exercises, p. 357 Select two or three.	Explain how to breathe from the diaphragm, and talk about the relationship between breathing properly and singing.
4. Vocalisation exercises, p. 384 Select two.	Encourage people to open their mouth and the back of their throat whilst singing. A large mirror or several small ones will let them see how they are really doing.
5. Chance chords, p. 377.	These help people relax further, stimulating participation unhampered by fear of failure.

6. Listening exercises, p. 384.	Develop sensitivity and awareness.
7. Sing a simple song based on major harmony 'Jesus, you're a wonder', CH.	This exposes group to basic harmonising.
Section II: Instruction	*10–15 minutes*
1. Teach a round. 'Rejoice in the Lord always', SOLW 10 'Seek ye first', SOLW 58.	Teach it to the group as a whole, all singing it a few times. Then divide into the two parts.
2. Teach a rhythmic song 'Neighbours', CH 'Psalm 8', CH 'Sanna', FS 1 'We will sing to the Lord our God', FS 13 *or* Teach a listening/repeating song 'The Spirit of the Lord', FS 107.	This will increase sensitivity.
Section III: Application/Creativity	*20–30 minutes*
1. Select one of the following, depending upon time and preference.	Since this is the first group meeting, participants may be too uncertain to develop anything on their own, even if aided by leaders. Work together as a large group, or sub-divide.
a. Teach two songs which will be used in a forthcoming worship service, or two songs which the group would be interested in learning (folk songs, etc.).	

b. Divide into four sections and learn the parts for a familiar hymn, then regroup to sing together. Alternatively, remain together, and let others listen while each section learns their part.

MUSIC WORKSHOP II: Exploratory — *Time: About 2 hours*

Purpose: To develop freedom in offering all of our humanity, our bodies, emotions, minds and voices, in worship.

Section I: Exercises and experimentation	*35–45 minutes*
1. Sing several familiar songs. Folk songs, lively hymns, perhaps a spontaneous verse song.	Pre-select fairly fast-moving songs with which people are comfortable.
2. Imagination Exercises Imaginary Catch, p. 364 The Runaway Balloon, p. 365.	These require activity besides singing. They help people realise they can offer to the Lord more than just their voices.
3. Sing 'Pullin' the weeds', FS 87 If seated, improvise hand actions for each verse. If standing, improvise simple mime actions for each verse.	Leaders choose the first few verses, then encourage people to offer their own. This song reinforces the idea that small routine activities are worthy of being offered to the Lord. It combines action and music, and stimulates spontaneity and participation.
4. Stand to sing and enact action song. 'Silver and gold', SOLW 50 'The butterfly song', SOLW 106 'He's my rock, my sword, my shield', FS 96: actions at end of chapter.	Further combines music and movement.

5. Sing a song involving people with each other personally.

   'Jesus, Jesus loves (*name*)', FS 83
   'We love the Lord', SOLW 112
   'One, two, three, Jesus loves me', FS 88

After people have re-seated themselves, begin this song without introduction, making it clear the group should join in. This type of song gives people a simple way to express caring and concern for each other and also quickens awareness of worship as a corporate activity.

Section II: Instruction

10–20 minutes

1. Teach a worship song and accompanying actions.

   'The Lord's Prayer' from *El Shaddai*, CH: actions included.
   'Clean hands', FS 94

Teach song first, then gestures. This familiarises people with gesture and movement in the context of worship.

2. Teach song for Section III, 1, if using song group doesn't know.

Preparation (if necessary) for next section.

Section III: Application/ Culmination

55–75 minutes, depending on project

1. Select one of the following, depending upon time and preference.

Provides opportunity for full use of the body in conjunction with music.

   a. Teach dance to 'This is the day', p. 256

   b. Teach dance chorus to 'Once no people', p. 260, with pre-arranged soloist to dance the verses.

   or

Divide into small groups and have each group work out a dance for one of the verses, then meet to dance all together.

2. Final song: select a well-known one with marked rhythm or improvisational potential.
   'All of my life' *or* 'Of my hands' with spontaneous actions

   'For you are my God' CH *or* 'Hymn of glory' CH with rhythmic movement or gentle clapping

   'Let us give thanks', SOLW 8 with rhythmic clap.

   Provides opportunity for people to move rhythmically while standing in place, or to clap in time, or to improvise gestures in a workshop context.

MUSIC WORKSHOP III: Experiential for a group that leads worship or as a worship centered activity for youth

Time: 1½ hours

Purpose: To develop sensitivity to leaders and others

This workshop is an extended version of Structure II, described in Workshops, Chapter 17.

Section I: Exercises and experimentation — *45–55 minutes*

1. Sing a few relaxed, well-known songs.
   Folk songs, lively hymns, perhaps a medley.

   Pre-select fairly fast-moving, familiar songs which people can sing easily.

2. Sing a song that involves actions or personal contact.

'The instrument song', CH 'Jesus took my burdens', FS 90	This helps people to relax, loosen up, enjoy themselves and each other.
or	
'Hey (*name*), do you love Jesus?', SOLW 109 'One, two, three, Jesus loves me', FS 88.	This gets people personally involved.
3. Sensitivity and following exercises	Omit discussion suggested in Exercises chapter.
Hand clapping, p. 368	Conclude this exercise by beginning a light hand clap that leads into the following song.
Sing 'I will sing', SOLW 7, accompanied by hand clap.	
Group sensitivity, p. 368.	This exercise leads directly into the following one.
The Ever-changing Object, p. 363	
Mirrors (basic), p. 368 *or* Movement, p. 368.	
4. Sing a two-part song	Develops listening sensitivity and awareness of parts balance.
'Rejoice in the Lord always', SOLW 10 'The Lord is my shepherd', SOLW 108.	
5. Sing a light, bouncy song	Leader begins song; this exercise determines how sensitive group is to mood set by leader.
'Allelu, allelu', FS 34 'Lu-ia, lu-ia', CH 'Thank you, Lord', SOLW 113.	

Section II: Development *35–45 minutes*

Select one of the following:

a. Prepare music for a service the group will be leading.

b. Work on *a capella* singing.

c. Learn new music or hymns, for new tunes for familiar hymns.

d. Break into twos or threes and work together in writing music or lyrics.

e. Have an instrumental rehearsal.

f. Use the time to work on a project already undertaken.

MUSIC: Warm up songs for music or worship workshops

Simple Songs

Give me oil in my lamp, SOLW 4

Thank you, thank you, Jesus, SOLW 18

The bell song, SOLW 53

Jesus is a friend of mine, SOLW 114

Jesus, you're a wonder, CH

I love my Lord, CH

I'm so glad I belong to Jesus, CH

He's able, CH

Whosoever will, CH

I will sing of the mercies, CH

Praise ye the Lord, CH

Glory to God, CH

The Lord is present, CH

Spontaneous Verse Songs

Oh! how good is the Lord, SOLW 6

I will sing, I will sing, SOLW 7

Come and go with me, SOLW 87

Hey, (*name*), do you love Jesus?, SOLW 109

Thank you, Lord, SOLW 113

(*Name*), Jesus loves you, FS 82

Pullin' the weeds, FS 87

Bless you, Jesus, FS 95

Jesus, you're a wonder, CH

Hand Action Songs

Silver and Gold, SOLW 50

The butterfly song, SOLW 106

One, two, three, Jesus loves me, FS 88

Jesus took my burdens, FS 90

Clean hands or dirty hands, FS 94

He's my rock, my sword, my shield, FS 96 (hand actions on following page)

God is our Father, CH

The instrument song, CH

Peter and James and John in a sailboat, CH

His banner over me

Rounds

Rejoice in the Lord always, SOLW 10

Father, we adore you, SOLW 26

He shall teach you all things, SOLW 41

Seek ye first, SOLW 58

Sing praise to the Lord for ever, FS 10

The light of Christ, FS 98

Hand Actions for 'He's my rock, my sword, my shield', FS 96

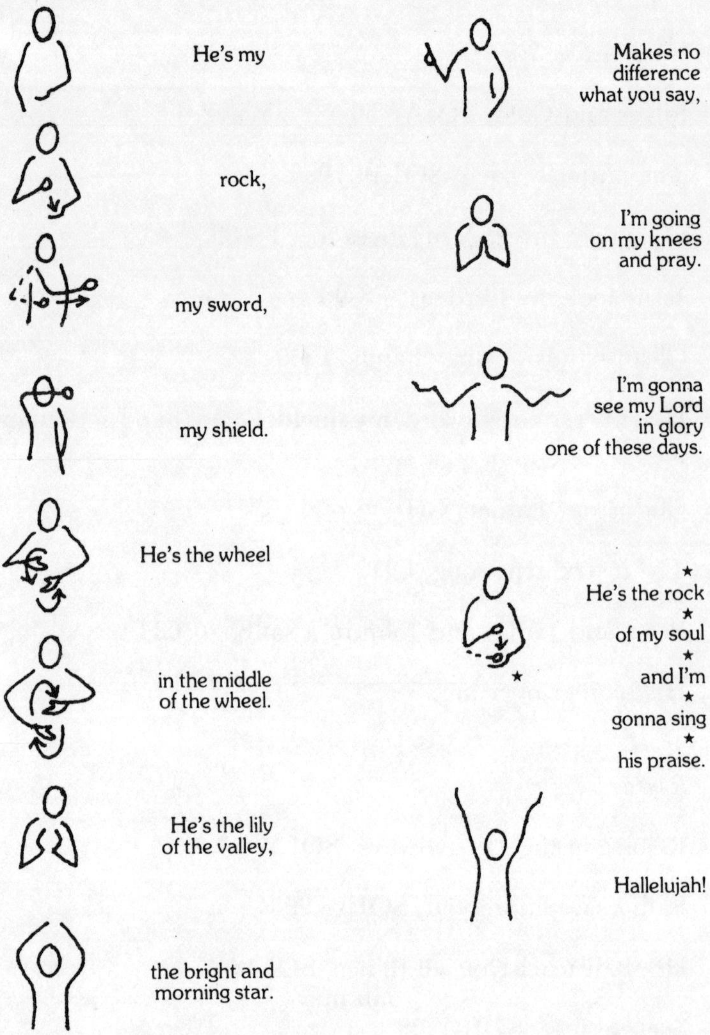

He's my
rock,
my sword,
my shield.
He's the wheel
in the middle of the wheel.
He's the lily of the valley,
the bright and morning star.
Makes no difference what you say,
I'm going on my knees and pray.
I'm gonna see my Lord in glory one of these days.
★ He's the rock ★ of my soul ★ and I'm ★ gonna sing ★ his praise.
★
Hallelujah!

CHAPTER 25

Art and Graphics Workshops

Introduction

Some religious traditions are lush in their expressions of beauty, with paintings, tile work, coloured glass, sculpture and statues, elaborately embroidered vestments made from sumptuous materials. Other traditions express beauty much more simply, perhaps through muted colours, flowers, dark woods. All traditions however, can benefit from folk artwork which has been tastefully integrated into the surroundings. Folk art adds visual enrichment, channels and directs thought, strengthens ties of familiarity and friendship, quickens appreciative awareness of the diversity within one's local group. When children see their drawings in a prominent location, obviously part of the worship or contributing to the instruction, they have a keen experience of themselves as a significant part of the larger church family and they realise that their contributions are welcomed and valued. Young and older adults, working together on a collage, get to know each other informally, learn to interact while completing a task, establish communication across age differences.

There has often been a place in church or community life for individual artists, but there have not always been many opportunities for groups. We believe that individuals and groups each make a unique offering and that both offerings are necessary. Through the skills and abilities of those gifted in painting, sculpture, design and needlecraft, the longings, hopes and passions experienced by all of humankind are communicated in particular fashion. The less sophisticated, technically more immature artworks fashioned by small groups and children embody another expression. They are tangible results of sharing and interdependency, of discussion and interaction. Both sorts of artwork deepen our worship, both help us focus more clearly on the God of all creation. In this book our emphasis is on the second category, that of group activity. We offer projects on which people can work together. The projects suggested are simple enough for the hesitant or inexperienced to find structure and direction, yet broad enough in scope for the more confident to be innovative.

Pointers

- The practical key to success is being sure that all necessary materials are in good supply and ready for the participants. Banner backings should be already prepared; scissors, pencils, etc. should be readily available. If the overall plan of the workshop is not geared to participants collecting their own materials, such as pine cones or shells for mobiles, be certain you have plenty. If paintings or drawings, wall hangings, collages or mobiles are to be used in worship or in an entertainment, allow plenty of time to hang them securely. Don't leave it until the end, planning to 'get there just a bit early'.
- Always stress the principle of simplicity in design.
- An appropriate scripture to use in workshops is Ephesians 2:10, *Jerusalem Bible:* 'We are God's work of art, created in Christ Jesus to live the good life as from the beginning he had meant us to live it.' This leads easily into a talk including any of the following: God's delight in fashioning us and his care for us; God's creating us in his image; awareness that the work of an artist is an expression of the artist's own personality; God is refining and reshaping us to his perfection; God has made us co-creators with him.

ART WORKSHOP STRUCTURE I: Introductory *Time: About 1 hour*

Purpose: To provide opportunity for people to experiment with basic artistic expression.

Projects: Leaders select one prior to workshop, and supply materials

1. Cinquain poem in conjunction with painting or collage
2. Wet-on-wet paintings
3. Collages

Section I: Introduction and discussion *15–20 minutes*

1. After general introduction, use one of the following to help people get to know each other and/or relax together.

   Name Game, p. 365 *or* Name Catch, p. 366
   Stick Game, p. 367 *or* Animal Game, p. 367

2. Explain project

3. Preliminary experimentation or discussion, if needed. Select from the following:

   Select or discuss scriptures
   Write cinquains
   Discuss theme of workshop and/or project

Section II: Project and sharing *40–45 minutes*

1. Work on and complete project.

2. Clean up.

3. Share as a group, reflecting on what people have made and/or talking about thoughts and feelings while working.

Instructions and Materials for Projects in Workshop Structure I

1. Cinquains
   a. Instructions: See Techniques, p. 386

   b. Materials
      scrap paper
      pens, pencils or felt pens

2. Painting wet-on-wet

   a. Instructions
      Cover paper with a light coat of water

      With brush full of paint, brush on 2 or 3 colours as desired. Colours will run and bleed together on already wet surface, hence term 'wet-on-wet'. The colours' bleeding can be somewhat controlled by the dampness of the surface; less damp – less runny; more damp – more runny.

      When painting is dry, add definitive lines with felt pens or with paint and paint brush.

   b. Materials
      good white paper or light card to paint on
      poster paints, tempera paints (mixed or powder) or water colours
      brushes and felt pens
      cups or containers for paints and water
      old rags to clean up spills
      old newspapers to protect tables
      paper scissors to cut paper into smaller pieces (if necessary)

3. Making a collage

   a. Instructions Cut out or tear out pictures from old magazines.

      Glue pictures on a piece of paper in desired arrangement.

   b. Materials
      old magazines
      paper scissors
      good paper on which to make collages
      School Glue or Pritt
      pens, pencils or felt pens

4. Combining techniques

   a. Instructions
      Write a cinquain about something in your surroundings. Do a painting, wet-on-wet (abstract or otherwise), and write a cinquain into the picture.

      Write a cinquain and illustrate it by making a collage from magazine pictures. Write cinquain on collage.

      Do a wet-on-wet painting as background for scripture or cinquain.

   b. Materials
      Any of above combination necessary
      Blu-Tack to display results.

ART WORKSHOP STRUCTURE II: Project oriented

Time: see below

Purpose: To accomplish project for use in worship, teaching or festivity

Projects: Leaders select one prior to workshop, and supply materials.

1. Mobiles
2. Wall hangings or banners
3. Paintings, collages, posters to develop theme

Suggested time structures: Two and one-half or three hours, on the same day.
One or two hours a day for two or three consecutive days.

Section I: Introduction and discussion *25–30 minutes*

1. After general introduction, select one of the following:
   a. If people don't know each other:

      Name Game, p. 365 *or* Name Catch, p. 366
      Stick Game, p. 367 *or* Animal Game, p. 367

or

Have each person share informally: names, where they live, why they attended workshop, etc.

b. If people do know each other, play a game just for relaxation:

The Stick Game, p. 367
What Are You Doing?, p. 366

2. Explain project.

3. Preliminary discussion
Consider theme of service or entertainment.
Consider scriptures, songs, stories, etc. which will stimulate ideas.

Section II: Project development *All remaining workshop time*

1. Divide into groups of 2–5 to work on projects.

2. Complete projects; clean up.

3. Re-group and share results.

4. Place or hang project, as appropriate.
Posters, collages, wall hangings, etc: Be sure they are well secured.
Banners: If parading with banners, ensure they are well fastened to poles.

Instructions and Materials for Projects in Workshop Structure II

1. Mobiles

a. Instructions (two people for each mobile)

See Illustration A

Choose one main bar. This will be the longest bar in the mobile.

Illustration A

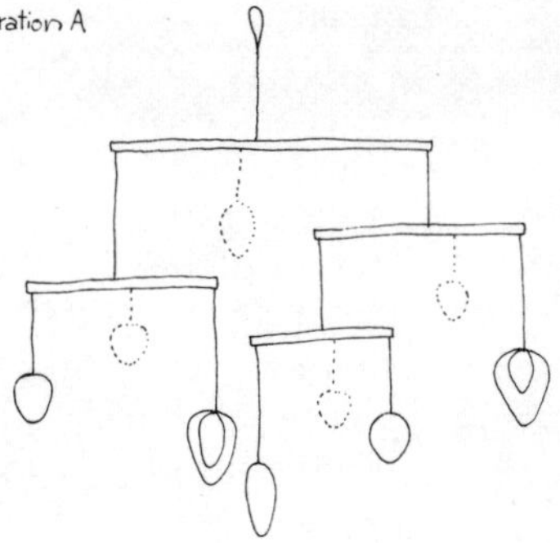

Choose a minimum of three smaller bars (branches, driftwood or dowels).

Choose a minimum of five objects (fir cones, sea shells, brightly coloured cards.

See Illustration B

Lay out bars of the mobile, beginning at top.

Illustration B

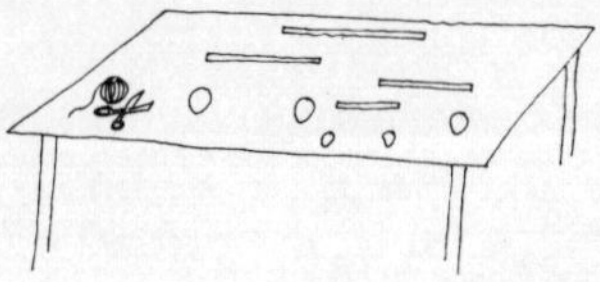

Lay out objects to hang from bars.

Cut lengths of string or twine and tie one to each object.

See Illustration C

Illustration C

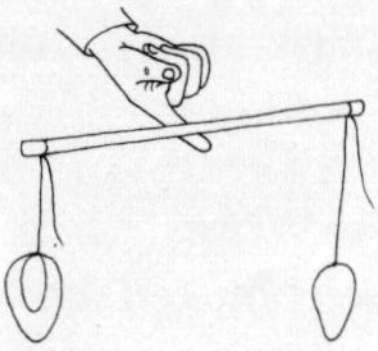

Tie objects and bars to main bar. Begin at *bottom* of mobile to do this. First tie objects to end of bar, then find balancing place, which is the point at which to tie the string to the bar. Find balancing place by laying bar on forefinger, then adjusting bar to right or left until it is perfectly balanced. Tie string at that place.

See Illustration A

For easy hanging, tie a loop in the final top string which holds the main bar (and thus the entire mobile).

b. Materials

Illustration D
Forest mobile

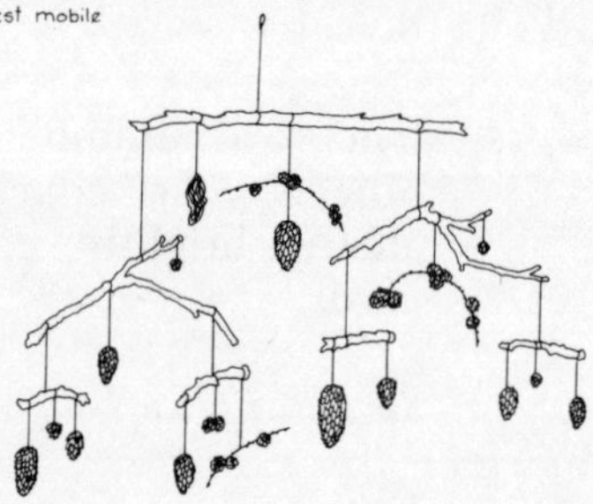

1) Forest mobile (see Illustration D)

tree branches
fir cones (various shapes, sizes, kinds), pieces of bark, other interesting objects from forest
jute garden twine
scissors

Illustration E
Seaside mobile

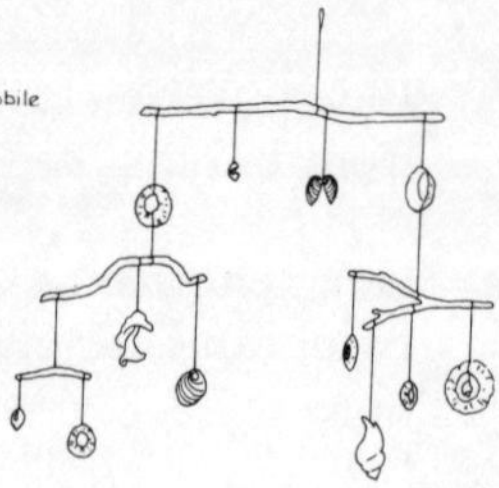

2) Seaside mobile (see Illustration E)

driftwood (various lengths, sizes)
sea shells with holes in them (to tie on strings)
sewing cotton
cotton

Illustration F
Coloured card mobile

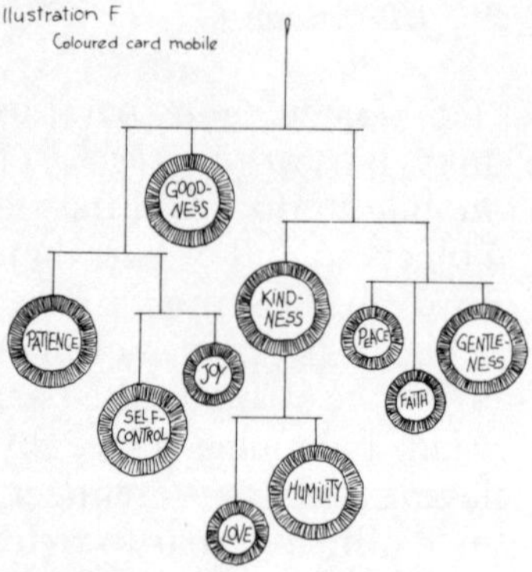

3) Coloured card mobile (see Illustration F)

small wooden dowels or sticks, or wires easy to bend yet strong enough to hold weight of objects which will hang from them

coloured card (or cartridge paper or paper plates which can be painted)
sewing cotton (or heavy thread)
scissors
Bible

Recommended supplementary resource: *Making mobiles*, A POCKET HOW TO DO IT book by STUDIO VISTA

2. Wall hangings or banners (see illustrations G, H, I, J)

a. Instructions (two – five people for each hanging)

To prepare backings:

This must be done before design is attached. It is best to do it before workshop meets.

Sew a casing at top; hem or ravel sides and bottom.

To make design:

Decide scripture, song text or theme; work out picture or design that you want to make in fabric.

Cut a piece of paper as large as the backing; use it to make a pattern of your design. Sketch shapes, letters, etc. lightly in pencil, and work out correct sizes and spacing. Trace outlines with felt pen. Cut out pattern, or wait and cut pattern and fabric design simultaneously.

Select fabric, limiting colours to two or three. Within this limitation, use a variety of shades, textures and prints.

Place pattern on fabric and cut out design. Arrange fabric design on backing in desired position; glue onto backing.

Slip pole through casing in the backing. Attach to each end of pole the string from which banner will hang.

b. Materials

fabric for backings (hessian, old sacks, old curtains)
fabric scraps to make design
School Glue, Pritt liquid or Wood Glue
fabric scissors
paper scissors
paper (good or scrap, A4 size and/or large pieces or rolls)
pencils
felt tip pens (to trace around the design on the paper pattern)

Bibles (preferably new translations)
poles (cane poles or old broomsticks, three – four feet in length, depending on width of hanging)
twine to attach to poles
drawing pins to attach twine to poles

Recommended supplementary resource: *Design in fabric and thread* by Aileen Murray, A POCKET HOW TO DO IT book by STUDIO VISTA

3. Paintings, collages, posters to develop theme
   See Instructions and Materials for Projects for Workshop Structure I, p. 457.

Illustration G

Backing: large, light green pillowcase cut in half
Design:
letters and leaves: dark green crimplene scraps
butterflies: white felt cut-outs over yellow fabric shapes
dots for 'i's, comma, daisy centres, and caterpillar: yellow felt
lines in leaves and butterfly bodies: yellow embroidery stitches

Illustration H

Backing: old, brown wool curtain

Letters: shades of yellow fabric scraps: prints, floral and solid (Striped fabric does not often make easily-read letters. Lines in the illustration are to indicate shade variation of solid colours.)

Illustration I

Backing: hessian

Design: fabric scraps of many patterns, textures, and colours

hair and woven belt: bits of wool plaited or tied

Illustration J

Backing: heavy-weave calico
Border: red velvet, machine stitched
Words: embroidered in red
Wind gusts: types of red velvet, hand stitched (not glued) around edges
Wind spirals: red cord attached by couching stitch

Additional Arts and Crafts Projects

- String paintings
- Tissue paper collages
- Texture collages (made from other than just fabric)
- Murals (each person painting a different section)
- Candle making
- Batik
- Patchwork: book covers, lampshades, cushion covers
- Bible covers
- Tie dyeing
- Needlepoint
- Embroidery: shirts, guitar straps, samplers, vestments
- Vestments for clergy

Additional Graphics Arts Projects

- Design for cover of service order or songsheet
- Illustrations, perhaps thematic, for calendar
- Large scale illustrations for stories which will be read aloud
- Greetings cards
- Design or symbol for church weekend, teaching series, holiday programme

CHAPTER 26

Writing Workshops

WRITING WORKSHOP I: Introductory *Time: 2 hours*

Purpose: To stimulate writing which is clear, concrete, and based on accurate perceptions.

Section I: Exercises and experimentation	*35–40 minutes*
1. Introduction Discuss the importance of accurate observation and clear description.	May read two different accounts of the same incident: one with concrete detail and one with generalities.
2. Blindfold Exercise, p. 327 Do this exercise just to the point of removing blindfolds *or* Concentration Game, p. 327.	Allow 30–35 minutes for Blindfold Exercise. Concentration Game takes only 20–25 minutes.
Section II: Instruction	*20 minutes*
1. Explain the cinquain/haiku forms. Give examples of these, written on large sheets of paper or blackboard. For cinquain, outline form as on p. 386. Haiku examples, p. 321.	

2. Each person writes a cinquain or haiku using their perceptions from either the Blindfold Exercise or the Concentration Game.

3. Those who wish to, share their poems. — Encourage everyone to share, but don't pressure any who feel reticent.

Section III: Application/Creativity — *60 minutes*

1. If group is larger than ten persons, divide into smaller groups of four or five for You Are There, p. 318. Each person tells story from the point-of-view of a different character.

2. Reassemble to share the results of writing.

WRITING WORKSHOP II: Project oriented

Time 1½ hours

Purpose: To write new material focusing on a particular theme for a worship service.

Section I: Warm up — *15 minutes*

1. Introduction to purpose of workshop.

2. Word Meditation
Everyone sits comfortably or lies on the floor. Close eyes and listen to readings. Instrumental music may be played softly in the background. — Read slowly, allowing time for reflection.

Readings:
John 1:1–4
John 1:14
Hebrews 4:12
Isaiah 55:10–11
Ecclesiastes 12:11
Isaiah 40:6–8
I John 1:1–4
Deuteronomy 30:11–14

Section II: Task accomplishment	*75 minutes*
1. Read the scripture readings for the service if these are prescribed. If not prescribed, determine the theme of the service and select readings.	In this column we construct an example of a service with these readings: Old Testament: Isaiah 9:2–7 Psalm 122 Epistle: Romans 12:9–21 Gospel: John 14
2. State the theme in one sentence, so that everyone has a clear understanding of it.	The Lord desires peace for his people.
3. Discuss the readings and theme. Determine what points in the readings should be emphasised. Decide on materials to be written for the service.	Decide to write first-person accounts of John 14 reading, an arrangement of the psalm, a structure for prayer.
4. Divide into small groups to write materials for the service.	
a. First-person accounts Follow the format of the You Are There exercise, p. 318. Paragraphs/poems written by the group may be read in conjunction with scripture reading and serve as stimulus for a sermon/teaching.	Individuals write the John 14 account from the point-of-view of Jesus and several of the disciples.

b. Arrange a psalm for a choral reading or a responsive reading. (See p. 323 for further development.)	Group arranges Psalm 122 for responsive reading with repeated chorus: 'Peace be within you'
c. Discuss prayer concerns. Compose a format for prayers, including specific prayer concerns and leaving time for spontaneous prayers.	Consider peace in the world, peace in your own nation, peace in your town or city, peace in your neighbourhood, peace in your families. These may include confessions of contributions to division, hatred and war and a statement of repentance. Prayers may focus on groups and organisations working for peace.
d. Write a poem or song on the theme. Select a refrain. All offer suggestions for lyrics. One person arranges stanzas. Group may work together on melody or ask one person to compose it.	Refrain: Peace I give you, my peace I leave you. *or* Blessed are the peacemakers. Leader may write suggestions for the first line of each verse: Jesus was the peacemaker of God. How can we be the peacemakers of God? Lord, let us be the peacemakers of God.

5. Small groups gather together and share fruits of their work.

Discuss arrangements for incorporating material into service.

Schedule a rehearsal before the service, to practise smooth flow from one thing to another.

CHAPTER 27

Children and Youth

Throughout the book we have indicated some of our concerns about the younger members of the church family. The topic is enormous however, and discussion could fill several volumes this size. Consequently, in this chapter we limit ourselves to examples of activity structures and general suggestions. Each structure represents a type of meeting or programme likely to be found or desired in local situations. Although these structures have been successful for us, and we offer them hoping they will be useful to you, we emphasise that it is not programmes but people, and the quality of love and friendship that they extend, that most powerfully and meaningfully influence young people's lives.

How do you decide what to do with or for children and youth? We bear in mind not only what they will enjoy, and sometimes what will keep them occupied!, but also whatever particular needs for teaching or guidance they may have at certain times. The contents of the Children's Holiday Programme listed below, for instance, were planned because of a factor in the larger church family. Members were from a plethora of national, social, cultural and denominational backgrounds. Such differences can be a source of conflict or a unique contribution to unity. We thought it essential that our children both recognise and deal positively with the fact of differences among people. It was with this in mind that we planned the programme's activities.

We are often flexible even when we have worked out a structure. Some discussions may need to carry on longer than planned; some stories may cry out for dramatic improvisation; on the Isle of Cumbrae in Scotland, a sunny day rather than a rainy one may require even greater changes! Don't bind yourselves to following a structure, yours or ours, when a change would seem to be more fruitful.

The chapter is divided into two sections, Children and Youth. The activities in the first section are, broadly speaking, suitable for children ages 5–11; those in the second section are intended for young people ages 12–17. Both sections include suggestions for Church School Lessons, Workshops and Holiday Programmes, and Additional Suggestions referring to teaching aids and materials in the book.

CHILDREN

STRUCTURE I: Church School Lesson *Time: 40–60 minutes*

Theme: God's love for the world

Materials: Large pieces of paper or blackboard
Paper for painting or drawing
Paints or crayons
Tape recorder or record player (optional)

Preparation: Write words to 'On tiptoe', FS 146 on large pieces of paper or blackboard.
Learn dance to 'On tiptoe'.

Structure

1. Teach song 'On tiptoe', FS 146

   Chat with children, noting that song chorus is from the Bible and reading or having someone read Romans 8:19. Discuss the song together, talking about the animals, creation, and being children of God.

2. Paint or draw

   Have each child paint or draw a picture illustrating the song.

   or

   Tape large sheets of paper together, hang them around room. Have children make a mural which illustrates song.

3. Teach dance, 'On tiptoe', p. 262

   Use record or tape, if desired.

4. Prayer

Pray together, asking one child to pray or encouraging each child to say a one line prayer. If children don't know how to pray spontaneously, help them.

Notes
This structure contains the following elements:

music
scripture
informal chatting and discussion
graphic expression
dance (vary with drama, mime, improvisation)
prayer

Many types of growth are encouraged by this variety of elements: spiritual, social, emotional, intellectual, artistic and motor coordination.
The lesson is shaped around a scripture-based song. Such songs are ideal vehicles for teaching the scriptures. Similar songs to use with this structure include:

The butterfly song, SOLW 106
The body song, SOLW 111
Wake up! SOLW 11
Ask and it shall be given you, FS 86
Peter and James and John in a sailboat, CH
The Wise Man Built His House Upon the Rock, FF Kit 1, 'All Aboard the Ark'
Abraham, father of the faithful, p. 297

More songs of this type are in the three song books.

STRUCTURE II: Workshop *Time: 1½–2 hours*

Purpose: To help children recognise God's love and presence in the people and things around them

Theme: The Kingdom of God is among us

Structure

1. Sing a few songs the children enjoy, chatting informally

together between songs. Sing add-a-verse songs and at least one hand action song; teach a new song. Encourage children to share thoughts about the songs or experiences the songs trigger. Songs we have used include:

Oh! how good is the Lord, SOLW 6
Thank you, thank you, Jesus, SOLW 18
I will sing, I will sing, SOLW 7
I'm not alone, FS 92
Jesus took my burdens, FS 90
Peter and James and John in a sailboat, CH
God is for me, CH

2. Read story, 'The Lost and Found Kingdom', p. 199, singing 'The butterfly song', SOLW 106 in the middle. (If children don't know the song, plan to teach it earlier or in the first part of the workshop.)

3. Select from the following, depending on your group:

   a. Chat further, asking the children if they have questions like Peter's. Discuss their questions, encouraging their answers to each other's questions as well as giving your own.

   b. Have children draw pictures based on the story yet putting in their own friends, their own parents or teachers, their own adventures. Share pictures together, then hang them.

   c. Improvise story, having the children retell it and act it out. ('The Lost and Found Kingdom' has little action, so doesn't lend itself to improvisation, yet other stories, including all those in this book, will be suitable for improvisation.) Alternatively, improvise a variation of story, with children putting in their own experiences and friendships.

   d. Have children make collages about the story.

4. Pray together, then finish with 'The Kingdom of God', SOLW 61.

Notes

Teaching comment: Peter, the boy in the story, was especially fortunate. Not all children have the benefits Peter did: loving family, helpful teacher, warm friendships, easy access to woods and meadows. If children in your group have been deprived of most of these benefits, help them to discover at least one which they have received (it may be your friendship!). Help them think about their present situation, help them discover how God is loving them now.

Elements: The workshop contains some of the same elements as the School Lesson; the chief difference is in the time factor. The longer amount of time available for the Workshop means that conversations can be more leisurely and projects developed more fully.

Variations: Many of the exercises, games, improvisations and workshop ideas suggested throughout the book are effective with children. Peruse them and build them into this structure.

STRUCTURE III: Holiday Programme *Time: 6 meetings 2–2½ hours each*

Purpose: To help children of varying ages and backgrounds appreciate their differences

Theme: Noah's Ark

Notes

Below is the programme as we did it with twenty children. We had two or three leaders for each meeting, and they participated in all activities along with the children. Occasionally an activity was too sophisticated for the younger children to accomplish individually, so leaders helped them directly by chatting with them, drawing out their thoughts, looking up their animals in the encyclopedia, reading the text to them, etc.

Although it's not listed in the structure, occasionally we had snacks between activities.

We found that using songs from a children's musical, rather than unrelated songs randomly selected, greatly contributed to thematic development as well as our enjoyment. Two such musical collections, based on the Noah's Ark theme, are:

> Mr. Noah, Fisherfolk Kit 1, 'All Aboard the Ark' (Celebration Publishing)
>
> Captain Noah and his Floating Zoo (Novello and Company Limited)

Following on this programme is a suggestion for the same structure with a different purpose and theme. We emphasise that the structure can be used with any number of topics and ideas and we stress that you should change or abridge it freely, as suits your own group.

Meeting 1: Getting Acquainted

1. Introduction

   Reading: 'Busy' from *Now We Are Six* by A. A. Milne

   We arranged the poem into a reading for three voices, the parts weaving in and out. Each leader took a part.

   Chat: Overview of programme

   Relating the adventures and changes in the reading to the children in the group, we emphasised that together we would discover new things about ourselves and each other. We noted that some discoveries would be surprising; and we indicated that our adventuring would take many forms, such as music, dance, drama, etc.

2. Small group sharings

   Dividing into as many small groups as there were leaders, we talked together about the following: favourite colour
   favourite game
   favourite place to visit
   what do you think you want to do when older

3. Two group storytelling

   Combining the smaller groups into two larger ones, we sat on the floor in circles. We made up stories, going round the circle with each person adding a section.

   Chat: Differences, when put together, can build something unique

   Noting that each of us was a different person, we acknowledged that the story we made together was quite different from the stories that each of us would have made on our own. Yet, because we were willing to work with what the person before us had said, and because we weren't each insisting on having our own story, together we had made a story that came from each of us yet belonged to all of us. It came from our differences, rather than our similarities.

4. Large group singing

Combining both groups into one, we sang three or four songs from the musical. The children knew one or two, and we taught one or two new ones.

Meeting 2: Getting to Know you

1. Song: Repeat one of the songs from the first meeting.

2. Animal Mimes

We played a version of the Stick Game, p. 367, with each person acting out an animal while using the stick.

3. Animal Hunt

Each child chose an animal they liked or wanted to know more about, then looked up that animal in the encyclopedia. They were asked to discover at least one entirely new fact, as well as something that amused or intrigued them. The children made notes of what they learned.

Re-grouping, each person shared with the others.

4. Animal Explorations

Improvs: Each person acted out their animal, then was paired with another person so the animals could interact.

Discussion: The group imagined situations in which certain animals might not get along together because of differing habits, such as owls and roosters, or differing inclinations, such as rabbits and foxes. Often something learned from the Animal Hunt contributed to the discussion.

5. What If This Happened on Noah's Ark?

   These improvisations were built around differences or conflict. Children were divided into small groups and dramatised the following:

   An animal becomes seasick
   Two animals argue about whether a window should be opened or closed
   A baby animal gets lost
   Three animals become bored with the rain and try to think of an entertaining occupation

   Re-grouping, we presented dramas for each other.

   Chat: What difficulties may people who are different have in getting along together? How can they learn to get along? Is there anything in the dramas that could apply to people? Is there anything that applies to us (our group) in particular?

6. Folk dance: 'Come go with me to the land', p. 258

7. Music: songs from the musical

Meeting 3: Make and Share

1. Art Adventure

   Project: Selecting from the following materials, each made anything they wanted:

   paper   tempera paints   magazines with pictures
   modelling clay
   shells   pencils   felt pens
   crayons   brushes and water   glue

   Some children carried on the animal theme, although instruction to do so was not given.

   One to one sharing: In groups of two, each person shared with the other what they had made, how they felt about it, what they liked, what they disliked (about their own work), if anything.

Group sharing: Seated in a circle on the floor, we all shared what we had made. Some children spoke, others said little, just offered their work for all to see. This led into:

2. Chat: We had all seen clearly that each piece of artwork was different from any other. Because each of us is in some way different from any other person, whatever we make shows those differences. Each piece of artwork was itself: there was nothing right or wrong, or particularly good or bad about any of it. The same is true of people: we aren't necessarily good or bad, right or wrong: we are all just ourselves, and different from each other. In talking and sharing we can see behind and beyond the differences and learn to appreciate each other.

3. Music

Since some of the children had written songs of their own, we sang those songs. This was a reinforcement to the Chat: the songs were all quite different, yet the group enjoyed singing them all. We saw that one person's songs didn't have to be like another's: in fact, as a group we were richer because of the variety.

We sang several songs from the musical, reviewing new ones learned earlier.

Meeting 4: Playing and Saying

1. Warm Ups

The animals in the following list are characters in the play we were going to work on, so as a group we improvised movement, sounds and speaking voices for these animals.

bears
giraffes
pigs
snails
rabbits

2. Drama: 'Animals'[1] Act IV from NOAH

In this humorous drama, God speaks to pairs of animals. He doesn't tell them outright that soon there will be a flood, but he does tell them to go to Noah's house. Each pair of animals has a different reason for not obeying God.

Improvs: Children selected animal parts they wanted to try, were divided into pairs and given scripts, then read and experimented with their parts.

Re-grouping, we talked about the improvisations, then each selected another part to try out. Re-grouping again, we talked further and then decided on definite parts for each person.

Rehearsal: Now sure of what part they would be playing, children again worked with scripts, learning their parts and practising their animal walks and voices. Young children, after a bit of improvisation in walk-on parts without lines, helped make Pig ears and noses, Rabbit ears, etc.

3. Music: We worked further on music with Noah theme.

Meeting 5: Getting it Together

1. Music: Further rehearsal on song
2. Drama: Further work on play, with leaders going round to pairs and helping when needed
3. Run-through of entire play

Meeting 6: An Evening with Noah and Friends

Presentation: Noah music and play for church family

Informal sharing: Children and leaders told others in the church family some of their experiences during the programme.

Alternate Suggestion for Children's Holiday Programme

Purpose: To help children become aware of the importance and necessity of interdependence

Theme: The human body

Elements

Drama: 'How Can the Body be Complete?', p. 237

Songs: The body song, SOLW 111
God has called you, SOLW 74
A new commandment, SOLW 66
We love the Lord, SOLW 112
Pullin' the weeds, FS 87
This is the day of the Lord, FS 14
Comfort ye, FS 69
The seed song, CH
Whosoever will, CH

Chats (Teaching points)

Meeting 1 (after Two group storytelling)
Similar to chat suggested, emphasising that without the contributions of each person, the story could not have been complete.

Meeting 2
Discussion: Organs and other parts of the body which are not at all alike are actually extremely important to each other. Imagine instances in which parts of the body didn't perform their proper function: if the nose wasn't taking in air, if the heart stopped pumping blood, if the fingers refused to obey the brain.

Chat: Similar to one suggested

Meeting 3
Similar to chat suggested, emphasising that each person is necessary and valuable in particular ways and that all are necessary. None are better than any others.

ADDITIONAL SUGGESTIONS

Teaching Aids

As stressed earlier, people learn in more depth when they participate directly in the learning process. 'Let Me In!', Variation 1 on p. 209 is a teaching aid for children that depends upon their participation.

'The Wise and Foolish Farmers', p. 210, 'The Amazing Change', p. 219 and 'Eli and Samuel' improvisation suggestion, p. 401 are others.

Material for Use with Children

The following material in this book is effective with children:

Readings

Let Us Rejoice!
Martha's Poem
all of the stories

Dance

This is the day
On tiptoe
Come go with me to that land

Mime and Drama

Peace! Be Still
Let Me In!
It's Impossible!
The Unforgiving Servant
The Wise and Foolish Farmers
The Amazing Change
Prodigal Son: foot mime, balloons
Eli and Samuel improv

YOUTH

STRUCTURE I: Youth Fellowship Activity or Church School Lessons

Theme: Gifts and their use *Time: 1½ hours or 4 one hour meetings*

Structure

1. Short teaching: How do we understand gifts?

   Base a short teaching on the following scriptures. Develop as many of the following points as desired.

   Scriptures: I Corinthians 12:27
   I Corinthians 14
   I Peter 4:10
   Romans 12
   Matthew 25:14–30

   Teaching points:

   Purpose of gifts: to strengthen entire group, rather than to glorify one individual

   Attitude towards gifts: tools for building, rather than spiritual merit badges or psychological reassurances about our own worth

   Use of gifts: service oriented, rather than competition oriented

2. Discussion: How do we recognise gifts?

   a. Gifts are sometimes disguised: Often what we consider our greatest weakness is actually our greatest strength. Discuss examples, including the following:

      Sensitivity: When directed only towards ourselves, our sensitivity may result in easily hurt feelings. When turned toward others, it can act as a catalyst to release or reassure them.

      Sense of humour: We may often make jokes to avoid facing things. This ability to laugh and make others laugh, when used constructively, can help break tensions during difficult moments or can help shy people relax.

   b. Listening to others: We may be uncertain about ourselves and our abilities, but believing and trusting what others tell us will help change our attitudes towards ourselves.

   c. Pursuing interests: Often we are attracted to certain activities because we are gifted in them. We should explore areas of interest, to see what will develop.

3. Small group work

Divide youth into small groups and give each group a situation. Individuals should think of what they could contribute to resolving the situation, then entire group should discuss situation, considering how to resolve it using the gifts of group members. Groups should be as aware as possible of everyone in the group, particularly drawing out those who may think they haven't anything to contribute.

Groups work out brief dramatic sketches, showing both situation and how they have decided to resolve or deal with it.

Possible situations:

Someone new comes into the group
Some people in the group find participation difficult
Someone is critical of the group
Someone makes a joke of everything
Someone takes over the group by demanding attention

Someone had made a commitment to the Lord but is going in the opposite direction
Someone who said they wanted to participate in the group now appears to be destroying it. They are angry, displeased about group activities, irritated with other group members
Someone in the group expresses doubt about their faith

4. Group sharing

Re-group and present sketches for each other. Have a discussion and response time and then end with prayers.

Notes

If people in the group play instruments, or if group is used to singing together unaccompanied, we suggest starting and/or ending with singing. Select songs that reinforce theme.

This structure contains the following elements:

instruction based on scripture
group discussion
small group interaction and dramatic improvisation
large group sharing
prayer

These elements nurture growth spiritually, intellectually, emotionally, socially and creatively.

Variation: Church School Lessons

Rearrange the content of Youth Fellowship Activity, Structure I, listed above, to develop a three or four week cumulative teaching for Christian education classes. Combine the teaching and discussion times and develop just one point each week. Use the scripture references as a study guide for the class, rather than just a reference for teachers, and build discussion of the scriptures into the general discussions. Work out dramatic improvisations for the Matthew scripture.

STRUCTURE II: Workshop

Since the structures in previous chapters are suitable for young people, we give no specific suggestion here. Youth however, are often especially interested in music, drama and dance. Arranging a series of cumulative workshops in which they explore techniques in those areas may be particularly effective.

STRUCTURE III: Holiday Programme

Time: Four meetings $1–1\frac{1}{2}$ hours each

Purpose: To help young people discover more about themselves as both individuals and members of a group

Theme: Identity

Notes

The young people participating in this programme had not previously met together as a group. They all attended the same school, and a few knew each other well, but most of the group did not know the others. They were keen to begin regular youth club meetings, so this programme was designed to lay a foundation for future meetings as a group. Initially the young people met on alternate days for a week; then their meetings settled into a weekly pattern. Additionally, they saw each other at worship services and in weekly church school classes.

Meeting 1: Who Am I?

1. The Stick Game, p. 367, using stick to express something about self.

2. Symbols

   Using crayons or coloured felt tip pens, draw symbols expressing four major influences in your life.

   Share pictures together, discussing what each has drawn.

Meeting 2: Who Am I? (continued)

1. Heroes and Heroines

   Prior to the group meeting, glue pictures from magazines and newspaper onto coloured card. The pictures should be of famous athletes, glamorous women, well-known actors and actresses, outstanding scientists or writers. Have some pictures of symbols as well: Superman's 'S' in its red and yellow triangle, cars, etc.

   When the young people arrive, have them walk around the room looking at the pictures as if in an art gallery. Then sit in a circle to discuss the following:

   What did the pictures mean to you?
   What do you think of the image presented by (*show specific pictures*)?
   What do the people or symbols represent to you?
   Who were your heroes when you were young?
   What does that reveal about what was important to you?
   Who are your heroes now? What does that reveal about you now?
   What place do heroes and models (examples) play in your life?
   Are your heroes accessible to you, or are they remote from you?
   Can they be involved with you personally? What are the advantages and disadvantages of proximity, in relationship to heroes and models?

2. Have each person choose pictures from magazines, then make collage which depicts as nearly as possible the heroes or symbols important to them now.

Meeting 3: Who Are You?

1. Give people time to think, then have each person share with the group one characteristic or aspect of each other person's personality that they particularly like or appreciate.

2. Using crayons or felt pens, draw a picture or symbol to represent each person in the group, including yourself. Then draw a wish for each person.

3. Share together the pictures and the thoughts behind them.

Meeting 4: Who Are We?

1. Small group improvs: Machines, p. 367

2. Large group sharing

   Re-group and present machines, then talk together about how the groups worked out their machines. Did one person have most of the ideas? Did any people feel left out or not listened to? Did one person seem to take over? Was it an enjoyable or a discomfiting experience? If groups worked together smoothly, what factors contributed? Help young people perceive that forming a group requires give and take, listening and responding, care and sensitivity. For most, these are deliberate actions, not spontaneous ones.

3. One-to-one exercise: Obstacle Walk, p. 388

   Prior to the meeting, set up an obstacle walk which the young people will not see.

   Divide group into pairs, have one person blind-folded and the other acting as leader. All pairs proceed to obstacle course and negotiate it. Have all pairs leave while walk is re-arranged, then have participants change roles: the former leader is now led. After all pairs have negotiated walk, remove all blindfolds.

4. Large group sharing

   Re-group and talk about leadership. Note that sometimes people change roles: those who lead in one instance may be followers in another, those who think they should always be leaders will have to learn to follow, those who think they will not or should not be leaders will have to be alert to changing roles.

   Talk about the group, discussing any of the following:

   > What obstacles do we put in front of others to prevent them from getting close to us? What do we want people to do about these obstacles?

What do we do when we run into peoples' obstacles? Do we go around them, do we stumble into them, do we act as if we're blindfolded and can't see them, do we expect someone else to lead us?

What obstacles could hinder the group from becoming unified?

Why do we want to be a group? What hopes do we have for the group?

ADDITIONAL SUGGESTIONS

Teaching Aids

The indirect approach is often the most effective way of teaching young people. They respond extremely well to *drama and music, storytelling and personal testimony, poetry, word pictures, photographs and films.* These are media that unlock what young people think, feel or question, and they are powerful yet subtle vehicles for challenging and directing youth.

In Chapter 1 we describe the *coffee-bar format*, a teaching approach we use often. It allows for both solo and group performances in the context of personal sharing and testimony, and it's possible to make strong points without sounding pedantic or pushy. *Arrangements* of poetry, music, dance, testimony/discussion, to develop a theme, are another effective way of communicating, useful in coffee-bars or youth clubs. 'Images', p. 281 and 'Identity', p. 280, are examples of these. *Dramatic teaching aids*, such as 'Let Me In!', p. 207 and 'The Obstacle Walk', p. 388 require direct participation but are nonetheless indirect as regards verbal instruction. When discussion follows, people teach themselves as the result of their own experience, rather than learning by assimilating someone else's information or viewpoint. At the same time, a sensitive group leader can draw out points of emphasis, based on members' experiences and comments.

Materials for Use with Youth

The following material in this book is effective with young people:

Readings

gooseberry pie
leaping
Ruth and Naomi
Revelation
Depressed Area
Friday
Jesus, keep me tender
As Peter
the self-giving God
The Woman at the Well
confession

Mime and Drama

The Sower and the Seed
Hands
Let Me In!
Prodigal Son: foot mime, circles, Family
On Tiptoe
Why Doesn't He Come?
The Unforgiving Servant
Abraham and Sarah
How Can the Body be Complete?
Scarfman improv
Identity
Images

Dance

Once no people
God has spoken
If I could get through
Come go with me to that land

NOTE

1. Available in Fisherfolk Kit 'The Ark Afloat' (Celebration Publishing).

PART IV Appendices

APPENDIX 1
GUIDE TO USING THE FOLK ARTS IN WORSHIP

This chart offers suggestions for the use of folk art material in each portion of a worship service.

PREPARATION

Media	*Type*	*Purpose*	*Example*
		PRELUDE TO WORSHIP	
MUSIC	Instrumental music	Establishes the tone of the service Provides time to collect thoughts	Any suitable music
	Solo song	States theme of service Focuses attention for beginning of service	Amazing grace, SOLW 5 Day by day, SOLW 67 Do you know? p. 285
	Entrance song	Announces beginning of service Heightens sense of expectancy	'Sanna, FS 1 Alleluia, sons of God arise, SOLW 86
		CALL TO WORSHIP	
READINGS	Solo reading	Focuses on theme of service Proclaims the Lord's presence	Come, Lord, p. 135 Endless Rejoicing, p. 134 Morning Song, p. 134
	Responsive reading	Involves congregation in beginning action of service	Let Us Rejoice, Let Us Be Glad, p. 137 Psalm 24, p. 136
	Choral reading	Heightens expectancy	Psalm 118, p. 148 Renewing the World, p. 146
DANCE/ MOVEMENT	Processional dance	Creates festive environment	Improvise dances to: Fear not, rejoice and be glad, SOLW 59 Morning has broken, SOLW 9
	Proclamation dance	Proclaims theme of service	Once no people, p. 260

Media	*Type*	*Purpose*	*Example*
THE MINISTRY OF THE WORD SCRIPTURE READINGS			
NOTE: Material may be used in addition to, or in place of, normal scripture readings.			
READINGS	Dramatic reading	Heightens drama of scripture	The Tax Question, p. 139
	Congregational reading	Involves all in scripture reading	Psalm 24, p. 136
	Choral reading	Brings out drama of scripture	Renewing the World, p. 146
	Meditation	Explores meaning of passage Provides time for reflection	I Stand and Knock, p. 141
POETRY	Solo poetry reading	Amplifies scripture reading	David Danced, p. 174
		Gives insight into personal response of scriptural character	The Woman at the Well, p. 177
		Applies scripture to personal experience	As Peter, p. 155
DRAMA	Congregational drama	Involves congregation in dramatic action	By Their Fruits Ye Shall Know Them, p. 243
	Scriptural drama	Dramatises situation described in scripture	The Unforgiving Servant, p. 233
	Humorous drama	Brings out humanity of biblical characters	Abraham and Sarah, p. 221
MIME			
NOTE: Many scriptures may be simply mimed as they are read.			
	Narrated Mime	Provides visual focus for reading Highlights certain actions Interprets meaning of scripture	The Wise and Foolish Farmer, p. 210
	Silent Mime	Enhances action	Prodigal Son (with balloons), p. 275
DANCE/ MOVEMENT	Interpretative dance	Gives visual focus for reading	Interpretative movement to Hosea 11:1–9
	Folk dance	Reiterates scriptural theme	Once no people, p. 260

Media	*Type*	*Purpose*	*Example*
MUSIC	Congregational song	Reiterates scriptural theme	God, make us your family, FS 67
	Solo song	Applies scripture to personal experience	Fear not, for I have redeemed you, CH
		INSTRUCTION	
READINGS	Dramatic reading	Introduces sermon/teaching	The Tax Question, p. 139
		Captures attention of congregation	
	Choral reading	Amplifies sermon theme	Wilderness Wanderers, p. 179
		Allows for reflection/meditation on theme	
POETRY	Solo poetry reading	Introduces theme of teaching	the self-giving God, p. 178
		Illustrates point in context of teaching	
		Describes situation of need	Depressed Area, p. 172
		Stimulates thinking of congregation	
		Introduces personal experience as stimulus for teaching	Jesus, keep me tender, p. 157
DRAMA	Scriptural drama	Provides stimulus for exposition of biblical theme	The Unforgiving Servant, p. 233 Ruth and Naomi, p. 227
	Contemporary drama	Illustrates present situation related to theme	How Can the Body be Complete?, p. 237
	Puppet drama	Involves children in teaching	The Amazing Change, p. 219
STORY	Participation story	Encourages participation by entire congregation	The Faithful God of Daniel, p. 194
	'Read-aloud' story	Engages children's imaginations	The Lost and Found Kingdom, p. 199
MIME	Narrated mime	Illustrates a particular need	Hands, p. 160
		Portrays specific teaching point	The Hat Race, p. 214
	Poetic mime	Stimulates thinking on teaching points	gooseberry pie, p. 284

Media	*Type*	*Purpose*	*Example*
DANCE/ MOVEMENT	Interpretative movement	Highlights particular situation	Interpretative movement to We Shall All Be Changed, p. 186
		Provides stimulus for teaching	
	Folk dance	Responds to homily	God has spoken, p. 253
MUSIC	Instrumental music	Allows time for response to spoken word	Any appropriate music
	Solo song	Applies message personally	Do you know?, p. 285
GRAPHICS	Overhead projector transparencies	Visual demonstration of teaching points	Illustration of Body of Christ, p. 126
	Slide show	Visually set mood or tone	
	Drawings	Spontaneously illustrate teaching points as teaching is being given	
ARRANGEMENTS	Multi-media presentations	Develops theme through combination of media	Tableaux of Faith, p. 291
		Involves several persons or groups	Identity, p. 280
		Provides complete teaching/ sermon in itself	Images, p. 281

PRAYER

PETITION/INTERCESSION

DIRECTED PRAYERS	Thematic prayers	Directs prayers according to theme	Litany of Resurrection, p. 167
	Prayer/Meditations	Elaborates on each section of prayer	The Kingdom Come, p. 163
POETRY	Solo poetry reading	Introduces personal application of theme in prayer	a prayer, p. 158
		Provides link between topics for prayer	Wind of Spirit, Wind of Change, p. 165
GRAPHICS	Slides	Visually presents concerns for intercessions	
	Drawings	Involves children in offering their concerns	

Media	*Type*	*Purpose*	*Example*
		CONFESSION	
READINGS	Congregational or group reading	Focuses thoughts on needs for confession	Psalm 51 reading, p. 144
POETRY	Solo poetry reading	Prelude to confession	confession, p. 158
			Coventry Cathedral, p. 182
			Litany to the Father, p. 159
DRAMA/MIME	Drama	Illustrates need for confession	The Unforgiving Servant, p. 233
	Mime	Portrays broken relationships and healing	Hands, p. 160
DANCE/ MOVEMENT	Interpretative dance	Provides time for meditation on relationships	Interpretative movement to We Shall All Be Changed, p. 186
GRAPHICS	Slides or drawings	Focuses on situations which require repentance	
		OFFERTORY/THANKSGIVING	
READINGS	Congregational reading	Draws congregation into offering thanks	Let Us Rejoice, Let Us Be Glad!, p. 137
POETRY	Solo poetry reading	Personally expresses thanksgiving	Lord of the Gentle Hands, p. 162
DANCE	Offertory dance	Visually portrays offering	Improvise dance to 'All of my life', SOLW 31
	Thanksgiving dance	Creates atmosphere of thanksgiving	God has spoken, p. 253

Appendix 2

The Folk Arts as Tools and Teaching Methods

Testimony

Use:

Informal sharing

Sermon aid

Teaching point emphasis

Examples:

Martha's childhood experience, Chapter 3, p. 42

Mike and Gary and the JONAH play, Chapter 4, p. 52

Purpose:

Adds personal dimension

Imparts practical experience

Helps interpret or apply scriptural principles or teaching points

Dialogue

Use and Examples:

Teaching device or sermon aid
Testimony sharing in coffee-bars: Pat and Jodi, Chapter 4, p. 57

Dramatic tool: 'Why Doesn't He Come?' p. 140

Style: Interview: one person asks another person questions

Exchange: two people converse together, including audience/congregation in their conversation
Note: When using either of these, avoid wandering dialogues by talking topic through beforehand.

Dramatic: seen or unseen speakers relate to each other or situation

Purpose: Informal speaking or presentation approach

Draws people into relationship existing between speakers

Poetry

Use and Examples: Accompaniment to personal testimony: 'As Peter' p. 155

Teaching point emphasis: 'The Woman at the Well' p. 177

Teaching or workshop device: Cinquains, p. 386; 'Lord of the Gentle Hands' p. 162

Style: Solo or group reading

Linked with music or sound effects

Purpose: Amplifies teaching or discussion point with another media

Draws out people's thoughts and feelings

Story

Use and Examples: Sermon aid: 'The Lost and Found Kingdom' p. 199

Teaching point emphasis: 'Samuel Merryweather' p. 197

Scripture presentation: 'The Faithful God of Daniel' p. 194

Style: Solo reader

Reader with mimists or actors

Group participation, with responses and/or hand actions

Illustrated while being told or read

Purpose: Elucidates scriptures or scriptural principles

Elucidates teaching point

Dramatises action

Instructs through visual perception (if enacted or illustrated)

Drama and Narrated Mime

Use and Examples: Sermon aid: 'It's Impossible!' p. 218; 'Hands' p. 160

Teaching point emphasis: 'The Hat Race' p. 214; 'Family' p. 272

Scripture presentation: 'Peace, Be Still' p. 231; 'Ruth and Naomi' p. 227

Style: Complete unit requiring no follow up

Incomplete unit, requiring interpretative talk

Unresolved situation, followed by talk or as springboard for discussion

Purpose: Elucidates scriptures or scriptural principles

Elucidates teaching point

Dramatises concepts

Instructs through visual perception

Mime, Movement and Dance

Use and Examples: Sermon aid: 'Let Me In!' p. 207

Teaching point emphasis: 'On Tiptoe' p. 205; 'On tiptoe' dance p. 262

Workshop or small group device: 'This is the day' p. 256

Style: Presentation linked with follow up

Group learning experience

Accompanied by sound effects, music or song

Purpose: Heightens or clarifies teaching point

Interprets scriptures

Group involvement

Instructs through visual perception

Puppetry

Use and Examples: Sermon aid: 'The Good Shepherd' p. 191

Teaching point emphasis: 'The Amazing Change' p. 219

Visual aid for story telling, interpreting songs or scripture: 'Eli and Samuel' suggestion, p. 401

Style: As simple or complex as desired (clothes peg puppets, paper bag puppets, ice cream stick puppets, cloth or sock puppets, papier-mâché puppets, etc.)

Purpose: Appeals to children

Children can participate in making puppets

Instructs through visual perception

Graphics

Use and Examples: Visual aid (See Chapter 8)

Type: Pictures

Illustrations

Wall hangings, p. 464

Spontaneous or prepared, to accompany stories

Mobiles, p. 462

Purpose: Heightens or reinforces teaching points and scriptural concepts

Audio-Visuals

Type and Purpose: Overhead projector: transparencies to illustrate teaching points, p. 126

Slides: accompanied by sound track, reading or music

to create an atmosphere
to emphasise teaching point
effective tools for meditation on particular themes or issues

Film: springboard for discussion or teaching point, educational aid

Arrangements

Combinations of the above forms. For Examples, see Appendix 1.

APPENDIX 3

Folk Arts in Festivity

When the church family or a fellowship group gathers to enjoy themselves, there is no form they must follow. They are free to create their own amusements and evolve their own traditions. Personal likes and dislikes, the contributions of each family and individual abilities will give each group's celebrations a distinctive flavour. These suggestions are designed to help groups discover their own special ways of celebrating. Some refer to materials in this book, others describe activities we've enjoyed in our own community and church family.

Storytelling

Most of the stories in Chapter 10 are suitable for festivity. Several employ techniques that can be used by any storyteller, such as the lap-mime or leading audience responses. Other techniques for entertainment evenings:

– Dramatised stories

Divide into several small groups, five to seven persons in each. Give each group a short children's storybook, an Arch Book or a fairy tale and allow about twenty minutes for them to work out a simple dramatisation. Reassemble and perform stories for each other.

– Characterisation

Read a well-known story (Paddington Bear, a Dr. Suess book, *The Narnia Tales* by C. S. Lewis) with people taking various parts. Create a special voice for each character.

– Illustrated stories

Whilst one person tells a story, another illustrates it on large pieces of paper.

Drama and Mime

Several dramas and mimes in the book have entertainment as well as teaching value. The 'On Tiptoe' Mime has enjoyable characterisation and can be presented with a minimum of rehearsal. 'The Unforgiving Servant', 'How Can the Body be Complete?' and the Prodigal Son Mimes require more preparation and can be rehearsed by a group for special presentation.

Equally entertaining is to improvise dramas. For each of the following, divide the group into small groups of five to seven. Allow about twenty minutes or so for groups to work out a drama, then reassemble and perform for each other.

– Paper Bag Dramatics

Give each small group a paper bag with several diverse objects in it (e.g., a dog's lead, a magazine, a wool scarf, a baby's bottle, a piece of paper with a telephone number on it). The groups create dramas using all the objects.

– Character Scramble

On small pieces of paper, write the names of characters, objects or animals (e.g., Julius Caesar, a rubber tree, a London taxi driver, a hungry tiger). Put the pieces of paper in a hat and have each person draw one. The groups improvise dramas using all the names they've picked.

– Change the Scene

Give each group the same story to enact, but assign each a different style of production or setting. For example, give all groups the story of the marriage feast in Luke 14:16–24. Ask one group to perform it as a silent movie, another as a clown act, another as a melodrama. Or give each group the story of Cinderella, but in differing contexts: a contemporary scene using current jargon, the traditional American West, a futuristic science fiction setting.

– Fancy Dress

Ask everyone to come as characters from favourite books: *Alice in Wonderland, Wind in the Willows, Robin Hood.* Read an episode from each book and have the various characters act it out.

Puppet Shows

These are longer term projects. With the help of adults, children can make their own puppets and either create a puppet show based on a familiar story or invent one of their own. 'The Amazing Change' and the Eli and Samuel improvisation suggestion are two examples. Stories with many characters are ideal for groups of children; 'The

Owl and the Pussycat', 'Peter and the Wolf', fairy tales and *The Narnia Tales* are excellent for puppet shows. See Appendix 2 and bibliography for more suggestions.

Music

For a music-making evening, gather a collection of percussion instruments: tambourine, wood sticks, bells, triangles, finger cymbals. Children can make shakers from margarine tubs filled with beans, grains, sugar, buttons. Ask people who play musical instruments to bring them and let everyone play along on familiar songs. Several exercises from the Music Workshops may be used in a festive music-making session.

Games

Games which families enjoy playing at parties or just for fun can become part of church family life at a games evening, wherein each family or individual introduces one of their favourites. If space and group size permit, divide into several small groups and play different games in different rooms of the church hall or a large home. Each group plays a game for twenty or thirty minutes, then the groups rotate[1] and play another. Musical chairs, Charades, What are you doing? p. 366, and other party games which accommodate large numbers are especially enjoyable.

Dance

Dances like 'This is the day', and 'Come go with me to that land' are casual and fun for festive evenings. Chapter 7 gives other suggestions for dance in festivity.

NOTES

1. The idea of rotating groups can be adapted to various activities. To explore several media, groups could rotate to different rooms with forty-five minute mini-workshops in music, dance, drama. Or each room could have a different story or a particular style of music for dancing. We've found this technique helpful in exposing large numbers of people to a variety of experiences whilst keeping groups small.

Appendix 4

The Family of God

The Riches of God's Promises and Provision

Renewing the World, p. 146	Group reading
Let Us Rejoice!, p. 137	Congregational reading
The Lost and Found Kingdom, p. 199	Story
Prodigal Son, pp. 267–278	Mimes, drama
Let Me In!, p. 207	Mime
The Good Shepherd, p. 191	Drama/Story
Tableaux of Faith, p. 291	Extended production
the self-giving God, p. 178	Poem
Litany to the Father, p. 159	Prayer poem
Lord of the Gentle Hands, p. 162	Prayer poem
God has spoken, p. 253	Song with dance
Once no people, p. 260	Song with dance

Human resistance and repentance

Psalm 51, p. 144	Group reading
Revelation, p. 151	Group reading

Wind of Spirit, p. 165	Narrated mime
Hands, p. 160	Narrated mime
Wilderness Wanderers, p. 179	Narrated mime
confession, p. 158	Prayer poem
As Peter, p. 155	Prayer poem

Family relationships

The Lost and Found Kingdom, p. 199	Story
The Hat Race, p. 214	Narrated mime
The Wise and Foolish Farmers, p. 210	Narrated mime
Prodigal Son, pp. 267–278	Mimes, Drama
The Unforgiving Servant, p. 233	Drama
Coventry Cathedral, p. 182	Poem
Jesus, keep me tender, p. 157	Prayer poem

Diversity and unity among God's people

Endless Rejoicing, p. 134	Proclamation
Ruth and Naomi, p. 227	Dramatic dialogue
How Can the Body be Complete?, p. 237	Drama
fitly joined, p. 181	Poem
Lord of the Gentle Hands, p. 162	Prayer poem
Prayer for Renewal, p. 163	Prayer poem

Bibliography and Resources

GENERAL

Bonhoeffer, Dietrich, *Life Together* (SCM Press Ltd., London, 1954).

Cox, Harvey, *Feast of Fools* (Harvard University Press London).

Gilliom, Bonnie Cherp, *Basic Movement Education for Children: Rationale and Teaching Units* (Addison-Wesley Publishing Company, London, 1970).

Hammarskjöld, Dag, *Markings* (Faber and Faber, London, 1964).

Haughton, Rosemary, *Tales from Eternity: The World of Fairytales and the Spiritual Search* (Seabury Press, New York, 1973).

L'Engle, Madeleine, *The Irrational Season* (The Seabury Press, New York, 1977).

McLelland, Joseph C., *The Clown and the Crocodile* (John Knox Press, Richmond, Virginia, 1970).

McLuhan, Marshall, *Understanding Media* (Routledge and Kegan Paul Limited, London, 1964; Sphere Books 1967; Abacus 1973).

Mead, Loren, ed., *Celebrations of Life from St. Stephen and the Incarnation* (The Seabury Press, New York, 1974).

Mearns, Hugh, *Creative Power: The Education of Youth in the Creative Arts* (Dover Books, distributed by Constable & Co.).

Nouwen, H., *With Open Hands* (Ave Maria Press, 1972).

O'Connor, Elisabeth, *Our Many Selves: A Handbook for Self-Discovery* (Harper and Row, Publishers, London, 1971).

Oden, William B., *Liturgy as Life-Journey* (Action House, Inc., Publishers, Los Angeles, California, 1976).

Reid, Gavin, *The Gagging of God* (Hodder and Stoughton, London, 1969).

Rookmaaker, H. R., *Modern Art and the Death of a Culture* (Inter-Varsity Press, London, 1970, 1975).

Routley, Erik, *Words Music and the Church* (Herbert Jenkins, Ltd., London, 1969).

Schmid, Jeannine, *Religion, Montessori, and the Home* (Benziger, Inc., New York, 1969, 1970).

Stevens, Roy, *Education and the Death of Love* (Epworth Press, London, 1978).

ART AND GRAPHICS

Birrell, Verla, *The Textile Arts, a Handbook of Fabric Structure and Design Processes: Ancient and Modern Weaving, Braiding, Printing, and other Textile Techniques* (Harper and Row, New York, 1959).

Dean, Beryl, *Church Needlework* (B. T. Batsford, London, 1961).

Ideas for Church Embroidery (B. T. Batsford, London, 1968).

Ferguson, George, *Signs and Symbols in Christian Art* (Oxford University Press, London, 1954, second edition, 1955).

Ireland, Marion P., *Textile Art in the Church* (Abingdon Press, Nashville, 1971).

Laliberte, Norman, and McIlhany, Sterling, *Banners and Hangings* (Reinhold Publishing Corp, New York, 1966).

Vienna, *Banners and Mobiles and Odds and Ends* (Morehouse-Barlow Co., New York, 1973).

Create and Celebrate (Morehouse-Barlow, New York, 1972).

White, Kathleen, *Design in Embroidery* (B. T. Batsford, London and Charles T. Brandford, Newton Center, Mass., 1969).

DANCE

Deiss, Lucien C. S. and Weyman, Gloria Gabriel, *Dancing for God* (World Library of Sacred Music, Cincinnati, 1965).

De Sola, Carla, *The Spirit Moves* (Liturgical Conference, 1221 Massachusetts Avenue N.W., Washington D.C. 20005, 1971).

Harris, Pitman and Walker, *Dance a While* (folk dance) (Burgess Publishing, 1969).

Long, Anne, *Praise Him in the Dance* (Hodder and Stoughton, London, 1976).

Ortegel, Sister Adelaide, *A Dancing People* (Center for Contemporary Celebration, P.O. Box 302, West Lafayette, Indiana 47906, 1976).

Taylor, Margaret Fisk, *A Time to Dance: Symbolic Movement in Worship* (The Sharing Co., 1976).

DRAMA

Bowskill, Derek, *Drama and the Teacher* (Sir Isaac Pitman and Sons Ltd., London, 1974).

Buerki, F. A., *Stagecraft for Nonprofessionals* (The University of Wisconsin Press, London, 1955, 1972).

Burbridge, Paul and Watts, Murray, *Time to Act* Sketches and Guidelines for Biblical Drama by Riding Lights, (Hodder and Stoughton, 1979).

Colson, Greta, *Voice Production and Speech* (Sir Isaac Pitman and Sons Ltd., London, 1973).

Speech Practice (Sir Isaac Pitman and Sons Ltd., London, 1973).

Hodgson, John, *The Uses of Drama* (Eyre Methuen Ltd., London, 1972).

and Richards, Ernest, *Improvisation* (Eyre Methuen Ltd., London, 1966).

Pisk, Litz, *The Actor and his Body* (George G. Harrop and Co. Ltd., London, 1975).

Scher, Anna and Verrall, Charles, *100 + Ideas for Drama* (Heinemann Educational Books, London, 1975).

Spolin, Viola, *Improvisations for the Theatre* (Sir Isaac Pitman and Sons Ltd., London, 1973).

Styan, J. L., *The Dramatic Experience* (Cambridge University Press, London, 1965).

MIME

Bruford, Rose, *Teaching Mime* (Methuen and Co. Ltd., London, 1958).

Kipnis, Claude, *The Mime Book* (Harper and Row, London, 1974).

Mendoza, George, *Marcel Marceau Alphabet Book*, *Marcel Marceau Counting Book* (Doubleday, New York, 1970).

See *A Dancing People,* Dance listing.

POETRY/WRITING

Carroll, James, *Tender of Wishes: Prayer Poems for Here and Now* (Newman Press, Paramus, New Jersey, 1969).

Elements of Hope, A Pastoral Education Book (Newman Press, New York).

Bernos de Gasztold, Carmen, translated by Rumer Godden, *Prayers from the Ark* (Macmillan and Co. Ltd., London, 1963).

Leedy, Jack J., ed., *Poetry the Healer* (J. B. Lippincott Company, Philadelphia, 1973).

Petty, Walter T. and Bowen, Mary, *Slithery Snakes and Other Aids to Children's Writing* (Appleton-Century-Crofts, New York, 1967).

Quoist, Michel, *Prayers of Life* (Gill and Macmillan, Dublin, 1965).

PUPPETRY

Engler, Larry and Fijan, Carol, *Making Puppets Come Alive* (David and Charles, Newton Abbot, 1973).

Kampmann, Lothar, *The World of Puppets* (Evans Brothers, Ltd., London, 1972).

Philpott, A. R., *Let's Make Puppets* (Evans).

Philpott, Violet and McNeil, Mary Jean, *The Know How Book of Puppets* (Usborne Publishing Ltd., 1975).

STORY

The Arch Books, *Daniel in the Lion's Den, The Silly Skyscraper, The Walls Came Tumbling Down*, etc. (Concordia Publishing House, London).

Carroll, James, *Wonder and Worship: Stories for Celebration* (Newman Press, Paramus, New Jersey, 1970).

Haughton, Rosemary, *The Carpenter's Son* (Macmillan Company, New York, 1965).

L'Engle, Madeline, *Dance in the Desert* (Farrar, Straus, and Giroux, New York, 1969).

Cry Hosanna by Betty Pulkingham and Mimi Farra (Hodder and Stoughton, 1980).

RESOURCE MATERIAL

Fisherfolk Kits: Collections of music, song, drama, mime, dance and readings
1. *All Aboard the Ark: Resources for family worship and teaching*
2. *Watch, Look, Listen: Resources for worship and teaching* (particularly appropriate to the Christmas season)

3. *The Stone Quarry and other dramas* (with production notes, teaching suggestions and scripture references)
4. *Sheep and other dramas* (as above)

Celebration Publishing, 57 Dorchester Road, Lytchett Minster, Poole, Dorset BH16 6JE.

SONGBOOKS

Cry Hosanna by Betty Pulkingham and Mimi Farra (Hodder and Stoughton, 1980).

Fresh Sounds by Betty Pulkingham and Jeanne Harper (Hodder and Stoughton, 1976).

Sound of Living Waters by Betty Pulkingham and Jeanne Harper (Hodder and Stoughton, 1974).

Hey Kids, Do You Love Jesus? (Celebration Records).

Index